Circles of Compensation

ECONOMIC GROWTH AND
THE GLOBALIZATION OF JAPAN

Kent E. Calder

STANFORD UNIVERSITY PRESS
Stanford, California

Published with support from the Johns Hopkins University/SAIS Reischauer Center for East Asian Studies.

Stanford University Press
Stanford, California

Printed in the United States of America on acid-free, archival-quality paper

Library of Congress Cataloging-in-Publication Data

Names: Calder, Kent E., author.
Title: Circles of compensation : economic growth and the globalization of Japan / Kent E. Calder.
Description: Stanford, California : Stanford University Press, 2017. | Includes bibliographical references and index.
Identifiers: LCCN 2017005239 (print) | LCCN 2017007919 (e-book) | ISBN 9780804798686 (cloth : alk. paper) | ISBN 9781503602441 (pbk : alk. paper) | ISBN 9781503602946 (e-book)
Subjects: LCSH: Japan—Economic policy. | Economic development—Japan. | Japan—Economic conditions. | Globalization—Economic aspects—Japan.
Classification: LCC HC462 .C28 2017 (print) | LCC HC462 (e-book) | DDC 330.952—dc23
LC record available at https://lccn.loc.gov/2017005239

Cover design: Bruce Lundquist
Typeset by Newgen in 10.5/13.5 Bembo

To the people of the Reischauer Center, past and present, who have so profoundly helped to shape the scholarship that I present today.

Contents

Figures

Tables

List of Abbreviations

BOJ	Bank of Japan
CME	Coordinated Market Economy
DPJ	Democratic Party of Japan
FDI	Foreign Direct Investment
FILP	Fiscal Investment and Loan Program
GDP	Gross Domestic Product
GOJ	Government of Japan
IBJ	Industrial Bank of Japan
IEA	International Energy Agency
IFDSA	Infrastructure Facilities Development Special Account
JANE	Japan Association of New Economy
LDP	Liberal Democratic Party
LME	Liberal Market Economy
LTCB	Long-Term Credit Bank of Japan
MAF	Ministry of Agriculture and Forestry
MAFF	Ministry of Agriculture, Forestry and Fisheries
METI	Ministry of Economy, Trade and Industry
MEXT	Ministry of Education, Culture, Sports, Science and Technology
MITI	Ministry of International Trade and Industry
MLIT	Ministry of Land, Infrastructure, Transport and Tourism
MOF	Ministry of Finance
NCB	Nippon Credit Bank

NRA	Nuclear Regulation Authority
NTT	Nippon Telegraph and Telephone
OECD	Organisation for Economic Co-operation and Development
SCAP	Supreme Commander for the Allied Powers
TPP	Trans-Pacific Partnership

Preface

Puzzles, we so often find, are catalysts for intellectual progress. They show us contradictions in the paradigms that we use to understand the world, and thus help us to refine and transform them. The ability to grasp and successfully resolve the puzzles we face is, I firmly believe, one of the most important skills that we can develop in life.

Puzzles were what drew me into the study of Japan, and its contradictory politics, well over four decades ago. I first arrived in Tokyo, as a boy of eight freshly arrived from the western United States, to find a city seemingly Western, and yet seemingly not. As I began the serious study of Japan's political economy fifteen years later, I saw a nation of massive scale growing at double-digit speed, yet nevertheless conforming to the norms of a world far less efficient or dynamic. And as I began field work three years shortly thereafter, I saw a country bereft of hydrocarbons suddenly convulsed by oil shocks, yet smoothly adjusting, without the social turmoil that wracked both the Group of 7 countries and much of the developing world.

More recently, as I began research on this book close to a decade ago, I observed the contrast between the turbulence of a globalizing post–Cold War world, racked by the Information Revolution as well as new security configurations, and the tranquility of Japan itself. Puzzled by all this, I began searching for a simple analytic paradigm that could account for the strange combination of change and continuity. Above all, I hoped that in its parsimony, abstraction, and fidelity to real experience, any new paradigm at which I arrived would travel outside the study of Japan, to secure relevance in the broader world.

I am grateful to the many researchers, students, colleagues, and friends who have supported me in this long quest. Sumiyo Nishizaki, Shinichiro Ichiyama, Kazuhiro Hasegawa, Gyunghee Kim, Meagan Foster Dick, Alexander Evans, Yun Han, Olivia Schieber, Sophie Yang, Azusa Donowaki, Mina Fukasawa, and Alicia Henry have all supported me in research at critical junctures. The Japan Foundation's Center for Global Partnership and the Reischauer Center of SAIS/Johns Hopkins University have generously provided financial support. Seminars at Oxford, Tokyo, Waseda, Seoul National, and Nanyang Universities have all provided useful feedback. The Stanford University Press team, beginning with Geoffrey Burn and including Jennifer Gavacs, Kate Wahl, James Holt, Emily Smith, Jay Harward, Olivia Bartz, and Carolyn Haley, has assured that editing and production would smoothly proceed. And support from mentors, colleagues, and friends, including Vali Nasr, Jessica Einhorn, Peter Lewis, John Harrington, John Roos, Francis Fukuyama, Leonard Lynn, Kurt Tong, Bill Grimes, Ulrike Schaede, Bill Brooks, and Rust Deming, as well as my family, has been crucial.

On a subject as complex and, yes, *puzzling* as this, I am sure that there are many imperfections and faults remaining. These I accept willingly as my own. I only hope that, through this comparative study of how nations and their citizens seek stability in a changing world, readers will find insights that resonate with and in some way enlarge upon their own.

Washington, D.C.
December 2016

Circles of Compensation

Introduction

Confronting the Paradox

Newly industrializing nations have faced a critical twofold imperative over the past century in their persistent efforts to catch global leaders: a challenge whose dimensions and resolution have been obscured in the arbitrary divisions of social science. On the one hand, they have faced the imperative of economic development through the use of state power.[1] On the other hand, they have faced the challenge of maintaining order in changing societies, so as to allow state-driven economic transformation to smoothly proceed.[2]

Since the late 1940s, these twin domestic imperatives of late development have been further complicated by the international context. The Cold War made domestic stability in developing nations increasingly important to superpowers like the United States, and provoked rival camps to compete in shaping local political-economic configurations. From the 1970s on, the politics of stable development also became interactive with international finance, as globalization began to link economies more tightly, and to magnify the international significance of domestic developments in any one country. The turbulence of the Mexican (1994–1995) and Asian financial crisis years (1997–1998) made these new realities starkly clear.[3] Increasingly, domestic transitions in the developing world came to take on a *two-level* character, interacting with both domestic and international politics, even as they also assumed simultaneous political and economic dimensions.

For more than two decades, political-economic transitions in the developing world have been underexamined empirically, and also undertheorized, due both to the complex interdisciplinary character of these late-development responses and the post–Cold War backlash against conservative Vietnam-era political-development studies. Academics, to be sure, have explored how development strategies are formulated, and how state capacity affects the implementation of those strategies.[4] Yet little attention has been given to how conflicts are neutralized, and political stability maintained in developing societies, at least those outside the Middle East. To the extent that sociopolitical conflict has been studied, priority has been given to understanding *ethnic* conflict. And even there, the persistent emphasis has been on causality rather than on modes of resolution.[5]

The Need for Two-Level Analysis

Particularly conspicuous has been the lack of both empirical research and theorizing regarding the concrete links between systemic changes in the global political economy and the domestic politics of individual nations. Analysts speak abstractly of two-level games.[6] Yet there remain all too few concrete studies of how transnational trade, as well as financial and intellectual flows, affect political-economic behavior at the national and subnational levels.

This paucity of two-level research is especially striking in view of the sweeping changes that have occurred in the global political economy since the mid-1970s.[7] With the coming of widespread jet travel, liberalized border procedures, and finally the Internet, transport and communications have changed enormously. Cross-border trade and financial transactions have grown explosively in their wake.

Just as paradoxical has been the recent failure of both academic and policy analysis to explore the continuing relevance of Japanese experience to late-developing nations, and to global affairs generally. Japan was, after all, the first non-Western industrial modernizer, whose dramatic economic and military successes evoked global interest and concern throughout the first three-quarters of the twentieth century. Japan's developmental experience attracted Sun Yat-sen, Zhou Enlai, Subhas Chandra Bose, and other Asian nationalists seeking a non-Western paradigm for their home country's future. Yet it also intrigued Western policy makers such as John Foster Dulles, seeking a non-Communist developmental alternative to China across the tense and bitter Cold War years.

American academics at the Mount Fuji conferences of that period pondered in detail the Japanese developmental model and its significance for the developing nations.[8] But few do so today. To the extent that the Japanese model is examined at all, it is considered almost exclusively for its relevance to the problems of the Group of 7 (G7) industrialized nations, or those of the Organisation for Economic Co-operation and Development (OECD). Yet the puzzles of Japan's past and present have clear relevance for all the world.

Nowhere does Japan present a more arresting puzzle than in its response to the socioeconomic globalization that has become pervasive in world affairs since the mid-1970s.[9] Japan has grown interdependent with the broader world in trade, finance, and technical-information flows. There are sharp differences, however, in inbound as opposed to outbound patterns, and a notable bias against in-depth dealings with frontier markets. Japan also retains distinctive domestic decision-making and information-processing institutions, which skew political-economic outcomes in counterintuitive ways that need to be better understood.

Japan's international trade and investment patterns illustrate the paradoxical profile of that country's economic globalization. Japan was the fourth largest exporter and importer in the world during 2015—a pattern roughly paralleling its standing as the third largest economy on earth in terms of nominal gross domestic product (GDP).[10] Fifty-seven percent of Japan's exports went to Japan's own Asian region—more diversified than Korea's 61.0 percent, but less than China's 43.0 percent. Conversely, only 3.6 percent of Japan's exports went to the globally distant African and South American continents, versus 5.7 percent for Korea and 8.4 percent for China.[11] So Japan was marginally less global in its trade than either Korea or China.

Japan is the world's fourth largest outbound international investor, with $113.6 billion in foreign direct investment (FDI) outflows in 2014.[12] That was a sharp increase of 102.0 percent over 2010—nearly four times the outflow from Korea, and slightly less than the flow from China.[13] Yet outbound FDI in the frontier African market was less than 1.0 percent of Japan's total, compared to 4.0 percent for China.[14] And FDI *inflow* into Japan in 2014 was only $2.1 billion—less than one-quarter of the flow into neighboring Korea, and less than one-sixtieth of the flow into China.[15] Japan's intake was only *one-quarter* of the GDP-proportional FDI flow into the United States.[16] Further, the inbound FDI total for Japan had *declined more than 80.0 percent* from the already minimal FDI inflows of 2009.[17]

The paradoxical profile of Japan's globalization extends beyond the economic, to the sociopolitical sphere as well. Japan has, for example, paid consistent homage to abstract symbols of globalism, like the United Nations. Some of its creative artists, such as orchestra conductor Seiji Ozawa, are world renowned, and Japanese architects, like Kenzō Tange have exceptional global prominence. Japan has also nurtured a few entrepreneurs, including Hiroshi Mikitani and Masayoshi Son, who engage creatively and dynamically with the broader world. In some sectors, such as automobiles and general trading, Japanese firms have developed formidably sophisticated approaches to international markets.

A more common pattern in many sectors, however, is a parochialism, defensiveness, and hesitancy in engaging with global markets and ideas. That parochialism is subtly obscured from Japanese public consciousness by the linguistic reality that "globalization" has no widely accepted translation in the Japanese language itself, apart from a vague "internationalization."[18] The parochialism underlying that linguistic ambiguity grew stronger over the first three decades of the recent era of globalization (roughly 1975–2005), even as the broader pace of international political-economic change accelerated worldwide.

Precisely when Japan needed to become more innovative and proactive, it grew more reactive, conventional, defensive, and risk averse, with little domestic objection to these tendencies. This evolution has had a devastating impact on Japan's economic and sociopolitical relations with the broader world, but is difficult to explain in terms of conventional categories—"state strategy" or "national identity," in particular. The mystery of Japan's hesitant and contradictory domestic response to the sweeping global changes since the 1970s deserves serious examination, which we intend to provide, in the context of a more comprehensive study of incentive structures and organizational behavior.

1

Paradox and Japanese Public Policy

For a century and more, from the mid-Meiji era in the 1890s until the collapse of its real estate bubble just over a century later, Japan's economy was a model for the world, recording some of the highest growth rates on earth. During those proud decades, Japan became the first non-Western nation to industrialize, and remained one of the few countries of Asia or Africa to avoid colonial subjugation by the West. After a dark imperialist interlude of its own during the early twentieth century, Japan resumed its high-speed economic growth as the Korean War began, at even higher rates than previously, recording remarkable equity of income distribution, as well.

The Puzzling Profile of Growth

Since 1990 the picture has been dramatically different. Real Japanese growth has averaged slightly less than one percent a year, compared to 2.5 percent for the United States, and 1.7 percent for the European Union.[1] Japanese growth has also been dramatically slower than that recorded in Japan's own recent past—4.4 percent for the 1980s[2] and around 9.7 percent for the high-growth period between 1955 and 1970.[3] Meanwhile, inequality in Japan has also dramatically intensified, and Japan has fallen from near the top to twenty-third internationally in per capita gross domestic product (GDP).[4]

Massive Pump Priming

Since the 1980s, in particular, Japan has frequently engaged in massive Keynesian pump priming—endorsed and approved by the international community. That quixotic effort has taken Japan's general government gross debt to 248 percent of GDP—the highest level on Earth.[5] In the twenty months following the 1985 Plaza Accord, under Finance Ministers Noboru Takeshita and Kiichi Miyazawa, the Japanese government implemented nearly ¥13 trillion in economic countermeasures to revive domestic demand.[6] Under the Structural Impediments Initiative of the early 1990s, established jointly with the United States to combat chronic trade imbalances, Japan committed itself to ¥430 trillion in additional fiscal pump priming over the decade following the October 1990 agreement.[7] During 1998–1999, the Keizō Obuchi government added nearly ¥42 trillion more in combating the Asian financial crisis, the bulk of it devoted to stimulative public works.[8]

Technological Strength

Japan also for many years made significant technological breakthroughs. Its automobile manufacturers gave birth to hybrid cars. Indeed, the chairman of Japan's top automobile manufacturer, Toyota Motor Corporation, Takeshi Uchiyamada, is the "father of the hybrid." Japan's steel companies pioneered in amorphous metals. Its construction firms developed the most advanced and efficient tunneling technology in the world. And Japan's consumer electronics led the drive to miniaturization as well, pioneering in development, for example, of the world's most minute and high-capacity random-access memories.[9]

Persistent Effort

There is no question that Japan—its leaders, its outstanding bureaucracy, and its formidably organized corporations—put enormous thought and effort, following the end of high growth, into the struggle for revival—more than two decades of sustained effort. Japan's leaders were essentially the same people and institutions that had sparked the miraculous expansion of previous decades. Time and again across the high-growth years—in 1958, 1965, 1974, and the early 1980s, just to name a few instances—they had succeeded in reviving the national economy and its remarkable, century-long path of exceptional dynamism. Yet this time it was not to be.

Why Sudden Stagnation?

Why, then, did a Japan that grew so explosively and consistently for more than a century suddenly find it so difficult to grow at all? Why was it abruptly outstripped by countries like the United States—not to mention its dynamic neighbors in Asia—which for so long seemed unable to even approach Japanese performance standards? And why did the pronounced relative shift in growth patterns—from exemplary growth to decidedly subpar, compared to both seemingly similar nations and its own past—occur when it did, with such abruptness? What are the necessary preconditions, including institutional transformation, for its long-term revival? And how important are inherited political culture and entrenched elites as constraints on needed change? Clearly in Japan's sudden and disturbing transition there is a paradox of major dimensions—for the world of practical affairs and that of social-science theory, as well.

Why No More Rapid Revival?

The Tokyo Stock Exchange's Nikkei 225 index average reached nearly 39,000 in late December 1989.[10] Twenty-five years later, despite massive stimulus efforts, a host of structural reform plans, and four major shifts in political power, the index still stood, near the end of 2016, at less than half that 1989 level.[11] Putative reformers ranging from Morihiro Hosokawa and Junichirō Koizumi to Yukio Hatoyama, Naoto Kan, and Yoshihiko Noda had come and gone, but none had achieved major structural change, despite changes in electoral and regulatory rules that should have significantly changed political-economic incentive structures. While Shinzō Abe, with his vaunted "three arrows," had temporarily rallied the stock market with aggressive monetary and fiscal easing, the "third arrow" of structural reform showed few signs of transforming Japan's domestic political economy, either. Growth continued on an uncertain trajectory, as suggested in Figure 1.1. Japan's balance of trade for goods position remained persistently in deficit, especially after the 2011 Fukushima nuclear accident, and even as Japan's neighbors, together with most advanced industrial nations, grew much more vigorously. In the second quarter of 2015, for example, Japan's economy shrank at an annualized rate of 0.7 percent, and its merchandise trade deficit remained at ¥406.6 billion, as exports failed to pick up despite a weakening yen.[12]

The Incongruous Contours of Policy

Together with paradoxes in the contours of growth—particularly its sustained rapidity for more than a century, followed by abrupt deceleration—Japan's recent history also exhibits anomalies in its pattern of policy formation. These may provide important insights into the puzzling patterns of growth and stagnation outlined above. One example in this regard is Japanese corporate

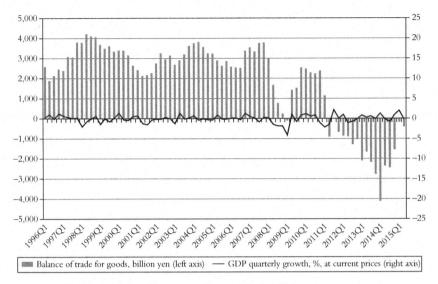

FIGURE 1.1   Economic struggles since collapse of the bubble

SOURCES: Ministry of Finance, "Table 6s-a-1 Current account (seasonally adjusted) (Quarterly Figures)," *Balance of Payments (Historical data)*; Cabinet Office, "Changes from the previous quarter (at current prices: seasonally adjusted series)," *Quarterly Estimates of GDP Jan.–Mar. 2016 (The 2nd Preliminary)*.

governance, and its sluggish, grudging transformation. In many parts of the world, change has been much more rapid than in Japan.

The emergence since the 1980s of a powerful global equity market has transformed incentives for the state worldwide, and presented political leaders with a "golden bargain"—the infusion of cheap and abundant capital into domestic markets, in return for reform of corporate governance and related regulatory innovations.[13] France and Korea have both embraced this opportunity and undertaken far-reaching reforms to make their firms more attractive to foreign capital. Japan, however, has not done so.

Japanese policies in a broad range of areas relating to globalization also contrast strikingly to those of many advanced industrialized nations to which Japan is otherwise similar. Transportation, real estate, agriculture, and housing are among the contrasting sectors. Japanese policies in most of these areas tend to be rigid, politicized, and parochial, although predictable and advantageous for long-standing participants, as we shall see concretely in Chapters 4 through 9. Change is occurring, but at glacial speed, considering the substantial changes in political-economic incentives, at both the global and national levels, that have occurred over the past generation.

Central Puzzles in the Contours of Policy

Japan's recent political-economic history exhibits three anomalies in its pattern of policy formation that may provide additional clues in resolving the central puzzle of abrupt growth deceleration.

(1) *The paradox of globalization response.*[14] In both elite political and mass public discourse, symbols of globalism have been popular in Japan throughout the postwar period: peace, the United Nations, and global responsibility, to name a few. Japan, as a "reactive state," has been relatively quick to respond, in rhetorical and in national-policy terms, to focused external pressure, or *gaiatsu*, that aligns with underlying cleavages in the domestic Japanese political economy.[15] Yet both policy in practice and the behavior of domestic enterprise have been slow to respond to the powerful winds of globalization that have transformed most of the world economy over the past three decades, despite Japan's high level of interdependence with the broader world in such strategic areas as finance.

Japanese ports and airports remain high-cost and domestically oriented; Japanese agriculture is also notably protectionist. Japanese regulatory policies in telecommunications and finance have been slow to respond to the revolutionary changes that have swept the world since the 1980s in those sectors. And Japanese education, like the professions, remains parochial, although these patterns are changing.

(2) *The paradox of cross-sectoral contrast.* Japan's public policies since at least the 1950s have exhibited sharp contrasts: a strong market orientation in directly traded sectors of the economy, and acceptance of widespread protection and inefficiency in many nontraded sectors. This bifurcated approach has involved low tariffs on industrial inputs in the traded sectors, and a determined effort to encourage higher value-added production in those sectors. At the same time, public policy in the nontraded portion of the economy has condoned highly protectionist and economically inefficient policies in areas like transportation, construction, agriculture, and services.

(3) *The paradox of inconsistency.* Japan, like most advanced societies, has meticulous rules for governing. In both international and domestic policy transactions, established insiders—those engaging systematically, over long periods, in routinized dealings with other legitimate policy actors—tend to be accorded favorable, consistent treatment. Japanese policy making, like Japanese social practice generally, tends to favor insiders against outsiders, be they foreign or domestic. It is also often slow to implement abstract global standards, even as many Japanese personally respect and idealize such norms.

It has been argued that Japanese politics is changing, growing less compensation oriented, and leading ultimately to a more neoliberal Japan.[16] Electoral politics has indeed arguably grown more fluid and pluralistic since the electoral reforms of 1994. Yet meaningful neoliberal structural reforms have been slow in coming, even when insistently pressed by forceful leaders such as Junichirō Koizumi and Shinzō Abe.

Problems for Analysis

Social-science theory since Aristotle suggests that the most powerful explanations are those that compare phenomena within a given category, and those that can account simultaneously for both similarities and differences in behavior.[17] Accounting for Japan's paradoxical recent growth patterns thus seems to be a promising catalyst for theory building, as it involves abrupt, discontinuous changes in a previously continuous variable. In many respects, Japan's complex growth profile appears to have the character ex post of a natural experiment.

Dual Patterns of Policy and Performance

An explanation for Japan's recent growth performance needs to account through a unified analysis for two separate and seemingly contradictory patterns: (1) the country's remarkably buoyant growth of the post–World War II high-growth years (1951–1990); and (2) Japan's subsequent stagnation (1990–present). If truly robust, a good explanation should also offer potentially verifiable predictions concerning a third analytical challenge: understanding preconditions and prospects for Japanese recovery.

There is considerable analysis regarding the causes of Japanese economic growth, in both mainstream economic and in political-economic literature. Yet most of it fails to anticipate, and cannot easily explain, the difficulties that subsequently transpired. There is much less consideration of the second and third problems—explaining Japan's recent stagnation and its prospects for recovery. Virtually none of the existing literature attempts to explain recent difficulties using the same variables as are considered in accounting for earlier success.

Muted Response to Globalization?

The recent period of stagnation in the Japanese domestic political economy also coincides with historic changes in the broader global system. Since the late 1970s, the information revolution has emerged with tremendous force, the world financial system has grown much more integrated, the Cold War has ended, the Internet revolution has transpired, and a huge number of new participants, concentrated especially in China, India, and the former Soviet bloc, have joined the world economy. How globalization is affecting the Japanese political economy, and why Japan is not responding more dynamically to global change, are thus also important issues for analysis that need serious consideration.

Insights from Existing Literature

Japan's growth pattern is distinctive, as has been suggested, for its discontinuous character. Most underlying macroeconomic and demographic parameters, such as savings rates and age structure, did not shift abruptly, suggesting the importance of more rapidly changing political-economic variables. It is thus to the political-economic literature that we turn first for causal insights regarding the puzzles at hand.

Our initial point of departure needs to be a consideration of microeconomic incentive structures and their relationship to social action. Classical economics, of course, begins with the rational actor as a basic paradigm, to which game theory adds important insights concerning how the incentives of individual actors interrelate to shape the logic of cooperation and conflict, where broader social relationships have continuity.[18] The basic rationale of games illustrates graphically, through problems like the prisoner's dilemma, the logic of conflict. The insights of Robert Axelrod and George Tsebelis, however, show us how, over time, iterations of a given social interaction, or game, make cooperation more likely, as do stable expectations regarding such interaction, helping to mitigate conflict where broader social relationships maintain continuity.[19] Those works also show us that cross-issue linkages among social problems can likewise facilitate cooperation. Yet Mancur Olson demonstrates, in his assessment of the free-rider problem, how the incentives for individuals to be a catalyst for collective action are nevertheless limited.[20]

Despite the logically convincing case which Olson makes that individual incentives for collective action should be limited, it is empirically clear in the real world that collective action in some situations is not only common, but also pervasive and persistent. *Why* such collaborative situations prevail, and *how* they are sustained is thus a paradox for organization theory, in the light of Olson's demonstration of the incentives to free-ride that should logically prevail.

Taken together, recent game-theoretic works demonstrate the underlying logic of the collaborative institutions that are so salient at the subnational level in Japan. They suggest the sort of functional roles in defusing risk, routinizing conflict, and discouraging free riders that such bodies could potentially play. Yet game theory itself is not well equipped to provide insights into broader macrosocietal *implications* of any specific interpersonal dealings within "circles of compensation" that actually occur. Achieving such deeper, more subtle insights requires more detailed, theory-guided empirical research.

An important secondary set of insights from existing literature is the extensive scholarly work regarding the impact of institutions on economic behavior, pioneered by such scholars as Oliver Williamson, Douglass North, George Stigler, Daron Acemoglu, James Robinson, Mancur Olson, and Elinor Ostrom.[21] One stream of the institutionalist literature has established that private bodies such as firms and industrial groups can improve efficiency and enhance growth by reducing transaction costs and diffusing risk. A second stream, however, pioneered by economists such as George Stigler, amplified by political economists like Daron Acemoglu and James Robinson, has shown in complementary fashion that public bodies have, through captive regulation, the potential to slow growth and increase inefficiency by allowing firms and other subnational actors to collect excessive rents. A third stream, represented by scholars like Mancur Olson, has stressed the perverse impact of intermediate bodies that bridge relations between state and society ("distributional coalitions") in inhibiting economic growth.[22] All three variants of institutionalist literature—explicating both the positive and the negative impacts of subnational institutions on growth—help us to understand the seemingly contradictory dynamics operating in the contemporary Japanese political economy.

Sociologists like Jeffrey Pfeffer, Gerald Salancik, and Neil Fligstein have shown, in complementary fashion to the institutional economists, how external pressures shape the internal behavior of firms, governments, and intermediate collective associations.[23] They help us to understand, by examining the varying external pressures on organizations, why markets are configured as they are, and also why different bodies respond so differently to stimulus from outside. Such sociological literature can be useful in assessing the role of Japanese intermediate organizations in shaping Japan's response, or the lack thereof, to globalization. Yet more theory-guided empirical work—especially concrete studies of the incentive structures prevailing in specific organizations at the interface of domestic and international—is needed to generate useful predictions of future behavior.

As a late developer, Japan—like several other European states, including Germany, Italy, and Spain—promoted corporatist modes of sociopolitical organization in order to simultaneously achieve both rapid growth and political stability.[24] Theory-guided literature on corporatism can thus generate important questions for research on the political economy of late development.[25] In particular, it mandates the study of how subnational bodies like agricultural cooperatives and business federations interact with government and each other to promote stability and growth.

Tracing and conceptualizing such neocorporatist interactions are a central concern of this research. They deserve special analytical precedence because they have so profoundly shaped the growth trajectories of so many "coordinated market economies" (CMEs).[26] They also help account for the success of many such nations in achieving rapid, capital-intensive heavy industrialization due to their ability to diffuse corporate risk and simultaneously accommodate mass social demands.

Beyond a review of abstract theoretical literature, it is also important to consider both conceptual and empirical insights provided by work that focuses more narrowly on the Japanese political economy itself. In addressing concretely the paradox of Japan's abrupt transition from growth to stagnation, it is especially useful to review related literature accounting for growth during the early post–World War II period, with a special focus on micro-level incentive structures.[27] Individuals do, after all, make the decisions that allocate resources and determine policy, albeit embedded within institutional parameters.

Perhaps the best-known classical work on Japanese economic growth is that of Kazushi Ohkawa and Henry Rosovsky, who stressed the importance of sectoral shifts in resource allocation that allowed Japan to enhance productivity and optimal use of capital.[28] Their work privileges a clearly macroeconomic variable: capital formation. Stressing trend acceleration in this key parameter, their work accounts elegantly for growth patterns in Japan through the Oil Shocks of the 1970s. For latter years, however, the fit between their independent variable and growth outcomes began to decline. And their analysis, focusing as it does on macro variables, has trouble explaining the abruptness of the transition to stagnation in the early 1990s. An additional dimension clearly needed to be added at the micro level.

The best-known political-economic work exploring Japan's distinctive growth model is that of Chalmers Johnson, presented in *MITI and the Japanese Miracle*.[29] Johnson argued that the origins of Japanese economic success across the high-growth period lay in distinctive patterns of "developmental," "plan-rational" economic management, that strategically exploited cross-sectoral synergies and long-term international competitive logic.[30] Developmental institutions, primarily bureaucratic, and appropriate strategy were critical variables, he maintained, in an analysis that entered the micropolitical realm, albeit without systematically considering micro-level incentive structures. Through a detailed and scholarly institutional history of Japan's trade ministry, however, he endeavored to show how a developmental strategy for achieving high growth might be successfully implemented.

The central problem with Johnson's analysis, often noted by critics at the time, was the substantial analytic leap involved in extrapolating from strategic decisions by the Ministry of International Trade and Industry (MITI) to the performance of the Japanese economy more generally.[31] This problem was implicit in the book title itself: *MITI and the Japanese Miracle*. Johnson did not establish systematically the relationship between the two central variables of his analysis. As the performance of the Japanese economy changed from positive to negative across the 1990s, his approach failed to account for the change, since the explanatory factor it privileged was the exemplary and unchanging structure of the Japanese industrial-policy bureaucracy itself. For years after the publication of his acclaimed volume, Johnson continued to assert dogmatically that Japan was vanquishing the outside world, even as Japanese advantages steadily and clearly eroded.

This book, like Johnson's, stresses the importance of understanding political-economic institutions in accounting for economic performance. It endeavors to transcend the problems his work presents by focusing on the *incentive structures* that operate within and between *institutions*, rather than on individual institutions alone. This book concentrates on financial institutions and hybrid public-private networks at the micro level that actually make or constrain decisions, rather than focusing exclusively on the functioning of formal government bureaucracies, or on their macro-level role in the broader national political economy.

Little work so far has considered new paradigms for Japanese economic activity, at either the macro or the micro level, that has taken place since the collapse of the "bubble" in the early 1990s. Among the few with pronounced sensitivity to the importance of micro-level incentive structures is Ulrike Schaede's *Choose and Focus*.[32] Based on detailed analysis of changing industrial architecture and corporate strategy during the first decade of the twenty-first century, Schaede's work argues that a new Japan is arising. While opening important new areas of empirical inquiry, Schaede's optimistic view fails to consider the sociopolitical forces and institutional developments that constrain structural change and response to globalization in Japan. These constraining elements include many of the collusive arrangements discussed in this volume, which stimulated speculative lending during the 1980s and 1990s, as well as institutional changes like collapse of the long-term credit banks, which sharply inhibited "patient-capital" investments in the years thereafter.

While most scholarly literature of the high-growth years focused on explaining Japanese economic successes directly, other authors adopted a more indirect approach, focusing on the relationship among political stability, regulatory institutions, and the microeconomic behavior of Japanese firms. The analytical objective was to understand political stability and other political processes, such as resource allocation. Such work proved to have relevance also in understanding the success of capital-intensive growth during the 1960s and 1970s. My two volumes of the late 1980s and the early 1990s, *Crisis and Compensation* and *Strategic Capitalism*, could be considered part of this genre, and their analysis a personal inspiration to the current work.[33] The research of Daniel Okimoto, Richard Samuels, and T. J. Pempel also addresses the interrelationship between Japan's economic growth and its political evolution, although with less explicit attention to the implications of political structures for economic growth.[34] Steven Vogel adds, importantly, that "the existing institutions of Japanese capitalism are shaping their own transformation," and begins to detail what the incentives and linkages between these embedded institutions and prospects for reform actually are, especially at the firm level.[35] He does not, however, probe at length how the incentive structures behind political as opposed to corporate behavior critically impede the process of reform.

Edward Lincoln, although an economist, did address many of the political structures that impeded Japanese economic growth during the 1990s, including farm cooperatives, lifetime employment, and the distribution system.[36] He lumped them together as "vested interests," however, and did not discuss in detail their often contrasting internal dynamics or incentives in detail. His analysis thus fails to provide a basis for explaining the frequently positive technical roles of non-governmental bodies; the incentives of their members; or the paradox that these organizations exerted a positive impact on growth in one era and a conversely negative impact in another period.

One of the few authors who has attempted to explain both the growth of the 1950s and 1960s and the intractable stagnation that followed is Richard Katz, in two general yet intellectually provocative recent works.[37] Katz adopts a chronological, political-economic approach, stressing how political clientelism has, over time, increasingly compromised economic management and rendered it ever more rigid and inefficient. His work does shed light at a general, anecdotal level on why the transition from growth to stagnation transpired. Yet it fails to identify in detail specific institutional variables at work, or the interrelationship between domestic incentive structures and broader forces operating in the global political economy.

Yves Tiberghien, like Katz, concerns himself in a penetrating way with the political economy of recent economic growth and stagnation in Japan.[38] In contrast to Katz, he does consider in detail the role of subnational factors, especially leadership, in shaping the puzzling and contradictory profiles of rigidity and reform that prevail in Japan. Yet Tiberghien cannot dwell, in his broad three-country study, on the specific institutions and embedded incentives that complicate the processes of reform and response to globalization within Japan itself.

Frances Rosenbluth and Michael Thies, like Margarita Estevez-Abe, in creative works replete with implications for the prospective long-term trajectory of the Japanese political economy, emphasize the important dualism between individual choice and institutional parameters that constrain it. They stress the importance, in particular, of electoral rules in configuring the incentives of Japanese politicians.[39] They all argue that the 1994 electoral reform, by changing the basis of Japanese Diet elections from a multi-member to a single-member district-based system, creates broader incentives for politicians that will ultimately lead to more market-oriented policy appeals. While these arguments have an abstract, long-term logic regarding party-political and electoral behavior, they do not consider sufficiently how intermediate organizations like agricultural cooperatives, religious groups, or industrial associations, standing between parties and the general public, will actively shape micropolitical preference structures.

What becomes apparent from previous analyses taken together is that accounting for Japan's stunning and globally important transition of the past quarter century, from growth to stagnation, is a complex, multivariate analytical process, just as forecasting prospects for Japan's recovery also is. Analysis naturally requires attention to macroeconomic changes, such as Ohkawa and Rosovsky emphasize. Yet analysis likewise needs to transcend the national level which is their central concern, and indeed that of virtually all the authors so far reviewed here.

Schaede, in contrast to the nationally oriented analysts mentioned above, considers in detail the mesopolitical "cooperative associations" of Japan.[40] These stand between the state, on the one hand, and a broader society, on the other, which includes the dynamic new market-oriented private firms now emerging in the electronic, pharmaceutical, and service industries, which Schaede also examines in separate research.[41] Schaede, together with William Grimes, notes in an additional volume the importance of intermediate institutions in channeling Japan's distinctive responses to global change, through a process of "permeable insulation."[42]

Schaede does not, however, concern herself in detail with the concrete institutions or incentive structures that mediate, and often constrain, globalization. As this book shows, there is powerful evidence that such intermediate bodies, in forms ranging from bankers' associations to agricultural cooperatives, do in fact profoundly transform the preference structures of members. This transformation renders such individuals quiescent and unresponsive to the broad electoral appeals whose recent importance Rosenbluth, Thies, and Estevez-Abe emphasize so strongly in their analyses.[43]

Broad shifts in global allocations of capital among nations appear to have affected Japan's growth path, especially in the increasingly integrated world political economy that began emerging in the late 1970s, and that gained increasing international salience in the early twenty-first century.[44] Yet those allocative shifts have been responsive not only to macroeconomic supply-demand relationships, but also to national financial regulatory patterns. They also remain responsive to political-economic incentives at the micro level, which are often embedded in durable subnational domestic institutions. Only an integrated approach—cognizant of international and domestic considerations, macro and micro, in both the economic and political spheres—can adequately explain the historic transition from growth to stagnation that has occurred in Japan over the past quarter century, or the complex and nuanced possibilities of reversing that development.

The Argument in Brief

This book explores how subnational institutions affect economic growth strategies and national response to globalization, with a special focus on post–World War II Japan. It focuses particularly on the intermediate organizations of civil society—many of them corporatist—that structure individual, corporate, and political incentives. These are not simply vested interests, and many perform important technical and administrative tasks. Banks play coordinating and connecting roles in many of them.

This book argues that these subnational institutions internalize benefits and externalize costs, thus orienting micro-level incentives of their members in a risk-and-reward-sharing fashion that can both encourage large-scale public-interest projects and support expansionary capital-investment-driven domestic growth strategies. At the same time these very "mesopolitical" institutions, through their parochial "in-group" orientation, insulate individual decision-makers from global pressures, and thus indirectly inhibit response to developments in the outside world.

To support its general argument, this book shows how distinctive subnational institutions, known as "circles of compensation," produce the collaborative, often efficient, yet distinctly parochial patterns of political-economic behavior such as often observed in Japan and other "cooperative market capitalist" systems. It contrasts them to the more consistently adverse "distributional coalitions," postulated by Mancur Olson to inhibit economic growth,[45] and the "vested interests" that are characterized by others in a similar vein.[46] This book explores the prevalence and functional role of circles of compensation within six sectors of the Japanese political economy, chosen for their putative roles in shaping growth and globalization patterns. Those focus sectors include (1) finance, (2) land policy, (3) agriculture, (4) energy, (5) transportation, and (6) communications. For control purposes, this book also briefly considers patterns of corporate behavior in two globalized industries—autos and electronics—where circles are less salient, as well as case histories of innovative, global Japanese firms, such as SoftBank and Rakuten, that have not been active in circles of compensation.

The research finds that circles of compensation in finance and land policy, for which banks are crucial connectors, have played central roles in shaping the contours of Japanese economic growth. The circles have done so in two ways: by diffusing the risk of large-scale capital investment through risk sharing, and by encouraging high leverage through the lending–real estate collateral link. By supporting risk sharing and high leverage, circles of compensation supported the rapid growth of such powerful heavy industries as steel, shipbuilding, and petrochemicals, which powered the high growth of the 1950s, 1960s, and early 1970s. Agricultural circles also played a supportive role by helping stabilize the political parameters supportive of capital-intensive industrialization, and by working to sustain high land prices that have in turn encouraged liberal lending by banks. Energy circles likewise aided for many years in relaxing resource and foreign-exchange constraints on growth, through wholesale introduction of nuclear power.

Even as they supported rapid growth for many years, the circles of compensation, through their risk-diffusion mechanisms, including government guarantees, also intensified moral hazard. As long as the Japanese system was insulated from the world through foreign-exchange controls, and had adequate credit-monitoring mechanisms, such as long-term credit banks, this risk was manageable. The circles were able to deal efficiently with excess capacity in shipbuilding during the 1970s, for example, through coordinated capacity reduction.[47] As financial globalization progressed during the 1980s, however, classical risk-monitoring and diffusion structures like the long-term credit banks and the Ministry of Finance convoy system lost their ability to stabilize the circles, leading to financial crisis, a credit crunch, falling land prices, and sharp growth declines. Moral hazard in the energy system, together with inadequate monitoring, led to crisis for the energy circles also, following the Fukushima disaster.

Circles of compensation have likewise helped configure Japan's response to globalization, it is argued, even as they have shaped domestic growth patterns, although different circles have been central in the two cases. Circles in transportation, agriculture, and communications have directly worked to insulate Japan from the world, and thus to directly inhibit and delay its response to globalization. Circles in finance, including the Ministry of Finance's convoy system, have likewise slowed the response of Japanese banks, insurance companies, and securities houses more indirectly, as well. Following collapse of the financial bubble during the early 1990s, the reluctance of the banks to lend intensified recession and deflation. Rigidities and hesitancy engendered by the circles have opened opportunities for foreign investors, who arbitraged the managed domestic markets that local players worked to preserve, often generating market-driven instability in their wake.

This book concludes that circles of compensation are so structurally embedded in most sectors of the Japanese political economy examined that it is unrealistic in the short to medium term to dismantle them. More productive is to adopt a gradualist approach—broadening the circles to encompass new groups, including foreigners; reviving the banks that frequently stand at the core of key circles; and ending gender discrimination. It is argued that worldwide best-practice search, with special reference to globally conscious European and Asian nations with communitarian traditions similar to those of Japan, could inspire further productive reforms in Japan itself.

In Conclusion

The Japanese political economy has experienced extraordinary variations in performance since Commodore Matthew Perry's "black ships" first arrived in 1853,[48] and remarkable variations even since the Oil Shocks of the 1970s. Japan's fortunes have been intertwined with many of the determining forces shaping our world, including war, industrial development, and globalization. In its interaction with those historic global forces, Japan's political–economic performance poses myriad empirical puzzles. These puzzles are classically excellent raw material for theory building, in both comparative and international political economy.

Despite the opportunities for social-science theory building that are created by the paradoxical aspects of Japanese public policy, Japan specialists have done remarkably little to capitalize on them.[49] Chalmers Johnson's concept of the developmental state, T. J. Pempel's "corporatism without labor," and the Ramseyer-Rosenbluth formulation of "Japan's political marketplace" have been among the prominent exceptions. Clearly there is room for more Japan-centric analysis that makes broader contributions to social-science theory, taking account of the deepening relationships that exist between Japan's domestic system at the micro level and the broader world outside.

The mesopolitical circles-of-compensation model developed here has unique heuristic and predictive value, because it recognizes both the prevailing *institutional structure* of late-developing cooperative market economies, with their strong corporatist tendencies, and the microeconomic *incentive structure* operating within such systems. The eclectic emphasis on rational choice subject to institutional constraint addresses the triple paradoxes presented earlier, in a parsimonious fashion that is also falsifiable, yet has not been heretofore concisely presented.

Among the most promising empirical puzzles posed by Japanese experience are Japan's fluctuating growth patterns of recent years, and its mixed response to globalization. Both are distinctive in comparative context. And both puzzles are related to subnational cooperative patterns embedded deep in the Japanese political economy, to whose conceptualization we now turn in greater detail.

The Circles-of-Compensation Concept

Comparative political economy has gradually, over the past half century, declared its independence from area studies and evolved into a theory-driven enterprise.[1] Specialists in Europe, Latin America, Africa, and even Southeast Asia, with their large number of country cases, have stood in the vanguard of such theory-driven comparative study, while the students of the large nations have lagged behind. Slowest to engage in active theory building have been specialists on large countries with complex languages not studied extensively in the West, including China, Indonesia, Korea, and Japan.

The recent performance of the Japanese political economy—both compared to its own recent past and to the trajectory of other advanced industrialized nations—is a study in striking paradox. That paradox has two central, and related, dimensions: Japan's recent inability to grow, and its recent inability to globalize. Innovation and structural change have both been difficult, and complacency has been rife. The paradox of Japanese public policy along these dual dimensions of growth and globalization has disturbing policy implications for all the world, and theoretical importance, as well. Its intellectual resolution could help generate ideas that, while born of Japanese experience, also have important heuristic implications internationally.

Many concepts have been imported from the study of other regions of the world into research on Japan, including class conflict, corporatism, and consociation. Yet all too few have traveled in the opposite direction.[2] The time is ripe for broader efforts by Japan specialists to fertilize their disciplines more generally.[3]

In this chapter we elaborate on a concept—circle of compensation—introduced briefly in Chapter 1, which has promise to help unravel the paradox of Japanese public policy, and at the same time contribute to broader social theory. It is a particular structural configuration within "compensation politics," which is "politics directed primarily toward advertising and satisfying demands for material satisfaction between grantors and supporters, as opposed to those politics oriented toward attaining non-material goals."[4] We define such circles of compensation more specifically as "networks of regular participants among which such interactions take place, in which members have reciprocal benefits and obligations."[5] Members can include both current and retired government officials, together with a wide variety of private citizens, often including financiers in central positions, although circles as a whole tend to be nonhierarchical in nature.

Outline of the Concept

Circles of compensation have five defining characteristics that allow one to recognize them by denotation. First, they have a *clearly defined set* of members, which to a significant extent persists over time. Second, this set is *expansible*—new members in principle can be admitted, although the assent of existing members is typically required. This expansibility gives the circle some flexibility in responding to—generally by co-opting—external pressures, provided that adequate resources are available within the circle to support expanded membership. Members can include both public- and private-sector actors.

Third, circles of compensation are *iterated*—that is, they persist over an extended set of transactions. They are thus, in the parlance of game theory, institutions—not simple one-act games.[6] The ongoing character of these circles enhances their flexibility, since members can in principle trade off preferences with other members over periods of time. Cross-issue trade-offs are also enhanced when circles become institutionalized. Fourth, the circles *allocate valued resources internally*, normally through a routinized, nonconflictual process, such as equal apportionment to all members, or through sequential apportionment, as under the *dangō* system of construction.[7] The circles thus incorporate both relationship-based and rules-based dimensions.[8] Government action can critically affect the level of resources to be allocated—through direct subsidies, tax policies, or regulation.

Fifth, circles of compensation *externalize costs* to nonmembers, thereby preserving harmony within the in-group that constitutes any given circle of compensation itself. Such entities naturally tend to be more sensitive to stimuli from other group members than from the outside, rendering them parochial.

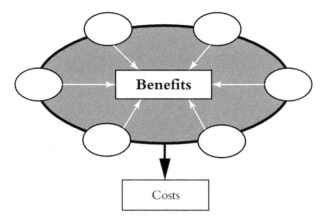

FIGURE 2.1   Circles of compensation—prevailing patterns of
benefit distribution

SOURCE: Author's illustration.

The general pattern of transactions within a circle of compensation, and
between such a circle and its socioeconomic environment, is presented in
Figure 2.1.

As suggested above, and in Figure 2.1, circles of compensation typically
operate in intimate, generally symbiotic relationship with government regulatory authorities. Indeed, in many cases government officials, or retired officials
in *amakudari* corporate positions, are best conceived as members of the circles
themselves. Those authorities can provide direct material benefits to members,
such as government loans or tax dispensations. They can regulate pricing,
license or inhibit entry of new members, confer special ascriptive benefits on
participants, and through various incentives influence the microeconomic behavior of members on such fateful decisions as capital investment. Government
authorities can also mobilize circle members to serve bureaucratic purposes,
such as, in the case of banks, underwriting government bond issues. And
they can help inhibit free-riding—the endemic problem of collective action
stressed by Mancur Olson. Circles of compensation involve flexible allocation
of benefits and costs among group members over time, and government can
help enforce predictable, long-term allocations, both formally and informally.

Circles of compensation tend to have a risk-diffusing, stability-inducing
bias, which reduces the incentives of participants to engage in radical innovation. Circles require stability and a consistent hierarchy among their participants to maintain cohesiveness. This is consistent with incremental innovation, complex manufacturing, and high levels of quality control, but not with
volatile paradigm shifts.[9]

Institutional Expressions

Circles of compensation have a common logical structure, outlined above. They assume a broad variety of institutional forms, which reflect the common logic as well as their varied political-economic contexts. Circles are also supported by a wide range of resource-allocation mechanisms. Over the following pages, we review and categorize the remarkable variation found worldwide, with a special concern for how circles are configured in Japan, the principal geographical focus of our research.

The most broadly researched and most commonly known variant of the circle of compensation is the cartel, which can be defined as a collaborative arrangement among competing individuals or organizations. Typically cartels conspire in economic affairs to stabilize or to raise prices, often by constraining output. They can also be used to allocate responsibilities in the industrial downsizing process, as through so-called recession cartels, or rationalization cartels.[10] Alternatively, they can be used to divide technical responsibilities in the process of scientific innovation, as through research cartels.[11] The notion can be extended to political or social spheres to denote collaborative arrangements among political competitors, such as the cartel of elites and cartel of anxiety, which Ralf Dahrendorf perceived in Weimar Germany.[12] All of these arrangements typically internalize benefits and externalize costs, exhibiting the trademark behavior of circles of compensation.

Industry associations also frequently exhibit functional traits of a circle of compensation, albeit in an institutionalized and multifunctional form.[13] Such associations have a group of members who band together for a common purpose, such as lobbying or adjusting industry capacity, internalizing the benefits of their actions. They also typically operate defensively to externalize costs— by raising prices, for example, to offset reductions in volumes of production. The functions of industry associations can overlap those of cartels, although the former are in general functionally broader and more versatile in their operations.

To operate successfully, a circle of compensation necessarily requires a stream of resources—preferably one that flows in a predictable manner to the circle for allocation purposes, and that is *not* accessible to outsiders. When such a predictable flow exists, and the allocation to individual recipients is not specified by an entitlement arrangement, the prospect that a circle of compensation will arise and persist is strong.

There are also a wide range of specialized, functionally oriented, and fundamentally productive collectivities—very common in Japan and similar coordinated market economies (CMEs)—that qualify, under the foregoing criteria, as circles of compensation. The very-large-scale integration (VLSI) "research cartel" of Japanese electronics firms, for example, worked effectively to develop the 64K dynamic random-access memory chip, as well as related production equipment.[14] Japan's Bond Issue Arrangement Committee (*Kisai Kai*) set corporate purchase allocations for corporate and government bonds, maintaining interest-rate stability in the face of massive bond issues within a highly regulated environment during the 1960s and 1970s.[15] A capital-investment council within the Japanese steel industry, composed of former Ministry of International Trade and Industry (MITI) vice ministers serving with each of the various top Japanese steel firms, determined steel-industry capacity expansions collectively for most of the high-growth years after 1960.[16]

A budgetary special account, whereby revenue is raised through some clearly specified transactional mechanism, and explicitly segregated from general revenues for a narrowly and clearly specified alternative purpose, is one such institutional mechanism for creating predictable, protected resource flows. Another is the government financial institution with explicitly and narrowly defined lending mandates. In the area of tax expenditures, narrowly targeted special-depreciation schedules fill a similar function. All of these distributive support mechanisms are widely used in cooperative market-capitalist nations with developmental aspirations, such as Japan.[17]

Geographical Distribution

Circles of compensation are not a uniquely Japanese phenomenon. In the form of cartels, they have been prominent in continental European industrial organization since the dawn of the industrial revolution in the second half of the nineteenth century. In the less structured form of industrial associations, they coordinate activities of the Swiss watchmaking industry to this day.[18] Danish and Dutch dairy- and livestock-industry promotion bodies have similar functions and characteristics, although they may be less prone to in-group discrimination than their Japanese counterparts, whose behavior is considered in Chapter 6. Both in Europe and elsewhere, circles of compensation are often prominent in heavy-industry sectors, characterized by lumpy, large-scale capital investments; high fixed costs; and sharply declining marginal costs—sectors such as steel, petrochemicals, and shipbuilding. As John Sutton notes, industrial cost structure, especially sunk costs, can be an important determinant of the organizational arrangements that are chosen.[19]

Circles of compensation are also of frequent importance in Asia. President Park Chung-hee self-consciously imitated Japanese agricultural cooperatives in his *saemaul* policies of the early 1970s. Kim Dae-jung revived the consociational model in initiating institutionalized labor-management cooperation during the Asian financial crisis of 1997–1998.[20] Under Deng Xiaoping and Mahathir Mohamad, both China and Malaysia also emulated Japanese models of industrial association and organization.[21] Turkey and India have done so, as well. In all these cases, risk diffusion and technical cooperation, so as to promote rapid, capital-intensive industrialization, were central objectives.

The Mediterranean world has also embraced corporatist variants, controversial as they have been, that represent permutations in the circles-of-compensation paradigm.[22] Benito Mussolini's Italy, Francisco Franco's Spain, and António Salazar's Portugal all were governed through consociational arrangements under which major groups were represented in national-level peak bargaining that aggregated interests among elites in a mutually cooperative way without mass political mobilization. This pattern was also typical for many years, before mass democracy emerged, in such Latin American technocracies as the Brazil of Ernesto Geisel and João Figueiredo (1974–1985).[23] Indeed, circles of compensation are a favored means of allocating political-economic resources in a wide range of transition economies where market mechanisms are still underdeveloped, and where their abrupt emergence would be socially destabilizing.

The Instructive Value of the Japanese Case

If circles of compensation are so globally pervasive, especially in transition economies, why do we focus on their manifestation in Japan? We do so for three major reasons. First, Japan has been, for the bulk of the past century and a half, both an economic success story and a major practitioner of this pattern of sociopolitical organization; its efforts at maximizing stability and economic growth through these mechanisms have thus been widely emulated elsewhere.[24] Korea under Park Chung-hee and China under Deng Xiaoping are cases where the Japanese socioeconomic model, broadly conceived, has been seriously referenced.[25]

Japanese circles of compensation are also unusually well developed institutionally, which makes them a uniquely accessible object of study. Japan has many formal industry associations, such as the Japanese Bankers Association and the National Federation of Agricultural Co-operative Associations (*Zen-Noh*), which are examined in Chapters 4 and 6, respectively. It also has an elaborate and formalized system of budgetary special accounts (*tokubetsu kaikei*), which are readily identifiable, easy to analyze, and substantive in their implications for policy and resource allocation.

Even though circles of compensation appear to be ubiquitous in Japan, they are also often misunderstood. There is a substantial literature on socioeconomic organization in Japan, as discussed in Chapter 1, replete with broadly discussed concepts such as "Japan, Incorporated," "ruling triumvirate," "*zaikai*," "*keiretsu*," and "*zoku*."[26] Yet this literature fails, in general, to address the crucial issue of micro-level incentive structures. Attention to incentives, discussed particularly in the latter section of this chapter, is essential in understanding patterns of stability and change in Japan.

Japanese circles of compensation are a compelling topic on which to focus, finally, because they have unusually important *global* implications for our twenty-first-century world. With a twelfth of global gross domestic product (GDP), Japan is the largest free-market economy in the world, apart from the United States. As such, it is large enough that many domestic institutions can comfortably focus on the domestic market alone. Many can give only moderate attention to international trade—less than 18 percent of GDP, compared to twice that share in neighboring Korea.[27]

It is therefore not surprising, given both insularity and often clientelistic regulation, that circles of compensation have come to enjoy enormous salience within the Japanese political economy, shaping both its domestic proclivities and its international orientation. As we shall see, such circles were central to Japan's highly leveraged bank-centric high growth for half a century after World War II, and the economic bubble's subsequent collapse. Over the early post–World War II years, the banking–land policy nexus, created and sustained by the circles, has fatefully shaped Japan's globally significant profile of growth and stagnation.

The circles also have a continuing impact on the ability of Japan to respond to global market forces, both through their perverse impact on distribution generally, and particularly in traditionally regulated service sectors like telecommunications. In such areas their risk-diffusing nature inhibits disruptive technological innovation and political-economic change. Precisely these micro-level rigidities within Japan delay resolution of debt problems, impede domestic absorption of capital, and hence render expansionary Japanese domestic fiscal policy unusually stimulative beyond Japanese shores, in an increasingly interdependent global financial system.

Both Japan's recent domestic struggles with globalization and its substantial resultant capital outflows are matters of critical importance to Japan itself. They are also matters of importance for the United States, with whom Japan is deeply interdependent, in both economic and security dimensions. Through that U.S.–Japan nexus, Japan's struggles to globalize are important for the world as a whole.[28]

Why Circles of Compensation Emerged Prominently in Japan

The pronounced salience of circles of compensation in Japan has deep roots in that nation's experience as a "late developer" internationally, albeit as a vanguard nation from an Asian regional perspective. Such circles were arguably central during the Meiji period to Japan's economic growth, its political stability, and on occasion its autonomy in international affairs. Japan emerged into the global political economy, after all, during the late nineteenth century—at the high noon of imperialism. It faced a stark set of alternatives: industrialize rapidly, with a strong military-industrial dimension, or fall under Western colonial dominance. The Meiji leaders chose the former course.

Japan's chosen course implied enduring three institutional imperatives, which the Meiji leaders themselves confronted: (1) trade protection for Japan's infant industries; (2) political stability, to instill national unity and confidence in the country's proactive course; and (3) risk diffusion, to encourage banks and industrialists to lend and invest the enormous sums needed to build optimal-scale steel mills, shipyards, and arsenals. Each of these challenges pointed to cooperatively oriented collective action—circles of compensation—as a solution, despite the clear long-term obstacles to effective collective action that Olson and others have emphasized.[29] These three challenges of Meiji gave birth to three functionally differentiated variants of the circles-of-compensation paradigm, still identifiable today. These are presented in Table 2.1.

In the international economic sphere, Japan's preferred response to the problem of trade competition, as in other late-industrializing nations, was trade protection through tariffs and quotas. The unequal treaties that were concluded with Western powers constrained that course, however, until 1911. As a consequence, Japan sought insulation from global competition more indirectly, through domestic collaboration—sectoral cooperative associations

TABLE 2.1

Three circles-of-compensation functional variants

Circle function	Challenges	Solutions
Protection	Foreign/domestic trade competition	Tariffs/quotas and industrial associations
Stabilization	Sociopolitical change	Corporatist civic institutions and agricultural associations; distributive benefits
Risk diffusion	Uncertainty/volatility investment scale	Cross-sectoral/intrasectoral groupings and government–business agreements

SOURCE: Author's illustration.

(*gyōkai*) that collaborated to restrict imports and to set prices, as needed.[30] These associations became a basic circles-of-compensation paradigm—observable in all the sectoral cases presented here.

The imperatives of limiting competition in the international sphere, so as to allow domestic corporate stakeholders to survive and prosper, had their distinct analogues at home within Japan. Private firms, often with government regulatory support, collaborated to neutralize competition and other forms of uncertainty in their business environment. Trade associations were often the preferred vehicle for this cooperation.[31]

In the political realm, the Meiji leadership responded to the challenge of maintaining stability amid rapid industrialization and social change with corporatist civic and agricultural associations, which emerged after 1890.[32] These new organizations were nominally private bodies with public functions, which mobilized grassroots political backing for the state and received subsidies, government loans, and often a subgovernance role in return. They included local chambers of commerce, post offices, and agricultural cooperatives, whose local notables became the core of support associations (*kōenkai*) for politicians as democracy began to emerge.

A third functional circles-of-compensation prototype—necessitated by the challenge of heavy industrialization—was the *risk-diffusion* variant. This permutation has taken on multiple institutional forms, and exists at various levels of economic organization. They include:

1. Cross-sectoral circles, such as the main-bank group (*keiretsu*) of the post–World War II era; or the financial clique (*zaibatsu*), its prewar variant;[33]

2. Intrasectoral circles, such as bond underwriting syndicates or financial consortia for large-scale industrial development projects.[34] In finance, such circles mobilized a wide variety of entities in risk diffusion, including insurance companies and trust banks, as well as long-term and commercial banks; and

3. Government–business collaborative arrangements, such as the long-standing convoy system in Japanese finance.

Prior to World War II, holding companies (*honsha*) provided the coordination mechanism for most risk-reduction circles of compensation. Accused of abetting the war effort, these ownership structures were formally dissolved in September 1946 by the Allied Occupation.[35] Over the ensuing decade, banks emerged as the core vehicle for coordination, as Chapter 3 points out in detail. Over the past half century and more, banks have continued to stand at the heart of Japanese finance, and of the most basic risk-reduction mechanisms in Japan, ranging from industrial groups to underwriting syndicates.

Circles of compensation have been a characteristic Japanese approach to resource allocation and corporate governance, since at least the Meiji era. They long held a powerful logic in Japan's economic development process, owing to their ability to promote rapid, highly leveraged growth, defuse intragroup conflict, and stabilize political-economic relationships, while reducing and externalizing risk, in the aggregate, for their participants. Yet in an increasingly globalized, volatile world, circles of compensation also generate subtle yet important risks for their members.

In a global world, both firms and governments need to respond flexibly, rapidly, and creatively to external challenge. Yet circles of compensation often reduce the incentives of their members to do so, particularly when entrepreneurial, individualistic action is optimal. Given these drawbacks, why do circles of compensation continue to play such a prominent role in Japan today?

Circles of compensation remain prominent in Japan, first of all, because they are deeply embedded historically—a product of the government's determined efforts to use them as a primary tool for achieving both high-speed economic development and concomitant political stability. The Meiji government used circles, at least from the early twentieth century, as a corporatist instrument of social control, in areas such as agriculture.[36] They were strengthened in sectors like finance and heavy industry during the 1930s, as instruments for Japan's military mobilization, and the related development of heavy industry, with banks playing an expanding role in the political economy.[37]

Bank-centric circles were greatly reinforced and given enhanced leverage by land policy during the postwar high-growth period, from the mid-1950s until the Oil Shock of 1973. Circles were also extended to a range of nontraded sectors like transportation and communications, from the 1950s through the 1990s. There they served as a means of enhancing political influence, and of collecting political rents on behalf of increasingly influential local interest groups.

A Meaning That Transcends Vested Interests

Circles of compensation remain formidable in Japan even though the high-growth era has ended. Many of them perform, after all, comprehensive and fundamental subgovernmental roles in sectors of continuing national importance, such as administration, interest aggregation, and technical services. More generally, their basic functions—distributing benefits internally, and externalizing costs—give them a powerful underlying attraction to members.

Circles of compensation, in short, are thus *far more* than conventional lobbying organizations.[38]

It is also true that circles often do safeguard powerful vested interests, through extensive and at times captive regulation, as well as the omnipresence of special accounts. The agricultural circles protect the affluence of farmers, for example, by guaranteeing high rice prices. Similarly, the transportation circles protect high airfares and inhibit competition that would impose major losses on embedded interest groups. Yet circles of compensation serve broader purposes.

Circles of compensation persist in Japan, first of all, because they perform significant and positive technical functions. Some of them work to incrementally develop advanced technology, as the VLSI project did. Others stabilize markets for government bonds. Still others coordinate investments in heavy industry, or work collaboratively to phase out sunset industries.[39]

Circles of compensation also persist in Japan, secondly, because they provide an efficient way for participants to reduce political-economic transaction costs. The country's formal policy processes are structurally complex, with multiple decision points that make reformist measures distressingly easy to veto.[40] The Japanese Diet is bicameral (in contrast to Korea's unicameral legislature, for example) with most legislation required to pass through both houses, as well as committees in each case, while also being vetted by a broad range of politicians and bureaucrats. Diet proceedings are divided into an average of three annual sessions, with legislation dying at the end of each session—in contrast to American legislative processes, for example, where bills continue to be live for up to two full years. Legislation can be either stopped or subverted at any number of points, making veto players unusually important.[41] Japanese circles of compensation, with their broad social networks and comprehensive functions, are well equipped to play this strategic defensive role.

A relative lack of sociopolitical pluralism, thirdly, also makes dismantling or altering the circles of compensation structurally difficult in Japan. The country is one of the most homogeneous, ethnically and socially speaking, in the world, with virtually no minority groups. In contrast to Korea, Germany, the United States, or even Meiji Japan, Japan today has no strong regionalist tendencies. To a greater degree than Scandinavia, Germany, Britain, or even the United States, Japan also lacks politically influential labor unions or non-governmental organizations. Its civil society is much more regulated and subject to state influence than in virtually any other industrialized democracy.[42]

A fourth reason that circles of compensation persist in Japan, despite their adverse recent implications for its globalization, and at times for economic growth, is that the country lacks the consistently strong executive leadership required to countervail or transform such collusive institutions. Part of the problem is structural—Japan is a parliamentary democracy in which the office of the prime minister, as chief executive, is structurally weak. With the party political system in transformation, the prime minister has typically also been politically weak, with seven different politicians serving in that office between 2006 and 2012. Shinzō Abe may be an exception in his recent tenure (since December 2012), but transforming the circles has nevertheless proved difficult even for him, as it also had been for such ambitious and articulate previous advocates of structural reform as Yasuhiro Nakasone and Junichirō Koizumi.

With circles of compensation deeply embedded, and attractive to their participants as well as other social groups, determined efforts would be needed to abolish or alter them. The challenge of transformation is compounded by the structural complexities of Japanese decision-making, the lack of pluralism in Japanese civil society, and the weakness—both structural and often political—of contemporary Japanese leadership. Thus, in the absence of enormous shocks from the outside, or transformative crisis from within, Japan may be condemned to live with circles of compensation—only gradually declining in political-economic salience—for some time to come, despite the drawbacks for the nation in its relations with the broader world. Yet the importance of such circles does vary by sector, and changes over time, making a refined sector-by-sector examination central to our analysis. Only by examining circles up close can we come to understand their current and future meaning for Japan and for world affairs more generally.

Case Selection

To best understand the meaning of the circles-of-compensation concept in the Japanese context, and to accurately assess the impact of such circles on the Japanese and global political economies, what sort of cases are most appropriate? We focus here on institutions for consociational coordination of interests in six sectors: (1) finance, (2) land and housing, (3) food supply, (4) energy, (5) transportation, and (6) communications. These sectors were chosen because of their pivotal relationship to both growth and globalization. Japan's distinctive "invest, then save" approach to economic development, bootstrapping high-speed growth through high, bank-administered industrial leverage, required sophisticated industrial-credit banks; credit policies predicated on rising land prices; and a stable political base.

Detailed studies of financial policies centered on banking, land policies centered on collateral, and agricultural policies centered on sustaining political support should yield fruitful insights into how high-growth policies were sustained at the micro level. Finance, land, and agriculture, after all, are sectors at once highly regulated and traditionally unexposed to global competitive pressures. The evolution of these three areas of the Japanese political economy also provides useful insights into Japan's overall ability to respond to globalization, since they are key indirect supports for manufacturing-sector competitiveness, and at the same time "gateways," where domestic Japan interfaces with the broader world. By considering these parochial sectors, pivotal battlefields in Japan's "managed globalization,"[43] it should thus be possible to develop a subtle and prospectively accurate prognosis regarding Japan's longer-term response to the powerful forces of globalization now transforming world affairs.

Energy, transport, and communications are also crucial "gateway" sectors. Energy engagement with the world is crucial because Japan is over 80 percent dependent on imports for its primary energy supply, with nuclear power being one of the few avenues for reducing that dependence. The reasons why communications and transportation profoundly influence a nation's ability to interact with the broader world are self-evident. The cost of telecommunications shapes a nation's propensity, as well as its economic ability, to reach out to other nations. The cost and availability of air travel and sea transportation impose similar constraints, as do education and cultural exchange.

The Importance of Counterfactuals

Understanding the impact that circles of compensation actually have on the Japanese political economy and its ability to interact with the broader world are, of course, central concerns of this research, within the context of a more abstract and general examination of collective action behavior around the world. Part of the analysis must thus involve concrete examination of specific circles and their functioning, along the lines outlined above, in areas where such institutions are powerful, with special attention to how they diffuse risk and conversely inhibit innovation and expanded outreach to the broader world. To fully understand the impact of circles of compensation, it is also important to consider counterfactual cases where they are weak or nonexistent.

The automotive industry and consumer electronics are two such sectors. Regulatory barriers to entry are relatively weak in both cases, and government plays little role in shaping market parameters—either in setting prices or in providing a market, or in protecting domestic firms from overseas competition. Industry associations in both cases are historically weak. Both industries, tellingly, have been at once proactive and successful at globalization. Toyota Motor Corporation and Panasonic Corporation, for example, have both succeeded—against vigorous competition—in becoming global leaders in their respective industries.

The counterexamples of autos and consumer electronics provide a hypothesis that can be productively explored in the cases to follow here: *Circles of compensation are a function of international isolation and high levels of regulation.* It should follow that as those variables decline in salience, circles of compensation themselves will decline in importance, improving prospects for globalization. Examining cases of Japanese firms operating in globalized sectors outside Japan, such as SoftBank, Daikin, Unicharm, and Rakuten, should allow us to test this proposition.[44]

Heuristic Value and Implications for Policy

The following chapters are replete with concrete applications of the circles-of-compensation concept, together with detailed assessment of the substantial policy implications which the unusual salience of this sociopolitical phenomenon in Japan have both for Japanese growth profiles and Japan's ties with the broader world. Suffice it to say here that circles are found in almost every walk of Japanese life, ranging from agriculture to transportation, finance, and manufacturing. The finance–land policy nexus that Japan sustained enabled the country's ambitious yet risky "invest, then save" strategy of the high-growth years. The circles-of-compensation concept has additional heuristic value in explaining the nontraded side of the Japanese political economy, where global market forces are naturally less salient than in Japan's direct involvements with international trade.

Circles of compensation enhance stability in human relationships while simultaneously intensifying parochialism. In the short run, they may inhibit economic efficiency, as they diffuse the risk to any one member of failing to respond to external challenge. Yet in the long run, circles also make megaprojects more possible—giant ventures ranging from massive steel mills to nuclear power plants and high-speed transport. Many of these megaprojects could otherwise not easily be realized, although they arguably contribute to social progress as a whole.

Circles of compensation are intrinsically attractive to participants, not least in economic terms, because they internalize the benefits of cooperation and reduce transaction costs. Through social cooperation among members, the circles raise production and distribution prices above levels that would prevail in the event of broader market competition, and reduce the need to go to outsiders for information and other valued resources. Conversely, circles externalize the costs of their existence by generating higher prices or greater scarcity for others. It is thus *non-member outsiders*—both foreign and domestic—who lack direct involvement with the circles—who ultimately *pay most of the short-run costs* of their exclusivity. The long-run costs of inadequate competition and information flow, however, such as low levels of innovation in response to environmental change, can ultimately be devastating for insiders, as well.

In Conclusion

The Japanese political economy exhibits paradoxical behavior in its growth patterns and response to globalization. It grew rapidly across the 1950s, 1960s, and early 1970s, but has stagnated along many dimensions since the early 1990s. The circles-of-compensation concept provides a potentially important tool for assessing and explaining such paradoxical, seemingly contradictory outcomes. In doing so, it helps us understand and explain some of the most distinctive and consequential dimensions of Japanese behavior, through a concept with potential applications elsewhere in the world, as well. Casual observation suggests particular heuristic value in understanding the development experience of late-industrializing CMEs in continental Europe, the Southern Cone of South America, Turkey, India, and Korea, as well as Japan.

Circles of compensation have five defining traits. They have a clearly defined set of members that is expansible, and interactions among circle members that are iterated. The circle allocates resources *internally*, externalizing costs to be absorbed by nonmembers. Such circles are thus inherently parochial and conservative in their response to outside forces.

Circles of compensation do help to promote stability and continuity. Yet they also engender resistance to reform. These circles could likewise presumptively impede structural change, even where adaptability is desperately needed, in response to threatening outside developments. How circles of compensation concretely shape Japan's response to emerging policy challenges, and hence Japan's broader vitality and role in world affairs, are subjects to which we now turn.

3

The Political Economy of Connectedness

In the following overview and six sector-specific chapters, we examine the concrete ways in which key Japanese socioeconomic sectors are regulated and organized internally, together with the implications of such organization for how those areas of the political economy function. We consider in succession the way in which the financial, land and housing, agricultural, energy, transportation, and communications sectors are configured, with special emphasis on how changes in finance are transforming the system as a whole.[1] We have chosen these cases because they are the key nonindustrial conduits through which the Japanese economy interacts with the world, thus configuring its response to globalization. We give special precedence to finance and land policies, because their synergistic relationship enabled the expansionary "invest, then save" policies of the high-growth years,[2] and also contributed centrally to Japan's "lost decade" of the 1990s and beyond. Indeed, ultimately dysfunctional networks linking banks, politics, and real estate also undermined the innovative "strategic capitalism" of the high-growth years, and impeded Japan's globalization over the subsequent decades.

Before we begin this sector-specific microanalysis, it is important to understand at a more general level why such subnational interconnectedness matters. We also need to understand what functional role interconnectedness serves, both for the sectors that we examine specifically and for the Japanese political economy as a whole. In the aggregate, the salience of circles of compensation in the important areas we examine has had, and continues to have, fateful implications for both Japanese globalization and for long-term national economic growth.

Many analysts have emphasized the pronounced domestic inter-connectedness—the "holistic character"—of Japanese society.[3] At the macro level, such notions as "Japan, Incorporated" and "cooperative capitalism," together with "J-firm" at the micro level, have been developed and invoked to describe this viscous quality. Analysts have also stressed again and again that comprehending how social networks actually operate within Japan, and in Japan's relations with the broader world, is fundamental to grasping how the political economy functions in reality.

The Critical Importance of Sectoral Linkages

Analysts have directed less attention to *why* interconnectedness matters in Japan, *where* it matters most, *how* social, political, and economic linkages among key sectors have evolved over time, and *what impact* intersectoral linkages have on the broader political economy. As we shall see in Chapter 4, Japan has traditionally had distinctive financial institutions, along with an admirably configured support structure for industrial lending, that stimulated rapid, investment-led economic growth. These highly leveraged institutions required stability and a variety of risk–diffusion mechanisms embedded broadly across the political economy in order to operate effectively. These risk-diffusion devices socialized the substantial risk implicit in large, long-term capital investment decisions, at the same time discouraging the micro-level risk-taking behavior needed to respond to volatile, dynamic outside stimuli like competition from abroad, or the sudden emergence of new foreign market opportunities.

Despite their real-world importance, the concrete configuration of leadership networks—both within individual sectors and across sectors—are all too infrequently considered. There are some exceptions; the study of *amakudari* ("descent from heaven"), for example, has attracted a good deal of attention.[4] Yet the human profile of Japan's "network society," as well as the functional significance of specific sociopolitical configurations within it, and their implications for growth and globalization, remains relatively unexplored.

Before considering the concrete profile of circles of compensation empirically, it is important to remember why social interconnectedness within the Japanese political economy matters analytically, and the research strategy that exploring it necessarily implies. Contemporary Japan, in contrast to most modern industrialized societies, is a distinctively *holistic* political economy, one in which the constituent parts—government, business, and a variety of subnational institutions—are deeply intertwined. As in the case of any high-performance vehicle, malfunction in any single dimension—beginning with land and financial policies, in the case of modern Japan—can have broad macro implications that are difficult to fathom without a combination of sectoral and macro analysis. In the Japanese case, however, these synergistic cross-sectoral implications are unusually large, for a variety of historically embedded reasons.

Japan is an island nation and highly homogeneous in ethnic terms. Its insularity and collective sense of connectivity were greatly enhanced by more than two centuries of isolation during the Edo period (1603–1868). More recent political-economic developments have further intensified the country's traditional holistic character. Following abrupt exposure to an imperialist West, war and high-speed growth progressively deepened the need felt by Japanese elites for domestic stability and risk-reduction mechanisms that at the same time would support rapid economic growth.

For nearly a century following the first arrival of Commodore Matthew Perry's black ships in 1853, Japan confronted a profound existential challenge in political-economic competition with the West that began at the high noon of imperialism during the late nineteenth century, and helped unify the nation. Japan responded with highly leveraged industrial strategies and supportive institutions, which in turn increased the political-economic importance of unity and stability still further. The country's semi-authoritarian government used corporatist tactics to unify the nation politically and administer it economically. These practices gave birth to a variety of sector-specific organizations with risk-sharing and resource-allocating capacity, dedicated to maintaining broader national stability. These included agricultural and industrial cooperatives, which we will examine extensively in Chapter 6. These stabilizing mechanisms were concentrated in the nontraded sectors of the political economy, with a few exceptions.

Japan's circles of compensation emerged in three waves from around 1900 into the 1950s. First there was the Meiji mobilization at the turn of the century, centering on agriculture and small business. Then there were the banking and industrial circles, formed as the country mobilized for war during the 1930s and early 1940s. Then there were the politicized circles, as in construction, that emerged as democracy unfolded and Japan's economy began growing during the first postwar decade (1945–1955). Circles have not been nearly as salient in most other late-developing nations, such as Korea and Singapore, because those other late developers did not confront institution-inspiring historical catalysts to the degree that Japan did.

Incentives and Their Institutional Context

Our particular concern, in examining the circles of compensation that so deeply influence the functioning of the Japanese domestic political economy, and its response to the broader world, is understanding the impact of such circles on the incentive structure of Japanese firms. As Douglass North, Oliver Williamson, and a series of distinguished institutional economists have observed, it is ultimately incentives that determine corporate and individual behavior.[5] And "institutions," as North points out, "define the incentive structure of a society."[6]

Iterative relationships, such as communal risk and reward sharing, alter incentive structures in fundamental ways. It is hence crucial, in understanding either current behavior or predicting the future, to understand the nature of the institutions that inspire micro-level incentive structure.

The "little platoons" of Japanese society, to paraphrase Edmund Burke,[7] matter functionally to the broader system. They matter, first of all, by making possible the expansionary, "invest, then save" economic development strategies, based on human linkages among bankers, industrial firms, bureaucrats, and politicians, that inspire high leverage and land-based collateral; these networks have prevailed across most of recent Japanese economic history. Those expansionary policies required sociopolitical stability allowing Japan to pursue the capital-intensive industrialization necessary to compete in the broader world.

Circles of compensation matter, in micro political-economic terms, because they diffuse risk, allowing corporations and individuals to act more decisively in their broader social relationships. The circles often serve as interest aggregators, allocating valued resources and responsibilities internally as informal surrogates for the government. Such circles likewise typically generate economic rents for participating members, affording them enhanced financial security and profits to be used for a variety of strategic purposes. The circles also often fill valuable technical functions, including research and development. Because of these diverse administrative and sociopolitical functions, circles of compensation are far more than simple vested interests.

For the better part of a century, from the early 1880s until the collapse of the Heisei financial bubble in the early 1990s, this combination of risk-reduction and rent-creation functions gave circles of compensation a vital role in supporting Japan's rapid, capital-intensive industrialization. They thus were enthusiastically embraced by government planners, bankers, and a wide variety of industrial leaders.

Circles of compensation also typically—although not universally—slow and often distort Japan's response to the pressures of globalization, owing to the pronounced in-group bias that they create, which redirects national attention from the international to the parochially domestic. This in-group bias is especially pronounced—and the corresponding circles created especially tight—at the intersection of agriculture, land, and finance, due to the political-economic salience of that intersection during the high-growth years, when both bank-centered finance and one-party dominance prevailed. Intimate political-economic networks were created then, through *amakudari*, campaign finance, and sociopolitical ties, which have cast their shadow over the Japanese political economy to this day.

The reduction of risk and the economic rents that circles generate among insiders create a natural bias toward transactions with other insiders—totally independent of cultural parochialism, which may intensify such biases still further. Where circles of compensation prevail, they slow the response of in-group members to outside stimuli, including new overseas market prospects or emerging overseas competition. Such myopia can be especially damaging as the pace of globalization and regional competition with Asia *both* accelerate, as they have since the 1990s.

Research Objectives

The central research objectives of this book are to explore the interrelated paradoxes of Japanese growth and globalization laid out in Chapter 1, which have led to unprecedented and persistent stagnation in one of the leading high-growth nations of the world. The specific sectors for examination in this section of the book are chosen for the light they shed on those basic puzzles. The following chapters examine in detail the circles of compensation that prevail in Japan within six sectors: finance, land and housing policy, agriculture, energy, transportation, and communications. Developments in these sectors have shaped both Japan's profile of growth since the 1990s, and its distinctive response to the challenges of globalization. The dialectic between continuity and reform within these sectors, situated as they are at the interface between domestic Japan and the broader world, will likely determine Japan's ability to grow and play a more integral role in global affairs in coming years.

Our sector-specific analysis begins with finance. Financial institutions and incentives have a powerful impact on individual action in any social system. Their operation has been especially central in Japan, due to its distinctive high-speed, capital-intensive industrialization strategy. That approach has often involved extremely high leverage, generated under an expansionary "invest, then save" approach that has required liberal credit extension by banks, col-lateralized by rapidly appreciating land assets. Declining flows into domestic real estate, due in substantial measure to expanded investment opportunities abroad, have significantly depressed domestic land prices, endangered banks, inhibited capital investment, and thus negatively influenced Japan's recent economic-growth trajectory. Perverse transformations in financial structure itself, including collapse of the long-term credit banks and a paucity of trans-parent credit-evaluation mechanisms, have complicated recovery still further.

Following finance, we look at land policy, because of its profound impact on Japanese corporate incentives flowing from (1) that sector's distinctive, little noticed, yet critically important relationship to finance; and (2) its profound impact on Japanese corporate incentives, flowing from the country's distinc-tive land-based collateral system (*tochi hon'isei*). For more than twelve hundred years, land has been the most fundamental store of wealth in Japan, and the de-terminant, in modern days, of borrowing capacity. How that collateral system has evolved, how the parochial set of incentives it has imparted to the Japanese political economy are configured, and why Japan's bank-centric, highly lever-aged growth policies make it so central to the political economy constitute fundamental topics for our sector-specific analysis. Although poorly under-stood outside Japan, land policy and related measures affecting land prices, such as favorable fixed-asset taxes and land-based collateral requirements, have fateful implications for Japan's ability to grow and prosper in an increasingly globalized world.

Following finance and land policy, we turn to a deeply related topic with similarly parochial implications: agriculture. Japan's rural policies are closely related to those governing land use, and deeply intertwined with the classical regard for *nōhonshugi*—the notion that agriculture is the root of the nation. As with respect to land policy, the collectivist institutions that regulate agriculture impart a parochial, inward-looking bias to Japanese policy making, even as they traditionally underpin high-speed growth strategies, based on high lever-age and one-party dominance. Japan's cooperative-market economic institu-tions also seriously complicate a cosmopolitan response to the broader world, even as globalization proceeds rapidly beyond Japan's complacent shores.

After agriculture, we consider energy. Given Japan's lack of hydrocarbon-based resources, its deepening dependence on the broader world for energy has been to some degree inevitable as its economy has grown. Since the late 1960s, however, nuclear power has provided a means of moderating that de-pendence and its macroeconomic implications. In Chapter 7 we explore how institutions of collective action made nuclear power more palatable as Japan's

energy demands rose, and how those institutions are coping with the Fukushima tragedy of March 2011. As in other sectors, a failure to engage in risky
innovation and structural change in the energy area, owing to the inhibiting
effect of existing circles of compensation, is depressing Japan's ability to grow
and globalize.

The concluding two sectors for examination are transportation and communications. Both are highly organized, highly regulated, traditionally stagnant, and notably parochial policy arenas that crucially affect Japan's ability
to globalize. Our analysis considers both the policy outputs emanating from
these sectors, such as the functioning of Japanese international airports, and
how circles of compensation within Japan have shaped those outputs, thereby
impeding Japan's ability to compete on a broader global stage.

Our central operating hypothesis, explored across the six sectors, is the following: *Circles of compensation systematically internalize reward and externalize risk,
introducing a parochial bias into both policy and corporate behavior that enhances in-
group solidarity, and reduces incentives to pursue outside initiatives, thus inhibiting both
individual and corporate responsiveness to globalization.* In an open world economy,
parochial bias also impedes innovation by slowing adaptation to stimuli beyond
one's circle of association. Parochialism also perpetuates, in the Japanese case,
an attachment to land-based credit evaluation that crippled Japanese banks as
land prices fell precipitously in the 1990s, following the liberalization of outward capital flows. That parochialism continues to inhibit economic revival in
the qualitatively different political-economic environment of the twenty-first
century.

To enhance the rigor of the hypothetical test, we explore not only sectors
where circles of compensation prevail in Japan, but also areas where they do
not. We likewise investigate policy profiles in comparable nations elsewhere,
where circles are not present. Although sectors without circles are relatively
unusual in a Japan that generally exhibits a stronger corporatist and collectivist cast than is common elsewhere, anomalous cases deepen—through
contrast—our understanding of just how circles of compensation actually do
shape sociopolitical behavior, in both Japan and elsewhere in the world.

4

Finance

Finance lies, together with land, at the heart of the Japanese political economy, and in a fateful relationship with it. The health of this sector—like that of real estate—has thus been central to the growth and political-economic stability of Japan as a whole throughout its modern history. Indeed, domestic finance, drawn from the frugal savings behavior of the Japanese people over six generations and more, generated the bulk of the capital formation behind Japanese economic growth from the 1890s up to the 1990s, leveraged by the real-asset collateral system.

To facilitate high-speed growth without falling into undue dependence on the outside world, Japan created institutions that brilliantly reduced the risk of heavy leverage, relegating foreign borrowing and risk-management techniques to a marginal role. Japan's own distinctive structures, forged in an earlier, more confrontational age, remain largely in place, even though the broader global context of Japanese finance has changed markedly since the 1970s. To a remarkable degree, the Japanese political economy still remains an atavistic Bankers' Kingdom, profoundly shaped by an embedded, finance-centric network of political-economic ties, with an economically outmoded yet politically influential land–finance nexus at its core.

Globalization, including the relaxation of long-standing barriers to outward-bound capital flows from Japan, has generated powerful market pressures since 1980 for the structural transformation of Japanese finance. The long-term credit banks have disappeared, while commercial and postal banking have been profoundly reconfigured, although deep resistance to

Anglo-American-style market practices remains. Japan has suffered from pronounced rigidities in domestic lending portfolios since collapse of the Heisei financial bubble, many relating to failure to either recognize and write off bad debts, or to sever traditional links between lending practices and the value of land. These rigidities have impeded economic reconstruction, perpetuated stagnation, and made it difficult for banks to support the domestic transformation in Japan's economy that globalization demands.

A more collectivist approach to finance than typical in the Anglo-Saxon world—circles of compensation—has been central to the evolution of Japanese finance since the Meiji era. In both socializing risk, so as to encourage capital investments (1890–1990), and in subsequently inhibiting efforts at structural change (1990–), cooperative capitalism has profoundly shaped the complex, contradictory profile of Japanese economic growth. Although a tradition of collaboration has not fundamentally changed, cross-sectoral circles of compensation in finance that traditionally promoted growth have conversely become in recent years a force for stagnation, impeding the structural changes and foreign investment that could otherwise help transform Japan.

Configuration of the Classic Circle

As in other sectors of the Japanese political economy, circles of compensation in finance have involved a diverse range of groups, many of them with seemingly contrasting interests, but with a common functional interest in dialogue and cooperation. Financial circles vary greatly in the scope and administrative level of their activities. As in other sectors, they share a common interest in sharing information, pooling risk, and reducing transaction costs. These circles thus have much more comprehensive functional roles than the lobbying that preoccupies classical vested interests,[1] although the circles do represent collective interests in the Japanese political process, as well.

The most important macro-level example of a financial circle of compensation—the Bankers' Kingdom mentioned above—is presented in Figure 4.1. It has dominated financial policy making in Japan since the late 1930s, and includes both private-sector actors and government agencies, in a broadly cooperative, risk-diffusing, horizontal set of relationships, often characterized by captive regulation. Some actors have recently changed, with the long-term credit banks disappearing at the dawn of the twenty-first century amid major commercial banking mergers. Their demise eroded the Japanese financial system's overall monitoring and financing capabilities with respect to large, long-term capital-investment projects. Yet the generally collaborative structure of the financial circle and its centrality in the overall Japanese political

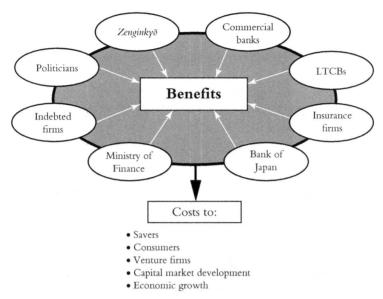

FIGURE 4.1   Circles of compensation in the Bankers' Kingdom

SOURCE: Author's illustration.

economy have persisted to a remarkable degree, perpetuating the land–finance linkages and the leveraged capital investment discussed in Chapter 3, which have been pillars of Japanese political-economic structure since the early postwar period.

The Japanese Bankers Association, *Zenginkyō*, was the key private-sector component in Japan's financial circle of compensation throughout the high-growth period (roughly 1951–1989). Finance in those years was highly regulated, so the Ministry of Finance (MOF) and the Bank of Japan (BOJ) had important formal roles as the responsible regulators. They conducted examinations of financial soundness, and formally determined interest rates. Intermittently, they also tried to control compensating balances demanded by the banks, and urged on by the politicians, although their efforts in that shadowy world of covert corporate transactions often proved unsuccessful.[2]

Imperfect as their dominance was, the financial regulators performed another important function: legitimizing the role of banks in the broader political economy, and facilitating their standing as connectors and supporters for the prevailing order of things. Many MOF alumni, for example, went into politics—three became prime ministers, and MOF alumni held a quarter of all ruling party Diet seats throughout most of the postwar period.[3] These former officials relied on their banking ties for support, and promoted banking interests and networks in return.

The prevailing financial regime of the high-growth period—its circle of compensation—was thus a cooperative form of negotiated, oligopolistic regulation that benefited capital-intensive industries like steel, shipbuilding, and chemicals as it suppressed long-term lending rates. It also advantaged city banks,[4] which supplied capital in volume to industry, while also aiding regional banks, which provided capital to the city banks through the short-term call market. The collaborative structure, involving regulatory barriers to entry against outside groups, and at times administered pricing, generated attractive profits for banks in the high-growth economy of the 1950s, 1960s, and 1970s, as indicated in Figure 4.2.

MOF and BOJ, which maintained a favorable regulatory umbrella for the private firms participating in the circle, were likewise beneficiaries. The circle

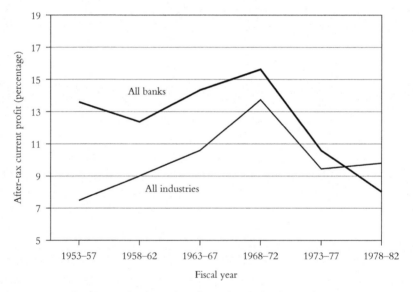

FIGURE 4.2   Banking and industrial profits in the Bankers' Kingdom

SOURCES: Reprint of Kent E. Calder, "Figure 5-2. Banking and Industrial Profits in the Bankers' Kingdom," *Strategic Capitalism: Private Business and Public Purpose in Japanese Industrial Finance* (Princeton, NJ: Princeton University Press, 1993), 139. Based on Akiyoshi Horiuchi, *Economic Growth and Financial Allocation in Postwar Japan* (Washington, DC: Brookings Institution, 1984), 23. Drawn from the following data: (1) Federation of Bankers Associations of Japan, *Analysis of Financial Statements of All Banks*; (2) Bank of Japan, *Financial Statements of Main Industrial Corporations* (excludes financial and insurance firms); and (3) Japan Development Bank, *Handbook of Financial Data of Industries*.

NOTE: Profit rates are after-tax current profits per capita account.

of compensation simplified financial regulation, transforming it into a collaborative process, and generated postretirement employment (*amakudari*) for government officials. It also assured a credible credit review process at the micro level, thanks to the systematic monitoring role of long-term credit banks, as well as *keiretsu* main banks.[5] As indicated in Figure 4.1, and as suggested also by the profitability statistics presented in Figure 4.2, however, the circle disadvantaged small business, individual consumers, and those lacking land collateral, who found it hard to obtain bank loans. It also tended to inhibit innovation and infant-industry development, except through the long-term credit banks, which collapsed in the late 1990s amid rising volatility in domestic financial markets.

The erosion of traditional risk-assessment mechanisms, such as those provided by the long-term credit banks, combined with the declining credibility of the convoy system amid abrupt and deflationary shifts in monetary policy, led to massive bad-debt problems, and to rising levels of toxicity at the Japanese banks.[6] That toxicity ultimately crippled both their profits and their ability to serve as constructive financial intermediaries. Yet the impressive and influential edifice that the Bankers' Kingdom had become—including its powerful political-economic networks—persisted in the political and institutional realms for a remarkably long period.

Functional Role of the Classic Circles

Japanese financial policies and institutions, in contrast to those of the Anglo-Saxon world, were traditionally designed to minimize competition and diffuse risk. They did so in order to amass large amounts of capital, and then channel it through organized suasion toward priority tasks of national development. The diffusion of risk in classical Japanese finance was far from a dirigiste process, and the organized private sector, configured by circles of compensation, played a pivotal role.[7]

Rather than a hierarchical arrangement, Japanese risk reduction historically took the form of more horizontal cooperative understandings. They involved commercial banks, long-term credit banks, and insurance companies, for example, as well as public authorities such as MOF and BOJ, in regulatory and legitimating roles. Real-estate-based collateral requirements engaged the political-economic interests of businessmen and politicians, further diffusing perceived risk, and reducing its burden on any given individual. Bond-issuing syndicates, especially those for government bonds, were an example of how risk diffusion through collective action worked in practice.[8]

How Cooperative Capitalism in Finance Emerged

The salience that circles of compensation hold in the Japanese political economy, and that banks hold in the Japanese financial system, is deeply embedded
in the history of Japan's economic development. To fully understand their
continuing political-economic role, it is important to examine how they came
to be. The cooperative risk–diffusion pattern in Japanese finance—and the
key role of private organizations like the Japanese Bankers Association in
supporting it—both have roots in the distinctive late-developer pattern of
Japanese economic evolution.[9] From the days of Japan's early industrialization
in the late nineteenth century, nearly half a century before the industrial-
policy bureaucracy emerged, public and private finance have been both crucial
to national growth and the object of formidable controversy. For both the
Tokugawa shogunate as it declined, and also for the infant Meiji government
as it began to rise after 1868, enhanced taxation, to cover the heavy dual costs
of economic development and national defense, were at once strategic and
politically delicate acts. So was the alternative: borrowing from domestic and
foreign sources.[10]

Finance, in a word, was both a valued and a contentious resource, in an
ambitious and rapidly expanding yet still relatively poor Japanese political
economy. Demand for capital far outstripped supply domestically, yet Japan
was loath to borrow from abroad, fearing Western imperialist designs. Cooperative institutional mechanisms within Japan for allocating capital thus became a means by which both government and private banks could exercise
leverage over borrowers, even as they gained the ability to collude in dealing
with those borrowers.

Central to the allocation of credit from the early days of the Meiji era to
the present, with a role embedded before industrial policy emerged, has been
the private banking system within Japan. Compared to most industrialized nations other than the United States, Japan has had a relatively large number of
private banks. It has also had a large and rapidly growing market for financial
services, since investment and trade finance have risen rapidly across most of
the past century. With investment and trade-financial demand rising rapidly
for most of the past century in Japan, the market for financial services there
has also been large and swift to grow.

In the Anglo-Saxon world, direct finance—through capital markets, with
securities firms as principal intermediaries—has historically been preeminent. In late-developing industrialized nations, however, such as Germany,
France, and Japan, indirect finance through intermediaries like industrial and

commercial banks has been far more common. With only a small number of actors (principally the banks) involved in mediating financial flows, both the incentives and the potential for collusion have been strong. Conversely, incentives for financial innovation, in response to deepening pressures from the broader world, have generally been weak.

As Yutaka Kosai and Yoshitaro Ogino point out, economic pressures toward competition within the Japanese banking system have historically been substantial. That was especially true during the high-growth period, when banks were competing fiercely to supply rapidly growing heavy-industry firms with capital.[11] Such competitive pressures have always inhibited bank profitability and even solvency, in the absence of public or private intervention to restrain competition. With self-regulation decidedly more congenial than outside regulation, Japan's private banks have had strong incentives to make their pricing decisions *collectively*, as through an industry association rather than individually. The technical need for cooperation in clearing operations has also naturally reinforced a broader political-economic bias toward collective action.

Private Banking Predates State Control

Japan's private banking system, as has been noted, is considerably older than the state regulative structure supervising it,[12] creating embedded institutional constraints on the public sector, and parallel traditions of private assertiveness. These embedded structural limits help to constrain any state capacity for strategy independent of the private sector. In view of this long-standing private-sector institutional strength, coupled with MOF opposition to outside intervention into MOF's established policy realm, METI industrial planners have only rarely been able to order the banks around. That reality has sharply constrained the sort of hierarchical, government-led allocation schemes casually postulated by Chalmers Johnson, but never empirically verified.[13]

Private bankers' associations also predate the establishment of modern central banking in Japan. This combination of historical precedence and embedded institutional strength long afforded the bankers leverage with both financial "regulators" and industrial "strategists,"[14] eroding any prospective hierarchical patterns in government–business relations. Indeed, Japan's first private bankers' association, the *Takuzen Kai*, was established by the great Meiji industrialist Shibusawa Eiichi in 1878, five years before the founding even of BOJ.[15] Formation of the *Takuzen Kai* also antedated by three years establishment of MOF's Banking Bureau, which soon after its foundation was frequently subjected to complex reorganizations and consolidations with other bureaus. The Banking Bureau did not decisively emerge as a coherent, independent entity within MOF until 1946.[16] Not surprisingly, it had trouble constraining the embedded influence of powerful, preexisting private financial institutions.

Venerable Private-Banking-Sector Cooperation

Taking initiative through private collective action, supported by congenial government regulation, is a venerable tradition in Japanese finance. Given the immense potential profits to be made through coordination, this pattern has become an enduring custom, as well. Indeed, early private bankers' associations worked to limit establishment of new, allegedly unsound banks, to put ceilings on deposit interest rates, and to regulate both call markets and general lending rates—long before public financial authorities began to actively regulate the financial system. Some elements of the Japanese government, although not necessarily the financial authorities, ultimately moved to legitimate and support these private initiatives. For almost forty years they continued to determine Japan's interest-rate structure through collective private action, albeit with tacit government acceptance.[17]

Emergence of the Bankers' Kingdom

In July 1937, full-scale war broke out between Japan and China. To more efficiently configure the Japanese economy for the conflict, the National Mobilization Law (*Kokka Sōdōin Hō*) was passed in the spring of 1938. This broad legislation provided the legal basis for wide-ranging "administrative guidance" of the banks by MOF and BOJ, in the form of ordinances authorized by the Mobilization Law. It also established the foundation for close cooperation among financial institutions, both public and private, thus laying a key foundation for the Bankers' Kingdom.[18]

During the ensuing years of conflict, private-sector yet highly regulated industry associations in steel, shipbuilding, and electric power, to name only the most conspicuous, grew rapidly in size and influence, strengthening the coherence of circles of compensation in those sectors. The associations, which lay at the heart of emerging circles, expanded their influence relative to individual firms, the banking community, and often enough also to the state itself. Indeed, they often acted as primary micro-level coordinators of the economy under wartime conditions, with implicit state assent.[19]

The coming of the Pacific War meant a further intensification of government controls with respect to both finance and industry. In February 1942, BOJ was greatly strengthened, under legislation based on the German *Reischsbankgesetz*. In August 1942, the government established nine "control associations," through ordinances based on the Mobilization Law, for six industries.[20] Through a separate but related ordinance, the new National Finance Control Association (*Zenkoku Kinyū Tōsei Kai*)—into which were merged all the preexisting private financial associations, private banks, and government institutions—coordinated lending authorizations and the concentration of savings for the war effort. Its crucial role in efficiently directing funds to strategically important heavy and chemical industries was given special coherence and legitimacy by government sanction.[21]

With demand for capital substantial relative to supply, the banks as a group enjoyed considerable leverage, even under wartime conditions; establishment of cooperative banking institutions like the National Finance Control Association enhanced their influence still further. The banks still faced political-economic competition from the *zaibatsu* holding companies (*honsha*) and the Wartime Finance Corporation during World War II itself.[22] Japan's surrender, followed by *zaibatsu* dissolution during 1946–1947, however, relieved that challenge. The Supreme Commander for the Allied Powers (SCAP) dismantled the holding companies but left the banks intact, perceiving them to be useful economic stabilizers in an uncertain transition period.

Early Postwar Favoritism Toward the Banks: Contrast to Germany

As Yoshikazu Miyazaki notes, the city banks of Japan were treated much more favorably by the Allies than their counterparts in West Germany.[23] Banks in Japan were, for example, given more favorable treatment than manufacturers in the early postwar evaluation of corporate assets for tax purposes,[24] a systematic preference not accorded their German counterparts. Procedures for ending wartime subsidies to military industry in Japan expressed the same systematic favoritism for private banks, contrasting sharply with the converse favoritism displayed in Germany toward manufacturers. Special losses of Japanese armaments firms, resulting from the ending of wartime subsidies, were not charged to the accounts of their former creditors, the banks. They were instead generally assessed against the firms' shareholders—in many cases the *zaibatsu* holding company giants disbanded by the Occupation.

The Japanese banks, which had found themselves in a favorable position under currency reform as debtors of their depositors, were also given preferential treatment as creditors of the armaments firms. In addition, the main banks of the former *zaibatsu* were not designated during the reforms of 1946–1948—either as holding companies or as companies subject to deconcentration. Instead, these banks emerged from the *zaibatsu* dissolution essentially untouched.[25] In Germany, by contrast, financial deconcentration went considerably further, giving rise to the so-called *Landesbank*, although the largest German banks were able during the 1950s and 1960s to regain a large measure of cohesion and much of their dominance over industry.

One might ask: Why were banks so explicitly favored in early postwar Japan, by both the Allied Occupation forces and the Japanese MOF? This systematic favoritism for banks in Japan stemmed partly from their ability to amass national savings at a time when only increased savings could restrain inflation and advance national productivity. Savings, however, could have been amassed through other types of financial intermediaries, as well, so it is important to consider the political dimension. General Douglas MacArthur, Supreme Commander of the Allied Powers in the Pacific, was said to be partial to banks and skeptical of securities firms as financial intermediaries, as his wife's family had taken substantial losses in the Wall Street crash of 1929.[26] Bankers' associations, both through their ability to exert pressure on policy makers and their ability to implement government objectives, were also key players, influential with both the SCAP and the Japanese government.

The bankers' associations worked to assure that (1) banks, rather than securities firms or other entities, became the principal coordinating force in postwar Japanese economic life, and (2) they were left with a general discretion to allocate credit on their own terms, serving as watchful monitors of industrial firms. Banks, with important lending risks that they constantly sought to defray through collective action, thus combined to play a key role in institutionalizing clear circles of compensation in Japanese finance, in cooperation with the government and supported by government regulation. Through political activism, in quiet support of one-party conservative dominance, the banks inhibited change in the early postwar system of indirect finance, reinforcing their role as the dominant purveyors of capital-investment funds, as Japan's economic growth began to accelerate.

A powerful Bankers' Kingdom thus gradually emerged after the war, helping Japan to defuse the risk implicit in high leverage, and to aggressively pursue heavy industrialization, dominated by private financial institutions. The Japanese banks were better able to collaborate than their more mutually competitive German counterparts, owing to greater continuity and political influence of the bankers' federations from the prewar and wartime years. The Bankers' Kingdom political-economic regime in Japan was reinforced by a real-estate collateral system that linked finance to the inexorably rising price of land, and to the political interests that promoted rising land prices and a dynamic, bank-centric "invest, then save" system of leveraged capital investment, as well.

Land and agricultural policies, discussed in Chapters 5 and 6, thus emerged as fundamental pillars of the new bank-centric Japanese political economy, sustained by one-party conservative political dominance. Meanwhile, institutional competitors of the banks, including *zaibatsu* holding companies, general trading firms, and the military, were largely dismantled by the SCAP, enhancing the influence of banks still further. During the high-growth period, from the late 1950s until the Oil Shocks of the 1970s, this Bankers' Kingdom, nourished by leveraged investment fueled by rising land prices, was felicitous for both Japanese growth and political-economic stability.

Government's Role as Creditor

Government fiscal and credit policies were similarly supportive of prevailing, highly differentiated circles of compensation. In fiscal 2015 there were fourteen special accounts (*tokubetsu kaikei*) maintained by MOF, with revenues explicitly segregated for narrowly and clearly defined alternative purposes. The energy measures special account (1974), for example, taxes electric-power consumption to provide for future power facilities development, traditionally nuclear. So-called social capital accounts tax road, port, and airport usage to provide for further construction.[27] Such earmarked expenditures, configured by the circles of compensation, are huge—four times the size of the national general account.[28]

Government lending programs have also traditionally been highly segmented and deeply integrated with circles of compensation. In 1992, for example, there were eleven government banks, with purposes so clearly specified that each attracted a different constituency. Tohoku/Hokkaido and Okinawa, for example, each had a government bank dedicated explicitly to funding their projects. This complex financial structure was simplified under the Koizumi administration (2001–2006), with the number of government lending institutions falling to eight by the end of Koizumi's tenure.[29] Yet that structure still remains more differentiated—and more tightly linked to collective corporate interest—than in most Western countries.

Rising Functional Role of the Japanese Bankers Association

Between 1945 and 1950, the private bankers' associations cooperated warily with government-led efforts at reconstruction, including the priority production policy of credit allocation (*keisha seisan hōshiki*). They concentrated on preserving their position as preeminent private financial intermediaries and did not challenge government preeminence in the credit-allocation process. After the outbreak of the Korean War, however, with investment demand rising, the bankers' associations, particularly the Japanese Bankers Association (*Zenginkyō*), took an increasingly protective role in allocating credit.[30] As the public financial authorities' own will and ability to allocate credit waned following the resignation of Governor Hisato Ichimada from BOJ in 1954, the role of private banking associations in the credit-allocation process became even stronger.

After 1958 the secretary general of *Zenginkyō*'s Capital Adjustment Committee also served on the Industrial Capital Subcommittee (*Sangyō Shikin Bukai*) of MITI's Industrial Structure Rationalization Council, evolving after 1964 into the Industrial Structure Deliberation Council (*Sangyō Kōzō Shingikai*). Throughout the high-growth period, the consolidated body remained the most authoritative voice on sectoral credit-allocation issues in Japan.

Through its membership on the Industrial Capital Subcommittee, *Zenginkyō* developed a formal, ongoing relationship with MITI, but without ever becoming MITI dominated. Indeed, *Zenginkyō* played a decisive and successful role during 1962–1964 in defeating MITI's efforts to centralize government control over credit allocation in its own hands.[31] The Japanese Bankers Association thus helped to assure that the circle of compensation in finance was dominated by financiers rather than industrial bureaucrats, and that the circle was wedded more closely to bankers' risk reduction than to industrial strategy, contrary to what Chalmers Johnson and his intellectual confederates maintained.[32]

Fierce "one-set" competition among industrial groups, as well as supportive international political-economic conditions, such as favorable access to U.S. and Southeast Asian markets, helped promote the stable, high-speed economic growth so greatly desired by Japanese bureaucrats, conservative politicians, and large portions of the general public. This bank-dominated political-economic regime, supported by government regulation but with independent capabilities of its own, was to fatefully configure the Japanese political economy in later years; its embedded influence with MOF, BOJ, *zaikai*, and the political world co-opted what little opposition it encountered. The Bankers' Kingdom helped the Japanese political economy, in particular, to defuse risk and aggressively pursue heavy industrialization during the 1950s and 1960s, even as the same institutions later inhibited structural change in response to globalization, and perpetuated economic stagnation by delaying the debt-restructuring process for more than a decade, during the 1990s and beyond.

Classical Circle-of-Compensation Outputs

Zenginkyō's recommendations to member banks during the high-growth years illustrate the typical operational bias of circles of compensation in the financial world.[33] Classical financial circles of compensation continued or expanded credit for existing recipients, and limited funds for newcomers, no matter how much long-run growth potential those newcomers might have. This conservative calculus *reduced risk* to participants and *externalized costs*—it hardly anticipated the future in any strategic fashion, as conventional wisdom suggests. Promising sectors such as electronics and telecommunications, for example, were largely ignored by *Zenginkyō* throughout the 1950s.

There is little evidence of a strategic approach to industrial transformation, such as MITI typically propounded, in the lending resolutions of the Japanese Bankers Association. Similarly, there was also little industrial-strategic intent in the regulation-oriented, risk-averse policies at MOF.[34] *Zenginkyō's* positions were likewise animated to some extent by political considerations: pressure from the Diet, particularly regarding the terms of small-business finance.

Across the two decades of the high-growth period and beyond, *Zenginkyō* has had administrative functions and technical responsibilities, such as check clearance, personal credit information, and bank-employee training,[35] that have made the Bankers' Kingdom far more than a simple vested-interest configuration. In response to Diet requests, conveyed by MOF, it agreed to "self-police" high-interest consumer loans (*sarakin*) (1981); and real-estate investments (July 1987). In the mid-1990s, *Zenginkyō* was also involved in cleaning up the *jūsen* housing-loan problem. In each case, the bankers' association sought, through collective action, to reduce the institutional risk confronted by the banks, but simultaneously to serve broader public purposes.

Zenginkyō, however, has also long been influential as a pressure group— primarily in defending private bank prerogatives, and in reducing the institutional risk that these firms confront. In the early 1960s, *Zenginkyō* broke MITI's major effort to usurp control of industrial credit, through its effective lobbying against the Special Measures Law for the Promotion of Designated Industries (*Tokushinhō*). Over more than two decades (1953–1974), it also successfully resisted proposals spearheaded by the Japan Socialist Party, with broader political backing, to limit large-scale lending to individual borrowers; ; many bankers of the period regarded this veto role as *Zenginkyō's* most important achievement.[36]

During the 1980s and early 1990s, *Zenginkyō* enjoyed additional policy successes—many of them engineered by its *Besshitsu* (Special Office). This small but formidable body informally participated in policy making by delivering "favorable" data and offering policy recommendations to bureaucrats at MOF.[37] It played a key role in defeating introduction of the green-card system for consolidating consumer-deposit accounting during the late 1980s, and in resolving the *jūsen* housing loan problem during the mid-1990s.

As one of the three largest financial supporters of the ruling Liberal Democratic Party throughout the high-growth years—a member of the powerful *Gosanke* (literally, "honorable trio")—together with the steel and electric-power federations, *Zenginkyō* generally wielded influence in the formation of policy that inhibited most other industries and even officials from challenging its prerogatives. During its thirty-five years of preeminence, dating from the early 1950s to the mid-1980s, the only less than complete successes for the federation were just two: its partial failure to check the expansion of postal savings, and to arrest the shift of corporate clients toward the securities industry, as liquidity rose in the broader financial system. Together the postal-savings program and the securities industry undermined banking's preeminence in Japanese corporate finance, and in the broader political economy. Ultimately, however, it was market and political pressures—rather than unilateral bureaucratic fiat—that allowed these challengers of banking preeminence to achieve some measure of initial success. The influence of the securities industry, however, was badly undermined by the collapse of the economic bubble and a series of scandals during the 1990s.

Junichirō Koizumi shifted the pendulum decisively back toward banking after 2001, enhancing the standing of *Zenginkyō* once again.[38] Koizumi's forceful attack on the postal-savings system, a most unusual confrontation with politically established interests, was enthusiastically supported by the banks, and they gained added stature from it. During the lost decade of the 1990s, however, banking profitability had significantly declined, hastening *Zenginkyō's* evolution into a technical organization, with notably reduced lobbying functions.[39] Three years of Democratic Party of Japan rule (2009–2012) further diminished their influence, and hastened *Zenginkyō's* transformation into a predominantly technical organization.

Zenginkyō did successfully retain policy relevance in the early twenty-first century by developing a new consumer-oriented agenda. It made proposals regarding revision of the insolvency law, risk-disclosure statements, and consumer-loan contracts, while proposing new accounting standards compatible with international rules, and options for reducing money-laundering problems. In the process of developing these agendas, it continued to play an important coordinating role within the financial world. It thus retained unusual *interest-aggregation functions*, even as its overall interest-articulation role in the Japanese political economy gradually declined.

The Mitigating Role of the Long-Term Credit Banks

The strong priority of Japan's classical Bankers' Kingdom actors, including banks, insurance companies, and industry associations, as well as the financial regulators at MOF and BOJ, was stability. Innovation, and even economic growth, was secondary to this stability imperative. The commercial bankers were primarily from legal backgrounds—mainly graduates of the Tokyo University law faculty, lacking much familiarity with the details of industrial organization and technology.

Twentieth-century Japan was, however, favored with one distinctive type of financial institution that bridged the yawning gap between banking capabilities and industrial development in a remarkable way. The long-term credit banks mobilized capital in huge quantities, closely monitored corporate performance, and provided practical, strategic advice to actors ranging from plant-floor managers to the chairman's suite. They were able to perform these critical hybrid functions because of both unique institutional characteristics and distinctive training programs and corporate culture.[40]

The first long-term credit bank, which spearheaded industrial innovation in Japan for fully a century, was the Industrial Bank of Japan (IBJ), founded in 1902.[41] Before World War II, the IBJ was a "special" public-private bank under government control, with the Treasury holding an important minority interest on behalf of the government.[42] During the war, IBJ assumed a central role in financing national military expansion in China and ultimately elsewhere in the Pacific. After the war it was modestly disciplined by SCAP, which cut its branch network, limited its debenture issues, and rendered it an unambiguously private institution, legally speaking, under the Long-Term Credit Bank Act of 1952.[43]

The Long-Term Credit Bank of Japan (LTCB) was also created in 1952, under the same legislation that formally privatized the IBJ. Like IBJ, the LTCB also initially financed large-scale capital-investment projects, particularly in shipbuilding, electronics, automobiles, and petrochemicals, also pioneering long-term financing of land reclamation and housing projects.[44] Five years later, in April 1957, a third long-term credit bank was founded: the Nippon Fudosan Bank, based on the remaining assets in Japan of the colonial-era Bank of Chosen, and specializing in financing large-scale real-estate transactions.[45]

The long-term credit banks were functionally complementary to rather than competitive with the commercial banks, spearheading changes in industrial structure and the development of new industries, even as the commercial banks labored to maintain the status quo. Their activist role in Japan's strategic capitalism of the high-growth period emerged from seven key realities, manifest most clearly at the largest institution, the IBJ:[46]

1. Unlike Japanese commercial banks like Mitsubishi, Mitsui, and Sumitomo, but similar to German universal banks, Japan's long-term credit banks were permitted to issue bonds and debentures.

2. Their access to individual and corporate deposits was severely restricted, with heavy restrictions placed on branch expansion. Accordingly, the long-term credit banks were highly dependent on government and corporate deposits, and hence more vulnerable than the commercial banks to outside influence and suggestion.

3. Their ability to loan money to others depended on the cooperation of other major financial power centers—MOF, the commercial banks, and the securities firms.

4. The long-term credit banks—particularly the IBJ—were widely perceived as neutral in the intense struggles among the major industrial groups with which the major commercial banks were engaged.

5. These banks, and the IBJ in particular, had unsurpassed technical expertise, particularly in credit evaluation, macroeconomic analysis, and large-scale project organization, at a time when public organizations like the Japan Development Bank were new, and the major private banks were still in a state of postwar disorganization and transition.

6. The IBJ, in particular, had sophisticated internal mechanisms for making industrial-credit decisions, including a highly regarded Planning Office attached directly to the office of the chairman, a sophisticated credit department for evaluating long-term risk, and the largest industrial research department among Japan's major financial institutions.[47]

7. The long-term credit banks—particularly the IBJ—had been unusually active politically. The IBJ, for example, was a consistent ally of growth-oriented Prime Minister Hayato Ikeda, and the bank's chairman, Sohei Nakayama, had been a key supporter of the economic expansionist Kakuei Tanaka in his campaign for the prime ministership in 1972.

Transformation in the Political Economy of Japanese Finance

Throughout the high-growth years from the Korean War until the two Oil Shocks of the 1970s, Japan's banking world established and consolidated, in cooperation with MOF, BOJ, and other financiers such as the insurers, a powerful and lucrative circle of compensation in Japanese finance. That circle dominated the provision of industrial credit, establishing and maintaining a strong structural bias toward indirect finance, through corporate debt mortgaged against rapidly appreciating land—within the Japanese financial system as a whole. The financial circle thereby played a key role in both supporting highly leveraged heavy industrialization and sustaining the political-economic preeminence of the Bankers' Kingdom within Japan, even as the broader global financial system embraced more-radical change.

The role of banking was unassailable in the political world of the late twentieth century, due to *Zenginkyō*'s powerful position in the Japanese political economy, together with the steel and electric-power associations.[48] These bodies provided critical direct funding for the ruling Liberal Democratic Party, while strongly supporting leveraged high-growth policies that benefited its powerful construction and real-estate constituencies, as well. Across the 1970s, however, as Japanese financial markets began to deepen and broaden, due to the rising liquidity that declining growth and rising domestic affluence combined to provide, a new power center in the financial world began emerging in the form of the securities industry.

Firms like Nomura, Daiwa, and Nikko made money by trading and underwriting stocks and bonds, both domestic and foreign.[49] Initially, the interests of the securities majors were interwoven with those of the banks, especially the IBJ, through narrowly focused mini circles of compensation like the Bond Issue Arrangement Committee (*Kisai Kai*), chaired by the IBJ, and later government bond-issuing syndicates.[50] The securities industry, however, had a distinctive bias toward growth and innovation, which the stability-oriented, risk-averse banks did not always share. Differences led to intermittent conflict across the 1980s—a rarity in sectors of the Japanese political economy dominated by circles of compensation.[51] Conversely, the securities complex, apart from the IBJ, could not provide the sort of detailed financial monitoring, based on intimate, ongoing human networks, which the classical Bankers' Kingdom did.

In the late 1970s, the risk-oriented securities firms played a fateful role in the most important policy change, in a political-economic sense, in postwar Japanese economic history—the December 1979 revision of the Foreign Exchange and Foreign Trade Control Law.[52] Undertaken only months before the election of Ronald Reagan as President of the United States, this development opened a vast new market in U.S. Treasuries for Japanese securities firms and insurance companies. It also, however, generated huge Japanese capital outflows, from what previously had been a "hermetically" sealed, exquisitely segmented, and fundamentally stable domestic financial system. Those flows ultimately undermined the very pillar of postwar finance: the land-standard system (*tochi hon'isei*), discussed more extensively in Chapter 5.

The result of this historic redirection of funds was ultimately enormous problems for the banks, including uncertainties in their credit monitoring and evaluation systems, as capital flowed away from domestic assets toward foreign securities, deflating overheated local real-estate values upon which bankers' lending decisions were traditionally based. Yet the banks, together with many politicians and land-rich investors, did not respond effectively to the new and dynamic shift in investment incentives which this deregulation implied. Their evaluation processes, after all, were ironically calcified, obscured by outdated criteria; and their confidence in the future dangerously mitigated by the normally felicitous circles of compensation in finance.

Circles of Compensation and the Globalization of Japanese Finance

The classical circle of compensation in Japanese finance included a variety of Japanese private banks (city, regional, and industrial); insurance companies; government regulators (MOF and BOJ); capital-intensive industrial firms; and a substantial part of the conservative political world. Landowners were also indirect beneficiaries, due to the traditional requirement of land-based collateral for bank loans. This circle was sustained for over two decades by a combination of favorable domestic regulation, high credit demand, and international financial controls that encouraged high corporate leverage while limiting the investment horizons of increasingly affluent domestic savers to domestic assets—first and foremost, real estate.

Following the relaxation of government controls on capital outflows during the early 1980s, Japanese savers confronted a much broader range of alternative investments than they had previously enjoyed, as suggested in Figure 4.3. In addition to Japanese land, stocks, and bonds, they also became able to invest in foreign assets, an option which they proceeded to actively exercise.[53] Foreign stock markets rose, and relatively less attractive Japanese land prices fell—a development that rapidly rendered the land-linked loan portfolios of Japanese banks increasingly toxic, and crippled their broader ability to support innovation and growth. The problem of bad debt was compounded by the inability of the classic Japanese credit evaluation system, centered on main-bank monitoring, to accurately assess risk in the increasingly fluid and volatile financial environment created by changing domestic markets, the decline of *keiretsu*, and deepening global financial integration.

(a)

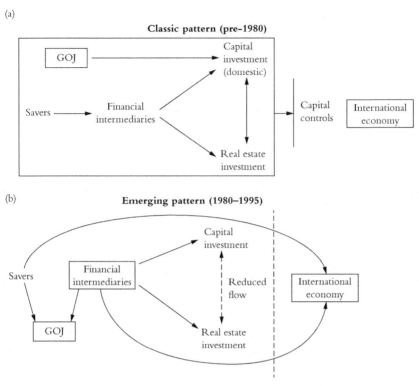

FIGURE 4.3   The challenge of financial liberalization to the Japanese domestic
political economy

SOURCE: Author's illustration.

Given the land-standard system, mandating that collateral be held in the
form of real estate, the diversion of Japanese savings from land to other investments thus created far-reaching structural problems for the Japanese political economy that generated a less felicitous response than pure free-market
models might predict. Land prices began to fall, and the institutional power
of Japanese banks, epitomized by *Zenginkyō*, prevented government from provoking foreclosures on the rising portfolios of toxic, real-estate secured domestic loans. A failure to write off bad loans continued for over a generation
to impede Japanese recovery, following the collapse of the 1980s real-estate
bubble. The problems of Japan's banks also impeded Japan's broader adjustment
to global economic pressures, because their formerly felicitous risk-sharing
features inhibited individual corporate risk taking. The disappearance of the
entrepreneurial long-term credit banks during and after the Asian financial
crisis compounded the challenge of structural adjustment.

Demise of the Long-Term Credit Banks and a Transformed Financial System

Japan's long-term credit banks were a key engine of innovation and growth, as well as a sensitive credit-assessment mechanism, throughout the post–World War II high-growth period, from the Korean War until the early 1970s.[54] They were dealt a heavy blow by the 1973 Oil Shock, when many of their largest industrial clients suddenly confronted drastically weakened markets and even bankruptcy, leading to sharp overall cutbacks in Japanese capital investment. The IBJ was dealt another heavy blow in 1979, when a $3.2 billion petrochemical complex in Iran that it had financed was halted, 80 percent complete, following the Iranian revolution.[55] The long-term credit banks did, however, continue to demonstrate their unusual restructuring expertise amid the Oil Shocks, with the IBJ successfully restructuring several troubled firms during the 1970s and 1980s, such as Toyo Soda Manufacturing, Nippon Soda, Keisei Electric Railway, and the Chisso chemical company.[56]

Despite their demonstrable expertise, formidable interpersonal networks, and extensive information flows, the long-term credit banks nevertheless faced an excruciating new external environment, as Japan's heavily regulated financial system began to liberalize. They had traditionally provided funds for massive, billion-dollar steel mills, petrochemical plants, and shipyards, with repayment periods measured in decades, even as they raised funds through the sale of one-, two-, three-, and five-year debentures.[57] As long as interest rates were stable, this mismatch in maturities was manageable. Yet rising liquidity and volatility in both domestic and international finance did not permit the luxury of such stable parameters. Like dinosaurs confronting a deepening Ice Age, the long-term credit banks, although remarkably prescient and nimble, faced increasingly serious environmental pressures, including growing volatility in deposit interest rates amid rising competition with their debentures. These new pressures threatened their very existence.[58]

The Asian financial crisis of 1997–1998 proved to be the last straw. In November, the Hokkaido Takushoku Bank, one of the top 20 banks that MOF had once proclaimed too big to fail, went abruptly bankrupt, followed by Yamaichi Securities, one of Japan's formidable top 4. This crisis prompted forced injections of government capital into the various Japanese banks in March 1998, followed by effective nationalization of the LTCB and the Nippon Credit Bank (NCB) later that same year.[59] Nationalization was, in theory, to last for as short a time as possible, although it proved difficult to unwind.[60]

In 2000 both of these institutions were sold back to the private sector—the LTCB to the Ripplewood Group, a conglomeration of foreign investors,[61] and NCB initially to a Japanese consortium (SoftBank and Orix Corporation, together with Tokio Marine and Fire Insurance). The consortium in turn sold to the Cerberus Group of foreign investors in 2003, which in turn resold to Barclays in 2013.[62] In 2002 the IBJ, succumbing to the same pressures that had doomed the LTCB and NCB earlier, sought safety in a duress merger with the Dai-Ichi Kangyo and Sanwa Banks, forming a Mizuho Bank that was truly too big to fail.[63]

The disappearance of the long-term credit banks left a gaping hole in the Japanese financial system, with consequences that were to haunt Japan for a decade or more. An important benchmark mechanism for credit evaluation, and a crucial engine of innovation, which had nurtured new industries insightfully throughout the postwar years, was destroyed. In the demise of the IBJ, one of the most important neutral coordinators for collective action across the Japanese political economy disappeared. Japan was, consequently, left with the more rigid and bureaucratized dimension of its banking system, even as it lost the financial institutions with the most intimate understanding of shop-floor dynamics and industrial change.

Some of the best entrepreneurs and financial analysts from the long-term credit banks left for a new breed of venture businesses that began to sprout up across Japan, short-circuiting the established commercial banks, so awash with toxic loans.[64] Some of these, such as Rakuten, founded by former IBJ executive Hiroshi Mikitani, were highly successful, and we discuss their stories in detail in Chapter 10.[65] Others, such as Livedoor, founded by Takafumi Horie, colloquially known as "Horiemon," succumbed to the temptations of the new, more freewheeling financial world, and failed. So the network and expertise of those immersed in the long-term credit bank experience lived on. Yet the demise of these institutions imposed critical costs on the Japanese financial system as a whole, ultimately reinforcing the continuing dominance of the classic Bankers' Kingdom and its static circles of compensation—a configuration both structurally insensitive to microeconomic risk and consequently disinclined to innovation.

In Conclusion

By the early twenty-first century, Japan was left with a rigid yet fragile domestic financial system, dominated by a circle of compensation that avoided the risk taking conducive to needed structural transformation. A crucial engine of innovation in the classic system—the long-term credit banks— had disappeared, even as the credit monitoring mechanisms implicit in the main-bank system were eroding. The evolving system exposed the country to powerful new international financial pressures, due to the dismantling of

foreign-exchange controls that had traditionally insulated domestic investors from the complex challenge of making globally oriented asset choices.
The fluid new environment erased many old benchmarks and institutions,
yet failed to give the remaining domestic financial actors adequate incentives
to adapt to the new challenges, and rendered traditional innovators like the
long-term credit banks unviable.

Japan's financial circles of compensation continued to channel the country's
high domestic savings into real estate and capital investments secured by land
at home, as it had done for half a century, even as those land prices began to
collapse after 1990. To make matters worse, the liberalization of restrictions
on outbound financial investment during the 1980s failed to provide domestic
Japanese banks and securities firms with clear parameters for adjusting to the
new global pressures and domestic challenges that were emerging. Internationalization during the 1980s ironically helped pave the way for the provincial, inward-looking stagnation of the two decades that was to follow, with
the problem exacerbated by domestic circles of compensation that diffused the
short-term risk of sustaining an increasingly adverse and dangerous status quo.

Financial developments have, for more than a century, been central in determining the broader course of the Japanese political economy. From the
Matsukata Deflation of the 1880s until the collapse of the Heisei financial
bubble in the early 1990s, private banks, in collaboration with government,
supplied capital and defused corporate risk, thus allowing capital-intensive industries like steel, shipbuilding, and petrochemicals to grow rapidly, with high
leverage. The land-standard system, by which firms borrowed against real-
estate collateral, with steadily rising value of its own, helped to make this heavy
financial leverage rational, and to defuse its related economic risk.

An implicit circle of compensation was thus forged among bankers, in-
dustrialists, real-estate interests, and conservative politicians, who sustained
and leveraged Japan's high-growth process. The Japanese Bankers Association,
Zenginkyō, lay at the center, helping to coordinate interest rates with BOJ and
MOF, with its central role justifying the appellation for the circle of "Bankers'
Kingdom." The network also helped direct credit flows. Long-term credit
banks, standing in a netherworld between industrial planners at MITI and the
Bankers' Kingdom, provided a modicum of innovative impulse.

Zenginkyō likewise performed more narrowly, as a smaller but more institutionalized circle of compensation, playing an important role in underwriting
and purchasing government debt, while also mediating a range of regulatory
issues between government bureaucrats and its own members. This system
remained stable as long as the Japanese financial system remained sealed off

from the world. Given the existence of exchange controls, and regulatory constraints on foreign investment, increasingly affluent domestic investors were deprived of attractive alternatives overseas to the land-based domestic investments that were central to the prevailing—and highly parochial—land-based financial system.

Financial liberalization within Japan during the 1980s and 1990s, together with the deepening globalization of international finance as a whole, threw the stable dynamics of a core Japanese circle of compensation, and the related credit monitoring systems of its banking participants, into painful confusion. Domestic investors, encouraged by securities firms, began to invest globally, finding domestic real-estate assets, inflated by the Heisei financial bubble of the 1980s, to be increasingly unattractive. Land prices within Japan collapsed. Yet the collaborative regulatory edifice of the Bankers' Kingdom, dominated by MOF's static "convoy system," impeded a reassessment and restructuring of the existing domestic order that was sufficiently responsive to global economic forces.

This domestic rigidity within Japan—intensified, ironically, by informal corporate risk-sharing, limited transparency, and the moral hazard of government guidance—inhibited foreclosure on bad debts, and rendered the prevailing financial system unsettlingly toxic, thus ultimately threatening the viability of numerous banks. New forms of direct finance began to emerge but were critically handicapped by Japan's underdeveloped mechanisms for credit evaluation, following the collapse of the long-term credit banks. Circles-of-compensation-induced rigidity within the financial system therefore helped provoke the protracted stagnation that has plagued the Japanese economy for decades.

Circles of compensation in finance have played a Janus-faced role over the years, both positive and negative. Felicitously, they defused risk during the high-growth years, facilitating explosive capital investment and successful heavy industrialization under the Income Doubling Plan. Perversely, however, those same circles obscured risk and compounded rigidity when structural reform became necessary during the lost decades to follow, due to their parochial vetoes on change. The most innovative element in the classic financial system—the long-term credit banks—fell victim to financial liberalization. Japan's banks and their regulators, through a perverse collaborative dynamic and an inadequate mechanism for risk evaluation, thus inhibited a dynamic Japanese national response to the globalization that became so imperative during the early twenty-first century. Through this process, finance helped precipitate the downward spiral from success to stagnation that has plagued Japan for decades.

Land and Housing

Land, like energy and food, is one of the delicate spheres of Japanese short-age and vulnerability—indeed, perhaps the most fundamental one of all. And throughout modern history, land's economic role has been tied intimately to finance, with land often serving as a powerful tool for credit creation. Japan, after all, is only the size of California, yet has a population over three times as large, and accounts for one-twelfth of global gross domestic product (GDP), mostly through manufacturing. The structure and operation of the Japanese political economy are colored profoundly by the pressure of a large popula-tion, intensified by rapid, finance-fueled economic growth for well over a century, on painfully finite parcels of land. The parochialism and rigidity of recent Japanese policy making in the face of globalization pressures has impor-tant roots in land policy, which ties national incentive structures and financial well-being more intimately to parochial goals like real-estate appreciation and local construction than to innovation, or to international commerce.

The powerful pressure of population on land is common sense to Japanese, whose instinctive characterization of their own country, despite its material affluence, is often as a *semai kuni* (narrow nation), bereft of resources. There are, in actuality, a few major countries more crowded than Japan, notably Ban-gladesh, South Korea, the Netherlands, Belgium, and a few city-states, such as Singapore. Yet Japan still ranks as the tenth most densely populated major nation on Earth, with 348 people per square kilometer.[1]

Compounding Japan's scarcity of land is the fact that the country is moun-tainous, thus complicating both agricultural and industrial pursuits, not to

mention ordinary life. Indeed, only around 21 percent of Japan's area is topo-
graphically suitable for housing, compared to 49 percent in the United States,
62 percent in France, and 64 percent in both Britain and Germany.[2] The only
other major, highly populated country as mountainous as Japan is neighboring
South Korea.

Land as the Standard of All Social Value

Neither Japan's high overall population density nor its ruggedly mountainous
topographical character can fully explain its distinctive patterns of land use
and land policy. Yet those physical endowments help create a distinctive and
predictable economic bias: They render habitable and arable land a scarce
resource—one that powerful groups in Japanese society naturally become preoccupied with controlling and allocating, to the exclusion of broader, more
cosmopolitan concerns.

The underlying physical scarcity of land informs the venerable and important principle of *tochi hon'isei* (land-standard system). That, in turn, has been
basic to Japanese political-economic thinking, and high among the priorities
of decision-makers nationwide—both public and private—since the eighth
century.[3] Since the 1950s, however, it has been harnessed powerfully to the
cause of economic development, and finally to speculation, driven by the politically configured financial incentives noted above. Land policy contributed
greatly to the ability of Japanese industrial firms during the 1950s, 1960s, and
1970s to avoid heavy dependence on foreign borrowing, while at the same
time investing and growing rapidly. Conversely, land policy also encouraged
the explosive borrowing that led to the economic bubble of the 1980s, its collapse, and the lost decade that followed.

Land as Leverage for Domestically Driven Industrial Finance

The dramatic story of the recent past has venerable origins. From the roots of
real-estate ownership in the Nara period, substantial land was owned by powerful Buddhist temples and Shinto shrines. Otherwise, until the end of the Edo
period in 1868, real estate was largely held by the state itself, including various
domain actors. The use of land as collateral for loans dates from the Edo period
(1603–1868), but became widespread during the Meiji era (1868–1912), as
Japan's industrialization gained momentum.[4]

Industrialists during the Meiji era began owning land as a reliable store of
value, rather than just a commodity for exchange. They borrowed money and
invested the profits of their ventures in more real estate to ensure financial leverage for future expansion, thus minimizing the need for foreign borrowing

that was pervasive in most of the rest of the developing world. Thus, the land standard was integrated systematically into the foundations of modern Japanese economic growth, simultaneously imparting a narrowly domestic bias to Japanese approaches to development beyond Japan's own shores. This parochial bias was compounded by foreign-exchange controls which prevented initially scarce capital from flowing to more remunerative applications overseas.

One of the principal reasons that land has been so important as a store of economic value in modern Japan has been that banks conventionally regard it as the main form of security for loans, reflecting the land–finance link that has grown increasingly important since industrialization began in the late nineteenth century. The Long-Term Credit Bank Law of 1952 explicitly required land as collateral on all extended loans of over six months' duration. Politicians and bureaucrats reinforce this bias by refusing to authorize alternate funding procedures. The reliance of firms on bank finance, as opposed to securities issues, likewise indirectly reinforces the land-value standard orientation that was classic even before the industrial era.

The political-economic consequences of the land–standard system are clear, and have created powerful constituencies for its perpetuation. Most important, the system gave large firms with substantial land holdings an asset cushion that encouraged them to aggressively undertake capital investments that might otherwise be considered reckless. In the early 1990s, for example, NTT had land assets with a market value estimated at almost $145 billion over book value; Tokyo Electric Power had an analogous "cushion" of nearly $61 billion, Toyota had $46 billion, and Kansai Electric Power had $39 billion.[5]

Policy Supports for the Land-Standard System

Japanese public policy from the 1950s into the 1990s worked to support the land-standard system in two synergistic ways: by increasing demand for land, and by constraining supply. The consequence, in the context of Japan's rapid economic growth of the postwar years, was an explosive rise in the price of land, expressed in a few simple statistics: (1) While a commodity costing $1 wholesale in 1956 was priced at $2 in 1990, a unit of urban land which $1 dollar in 1956 was priced at $145 in 1990;[6] (2) in *one* year (1987), the corporate capital gains generated through land-price increases amounted to ¥416 trillion for Japan as a whole—about 20 percent greater than Japan's *entire* GDP in that year;[7] and (3) at its high point, the value of the land inside the Imperial Palace moat in Tokyo was greater than that of the entire state of California.[8]

On the demand side, expansionary monetary policies naturally enhanced demand for real-estate assets, as did the heavy concentration, in the fiscal sphere, of public-works spending in the Japanese national budget.[9] Agricultural price supports likewise indirectly increased the shadow value of farmland.[10] So did legally explicit requirements for land collateral, such as that provided under the 1952 Long-Term Credit Bank Law.[11] The rising price of land in turn provided collateral for expanded bank loans to support capital investment, facilitating Japan's distinctive "invest, then save" political-economic behavior, which powerfully accelerated economic growth without heavy foreign borrowing.

The Japanese government's role in constricting the supply of land available for development, and thus accelerating land-price increases, was largely one of omission. It set initial policies that incentivized the concept of land as an asset, and then remained inactive until the early 1990s, under the logic that it could do nothing to breach constitutional provisions guaranteeing the right to own property as inviolable.[12] Three policies were centrally responsible for constraining the supply of land available for development: (1) the Land and House Lease Law; (2) the inheritance-tax system; and (3) the property-tax system, especially the fixed-asset tax.

The Land and House Lease Law indirectly increased the price of land, due to the strong tenant rights that it established. The ability of a landowner to evict tenants was highly restricted, making it difficult to quickly and flexibly sell land in the event of rapid price increases. The inheritance tax, while in principle forcing land sales because of the high rates for intergenerational transfers, in reality was modified by the operating practice of valuing land for tax purposes at only 70 to 80 percent of the government benchmark price, which was itself only about 70 percent of the market price.[13]

Japan's modern property-tax system, which has maintained rates at remarkably low levels throughout most of the post–World War II period, is a third pillar of the venerable *tochi hon'isei* order that has so profoundly shaped Japanese political-economic development. Real-estate prices have traditionally been very high in Japan, but real-estate tax revenue has nevertheless been much lower than in either the United States or Britain.[14] The effective rate of the real-estate tax fell as low as 0.05 percent of the market value of land, compared to a rate of close to 1.00 percent in other developed countries.[15] The highly decentralized property-tax system, which places primary responsibility for determining tax levels on local governments that have tended to be especially deferential to real-estate interests, was established in 1950 as part of tax reforms recommended by the Occupation-era Shoup Mission.[16]

The position of land as a privileged asset was also reinforced by a series of policy steps introducing favorable tax treatment for farmland, thus increasing

demand, reducing supply, and inflating overall land prices. These supportive
measures began in 1964,[17] and included prominently the Production Greening
Law (*Seisan Ryokuchi Hō*) of 1974,[18] and the Price Reduction Ordinance (*Jōrei
Gengaku Seido*) of 1976.[19] Under these laws, urban development is restricted
in areas covered for periods of thirty years, artificially curtailing the supply of
land for urban development, and putting upward pressure on prevailing land
prices.[20] Reduced inheritance tax on land transfers also for many years helped
to keep land prices high.

Policy Constraints Emerge

As land-price rises accelerated in the late 1980s, social pressure to curb their
further ascent began to build. In 1989 the Basic Land Law (*Tochi Kihonhō*) was
passed, to curb land speculation and to raise land taxes to levels reflecting land-
price trends in the real economy. In 1992 a land-value tax came into effect, and
in 1994 tax breaks on agricultural land in urban areas were reduced.[21]

These measures helped brake and ultimately reverse the inexorable land-
price increases that had continued since the Korean War. Yet these steps were
marginal changes from a policy standpoint. They left Japan's basic embedded
policy stance of privileging land assets and their development, according lesser
priority to more-cosmopolitan incentives, fundamentally unchanged.

The Land-Driven Capital Investment Cycle

As indicated above, a land-standard system, existentially rooted in Japan's geo-
graphic configuration, with its ineluctable pressures of population and affluence against finite space, has expressed itself repeatedly across Japanese history.
That long-standing proclivity has been reinforced by a wide range of legislation and administrative guidance from the bureaucracy since the early postwar
years. Public works and agricultural price-support policies, for example, have
increased demand for real estate. Meanwhile, tax disincentives for development have reduced supply.

The land standard has also proven to be a powerful tool for credit creation.
As a decimated global power with revived economic ambitions in the wake
of World War II, Japan desperately wanted to advance rapidly, but without
undue reliance on the broader world. The land-standard system proved to be
a powerful tool for bootstrapping that effort, by supporting and legitimating
a unique "invest, then save" approach to capital investment and economic
growth.[22]

Following Dodge Line retrenchment and the economic boom of the
Korean War years that ensued, Japan maintained a relatively high basic level

of domestic savings. One key developmental challenge was mobilizing that savings, and then harnessing it to rapidly build plant and infrastructure. In contrast to conventional wisdom, this was *not* simply a matter of MITI developmental fiat.[23] The land standard generated a crucial link by providing a collateral base whose value was continually rising, justifying expanded-borrow asset-based bank lending as well. The stimulative effect of rising land prices on Japanese capital investment over the high-growth decades between 1955 and 1990 is clear from Figure 5.1. Conversely, the deflationary pressures exerted by falling land prices since the early 1990s are apparent, as well.

The land price–capital investment interactive dynamic has also had major implications for Japanese growth. When land prices rose, their synergistic interaction with capital investment created great surges in corporate investment, much of it leveraged with heavy domestic bank borrowing. During the early 1960s, for example, following announcement of the Income Doubling

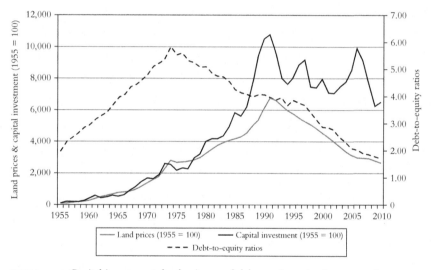

FIGURE 5.1   Capital investment, land prices, and debt-equity ratios in postwar Japan, 1955–2010

sources: Ministry of Internal Affairs and Communications Statistics Bureau, "22–20 Urban Land Price Index—All Urban Land, 6 Major Cities and excluding 6 Large Cities (1955–2005)," *Historical Statistics of Japan* [for 1955–2005]; Ministry of Internal Affairs and Communications Statistics Bureau, "17–12 Urban Land Price Index," *Japan Statistical Yearbook 2015* [for 2006–2010]; Ministry of Finance Policy Research Institute, "Assets, All Industries (except Finance and Insurance)," "Liabilities, All Industries (except Finance and Insurance)," and "Investment in plant and equipment and inventories," in *Financial Statements Statistics of Corporations by Industry, Quarterly.*

notes: 1) "Capital investment" is defined here as investment in plant and equipment, excluding software, for 1955–2000 and investment in plant and equipment, including software, for 2001–2010. 2) "Debt-to-equity ratio" is defined here as (Liquid Liabilities + Fixed Liabilities) ÷ (Total Assets – Total Liabilities), calculated by the author with Ministry of Finance data. 3) Q4 data is used here to represent year-end financial position.

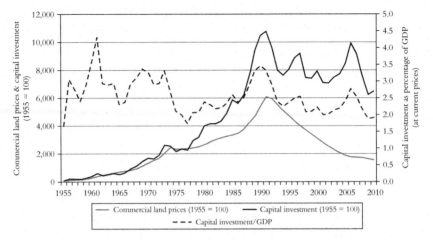

FIGURE 5.2   Capital investment share of GDP and commercial land prices, 1955–2010

SOURCES: Ministry of Internal Affairs and Communications Statistics Bureau, "22–20 Urban Land Price Index—All Urban Land, 6 Major Cities and excluding 6 Large Cities (1955–2005)," *Historical Statistics of Japan* [for 1955–2005]; Ministry of Internal Affairs and Communications Statistics Bureau, "17–12 Urban Land Price Index," *Japan Statistical Yearbook 2015* [for 2006–2010]; Ministry of Finance Policy Research Institute, "Investment in plant and equipment and inventories," *Financial Statements Statistics of Corporations by Industry, Quarterly*; Ministry of Internal Affairs and Communications Statistics Bureau, "3–1 Gross Domestic Expenditure (At Current Prices, At Constant Prices, Deflators)-68SNA, Benchmark year = 1990 (C.Y. 1955–1998, F.Y. 1955–1998)," *Historical Statistics of Japan* [for 1955–1998]; Ministry of Internal Affairs and Communications Statistics Bureau, "3–1 Gross Domestic Product (Expenditure Approach) At Current Prices," *Japan Statistical Yearbook 2016* [for 1999–2010].

NOTES: Nominal GDP figures are used here for two reasons: 1) the Government of Japan reported real GDP figures before 1998 with 1990 market prices and figures after 1998 with 2005 market prices; 2) capital investment amounts were reported in nominal terms.

Plan, capital investment exceeded 4 percent of GDP, with price increases for commercial land reaching 21 percent annually.[24] These real-estate-stimulated capital investment surges became, as suggested in Figure 5.2, one of Japan's most important drivers for economic growth, in a political economy far *less* dependent on exports than its Northeast Asian neighbors.[25]

Incentive Structures, Land Allocation, and Housing

Across a century and more of high-speed Japanese economic growth, stretching from the aftermath of the Matsukata Deflation in the 1880s until the collapse of the massive Heisei real-estate bubble in the early 1990s, real-estate prices persistently rose at a rapid rate, much more quickly than the incomes of prospective home buyers, and closely correlated with bank lending, as indicated in Figure 5.3. This pattern, from a consumer standpoint, paradoxically attracted little mainstream political opposition. It did, however, attract eager support from the ruling Liberal Democratic Party (LDP), despite its inegalitarian implications for Japan's democratic society. Japanese real estate, after all,

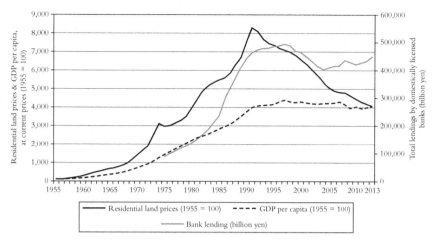

FIGURE 5.3   Japanese land prices, bank lending, and GDP per capita in comparative perspective, 1955–2013

SOURCES: Ministry of Internal Affairs and Communications Statistics Bureau, "22–20 Urban Land Price Index—All Urban Land, 6 Major Cities and excluding 6 Large Cities (1955–2005)," *Historical Statistics of Japan* [for 1955–2005]; Ministry of Internal Affairs and Communications Statistics Bureau, "17–12 Urban Land Price Index," *Japan Statistical Yearbook 2015* [for 2006–2010]; Ministry of Internal Affairs and Communications Statistics Bureau, "3–1 Gross Domestic Expenditure (At Current Prices, At Constant Prices, Deflators)-68SNA, Benchmark year = 1990 (C.Y. 1955–1998, F.Y. 1955–1998)," *Historical Statistics of Japan* [for 1955–1998]; Ministry of Internal Affairs and Communications Statistics Bureau, "3–1 Gross Domestic Product (Expenditure Approach) At Current Prices," *Japan Statistical Yearbook 2016* [for 1999–2013]; Ministry of Internal Affairs and Communications Statistics Bureau, "2–1 Total Population B 1920–2013," *Japan Statistical Yearbook 2015*; Ministry of Internal Affairs and Communications Statistics Bureau, "14–3-a Assets and Liabilities of Domestically Licensed Banks—Banking Accounts (1975–2005)," *Historical Statistics of Japan* [for 1975–2005]; Ministry of Internal Affairs and Communications Statistics Bureau, "14–2 Assets and Liabilities of Domestically Licensed Banks A Banking Accounts," *Japan Statistical Yearbook 2011* [for 2006–2009]; Ministry of Internal Affairs and Communications Statistics Bureau "14–2 Assets and Liabilities of Domestically Licensed Banks A Banking Accounts," *Japan Statistical Yearbook 2014* [for 2010–2013].

served dual purposes for its owners: (1) as a reliable store of value; and (2) as a favored collateral for bank loans. Land was, throughout the high-growth period, more predictably remunerative than more flexible or cosmopolitan asset choices, either at home or abroad.

This deep and synergistic political-economic relationship among economic growth, financial leverage, land prices, and stable conservative political dominance continued as long as capital controls sealed off the Japanese financial system from the broader world. The end of isolation, however, brought ultimately fateful change. As Figure 5.3 indicates, 1991—only a decade after the removal of foreign-exchange controls—was a key watershed year, with respect to both land prices and per-capita GDP growth. From 1991, with capital flowing increasingly outward from Japan rather than into domestic assets, land prices began to fall precipitously—a trend that continued for more than two full decades. Although per-capita GDP did not fall appreciably, its rate of increase abruptly flattened out.

We have already seen the devastating implications for Japan's banks and for general investors in recent years of the intimate land–finance link that prevailed throughout the high-growth period. Until the collapse of the real-estate bubble during the 1990s, however, both businesses and wealthy individuals desiring to borrow money consistently put priority on possessing land. Because land was in short supply during the high-growth period, and a valued corporate asset, investors forced the price of real estate ever higher, pushing it increasingly beyond the purchasing ability of many citizens, even for housing. As Figure 5.3 makes clear, land-price increases steadily outstripped increases in per-capita GDP from the mid-1950s until 1990. The land-standard system thus exacerbated a bias toward land ownership for speculative and industrial use by large corporations at the expense of individual housing. Large industrial and trading firms increasingly crowded out home buyers and small investors.

The traditional pattern of relentless land-price increases, persistently exceeding individual income growth, abated with the collapse of the Japanese macroeconomic bubble after 1990. By 2010 land prices had fallen to the long-term per-capita GDP growth trend line, as investors rushed toward alternative assets, including U.S. Treasury bills and other foreign securities. Liberalization of foreign-exchange controls, after all, had allowed Japanese residents to broaden their investment horizons to the wider world.

Windfall profits from the land-standard system, flowing from growth-fueled demand and constrained investment options, had thus mainly dissipated. Yet the standard itself remained largely in place, owing to institutional rigidities and the political-economic costs of disrupting an established circle of compensation. Land-based circles thus continued to profoundly affect the overall operation of the Japanese political economy, although with converse growth implications to the previous pattern. Real economic growth averaged 4.4 percent over the decade of the 1980s, but dropped to only 1.5 percent during the 1990s, following the collapse of the bubble, and to just 0.6 percent during the 2000s.[26] Declining real-estate prices, despite determined support efforts from banks, developers, and government, were both a basic cause and a consequence of two decades of stagnation.

High growth and rapid land-price increases prevailed at times in prewar Japan, to be sure, especially during and just after World War I. Yet this pattern of active and systematic land investment—together with the parochial incentive structure for business and bureaucracy that accompanied an institutionalized land standard—became much more highly developed in the Japan of the post–World War II high-growth period than had ever been true previously, due to the support it gave for enhanced financial leverage. Supply and demand for real estate became much more systematically shaped by policy than had ever been before.

This historic post–World War II pattern was largely due to an additional catalytic factor in the land-standard political-economic equation: the emergence of real-estate-oriented party politicians. This pattern was epitomized by Kakuei Tanaka, who played a key role in defining land policy for nearly four decades.[27] During the 1960s and 1970s, in particular, such figures supported both stimulative macroeconomic policies and a series of sectoral measures supporting land prices by restricting supply of urban land for development.

To be sure, there had previously been real-estate-oriented politicians, such as Takashi Hara, during the days of Taishō democracy before World War II.[28] Yet over the first post–World War II decade they gained far greater scope than previously. Three factors were at work: (1) the dissolution of the Home Ministry at the end of 1947; (2) the advent soon thereafter of a new and poorly institutionalized Construction Ministry over which politicians could readily wield influence; and (3) a sudden acceleration during 1951 of government revenues and economic growth, fueled by the Korean War boom.

Together, these three developments generated immense new opportunities for political entrepreneurship at the interface of construction and land-policy management. With factional and party-political competition also intensifying, politicians had strong incentives to harness real-estate ventures as a vehicle for raising needed political support funds, as well as for personal aggrandizement. The land standard previously embraced by big business found powerful political support, as well, its negative implications for new housing-market entrants and for used-housing transactions notwithstanding.

Political Imperatives That Economic Incentives Generate

The economic incentives of the high-growth years, stretching four decades from the mid-1950s into the 1990s, were crystal clear: large private firms should invest in real estate, and then harness the rapidly appreciating assets as collateral for loans financing ambitious capital investments in industry. To render those capital investments more efficient, supportive infrastructure, much of it greenfield construction, was needed. Facilitating this construction was the collective responsibility of bureaucrats and politicians who authorized and formulated the related government budgets.

Politicians were pivotal in bringing to pass the large public infrastructural projects—ports, airports, and highways. These in turn made the massive private investments of the high-growth years in steel, petrochemicals, and shipbuilding economically feasible. Diet members also had strong personal incentives to become catalysts in such ventures. Industry-linked public-works investments, after all, had a powerful stimulative effect on local land prices, which benefited business backers of the politicians, while aiding construction company supporters and local communities, as well.

The huge Nippon Steel production complex at Kimitsu in Chiba Prefecture, like the massive petrochemical complexes along the Inland Sea, involving ports, highways, and railway lines, as well as heavy-industrial facilities, were cases in point. Political incentives were powerfully aligned in such cases with the imperatives of high-speed economic growth—adverse social consequences such as air and water pollution notwithstanding. Many politicians and businessmen, transfixed by the attractions of domestic real-estate investment, developed increasingly intimate ties, and often became myopic about international concerns, even as globalization quietly began to unfold in the wider world beyond Japanese shores.[29]

Profile of the Charmed Circle

Land-related political-economic ties deepened from the 1960s on—precisely during the period when economic relations in the West were growing globally more cosmopolitan. Yet Japan's land standard (*tochi hon'isei*), on which today's real-estate-related circles of compensation are based, has political-economic origins that stretch back well over 1200 years. The Japanese elites gained ever deeper stakes in rising land prices over the century and more of sustained modern economic growth that began with the end of the Matsukata Deflation (1882–1885), and accelerated, following World War II, until the collapse of the Shōwa and Heisei bubble (1987–1990). As indicated in Figure 5.4, an extraordinarily broad range of interests—almost entirely domestic—have come to share a common stake in stable and rising Japanese land prices, irrespective of broader social costs and foregone opportunities to deepen broader global interdependence. Their interests became deeply fused during the high-growth years, with stable land prices, protected by regulation and fiscal expansion, serving as a common motive for cooperation.

Real-estate interests—developers, in particular—were natural early beneficiaries of Japanese land policies, particularly in their post–World War II incarnation, as the suburbs of Japan's great cities were emerging.[30] Many of these entrepreneurs—men like Yoshiaki Tsutsumi, president of Seibu Railway,[31] Keita Gotō of the Tokyu Group,[32] and Kenji Osano, president of the Kokusai Kogyo motor-transport conglomerate,[33] were in the transportation sector,

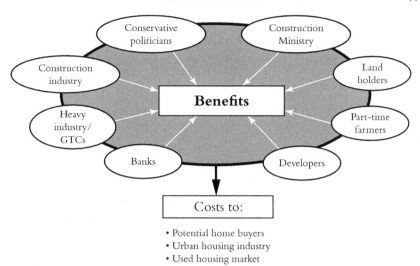

FIGURE 5.4   Circles of compensation in land policy

SOURCE: Author's illustration.
NOTE: "GTC" denotes "general trading company."

with hotel interests, as well. They capitalized on and gained a strong stake in rising land prices by engaging in business lines, such as railway and motor transport, that involved both substantial real-estate purchases and synergistically stimulated price increases in domestic land. Tax, zoning, and collateral regulations, together with distributive benefits conferred through the public-works budget, gave these developers strong common interests with politicians, bureaucrats, and other more conventional businesspeople.

Working closely with the developers were Japan's construction companies, both large and small, which prospered greatly during the high-growth years. They were, after all, the firms that implemented the actual construction projects. The leaders, such as Kajima Corporation, Kumagai Gumi, and Nishimatsu Construction, grew to become some of the leading enterprises in Japan. Smaller firms were often nevertheless highly important in local areas, especially to local Diet members, and were frequently central participants in public-works construction projects that such politicians and their constituents valued.

In the land-policy area, government has played a powerful role in sustaining and strengthening circles of compensation, both by regulating property development and by providing distributive benefits, especially by authorizing public works. Conservative political allies of the developers and construction companies, led by Kakuei Tanaka, held parallel and synergistic interests with those firms, in both dimensions. Because they were technically government officials, politicians could help shape the contours of regulation, especially at agencies like the Ministry of Construction. There they held sway over bureaucratic regulators, both by influencing personnel appointments and by preparing postretirement "landing spots" for former officials.

Politicians also held the power to determine the scale and distribution of public-works budgets. That influence in turn shaped land prices, particularly in the areas given enhanced access to the broader world by new roads, railways, and bridges. Just as important, from a business perspective, politicians could also determine through their Diet and prefectural deliberations the *timing* of new infrastructural projects, thus exercising substantial impact on land prices in local areas.

Large industrialists were also significant participants in land-policy circles of compensation, although their economic interests were typically not bound so tightly to politics as those of the developers. The central activities of big business far transcended real estate, which, except during speculative periods such as the late 1980s, was not too central to their commercial operations. Manufacturers did, however, need real estate as a physical base for their factories, and found rising real-estate prices useful as collateral for the expanding loans they persistently sought from financial institutions throughout the high-growth period.

As real-estate prices began to moderate during the early 1990s, some new members of the land-policy circle of compensation became more prominent. Most dynamic were the urban real-estate developers, such as Mitsui Fudosan; Mitsubishi Estate; and Mori Building. Taking advantage of the stable land prices, low interest rates, and the strong upscale consumer power of the post-bubble era, these developers built such stylish, new, diversified, leisure and office complexes in Tokyo as Shiodome City Center (Mitsui, 2000), Roppongi Hills (Mori, 2003), Tokyo Midtown (Mitsui, 2007), and the Toranomon Hills complex (Mori, 2014).[34] These developers also capitalized on the new economic environment of the post-high-growth era, as well as favorable tax policies, to engage in smaller-scale condominium development across Japan.

General trading companies (*sōgō shōsha*) have increasingly held interests similar to those of the developers and the manufacturers in the price of land, particularly within the context of their respective industrial groups. Sometimes, particularly since the late 1980s, when real-estate prices peaked, the trading companies have engaged directly and actively in real-estate development, as Itochu and Marubeni have done through their property-development subsidiaries.[35] In addition, the *sōgō shōsha* sold construction materials to developers and construction firms, thus serving as important members of the land-policy circles of compensation in a variety of ways.

Banks have likewise traditionally been central members of the land-policy circle, lending the money to finance real-estate development projects. During the high-growth years of the 1950s, 1960s, and early 1970s, their principal focus was financing capital investment in manufacturing, with real-estate finance remaining secondary. As alternative opportunities in manufacturing and international trade became less attractive during the 1980s, however, with Japan's economic growth gradually decelerating, the banks—especially smaller regional banks, which had more surplus funds to lend—shifted their focus increasingly toward real estate, often in speculative fashion. During the real-estate bubble of the late 1980s, the banks became central players in the land-policy circle of compensation, with many of them being badly hurt when the real-estate bubble collapsed a few years later.

Farmers also played a role, albeit generally passive and peripheral, in the land-policy circles of compensation. They were, after all, among the principal owners of land, especially in outlying areas that increasingly became targets for development as Japan's economy expanded over the 1960s and 1970s. They had a special interest in keeping land taxes low in suburban areas, so that they could keep resale prices high while flexibly retaining their property, in order to capitalize on rising land prices.

Outsiders

Soaring land prices did not benefit everyone in Japan. Indeed, they were perverse for new, individual would-be land owners, without much property, including young people. Rapidly rising land prices were also generally perverse for housing development, as well as the provision of public green space, since high prices discouraged such communal use of land. Japan's compulsive domestic real-estate orientation narrowed national horizons, inhibiting broader international concerns and slowing response to globalization.

Japan's land-related circles of compensation thus created a strong bias toward domestic commercial and industrial uses of real estate, often speculative and construction driven. This orientation made it difficult for consumer-friendly policy approaches, with a priority on housing supply rather than construction for its own sake, to gain traction. And government, in contrast to patterns in Singapore or heavily populated Western nations like the Netherlands, was slow to intervene on the consumer side in many areas: proactive public housing; incentives for affordable secondhand housing; and urban-planning programs, to name a few.[36]

Even the LDP's political opposition failed to make Japan's deplorable housing conditions a centerpiece in their indictment of conservative rule. Indeed, the Democratic Party of Japan (DPJ) failed to pursue systematic urban planning even during its 2009–2012 tenure in national political power. Due to political divisions within its ranks, and a philosophical bias against social-infrastructure investment, the DPJ gave priority to direct subsidies to individuals, such as children's allowances and household income subsidies to farmers, rather than tax-policy innovations such as mortgage deductions or direct support for decent, affordable housing.[37]

How Circles of Compensation in Land and Housing Policy Emerged

The institutional configurations described above, that came to dominate Japanese land policy by the 1970s, did not exist in 1945, in contrast to more venerable circles of compensation prevailing in finance, industry, and agriculture. During the pre–World War II period, bureaucrats, especially those of the Home Ministry, typically monopolized the process of land-use policy formation, while also controlling allocation of public-works budgets. They achieved considerable success in managing a coherent, organized recovery from the Great Kanto Earthquake of 1923, epitomized in the construction amid the ruins of a broad, straight, and majestic four-lane Shōwa Dōri avenue from Tokyo Station to Ueno.[38]

Similarly, the Home Ministry bureaucrats also began, from late 1945 on, to coordinate the land-use side of post–World War II rebuilding efforts, epitomized in the clearing of plazas in front of the Shinjuku, Shibuya, and Gotanda stations in Tokyo.[39] In this effort the bureaucrats were aided by major new legislation—the National Reconstruction Land Policy (*Fukkō Kokudo Keikaku*) and the Special City Planning Law—both promulgated in 1946.[40] Although Home Ministry officials were never able to implement the grandiose wartime plans they had harbored for the future of Tokyo,[41] they were nevertheless able to record significant, albeit modest, successes before the Ministry was abolished at the end of 1947.

Early Post–World War II Transformations

Three major events helped bring the Japanese land-policy circle of compensation as presently configured into existence. The first development was the advent of fully democratic party politics, with the elections of April 10, 1946. These and ensuing elections created a party-political class that was internally competitive, especially within conservative ranks, and that desperately needed political funding for survival. Expanding public-works spending that enriched both big business and construction interests naturally proved attractive to these competitive, insecure politicians.

A second development accelerating transfer of control over land policy from purely bureaucratic hands into those of a less hierarchical and much more politicized circle of compensation was the dissolution of the Home Ministry in December 1947. That development, ordered by the Allied Occupation as part of the Supreme Commander for the Allied Powers' effort to dismantle authoritarian structures of the wartime years, created a gaping institutional vacuum in local communities across Japan. Within that context, newly empowered democratic politicians such as Kakuei Tanaka, struggling for survival on the fluid and chaotic early postwar political battlefield of Niigata Prefecture, rose to achieve new, unprecedented policy influence. In one important early indication of their pro-construction bias, the politicians succeeded in having the Public Works Bureau (*Doboku Kyoku*) of the Home Ministry elevated from its scheduled agency status to ministerial rank, creating a new, politicized, and increasingly powerful Ministry of Construction.[42]

Deepening Domestic Construction Bias

These institutional changes helped impart a strong *construction* bias that has been a hallmark of Japanese housing policy since the 1950s. Rather than putting priority on public housing, as Singapore and many European countries have done, postwar Japan has aggressively subsidized *new construction* of housing by private contractors. This orientation has its roots in the Public Housing Law (*Kōei Jūtaku Hō*) of 1951. This historic member bill, proposed and orchestrated by Tanaka himself, preempted parallel welfare-oriented legislation by the bureaucrats of the Ministry of Health and Welfare, placing responsibility for housing policies in a new Ministry of Construction.[43]

The construction bias that was pioneered in the 1951 legislation resonated synergistically with the land-centric orientation of Japanese public policy more generally, and was deepened in a series of related policy steps over the ensuing three decades. In 1966 the Housing Construction Planning Law was passed, which established housing construction programs using loans from the Housing Loan Corporation (*Jūtaku Kinyū Kōko*) as a policy goal, with annual targets established.[44] This legislative development led, by the 1970s, to "home ownership through new housing construction" (*mochi ie seisaku*) being established as a key tool of macroeconomic stimulus, as capital investment in industry waned.[45]

In another fateful development, demonstrating rising politicization of land policy, the fledgling construction lobby in the Diet secured the designation of *twenty-two* special-development areas for TVA-style hydroelectric power development under the comprehensive national land development program of 1953–1958, when only a tenth as many had been initially contemplated by the bureaucrats.[46] Across the high-growth years to follow, political entrepreneurs engineered ever more ambitious national land-use development schemes. These culminated in Tanaka's massive Plan for Remodeling the Japanese Archipelago (*Nihon Rettō Kaizō Ron*) of 1972, designed to spread factories and infrastructure to the farthest corners of the country.[47] Like the 1951 Public Housing Law, these measures attempted to link public welfare and economic growth to private construction, and to a rising value for land, rather than to the more direct housing and consumer-support measures common in the West.

High Growth as a Catalyst

A third development that helped fuse real-estate, financial, political, agricultural, and bureaucratic interests, thus giving rise to the contemporary land-policy circle of compensation, was the advent of high growth following the outbreak of the Korean War in June 1950. The outbreak of war led to huge offshore procurements in Japan, the closest nation to the conflict zone, and to a sudden acceleration of Japanese economic growth.[48] Tepid real growth of only 2.2 percent in 1949 was followed by 11.0 percent GDP expansion in 1950, driven by wartime demand. Average growth of 10.8 percent across the 1950s as a whole was followed by 10.5 percent average expansion during the 1960s.[49]

The sustained hyper-growth of the 1950s, 1960s, and early 1970s encouraged manufacturers to accelerate capital investments in industry far beyond original expectations, making them ever more reliant on a rising price of land as both a source of leverage and a store of value.[50] The Korean War and to some extent the Vietnam War also encouraged politicians to work with construction interests to mastermind expanded public-works projects, especially roads, ports, and airports to serve the U.S. and Japanese militaries—a process which itself further accelerated growth. Housing investment policies, which stressed new private construction, subsidized by government, and discriminated against alternative investments in used-housing stock or public construction, were also a key part of this land-oriented stimulus, especially following the Oil Shocks of the 1970s.[51] Economic expansion, in short, became the final catalyst for an obsessive land-standard bias. It also catalyzed parochial land-use circles of compensation, aligning bankers, industrialists, farmers, and politicians with real-estate and construction interests. Together they could capture the rich dividends of growth, defuse the attendant risk of rising leverage, and preempt alternative means of promoting public welfare, including interdependence with the broader world.

Policy Consequences

The fateful coincidence of democratic political reforms (1945–1948), the dissolution of the Home Ministry (1947), and the onset of rapid economic growth (from 1951) thus gave rise to parochial, politically dominated land-policy circles of compensation, preoccupied with domestic real-estate investment. As a product of post–World War II political-economic developments, rather than the mobilization for war itself (in contrast to patterns in finance and agriculture), these circles in the land-policy area were less formal, in an institutional sense, than their counterparts in finance and agriculture. Yet they were no less integrated, in real-world political-economic terms. The land-policy circles were, however, more grounded in informal personal networks, linking politicians, construction companies, banking, construction-sector bureaucrats, and business, than in well-defined business associations with clear legal mandates. They were relatively recent creatures of the high-growth years (1950s–1970s), unlike their counterparts in most other sectors, which were a generation or more older.

Despite their recent provenance, land-policy circles steadily gained in influence within the domestic Japanese political economy, from the 1950s until the collapse of the real-estate bubble in the early 1990s. That influence was epitomized in the rise of the Tanaka faction of the ruling LDP. As Tanaka rose politically, from Minister of Posts and Telecommunications (1957–1958) to Minister of Finance (1962–1965), to LDP Secretary General (1965–1966), to MITI Minister (1971–1972), and finally to Prime Minister (1972–1974), the land-policy circle of compensation itself gained increasing political-economic prominence.[52] Several consecutive ministers of construction from the Tanaka faction during the 1970–1976 period helped to consolidate the circle of compensation politically, and to endow its members with decisive policy influence.

The land-policy circle's efficacy went far beyond arranging the details of construction contracts. The Tanaka faction at its core also included high-level alumni of the Ministry of Finance, as well as MITI and other economic ministries. It was thus able to inspire macroeconomic stimulus and regional development policies that leveraged its ability to promote construction projects as well.[53] The circle's influence thus lay in its *systemic* capabilities—centering on a unique ability to organize projects across an otherwise fragmented and

stovepiped Japanese political economy. It became a *subgovernment*, with functional roles, including de facto administration, that greatly transcended the
normal definition of vested interest. The simple potency of the land-policy
circle on domestic matters simultaneously rendered the Japanese system insensitive, however, to international concerns, and sharply skewed and delayed its
response to globalization. Smaller Japanese banks, for example, were slow in
their development of sophisticated credit-risk analysis, due to their persistent
insistence on land-collateralized lending.

The rising influence of the land-policy circle of compensation is best seen
by contrasting land policies of the period before its emergence, when bureaucrats clearly dominated land allocation, with developments thereafter. Until
the dissolution of the Home Ministry in late 1947, land-use planning was systematic, with little apparent distortion from political influence. A clear example was the National Land Planning Ordinance (*Kokudo Keikaku Settei Yōkō*)
of September 1940.[54] Early postwar reconstruction in Tokyo (1946–1947),
such as the clearing of large public squares in front of the Shinjuku, Shibuya,
and Gotanda stations, also had this technocratic flavor.[55]

Since the dissolution of the Home Ministry in late 1947, however, Japanese
land policies have been strikingly divergent both from major patterns in Japan's
own past and also from patterns in other densely populated nations of the
industrialized world, due in part to a sharp decline in bureaucratic autonomy
from political pressure. There has been substantially less effective zoning or
green-space allocation than previously, and the plans developed have been
emasculated by interest-group pressure, or transformed into broadly inclusive
industry-development schemes.[56] The state has found it difficult to compel the
private sector to make compulsory land contributions for public purposes like
parks, as it was able to do during the prewar period. Politics has also severely
circumscribed the power of eminent domain, and encouraged landowners to
demand high levels of compensation in return for ceding their property to
public purposes.

Japanese tax policies, reinforcing the land-value standard, have operated
until recently to accelerate the rate of land-price increase and also to encourage industrial and agricultural development, at the expense of increased
investment in housing stock. There continues, for example, to be preferential
taxation on agricultural land in urban areas, as noted above. This practice
arbitrarily reduces taxes on land where even minimal quantities of vegetables
are planted, regardless of location—encouraging both land hoarding and inefficient low-density land use.[57] Land authorized for rice cultivation in one
of Japan's major urban areas, for example, is taxed at less than half the rate of

comparable urban land designated for housing, while land on which vegetables are cultivated is taxed at less than one-fifth the rate for housing land.[58] In late 2015 the Abe administration proposed to double the low property tax on idle farmland, and to consider raising the inheritance tax on such land, but any changes were to be introduced in 2017 or later.[59]

High taxes on the sale of land, Japan's distinctive response to the huge land-price increases of the early 1970s, have conversely often stimulated such price increases in the short run by artificially restricting the supply of available land. They have also encouraged speculators, contrary to policy intent, even when substantial underlying demand has existed.[60] Rent controls and other constraints on landlord use of rental property have similarly created strong disincentives to develop high-quality rental housing, as did government credit policies until the early 1970s.[61] In contrast to the United States and most other industrialized nations, interest expenses on primary residences are still not tax deductible in Japan, although different incentives encourage purchase of new contractor-built homes, while also supporting investment in corporate-employee housing (*shataku*).[62] This perverse tax policy discourages Japanese from investing in home improvements and from buying "secondhand" homes.[63]

The era of explosive Japanese domestic growth, which sent industrial borrowing and real-estate prices soaring while fusing industrial, political, and financial interests together in support of the land-value standard, is over. Yet the institutions and social networks forged in that era remain, with their natural stake in self-preservation. The land-policy circle of compensation remains a major reason why the instinctive recipe of the Japanese political economy for national revival, as in the case of Abenomics, is so consistently fiscal and monetary expansion is largely devoid of structural reform.

In Conclusion

Japan is a nation with high population density and limited arable, habitable land, although not nearly as unique in these two respects as conventional wisdom suggests. There are other crowded nations, including the Netherlands, South Korea, and Singapore, that have systematic and technocratically driven land-use planning processes. Japan's land-use and housing-policy profile, by contrast, has been strongly shaped since the late 1940s by the influence of politics generally, and particularly by conservative circles of compensation.

There is little written about Japanese land and housing policies—in English, or even in Japanese-language scholarly literature. Such literature as exists is largely technical, and gives limited attention to political-economic matters. Yet despite the lack of broad scholarly attention, the substantive implications of land and housing policies for how the Japanese political economy actually operates are profound. They are a central reason for the parochialism, obliviousness to global concerns, and expansionary macroeconomic bias that often pervades Japanese policymaking.

The land-standard system has been a pillar of lending practices, as well as assessment of personal and corporate worth, throughout modern Japanese history. Public policies in a broad range of areas, including finance and agriculture, have supported it, and in turn been shaped by it. The land standard for many years had a self-reinforcing effect, synergistic with Japanese economic expansion, by which economic growth and monetary expansion triggered higher and higher land prices. Those in turn allowed greater corporate leverage and facilitated capital-intensive industrialization.

The dominant circle of compensation in the land-use area includes developers, construction companies, manufacturers, general trading companies, banks, farmers, and conservative politicians. All traditionally have an economic stake in rapidly rising land prices, as well as the priority use of land for commercial and industrial purposes, and housing policies oriented toward new construction. They do not, as a rule, directly oppose consumer-oriented housing policies.

Yet the bias of Japan's land policies toward aggressive, construction-oriented real-estate development renders alternative, community-oriented uses of green space economically unattractive, and trading in older buildings less active. This construction bias also results in tax policies that privilege development and create shortages of land for immediate development. That shortage in turn generates longer-term momentum for sustained land-price increases.

As in other policy areas, the existence of land-policy circles of compensation internalizes gains to the circle—in this case, through increases in real-estate prices that benefit all members of the circle. Since the early 1990s, land-policy circles have also filled the defensive function of minimizing short-term land-price reductions. As in other sectors, the circle also externalizes costs—by generating high land prices, for example, that systematically disadvantage first-time home buyers and prospective public uses of green space, such as parks, as well as service industries and entrepreneurs who lack substantial land assets.

The existence of the land-policy circle of compensation has also intensified the conservative and parochial bias of Japanese policy making, making businesspeople more reluctant to risk economic involvement abroad, outside of manufacturing and real estate. The standard has thus tended to impede globalization, and to discourage the redeployment of domestic assets to uses enhancing international competitiveness and consumer welfare, particularly since the collapse of the land-price bubble in the early 1990s.

Since the collapse of the Heisei financial bubble in the early 1990s, the perversities of the land-policy circle of compensation, in both the domestic and international dimensions, have shown themselves clearly. Nevertheless they have engendered only a tepid response even from ostensibly progressive elements of the political spectrum, and despite the rise of those elements to political power during the 2009–2012 period. Deeply embedded within the structure of the Japanese political economy, the land-policy circle of compensation has exerted strong influence on national policy profiles. It is to the related sector of agriculture that we now turn.

Food Supply

Food supply, of course, is a fundamental human need that can in principle be supplied by market mechanisms. In crowded, resource-poor Japan, however, market-based supply inevitably involves high levels of imports, with "food security" implications in potential tension with transnational interdependence. Political processes transform both production and distribution in distinctive ways. They create and help sustain circles of compensation similar to those prevailing in so many other economic sectors, with fateful implications for both Japanese consumers and their nation's broader ability to globalize. Considering the small and declining share that farmers and farming represent in the Japanese workforce and gross domestic product (GDP), those circles remain remarkably potent within the Japanese domestic political economy.[1]

Japan has, for example, some of the highest rice prices in the world. Yet it fails to import rice in significant amounts. "High support levels and limited market orientation," as the OECD has characterized it, it, typify many other areas of Japanese agriculture, as well.[2] This chapter considers the role of circles of compensation in both the production and distribution of food in Japan, how these distinctive patterns came to be, and their broader political-economic consequences for the Japanese political economy—impeding true globalization, in an otherwise increasingly borderless world.

Root of the Nation: The Common Face of Varied Agricultural Incentives

As with respect to energy and land, Japan's overall national circumstances have inevitably made food a scarce, valued resource that tempts powerful political and business interests to intervene in its production and distribution. With a population of over 120 million people, inhabiting a nation the size of California, Japan finds it virtually impossible to produce a full range of basic foodstuffs to feed its people. It is inevitably faced with a persistent challenge of assuring food security.

From very early times, due to the persistent pressure of high population on scarce land, the notion of *nōhonshugi*, or "agriculture as the root of the nation," has been implicit in popular consciousness and policy—not only in Japan, but across East Asia as a whole.[3] The notion is that agriculture serves as the cornerstone of prosperity, and indeed of human existence, making abundance on the land and affluence in other sectors inseparable. This concept of rural–industrial interdependence lay behind the early agglomeration of agriculture, industry, and distribution in Japanese bureaucratic management. Indeed, it was not until 1925, as Chalmers Johnson points out, that Japan even established separate ministries for industry and agriculture.[4]

The elemental imperative of assuring food security provided a natural social rationale in early modern Japan for establishing broad-based, cross-sectoral circles of compensation—encompassing food production, distribution, and even the manufacturing of agricultural inputs, such as fertilizer and farming equipment. As in other policy areas, these circles internalized the benefits of supply and distribution among their members, while similarly externalizing related costs. They thus embedded a parochial bias that both stabilized agricultural life and simultaneously rendered it less responsive to broader national and international forces that might destabilize prices, supply, or rural livelihood in general. Political-economic uncertainties on the land, in short, threatened to provoke broader uncertainties—in real estate, finance, politics, and ultimately economic growth itself, since all these dimensions of the Japanese political economy were linked holistically with one another.

The Rise of Agricultural Corporatism

The Meiji government quickly absorbed the solipsistic logic of industrial-agrarian synergy, establishing a variety of corporatist organizations in the 1890s and 1900s to simultaneously aid the countryside and co-opt political-economic dissatisfaction there, while also promoting industrial development.[5] These new bodies included the *nōkai*, or agricultural voluntary associations, and the "industrial associations" (*sangyō kumiai*), both established by Diet legislation in 1900. The latter were, despite their appellation, modeled after German agricultural cooperatives designed to improve agricultural-tenant productivity, and were distinct from the sectoral cooperative associations (*gyōkai*) that emerged a generation later across Japanese industry and finance.

The two types of corporatist rural production and distribution societies developed in parallel, with the *sangyō kumiai* soon distributing fertilizers and, from 1906, credit services to farmers. The *nōkai*, in which participation for farmers became mandatory during 1905, meanwhile concentrated on agricultural education and extension services. In 1931 the *sangyō kumiai* also obtained a monopoly on rice purchases from farmers, as well as exclusive rights to handle the sale of rice by farmers to both the government and private retailers.

Meanwhile, as the *nōkai* and *sangyō kumiai* were evolving under government aegis across the turbulent early twentieth century, a related public-welfare society with agricultural interests was developing from the grassroots. In 1922 the Livelihood Cooperative Association (*seikatsu kyōdō kumiai*, or *seikyō* for short) was established in response to the rapidly rising food prices of the World War I years, which precipitated the widespread rice-price riots of 1918. Led by Toyohiko Kagawa, a social activist educated at Princeton Theological Seminary, and backed by nascent labor unions, *seikyō* distributed food and other necessities of life at reasonable prices to workers and other urban dwellers.[6] Kagawa also participated in the semiofficial agricultural movement, organized ostensibly to improve the moral and spiritual lives of the rural populace, illustrating the close interrelationship between the urban consumer-based *seikyō* and their agricultural counterparts during the pre–World War II period.[7]

In 1942, under the deepening pressures of the Pacific War, which mandated increased agricultural supply with reduced labor input, the two types of cooperatives most directly related to farm production merged, under explicit state control. In the same year, a newly promulgated Food Control Law authorized the Ministry of Agriculture and Forestry (MAF) to pay farmers directly for their produce, bypassing landlords, and effectively displacing those parasitic forces from the agricultural economy. The foundations of postwar, state-dominated circles of compensation in agriculture were thus firmly laid. In 1947 those links were strengthened when MAF made *nōkyō* the exclusive distributors of grain in Japan. In the same year, the cabinet of Socialist Tetsu Katayama also proposed a formal legal role for *seikyō*, incorporating it under the Ministry of Health and Welfare (MHW).

The bureaucratic linkages with agriculture—and MAF's founding role in the emerging food-sector circle of compensation—were forged during and just after World War II. Yet direct, ongoing connections between the food economy and the political world were slower to emerge. To be sure, *Seiyūkai* politicians had begun to develop formidable patronage political ties with the countryside during the days of Taishō democracy (1912–1926).[8] Yet relationships between farmers and political parties did not really begin to assume systematic, institutionalized form for more than two decades thereafter.

A major catalyst was the serious economic difficulty that the *nōkyō* experienced following the deflationary Dodge Line of 1949. By 1951, 2,600 local branches of *nōkyō*, which had prospered mightily during the food shortages of the early postwar years, had gone bankrupt. The rest were desperately in search of new commercial opportunities that would enable them to survive.

The Paradoxical Political Imperatives of the "Steel and Rice" Coalition

Across Japanese political history, as in Germany and several other late industrializing nations,[9] a recurring pattern is a "steel and rice coalition." As suggested above, such an alliance of elite agricultural and industrial interests prevailed during most of Japan's pre–World War II industrialization, from the Meiji Restoration until 1945. In its postwar incarnation, industry provided campaign finance, while agriculture turned out voters in large numbers.[10]

An incongruously conservative Liberal Party government, led by Shigeru Yoshida, consolidated power in Japan early in 1949, just as the Communist revolution in China was unfolding, amid a powerful countersurge of radical leftist sentiment and activism within Japan, as well.[11] The precariously dominant new ruling party was tempted to harness such an economically important and politically legitimate entity as *nōkyō,* representative of agricultural interests, for political purposes. The Liberals did so by introducing ambitious new support policies for the turbulent countryside—an anomalous yet crucial swing constituency for them at the time, in their efforts to create a stable coalition supportive of heavy-industry-driven economic growth. As economic growth accelerated across the 1950s, driven by surging investment in steel, shipbuilding, petrochemicals, and other capital-intensive sectors, debt-to-equity ratios rose sharply, while the political-economic connections among finance, real-estate collateral, and agriculture grew steadily tighter; agricultural support for the ruling party thus grew progressively more crucial.

The ruling Liberals and their circle also funneled heavy support through the agricultural cooperatives. Between 1951 and 1955, the Japanese government provided over ¥3 billion to support local *nōkyō*, with subsidies rising to over half of MAF's entire budget.[12] In 1954 MAF also authorized creation of a national peak organization for *nōkyō*, the Agricultural Cooperatives Central Association (*Nōkyō Chūōkai*), to serve as a central point of liaison with the government.

After a turbulent and uncertain democratic-socialist interlude during the early Allied occupation, Japanese governments began organizing their countryside, transforming the *nōkyō* into a corporatist vehicle for binding farmers to the political fortunes of the newly dominant ruling party—highly conservative, despite its Liberal appellation.[13] Through three major revisions of the Agricultural Cooperative Association Law, whose original 1947 version had been passed under the Socialist Katayama administration, the Liberals during the 1949–1951 period greatly strengthened the corporatist intermediary role of the *nōkyō*. Their new measures included (1) allowing the cooperatives to combine buying and selling functions (May 1949); (2) permitting the cooperatives to handle sales of fertilizer to farmers (May 1950); and (3) allowing farmers to reinvest dividends from their own commercial operations in their local *nōkyō* branch, without being taxed.[14]

Consumer Groups and the Conservative Agricultural Circle

The objectives of consumer-livelihood cooperatives (*seikyō*) were broadly parallel to those of their agricultural cousins (*nōkyō*) in classical terms—the stable production and supply of livelihood necessities. Yet the architects of Japan's postwar political order responded very differently to urban-based *seikyō* than they had to the rural *nōkyō* for four basic reasons. First, *seikyō* remained, in the early postwar years, relatively small and weak organizationally, lacking strong roots in a countryside made affluent by early postwar food shortages. Second, *seikyō*—like most primarily urban groups—loosely amalgamated complex, cross-cutting interests that were inherently difficult to organize, in contrast to the simpler profile of the countryside—it was hence a less coherent political partner.[15] Third, the Liberals (actually, deceptively named conservatives) had a serious conflict of interest. They maintained strong ties with small-scale urban merchants, who felt that *seikyō* were undercutting their own economic livelihood. And, finally, *seikyō* members, for their part, were either oblivious of or unreceptive to being used as a political force. This inclination was strengthened by the reality that most *seikyō* members were female, in a country where women had exercised the franchise only since 1946.

The Anti-Globalist Cast of Communalism

The political predilection that both *nōkyō* and *seikyō* shared, together with Japanese consumers more generally, was ultimately a protectionist impulse, rooted in elemental economic insecurity. It was a feeling that, in a volatile, uncertain world, national prosperity, health, and environmental protection all mandated reliance on *nearby* players with whom consumers could share communal contact—even when the output of those neighbors was relatively more expensive than the produce of efficient foreigners farther away. As Steven Vogel has pointed out, "Japanese consumers and consumer groups do not hold the expected preferences for liberalization. They value social stability, product safety, and/or environmental protection over economic efficiency, and they sympathize with producer groups such as farmers and retailers."[16] Both sides of the supply-demand equation in the Japanese agricultural sector thus traditionally view global interdependence in foodstuffs with some trepidation.

This orientation has been amplified by Japan's mass media, much of which has a traditionally populist cast and policy-conformist orientation.[17] Concrete steps toward liberalization are also impeded by the complexity of Diet procedures.[18] These give leverage to veto players with intense preferences, including members of the agricultural circle of compensation.

Japan's parochial orientation on agricultural matters long ago gave the Japanese food economy and its distribution system a protectionist value bias that has consistently impeded true Japanese globalization over the years. Agricultural producers and distributors have a persistent tendency to favor nearby domestic producers over the international market. That bias has been strongly reinforced by the structure of the domestic food economy, in which circles of compensation centering on *nōkyō* and *seikyō* dominate both production and distribution.

A Common Overall Pattern and Two Contrasting Variants

An integrated and consistently parochial conception of domestic agricultural interests—producer, distributor, and consumer as one—has been traditional in Japan since ancient times. Indeed, the widely supported concept of *nōhonshugi* itself, with venerable roots, within a community of shared welfare concerns, implies that consumers defer to producer concerns. Inside the agricultural economy itself, the strong structural interdependence of farmer and bureaucratic interests dates from the dawn of the twentieth century, when the *nōkai* and *sangyō kumiai* were both founded.

That interdependence was strengthened greatly by the pressures of World War II mobilization, which produced the 1942 Food Control Law in an effort to more efficiently feed the troops. Following the war, conservative politicians became clear members of the agricultural compensation circle, in response to the farming crisis of the late 1940s. They seized the opportunity to rescue the nearly bankrupt *nōkyō* amid the Dodge Line–induced depression of 1949, as Yoshida's Liberal Party sought to consolidate its precarious rule.[19]

Within this venerable tradition of broad-based support for agriculture in Japan, two politically contrasting yet economically complementary streams of compensation in food production and distribution emerged in the early post–World War II period: (1) a conservative variant, based on the *nōkyō;* and (2) a left-oriented version, based on the *seikyō*. The former was more directly influential politically, since the conservatives (i.e., the Liberal Party) were in power after 1949, and received the bulk of government resources. Yet both variants had parallel anti-foreign-trade biases, thus intensifying the overall protectionist hue of Japanese agricultural policies, and embedding protectionist policies thereafter highly resistant to change. The parallel biases of left and right also privileged producer interests. These commonalities make it legitimate to speak of a common agricultural circle of compensation, transcending ideology and partisan politics, as presented in Figure 6.1.

The Nōkyō Variant: Parochialism of the Right

In the food production and distribution circle of compensation, the agricultural cooperatives loomed very large. By the mid-1990s, they handled 95 percent of all the rice marketed in Japan, while channeling 80 percent of Japanese agricultural subsidies.[20] Ninety-nine percent of Japanese farm households (both full-time and part-time) were members of the circle, together with nearly three million associate members attracted by the nonagricultural

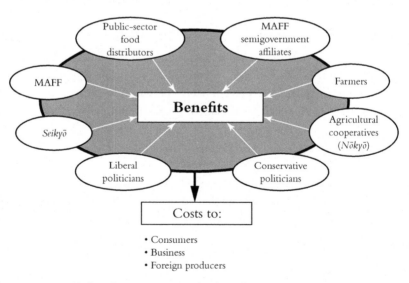

FIGURE 6.1   Circles of compensation in food supply

SOURCE: Author's illustration.

benefits of membership, such as attractive credit opportunities and easy access to discount airline tickets. By 1990 the Central Union of Agricultural Co-operatives (JA-Zenchu, *nōkyō*'s umbrella federation), boasted 8.5 million members, and a staff of 375,000, making it the third-largest non-governmental employer in Japan.

Japan Agricultural Cooperatives (also known as JA or *nōkyō*), as noted earlier, have traditionally provided a wide range of services for farmers, who continue to be heavily subsidized and otherwise supported by government.[21] JA has supplied everything from fertilizer and insurance to discount hotels in Waikiki and funeral services to members.[22] These varied services make membership in and political cooperation with *nōkyō* attractive for even part-time farmers, who still comprise over 70 percent of Japan's farming population. They also render the organization more broadly influential in society.[23] Because of its varied functional roles, JA must be seen as a dual entity: both a multifaceted service provider and a politically formidable interest group. At the local level, farmers participate in one or both of two co-op varieties: around seven hundred large, multifunctional service-providing co-ops (*sōgō kumiai*), and smaller, commodity-specific co-ops (*senmon kumiai*).

At the national level, JA is grouped into four major federations, which specialize in finance, insurance, distribution, and political action. Perhaps the most economically prominent is the Norinchukin Bank, with total assets nearly ¥100 trillion and over 3,500 employees.[24] Norinchukin Bank invests heavily in government bonds. It is thus greatly appreciated by the Ministry of Finance (MOF), another indirect affiliate of the agricultural circle, although Norinchukin Bank suffered, like its mutual-insurance partner Zenkyoren, during the awkward financial liberalization of the 1990s.[25] Both Norinchukin Bank and Zenkyoren had relied heavily on MOF's "convoy system" of supervised lending, lacked adequate internal credit-monitoring systems, and suffered from a high level of nonperforming real-estate debt after the Japanese financial bubble collapsed during the early 1990s.

A third key federation and member of the agricultural circle of compensation has been *nōkyō*'s affiliated trading firm, Zen-Noh. It handles around 90 percent of the chemical fertilizer, 60 percent of the pesticides, 55 percent of the farm machinery, and 30 percent of the animal feed that are sold in Japan.[26] Zen-Noh is joined in the charmed agricultural compensation circle by commercial suppliers such as tractor manufacturers, chemical producers, and petroleum refiners.

Conservative politicians and agricultural bureaucrats, including members of the Ministry of Agriculture, Forestry and Fisheries (MAFF)-affiliated semipublic corporations, are also key members of the agricultural circle of compensation. Politicians, who keep subsidies coming and rice prices high, draw on *nōkyō* members for electoral support, through the fourth and most powerful agricultural federation, JA-Zenchu. Nearly 65 percent of Diet members affiliating with the Liberal Democratic Party, which has dominated Japanese politics for more than half a century, have at least a nominal relationship to JA-Zenchu. This political powerhouse also holds strong ties to the Democratic Party of Japan, which ruled during 2009–2012.

MAFF is the central policy-making entity within the circle, and plays a key role in sustaining the complex pattern of political-economic understandings implicit in the circle itself. With over seventeen thousand career officials, or nearly four times as many as METI, MAFF is one of the larger ministries in the Japanese government.[27] It works closely with an additional sixty thousand agriculture-related officials in local governments, who help administer many of its policies. MAFF, which administers 125 laws, also has an extremely broad sphere of regulatory authority within the food economy, aided by a wide range of affiliated semigovernmental agencies that help enforce its policies.

Regulation, often captive, thus gives critical coherence to the agricultural circles of compensation.[28] Price supports, subsidies, and quotas are among alternate tools used to both provide benefits to members of the charmed circle, and to impose costs on those outside it. *Amakudari* is another tool that MAFF, like other major ministries, invokes frequently to give coherence to the agricultural circle of compensation.

MAFF's semigovernmental affiliates are among the most extensive of any ministry in Japan, and a major technical support to other elements in the *nōkyō* circle of compensation.[29] They include bodies such as the Japanese Agricultural Standards Association (*Nihon Nōrin Kikaku Kyōkai*); public-relations operations like the Hometown Information Center (*Furusato Jōhō Senta*); and distributors such as the Agriculture and Livestock Industries Corporation (*Nōchikusangyō Shinkō Kikō*), responsible for supervising designated dairy-product imports.[30] Nōkyō's close collaborators also include the Japan Racing Association (*Nihon Chūō Keibakai*), which holds a monopoly on horse racing in Japan, and thus generates substantial revenues available to the ministry, outside the constraining purview of MOF.

Virtually all of these semigovernmental entities employ substantial numbers of retired MAFF bureaucrats in senior leadership and advisory capacities.[31] *Amakudari,* or "descent from heaven," thus provides an important supplement to the often modest lifetime income of these officials, both through substantial salaries and generous retirement payments upon re-retiring from their new, second-career organizations. MAFF officials consequently hold a strong vested interest in preserving the broad functions of their semigovernmental affiliate bodies, whose standing is predicated on substantial public intervention in the food economy.

The Seikyō Variant: Parochialism of the Left

Seikyō concerns itself with food distribution and, to some extent, with production as well, together with broader social issues.[32] It has an alternate group of affiliates to *nōkyō*, which constitute *seikyō's* own distinctive circle of compensation. These affiliates include student groups, health- and safety-oriented non-governmental organizations (NGOs), MHW (*seikyō's* supervisory ministry), a modest group of progressive farmers, and many left-oriented politicians, including particularly members of the Communist and Social Democratic parties. Among its administrative staff, *seikyō*—one of Japan's largest food distributors—is also said to number retired officials of MAFF, just as at right-oriented *nōkyō*.

Outsiders

As in the case of circles of compensation elsewhere in the Japanese political economy, those existing within the food sector operate to internalize benefits within their circles and to externalize or generalize costs. They thus tend to have a distinctive parochial bias. Those who are not members of these compensation circles end up paying significant penalties for their failure to join them, which the political system generally does not countervail.

In the case of agriculture, these negative externalities, imposed on the broader public beyond the food production and distribution economy itself, include higher food prices, and lack of access to lower-cost (and at times higher-quality) imported food. The *nōkyō* and the *seikyō*, to be sure, privilege slightly different domestic constituencies, and the *nōkyō* are more closely connected with dominant conservative political forces. Yet both circles operate to intensify agricultural protectionism, and thus to help isolate Japan's food economy from the broader world. In so doing, they also seriously complicate broader Japanese efforts to conclude regional and global trade agreements, where flexibility on agricultural issues often proves central to broader negotiating progress. In a variety of ways, agricultural circles of compensation impede Japan's political-economic integration with the broader world.

Policy Outcomes

Since the late 1940s, as a result of broad-based collective political support—
often urban as well as rural—Japan has developed a structure of policy supports for agriculture which is one of the most elaborate and costly in the
world.[33] This high level of protection has been remarkably persistent in the
face of strengthening liberalization trends elsewhere—the public protestations
against *nōkyō,* and the remonstrations of the Japanese government notwithstanding. By 2014 Japan's producer-support estimate ratio, at 49 percent, stood
at nearly three times the OECD average, and were actually higher than in
2008, as indicated in Figure 6.2.

Japan's interventionist agricultural policies, sustained by the parochial food-
economy circles of compensation, have three fundamental pillars, all related
to rice, Japan's principal foodstuff: (1) rice market intervention, (2) budgetary
subsidies, and (3) import barriers.[34] The first involves government distribution of rice, through the Food Agency.[35] The second involves heavy price
supports for Japan's generally noncompetitive agriculture, beginning with
rice. The third for many years involved strong Japanese governmental insistence on highly restrictive quotas, although in recent years MAFF has fallen

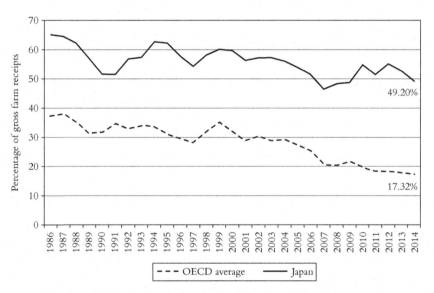

FIGURE 6.2   Japan's high producer support estimate levels, 1986–2014

SOURCE: Organisation for Economic Co-operation and Development (OECD), "Figure 2.1. OECD: level and
composition of Producer Support Estimate, 1986–2014" and "Figure 13.1. Japan: PSE level and composition by
support categories, 1986–2014," *Agricultural Policy Monitoring and Evaluation 2015* (Paris: OECD Publishing, 2015),
doi: 10.1787/agr_pol-2015-en.

back on tariffication, on an ever-shrinking, albeit still substantial, range of commodities.

Continuing Japanese agricultural protectionism, however, emphatically includes rice, on which a prohibitive off-quota tariff equivalent still remained, even in the wake of the abortive October 2015 Trans-Pacific Partnership (TPP) multilateral agreement. Japan also continues to use quotas or related mechanisms to protect wheat and wheat flour, butter, barley, starch, milk powder, and sugar. Japan likewise retains high, if declining, tariffs on beef, oranges, cheese, apples, and wine. The United States' withdrawal from the TPP following the American 2016 presidential election clearly reinforced the latent defensive capabilities of protectionist agricultural groups in Japan.

The insulation from world markets that circles of compensation have provided to Japanese farmers for over half a century, and the cost to which Japanese consumers have been oblivious, is graphically illustrated in the case of rice, a commodity constituting almost one-third of Japan's cultivated-crop output by value.[36] During the 1950s Japanese support for rice was not exceptional, and Japanese commodity supports were generally lower than those of major Western European nations.[37]

That pattern, however, was soon to change. Japanese domestic rice prices began diverging significantly from world markets in the early 1960s—when Japanese producer prices began escalating sharply, despite weaknesses in the global market. They rose rapidly during 1961–1968, and again during 1973–1975, reaching over ¥18,000/60kg in the mid-1980s, as indicated in Figure 6.3. Although international rice prices measured in yen per sixty kilogram units, have recently fallen to one-third of prevailing levels in the mid-1970s, Japanese rice prices even today remain close to their high points, as Figure 6.3 again suggests, despite powerful market pressures to the contrary.

In rice and most other commodities, Japan has not been notably responsive to global pressures. Despite the introduction in 1995 of market mechanisms for price setting, it made little progress over the ensuing two decades in cutting its overall level of producer support, or in reducing the most distorting forms of assistance, despite the strong international pressure flowing from Japan's persistently large overall trade surpluses.[38] The Japanese government has continued to spend nearly 30 percent of MAFF budget on agricultural subsidies, despite both strong international pressure and also rising domestic fiscal pressures stemming from large national budget deficits.[39] These supports made Japan's subsidies to its farmers greater than half of the entire contribution made by the twenty-eight members of the European Union in 2010.[40] In fact, without tariff and price support protection, Japan's agricultural GDP could have been nil.[41]

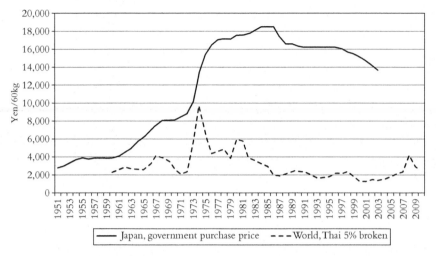

FIGURE 6.3   The high producer price of rice in Japan, 1960–2010

SOURCES: Ministry of Agriculture, Forestry and Fisheries, "1–1 Beikoku Seifu Kaiire Kakaku Nensanbetsu (Shōwa 26—Heisei 20) Kuni no Kokuji Kakaku (Seisansha Tedori Kakaku) [Rice Government Purchase Price, 1951–2008, Producer Price]," *Shokuryō Tōkei Nenpō Heisei 20-nen [Annual Report on Food Supply 2008]*; World Bank, "Rice, Thailand, 5%, $/mt, current (RICE_05)," *Global Economic Monitor (GEM) Commodities*; Ministry of Internal Affairs and Communications Statistics Bureau, "18–8 Foreign Exchange Rates (1950–2005)," *Historical Statistics of Japan* [for 1960–2005]; Ministry of Internal Affairs and Communications Statistics Bureau, "15–15 Foreign Exchange Rates," *Japan Statistical Yearbook 2015* [for 2006–2010].

NOTES: 1) Due to change in the Law for Stabilization of Supply, Demand, and Price of Staple Food during April 2004, the purchase price of rice set by the government has since then been based on bids. Therefore, Japan's government purchase prices are only available for 1951–2003. 2) World Bank releases rice prices in U.S. dollar per metric ton. Conversions were made by the author using official exchange rates released by the Japanese government.

A Tortuous Struggle for Globalization

Since the early 1970s, massive trade surpluses have intensified pressures against Japan for trade liberalization. Nowhere has the economic logic for such liberalization been stronger than in agriculture. Japan has one of the largest agricultural markets in the world, but one that nevertheless restricts imports in important areas, from nations throughout the world. As noted in Figure 6.3, since 1975 Japanese domestic producer rice prices have averaged around six times the global price. Yet imports have rarely exceeded 10 percent of consumption, as indicated in Figure 6.4.

A Changing Socioeconomic Equation

Circles of compensation have inhibited the economically rational integration of Japanese agriculture with the broader world by rendering the incentives of domestic actors considerably more parochial. The circles thus tend to both encourage and sustain agricultural protectionism and captive regulation in many

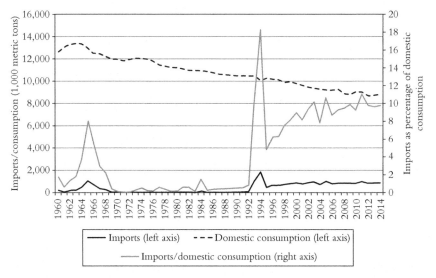

FIGURE 6.4   The declining share of rice in Japan's agricultural imports

SOURCES: Ministry of Agriculture, Forestry and Fisheries, "2 Yunyūryō [Imports]," *Heisei 26-nendo Shokuryō Jukyūhyō [Food Demand and Supply Table FY2014]*; Ministry of Agriculture, Forestry and Fisheries, "2 Kokunai Shōhi Shimukeryō [Domestic Consumption]," *Heisei 26-nendo Shokuryō Jukyūhyō [Food Demand and Supply Table FY2014]*.

dimensions, and also to conversely inhibit liberal trade flows. Such institutions thus have a powerful regulatory force of their own. They rest, however, on socioeconomic pillars that are gradually beginning to shift.

One important change is demographic. Nearly 62 percent of Japanese commercial farm workers are now over sixty-five years old. This share has doubled from only 33 percent in 1990.[42] Thus, the share of farmers who have just left the agricultural workforce, or who are about to leave it, is rapidly rising.

Statistics indicate, secondly, that the *share* of full-time farmers in Japan has begun to slowly rise, even as the total number of farmer households declines, as the countryside ages.[43] Since the mid-1970s, this share has tripled, as Figure 6.5 suggests, from around 10 to nearly 30 percent.[44] More and more farmers are gaining strong stakes in farming itself, as opposed to just casually collecting farm income, while pursuing multiple careers in which they hold limited individual stakes.

A third and final, increasingly important socioeconomic reality in Japan is that farms remain small. The average Japanese farm, for example, is only 1/148 the size of its counterpart in the United States, or 1/37 the scale of an average French farm, as shown in Table 6.1. There is thus ample room for consolidation, allowing enhanced profits for the rising corps of full-time farmers.

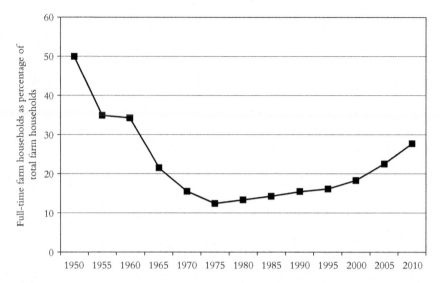

FIGURE 6.5   The fall and rise of full-time farming: Full-time farm households as
a percentage of total farm households

SOURCE: Ministry of Internal Affairs and Communications Statistics Bureau, "7–1 Farm Households by Degree
of Engagement and Size of Operating Cultivated Land," *Japan Statistical Yearbook 2011*.

TABLE 6.1

Japanese farm sizes in comparative perspective:
Average size of agricultural holding, by decade
(unit: hectare)

Country	1960	1970	1980	1990	2000
France	18.8	22.1	26.2	31.5	45.0
Japan	1.2	1.0	1.0	1.2	1.2
United States	122.6	157.6	168.1	187.0	178.4

SOURCE: Sarah K. Lowder, Jacob Skoet, and Saumya Singh,
"What Do We Really Know about the Number and Distribution of
Farms and Family Farms in the World? Background Paper for *The
State of Food and Agriculture 2014*" (ESA Working Paper No. 14–02,
Agricultural Development Economics Division, Food and Agriculture
Organization of the United Nations, Rome, 2014), Annex 4, http://
www.fao.org/docrep/019/i3729e/i3729e.pdf.

Incremental Policy Change

This changing political-economic logic in the Japanese countryside helped support the revocation in 1995 of the 1942 Food Control Law (*Shokuryō Kanri Hō*),
even though that new legislation appears to have materialized mainly due to
foreign pressure.[45] This new logic also supported ambitious policies of Prime

Minister Shinzō Abe after his cabinet took office in December 2012.[46] To encourage more-efficient land ownership and management practices, such as the
liberalization of regulations on farmland leasing, the Abe administration introduced a new system of prefectural land-consolidation banks.[47] The Abe administration also implemented programs including partial deregulation of private-
sector corporate participation in the agricultural sector, as well as support for
farmers who produce for export and take on new ventures outside simple farm
production, such as food processing, agricultural marketing, and agritourism.
The MAFF terms this approach the "sixth industrialization" of agriculture.[48]

Abe also worked to intensify the pace of agricultural change by supporting Japan's participation in the TPP trade liberalization talks. In early 2015
he boldly moved to deprive the JA-Zenchu of its auditing power, with new
legislation that nevertheless left Zen-Noh with distributional monopolies for
farm products.[49] This legislation was passed in September 2015 and became
operative in April 2016.[50]

The pace of policy reform in agriculture accelerated during 2015–2016,
with Prime Minister Shinzō Abe, in particular, capitalizing on a combination
of foreign pressure and socioeconomic change in the countryside to achieve
some incremental reforms. Japan's underlying vulnerabilities with respect to
food supply, however, have not changed. The broad network of human ties
and interlocking economic incentives that constitute the agricultural circle of
compensation continues to persist.[51] The overall pace of transformation in the
countryside thus remains slow,[52] with incentives for further change being reduced by the American rejection in early 2017 of the multilateral TPP agreement. As throughout modern Japanese history, especially since the dark days of
World War II, the incentives implicit in the circles of mutual convenience and
support prevailing within Japan continue to inhibit positive political-economic
response to the broader pressures of globalization, especially when liberalization steps are not met with supportive response from abroad.

In Conclusion

As an economically advanced yet heavily populated and mountainous island
country, Japan has an inherent national vulnerability with respect to food supply. That congenital shortfall conversely represents a commercial opportunity
for trading partners. Japan also harbors a deeply rooted domestic consciousness, dating from ancient times, that abundance and prosperity in agriculture
are fundamental aspects of national security.

Across the early twentieth century, building on traditional *nōhonshugi* consciousness and political exigencies such as mobilization for war, highly regulated

subnational institutions supportive of both domestic agriculture and local food distributors gradually emerged in Japan. Those institutions were welded into an increasingly coherent and routinized circle of compensation, linking producers, distributors, bureaucrats, and politicians, following the consolidation of conservative rule in 1949, amid the agricultural depression that preceded the Korean War. Government subsidies for agriculture were sharply increased; *nōkyō* were given increasingly strategic functions in distributing fertilizer and credit on favorable terms to farmers; and their overall highly regulated structure was consolidated to align it more closely with nationwide conservative political interests. All these developments, reinforced by *amakudari* networks of personal interdependence, insulated Japan securely from the global market pressures that were to emerge during the 1970s and thereafter, even as they also created an orderly domestic balance between supply and demand.

Early in the twentieth century, a left-oriented circle of agricultural and food-product compensation, parallel to that of the *nōkyō,* evolved from the grassroots in urban Japan, taking the form of the *seikyō* livelihood cooperatives. The *seikyō* gained some state-related legitimacy during the progressive Katayama-Ashida years (1947−1948), becoming affiliated with MHW. Yet they failed to join the conservative food-economy circle of compensation following the right-of-center political revival of late 1949. Although distant politically from the conservative *nōkyō,* and not nearly so complicit in government regulation, *seikyō* have shared the parochial trade-policy stance of their rural cousins. They have been supportive of domestic agricultural production and skeptical of imports, while privileging health and safety considerations above economic efficiency. The broad consensus of the left and the right-oriented agricultural NGOs, until very recently on the virtues of protectionism, has been a key reason for their enduring political strength, even as the farming share of both the national workforce and GDP has declined to miniscule levels. Demography and the rising role of full-time farmers have begun to erode this pattern, but only slowly, and at the margins.

The subnational circles of compensation in the Japanese food economy have helped provoke three distinctive policy outcomes that impede Japan's globalization: (1) attempts at self-sufficiency in rice, through high producer prices; (2) high subsidies in multiple commodities, absorbing the bulk of the MAFF budget; and (3) import barriers, centering on rice, but extending broadly across the food economy. These parochial policies have, in classic circle-of-compensation fashion, internalized the dubious social benefits of a protected, high-cost food economy among producers and selected distributors, while externalizing and generalizing costs to Japanese consumers, as well as to the international community.

Embedded linkages through the political process and the mass media between consumers and the food-economy circle, developed over many decades, have reinforced a pervasive national sense of vulnerability with respect to food security. Japanese consumers have paradoxically accepted many of the protectionist parameters of their food economy, even when those parameters stand in tension with broader consumer economic interests. Agricultural circles of compensation, reinforced by parochial regulation and complex legislative processes, thus clearly impede Japan's opening to the broader world, yet continue to inhibit domestic change, as well.

Energy

Energy security has been one of modern Japan's most intense and strategically important obsessions over more than a century of rapid growth.[1] Shortages forced Japan to deepen often uncomfortable economic interdependence with a broader world, over which it had distinctly limited control. Throughout its modern history, a Japan that finds structural change painful, globalization challenging, and self-reliance attractive has been seeking domestically acceptable formulas for securing the energy it needs without major disruption of its traditional decision-making and resource-allocation processes. As in so many sectors, it has sought autarkic solutions, to protect itself against the volatility and uncertainty of the surrounding world.

Japan is by no means devoid of domestic energy reserves. As late as 1890, the country was a major exporter of coal, mainly to Shanghai, Hong Kong, and Singapore, to fuel steamships throughout the Western Pacific. Yet by the dawn of the twentieth century, the insatiable demands flowing from its accelerating economic growth had outstripped Japan's finite supplies, generating a chronic vulnerability that ultimately led the country down a tortured road to war in 1941.[2]

After a decade of hiatus amid the bitter Pacific conflict and its aftermath, Japan's explosive economic growth resumed with the onset of the Korean War and expanding offshore procurements to support the United Nations forces, deepening the dilemma of energy security once again. Resolution turned in the direction of nuclear power—Japan's bitter experience with Hiroshima and Nagasaki notwithstanding. This chapter tells the story of that politically puzzling yet economically rational development, which has proven to be fatefully significant for the Japanese energy economy, Japan's growth profile, and Japan's relationship to the globalization process.

A New, Postwar Deus Ex Machina

Modern Japan has been chronically energy-insecure since the early twentieth century, and until 1945 often pursued regionally disruptive political-military actions to assuage that insecurity. A new potential deus ex machina appeared soon after the Korean War, initially in the form of "atoms for peace." In a landmark December 1953 speech at the United Nations, soon after the Korean War armistice, Dwight D. Eisenhower "pledged to spread the benefits of peaceful atomic power both at home and abroad."[3] Japan—not surprisingly, given its energy insecurities and its distinction as the sole victim of the military use of atomic power—became a priority potential customer.

Given the heritage of Hiroshima and Nagasaki, Japanese public opinion was at first intensely skeptical. Aversion to nuclear power had been intensified by the rash of candid, post-censorship reports of the 1945 bombings that followed the end of U.S. occupation censorship in late April 1952. This initial nuclear aversion was exacerbated further in March 1954, when fallout from U.S. hydrogen bomb tests in the Marshall Islands contaminated twenty-three Japanese fishermen aboard the *Daigo Fukuryū Maru* ("Lucky Dragon no. 5"), which was sailing eighty-five miles away from the detonation and outside the designated danger zone.[4] By 1955, fully 32 million people, or one-third of Japan's entire population, had signed petitions against hydrogen bombs.[5]

The United States was nevertheless intent on countering Japan's "nuclear allergy" with an active campaign to promote the peaceful uses of nuclear energy in the country. Beginning in November 1955, exhibits cosponsored by the U.S. government and the *Yomiuri Shimbun* newspaper were held around Japan to highlight the peaceful use of nuclear power for generating electricity, treating cancer, preserving food, controlling insects, and advancing scientific research. In Kyoto fully 155,000 people came out in snow and rain to attend.[6]

In 1954, the Japanese government began funding its own civilian nuclear research program. In December 1955, the Diet passed the Atomic Energy Basic Law, establishing the Japan Atomic Energy Commission (JAEC). Matsutarō Shōriki, president of the *Yomiuri Shimbun*, became minister of state for atomic energy, as well as the first chair of the JAEC. Meanwhile, in July 1955 the United States commenced its own first commercial nuclear power; and a year later, President Eisenhower informed the United Nations that the U.S. had agreed with thirty-seven nations to build atomic reactors and was negotiating with fourteen more.[7]

Despite Japan's lingering nuclear aversion, there was substantial latent support for nuclear power among Japanese scientists, electric-power company executives, and conservative politicians, such as Prime-Minister-to-be Yasuhiro Nakasone.[8] Nuclear power, after all, largely freed Japan from the energy constraints that would otherwise shackle that hydrocarbon-poor nation's economic growth. It did require huge, lumpy capital investments in nuclear plants and equipment, but the powerful Bankers' Kingdom, with its long-term credit banks, could handle those.

Nakasone was among the first Japanese political figures to follow Washington's lead into the civilian nuclear arena. Japan purchased its first commercial reactor from Britain in 1956,[9] but soon thereafter shifted to U.S.-designed light-water reactors. By mid-1957, the government had contracted to buy twenty more reactors, almost all of them American.[10]

Given strong U.S. and Japanese government backing, as well as an active public relations campaign in support of peaceful nuclear energy, and the unexpected award of a Nobel Prize in Physics to Japanese scientist Hideki Yukawa, Japanese public opinion toward civilian use of nuclear power underwent a remarkable shift.[11] In 1956, 70 percent of the Japanese people equated "atom" with "harmful," according to one classified U.S. public opinion study.[12] By 1958, however, that number had dropped by more than half, to 30 percent.[13] Wanting their country to become a major, technologically advanced industrial power, and highly conscious of Japan's lack of energy resources, the Japanese public allowed itself to be convinced that nuclear power was safe and clean, the lingering memory of Hiroshima and Nagasaki notwithstanding.

Incentive Structures and Nuclear Power

By the late 1950s, Japan was politically ready to build nuclear-power plants, and thereby to alleviate its chronic energy insecurities through reduced reliance on imported fossil fuels. Through nuclear power, Japan could rapidly achieve its fervently desired economic prosperity, sustaining double-digit growth without unmanageable resource and foreign-exchange constraints. In October 1963 the Tokaimura experimental reactor near Tokyo was connected to the grid, and in March 1970 the first full-scale nuclear plant, at Tsuruga on the Sea of Japan, became operational.[14] Over the ensuing forty years, Japan constructed sixty reactors,[15] and came to depend on nuclear power for a quarter of its total electricity, one of the highest ratios in the world, as indicated in Figure 7.1.[16]

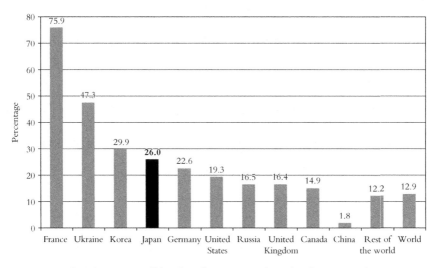

FIGURE 7.1   Japan's strong traditional nuclear power orientation in comparative perspective

SOURCE: International Energy Agency (IEA), "% of Nuclear in Total Domestic Electricity Generation," in *Key World Energy Statistics 2012* (Paris: 2013), 17, doi: 10.1787/key_energ_stat-2012-en.
NOTES: Figures indicate 2010 data.

In developing nuclear power, Japan's electric utilities, in cooperation with government, overcame major political-economic challenges—high up-front fixed costs, latent local opposition, and regulatory obstacles among them. The utilities enjoyed substantial public and private support, however, in their difficult nuclear undertakings—support intensified by Japan's underlying energy insecurities and ambivalence regarding heavy foreign energy reliance. Understanding both why Japan's power producers were motivated to pursue nuclear power so vigorously, and also how they went about overcoming the obstacles in their way, is crucial to grasping why nuclear power became so prominent in post–World War II Japan, particularly from the 1970s on.

The Domestic Sources of Japan's Nuclear Orientation

At the macro level, the motives for embracing nuclear power are clear: energy security and environmental protection. Japan imports 94 percent of its oil,[17] over 80 percent of which flows along the vulnerable seven-thousand-mile energy sea lanes from the Middle East.[18] Building a massive industrial infrastructure generating one-twelfth of global gross domestic product in an island archipelago the size of California—with many of the traditional key industries, like steel and petrochemicals, being highly polluting—has generated strong environmental imperatives, as well. Whatever its defects in other spheres, nuclear plants provided large amounts of power without carbon dioxide emissions.

Yet these macro imperatives that would suggest the utility of embracing the nuclear option are underpredictive: They do not adequately explain the *timing* of nuclear power's introduction into Japan; the distinctive geographical *distribution* within the country; the pattern of *local support and opposition*; or the *tactics* employed to assure that public assent was achieved. To fully understand the profile of nuclear-power usage in Japan, an examination of concrete incentives at the micro level, and how they relate to circles of compensation, with their unique risk-diffusion qualities, is required.

The cost structure of nuclear-power generation is fundamental to the interest of the Japanese electric utilities in introducing nuclear power, as well as their tactics for doing so. Building nuclear plants is extremely expensive—as much as 70 percent of the ultimate cost of the electricity provided.[19] And optimal operating efficiencies have traditionally been obtained with large-scale nuclear reactors such as the AP1000, made by Westinghouse, whose construction costs typically run in the billions of dollars.[20]

Building nuclear plants has always involved substantial political risk, a commodity difficult to quantify. Few communities are eager to host nuclear plants in their backyards, due to the small yet potentially devastating prospect that something might go wrong. Power companies need to offer transfer payments to offset this risk. They also need to deal with regulatory hurdles and delays. And they of course must compensate victims in the event of harmful radioactive leakage.

Compared to construction costs, the marginal costs of running nuclear plants are extremely low, once the plants begin operation. Costs depend, of course, to some extent on the efficiency of the technology employed, as well as the price of fuel. Yet compared to gas- or oil-fired facilities, the costs of operating nuclear plants are extremely low. The share of fuel in electric-power production costs, in particular, is extremely low in the case of nuclear. According to one recent study, in Japan, to build a typical natural gas plant (combined-cycle gas turbine) and a typical nuclear plant (advanced light-water reactor) needs $13.96 per megawatt-hour (MWh) and $45.92/MWh, respectively at 7 percent discount rate. In contrast, the fuel cost of a natural gas plant is $104.07/MWh, more than seven times fuel and waste costs of a nuclear plant combined ($14.15/MWh).[21]

Although the marginal costs of running nuclear plans in Japan—once constructed and operating—are extremely low, utility prices are traditionally high. As indicated in Figure 7.2a, electricity prices paid by industry in Japan during recent years were the highest among comparable industrialized nations, as they have consistently been since the early 1980s. Those costs were around three times comparable rates in the United States, according to the OECD.

Electric prices paid by the household sector, shown in Figure 7.2b, have also been higher than in the same three nations, except in Germany, since around 2003. Germany is a special case, due to its powerful environmental movement, led by the Greens, which since around 2000 has advocated using the price mechanism to promote alternative-energy development and to constrain overall energy use. Household energy prices in France, Korea, and the United States remain consistently lower than in Japan.

The Political Imperatives That Economic Incentives Create

Nuclear-power plants, as discussed above, entail high initial fixed costs for capital investment and construction. Yet they also involve low variable costs for actually running such facilities. Such variable costs become progressively more attractive—relative to other means of generating electric power—the higher the cost of non-nuclear fuel alternatives, and the longer a given nuclear-power plant has been in operation. High rates of return are needed in the case of nuclear power to induce initial investment, and to provoke the inevitably complicated efforts to neutralize community ambivalence. Predictable regulatory environments, liability regimes, and financing parameters—not to mention utility rates—are also extremely important in making nuclear power practical for the overall community, even though it is intrinsically attractive to producers in terms of narrow cost-competitiveness. In a word, *stability* in political-economic parameters, both at the national and local levels, is essential to the feasibility of nuclear generation, which entails potentially high-cost, albeit low-probability, risks.

The importance of stability in the political dimension of nuclear power in Japan has risen sharply since the advent of commercial nuclear plants in the late 1960s, as nuclear regulation has grown more politicized, and the number of locations in which new nuclear plants are being built has steadily increased. There was a notably pronounced period of politicization in nuclear administration from the mid-1960s until around 1990. Japan's nuclear-plant construction actually began in the 1960s, with the first nuclear plant, Tokai-1, started in March 1961 and coming onstream in July 1966.[22]

More than 85 percent of Japan's nuclear-power plants were completed in the three decades thereafter, as noted in Figure 7.3. That period was one of enormous fluidity in the economic parameters of Japanese energy supply—two

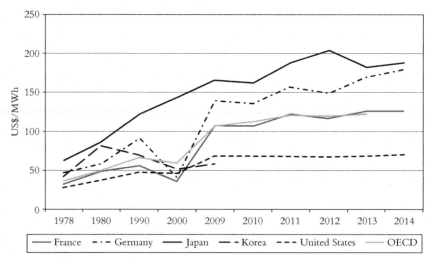

FIGURE 7.2a   Electricity prices for industry (US$/MWh)

SOURCE: IEA, "Table 3.5 Electricity prices for industry in US dollars/MWh," *Electricity Information 2015* (Paris: IEA, 2015), III.57, doi: 10.1787/electricity-2015-en.

NOTES: 1) Korea has not reported electricity prices for industry since 2010. 2) There is no figure for OECD 2014 average, as not all OECD members had reported relevant 2014 figures at the time of publication.

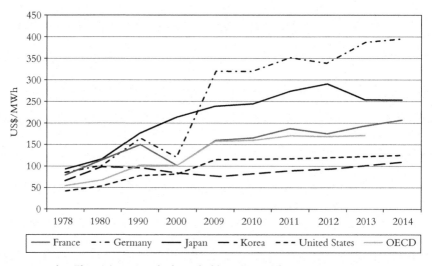

FIGURE 7.2b   Electricity prices for households (US$/MWh)

SOURCE: IEA, "Table 3.7 Electricity prices for households in US dollars/MWh," *Electricity Information 2015* (Paris: IEA, 2015), III.58, doi: 10.1787/electricity-2015-en.

NOTE: There is no figure for OECD 2014 average, as not all OECD members had reported relevant 2014 figures at the time of publication.

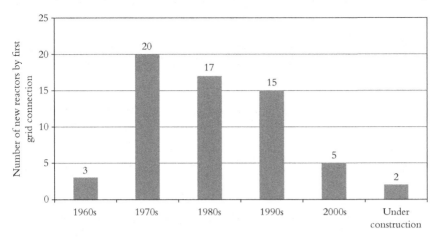

FIGURE 7.3   Japan's nuclear power plants

SOURCE: International Atomic Energy Agency (IAEA), "Country Statistics—Japan," *Power Reactor Information System (PRIS)*, updated July 6, 2016, http://www.iaea.org/PRIS/CountryStatistics/CountryDetails.aspx?current=JP.

Oil Shocks, coupled with rapid shifts in energy prices and exchange rates—as well as a broadening geographical ambit for power-plant location, and deepening politicization of energy policy making. These developments in the aggregate made stable political parameters and business-government relationships at once more imperative and more difficult to achieve, as the nuclear industry spread ever more broadly across a Japan where the general public was growing increasingly judgmental regarding public-policy outputs. The imperatives of economic growth and energy security in a globalizing world threatened to run head on into public opinion.

As indicated in Figure 7.4, commercial nuclear power first emerged in northern Japan, at the Tokai-1 plant in Ibaragi Prefecture near Tokyo (construction begun in 1961, commercial operation from 1966) and the Tsuruga-1 plant in Fukui Prefecture on the Sea of Japan (begun 1966, completed 1970).[23] Next came Mihama-1 in 1970, also on the Sea of Japan, and the great Fukushima complex on the northeastern coast, opened in 1971, followed later by nuclear plants in Kyushu, Niigata, and elsewhere.[24] More than ten of the coastal provinces of Japan now host them, although only about one-quarter of the new sites have established since 1990. Increasingly, new plants have been added on existing sites, leading to massive, multireactor complexes like Kashiwazaki, Mihama, and Fukushima.

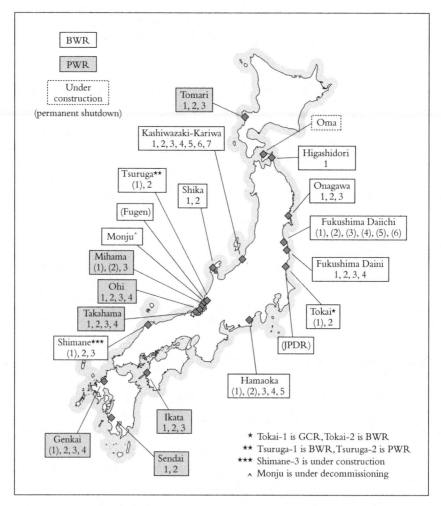

FIGURE 7.4   Spread of nuclear plants along Japan's coastline (as of April 2016)

SOURCE: Author's illustration based on International Atomic Energy Agency, "Country Statistics—Japan," *Power Reactor Information System.*

Why Circles of Compensation in Electric Power Were Initially Weak

A stable supply of nuclear power had a compelling strategic logic for Japanese business and bureaucratic elites, intent as they were for half a century after World War II on high-speed economic growth. Yet broader support for that risky course did not emerge spontaneously. It required political-economic antecedents at the grassroots level, such as circles of compensation. These distinctive configurations, as we have seen in areas ranging from agriculture to transport and finance, are not merely ad hoc responses to socioeconomic challenge. They involve political, bureaucratic, business, and sometimes mass-popular cooperation in the creation of consensual mechanisms for addressing potentially conflictual public-policy problems. They generally necessitate the creation of new institutions that apportion responsibility and allocate resources broadly, so as to avoid or ameliorate conflict and risk. Such resource-allocating and risk-diffusion institutions typically endure for extended periods, helping to stabilize political-economic interactions far beyond the specific functional problems they address. They may also, however, have important international implications, as we have seen in such sectors, as finance and agriculture.

Circles of compensation were not yet well developed in the electric-power industry until the 1970s, despite their transcendent strategic logic in high-growth postwar Japan, for four basic reasons:

(1) *Lack of embedded institutions.* In contrast to the steel and banking sectors, little embedded corporatist infrastructure remained from the wartime years. *Nippon Hassoden*, the principal wartime atavism in electric power, was abolished in 1950, together with the Ministry of Communications (*Teishin Shō*). An independent Public Utilities Commission was established to oversee the electric and gas companies, with generating facilities coming into the hands of nine public-stock companies, each with a regional monopoly.[25]

(2) *Lack of corporate incentive.* Japanese electric-power companies have long had powerful incentives to build nuclear plants, and to keep them in operation as long as possible. Those incentives to build nuclear date from the days of Eisenhower's "atoms for peace" proposals in the 1950s. Nuclear plants have long been considered highly profitable, and the longer they run, the more profitable they become, especially after being fully amortized.[26] Until the 1970s, however, electric utilities felt little need to mobilize broad social coalitions to support their plant-siting proposals, both because the fossil-fuel plants on which they principally relied raised few local anxieties, and also because most local communities in Japan were not politically active.

(3) *Underdevelopment of the nuclear sector.* Nuclear plants were still mostly on the drawing board until the 1970s. Japan's first experimental reactor, at To-kaimura, was not connected to the grid until 1963, and the first commercial plant (Tokai-1) was not opened until 1966. Japan did not open its first full-fledged nuclear-plant complex (Mihama) until 1970.[27]

(4) *Weakness of the anti-nuclear-power movement.* During the 1960s, the influence of the anti-nuclear-power movement was not significant. Local communities were enthusiastic to have nuclear plants that could help stimulate their local economies. To the extent that they sought compensation from the power companies, the communities were mainly concerned about property and fishing rights, with the danger of radiation virtually absent from their consciousness. At the national level, the anti-nuclear-weapons movement (*gensuibaku kinshi undō*), such as it was, was not associated with opposition to civilian nuclear power. And in the 1960s, nationally mobile anti-nuclear activists did not participate in local anti-nuclear movements of any sort.

How and Why Circles of Compensation Finally Emerged

Japan's energy circumstances fundamentally changed as oil prices rose in the early 1970s, making large-scale, environmentally friendly power generation increasingly important, and thus inspiring the emergence of newly institutionalized, semicorporatist mechanisms for consensual conflict resolution in the Japanese electric-power sector. These new mechanisms were identifiable circles of compensation that both distributed benefits to supporters of nuclear power—especially local communities—and diffused the political risks of accepting nuclear plants. The changes that inspired emergence of these circles occurred along three dimensions: economic, strategic, and political.

The earliest and clearest driving force was economic: Japan was growing explosively—at double-digit rates in the half decade before the 1973 Oil Shock—and desperately needed more electric power. In a crowded nation the size of California—with three times California's population—and with virtually no domestic fossil-fuel supplies, nuclear power seemed attractive as an alternative to the status quo. This appeal increased sharply over the 1970s, as the Shah of Iran quadrupled the price of oil (1973), and then fell from power (1979), creating chronic Middle East uncertainties of a different kind.

A second driver was strategic. Japan's prospective fossil-fuel supplies were seven thousand miles away, in an unstable Middle East. Particularly after the Arab oil embargo of 1973, the self-sufficiency afforded by nuclear power appeared highly attractive. Yet nuclear power—attractive as it was strategically—was also prospectively controversial, requiring new, consensual approaches to conflict resolution, such as circles of compensation provided.

A third driver was political. Japan at the end of the 1960s was entering a turbulent period of domestic political crisis, in which populist interest groups, NGOs, and mass media were growing more influential.[28] Consensual mechanisms were needed that could at once help implement citizen demands and also neutralize pressures for radical political change.

In response to the foregoing pressures, a new framework for compensation was established, in the form of the three electric-power-generation laws (*Dengen Sanpō*). These were promulgated during the prime ministership of Kakuei Tanaka in 1974, at Tanaka's personal instigation.[29] The first of these laws established a taxation system, generating revenue drawn from a surcharge on utility fees, to support popular acceptance of nuclear power, and to compensate for negative externalities. The second law created a special account to sequester the earmarked level of general electric-utility fees. The third law allowed for the construction, using revenue from the special account, of compensatory public facilities (including roads, sports complexes, and citizen meeting halls) for areas surrounding new nuclear plants.[30]

The three laws together provided a framework within which interest groups could petition for financial support to offset the costs and dangers associated with the introduction of nuclear power. These laws represented two imperatives: (1) the classic "compensation amid crisis," impelled by the shared business, bureaucratic, and conservative political desires to stabilize the prevailing political order; and also (2) the creation of a consensual, institutionalized framework for nuclear-site decision-making that could smoothly facilitate the introduction of much-needed nuclear power. The three laws created the rules for a unique new "compensation politics" game in the electric-utility area, institutionally bounded by the energy-sector circle of compensation.

The game gained new intensity after a series of nuclear mishaps, which bred a rising protest movement amid the growing national reliance on nuclear power. First, in September 1974, the nuclear-powered ship *Mutsu* began leaking radiation, making national headlines and triggering a local backlash that impelled local fishing and civic groups to refuse *Mutsu* reentry into its home port of Ohminato.[31] This mishap gave rise to the first nationwide anti-nuclear-power conference, held in Kyoto in August 1975.[32]

The *Mutsu* incident was followed by the March 1979 Three Mile Island accident in the United States, which gave birth to a new, unsettling term for the protesters' lexicon: *Anzen Shinwa* ("safety myth"). Then in April 1981 radiation leakage at the Tsuruga nuclear plant in Fukui Prefecture, and later at Tokai, Ibaraki Prefecture (1997 and 1999), gave further momentum to the anti-nuclear movement.[33] Yet still the nuclear building program moved forward, with formidable political support.

Key Members of the Circles

To provide stability and predictability to the firms that supply nuclear power, and thereby reduce debilitating risks in the face of rising politicization, circles of compensation became indispensable. They provided "win–win" incentives to all the key players, through a mix of subsidies and favorable regulation, while also supplying much-needed technical expertise. To forge such support bases for reactor siting—coalitions including members with both technical skills and political clout, that simultaneously exhibited a communalistic, altruistic cast—electric-power producers from the 1970s on began to build circles of compensation with local economic and political interests that could systematically aggregate and distribute benefits to members. The typical configuration of interests is presented in Figure 7.5. It is noteworthy that these cooperative institutions emerged significantly later in the power industry than in areas such as agriculture (mid-Meiji) or banking (early Shōwa), because of the later development of the nuclear-power sector and the different incentives for collective action that prevailed.

Nuclear-energy circles of compensation traditionally included the following constituencies:

(1) *Citizens living and working near nuclear plants.* All of these plants, as noted in Figure 7.4, are located in outlying areas along Japan's coast, because access to large volumes of water is important to the functioning of such a facility. Most reactor sites thus have fishing and farming communities nearby, although overall surrounding population density is relatively low. As their livelihoods could be gravely affected by nuclear accidents, these citizen groups

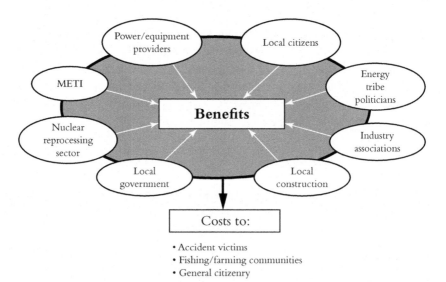

FIGURE 7.5   Circles of compensation in nuclear energy

SOURCE: Author's illustration.

typically seek and receive transfer payments to obtain their acquiescence in the location of nuclear plants to their area, which are usually provided through local agricultural or fishery associations.[34] Power companies also typically provide extensive employment opportunities to local residents,[35] as well as side benefits such as discounted electric-power rates and monopolistic business rights, including those for dry cleaning and catering services.[36]

(2) *Local governments.* Nuclear plants are typically located in isolated, depressed, lower-income areas with little industry, with declining, increasingly elderly populations and few alternative long-term economic options. The local governments in such areas often have extensive welfare burdens, and a limited local tax base. Their ability to provide local services and to attract new industry is also constrained by highly centralized Japanese administrative practices, including centralized distribution of tax revenue.

Financial support from power companies, either in the form of subsidies or of tax payments on nuclear-power facilities, thus provides indispensable financial wherewithal for local governments hosting nuclear plants—especially important because it provides discretionary income to these bodies that flows in without any additional taxation. In many local communities hosting nuclear plants, payments from the power companies provide half or more of local government revenue.[37] When the power companies make arrangements to enter a community, they provide support over long periods of time—often as long as forty-five years, extending from as long as ten years before the start of actual power-plant operation, through the entire working life of the plant in question.[38]

(3) *Bureaucrats regulating the nuclear industry.* Electric power is among the most highly regulated sectors of the Japanese economy, with government having exercised considerable discretion in how regulations are administered. A single bureaucratic entity—METI—administers utility rates, non-nuclear safety inspections, and depreciation schedules for capital investment, while also providing concessionary loans through affiliated government development banks.[39] Since September 2012, the Nuclear Regulation Authority (NRA), an external affiliate of the Ministry of the Environment, has supervised safety issues with respect to Japan's nuclear-power industry,[40] although traditional relations between METI and the power companies remain in other areas. METI often calls on the utilities to perform broader social functions, such as support for overseas economic development missions and cultural exchange. The power companies, for their part, traditionally employ senior bureaucrats, upon retirement, to fill strategic senior posts.[41]

(4) *The nuclear-reprocessing sector.* Nuclear power is a sector with *enormous* risk, and enormous externalities—technological innovation, waste storage, and waste disposal among them. Although METI is the responsible ministry for administering the day-to-day operations of the nuclear-power sector, apart from safety, a separate ministry, the Ministry of Education, Culture, Sports, Science and Technology (MEXT), oversees these other activities, with the assistance of a specialized public entity, Japan Nuclear Fuel Ltd. (*Nihon Gennen*). That corporation administers Japan's ambitious and massive energy-reprocessing program, including elaborate facilities at Rokkasho, with the financial support of both the national government and the private power companies.[42] Accidents at reprocessing facilities, at experimental fast-breeder reactors such as Monju,[43] and at conventional light-water reactors such as Fukushima Daiichi have, however, cast doubt on long-term prospects for the program, and led to the December 2016 national-government decision to ultimately decommission Monju.[44]

(5) *Industry associations.* The electric-power industry has an especially powerful and active industry affiliate, the Federation of Electric Power Companies (*Nihon Denki Jigyō Rengōkai*, or *Denjiren*). Its member firms have traditionally had their own distinct operating areas, thus avoiding direct competition with one another. Indeed, due to long-standing technical segmentation (separate cycle frequencies—sixty versus fifty cycle), it has been very difficult to transmit more than a small amount of power from western to eastern Japan, and vice versa. This incompatibility created major problems in moderating power shortages in eastern Japan following the massive March 2011 earthquake and tsunami.[45]

In response to the "3/11 crisis," the resulting political vulnerability of the major power companies, and the rising desires of varied groups across Japan for more competitive electricity pricing, the Abe cabinet approved historic proposals for electric-power reform. These set three central policy objectives: (1) securing a stable electricity supply, (2) suppressing electricity rates to the maximum extent possible, and (3) expanding choice for consumers, as well as business opportunities.[46] New legislations passed during 2013–2015 provided for full liberalization of electricity retail business by April 2016; and unbundling of electric-power transmission and generation sectors and full liberalization of retail electricity rates by 2020.[47] And establishment of the Organization for Cross-regional Coordination of Transmission Operators in April 2015, explicitly designed to coordinate cross-regional power transmission, could well also have a stabilizing effect on existing industrial relationships. Power-generating and power-transmitting companies, however, are being permitted to retain

capital ties through holding company relationships, allowing cooperative relations among power-sector actors to continue, albeit in attenuated form.[48]

In this changing political–economic context, the *Denjiren* continues to play
a major role in Japan's nuclear circle of compensation. It assumes the central
role in assisting the Japan Business Federation (*Nippon Keizai Dantai Rengōkai*,
or *Keidanren*), its umbrella federation at the national level, to raise funds for
projects of national importance—ranging from electoral campaigns to rebuilding the Ise Shrine to foreign university contributions. *Keidanren* in return
supports the power companies' nuclear aspirations, including reprocessing, at
the national policy level. *Denjiren* also helps the individual power companies
in persuading local communities to agree to site locations in their area. It is
likewise said to have played a role in raising funds to assist victims of the March
2011 Fukushima disaster,[49] although its heretofore substantial influence in the
Japanese political economy as a whole has doubtless been undermined by the
straitened economic circumstances of Tokyo Electric Power, heretofore its
dominant member.

(6) *Construction interests*. The construction cost of a new nuclear plant in
Japan is roughly $5 billion.[50] During the 1970s, there were twenty new re-
actors built in Japan, at ten different locations, and the pace of construction
continued at nearly that rate for another two decades thereafter, as noted in
Figure 7.3. Apart from reactors themselves, the construction of greenfield
nuclear plants also stimulated substantial related construction: roads, bridges,
and telecommunications lines. It also spawned compensatory local public
works—hospitals, community halls, and schools. All were provided by the
power companies to appease local host communities, in return for their acceptance of the nuclear plants.

(7) *Politicians*. The electric-power industry, and especially the nuclear-power
sector, is highly regulated. Yet since the 1970s politicians have gained increasing influence over regulators, which in the case of Japanese nuclear power have
been traditionally mainly from METI.[51] During the mid-1970s, for example,
when many of the most important siting decisions were made, the Administrative Vice-Minister of MITI, Keiichi Konaga, was the former secretary
of Japanese Prime Minister Kakuei Tanaka. Politicians such as Tanaka also
had close ties to construction interests; indeed, Tanaka himself was a former
construction-company president.

(8) *Power companies*. The electric-power companies of Japan remit enormous side payments to a broad range of sociopolitical groups, in return for

their services and support in nuclear-plant construction and operation. As the aftermath of the 2011 Fukushima crisis makes clear, there is latent risk in nuclear-power production that can sharply undermine or destroy any prospective corporate financial gain. Even assuming smooth, uneventful operation, nuclear power involves substantial life-cycle costs for safety, spent-fuel storage, and decommissioning.

When all these prospective costs are factored in, alternatives to nuclear power are arguably more competitive with the nuclear option, from a corporate standpoint, than had been true previously. METI, for example, estimated in 2011 that atomic power would cost 8.9 per kilowatt-hour (kWh) in 2030. Four years after Fukushima, METI raised the estimate to ¥10.3, factoring in decommissioning costs and new safety measures. In comparison, METI estimates coal-fired power will cost ¥12.9 per kWh, and ¥13.4 for liquefied natural gas, up to ¥16.4 for solar, and up to ¥16.8 for geothermal power.[52]

Negative externalities, however, are difficult to quantify, as it is generally uncertain when and how they might materialize. When marginal operating costs alone are considered, nuclear power has decisive costs advantages, which tend to grow larger, in the short run, as the operating life of nuclear plants is extended. To the extent that firms can limit their liability to only operating costs, nuclear power thus has great advantages for electric-utility firms, as well. These advantages have been growing greater in recent years, as plants become fully depreciated, and that situation bolstered the profitability of such firms considerably in the years before the tsunami of 2011.

Although electric utilities, METI, and local communities hosting nuclear facilities all lie traditionally at the heart of nuclear energy circles of compensation, other actors are also involved. As indicated in Figure 7.5, the nuclear-reprocessing sector and affiliated science and technology bureaucrats, concentrated at MEXT, are also participants. They have inspired future-oriented projects such as the Rokkasho nuclear-reprocessing facility in Aomori Prefecture, dedicated to reducing nuclear waste and generating increased energy—through converting a mixture of spent fuel and plutonium (mixed-oxide [MOX] fuel) into additional energy.

Outsiders

The essence of circles of compensation is to systematically *internalize* benefits and *externalize* costs. In the case of nuclear power, the short-term benefits captured by circles have traditionally been large—huge up-front construction opportunities, low operating costs, low carbon dioxide emissions, and large support payments to local communities. The externalized costs have been diffuse, difficult to quantify, and long term—the risk of accidents, together with the troubling but easily neglected back-end problems of spent-fuel storage and final decommissioning.

It is thus difficult to define in normal circumstances exactly who is *outside* the nuclear circle of compensation. That is one of the reasons opposition to nuclear power has historically been limited. As evident in the case of Fukushima, however, in the case of accidents the explicit exclusion of much of the general public from the benefits generated by nuclear circles of compensation can become dramatically clear, And a negative general perception of nuclear power can consequently continue for some time, as post-3/11 experience makes clear.

Post-Fukushima Prospects

Even four years after the Fukushima nuclear accident of March 2011, there was an understandably strong general public backlash against nuclear power in Japan. In August 2015, for example, 57 percent of the Japanese public opposed Kyushu Electric Power's restart of its Sendai nuclear-power plant, with only 30 percent in favor, even though the plant was not even near an earthquake fault line, and had undergone years of safety testing and certification.[53] Nevertheless, the Sendai #1 unit returned to full commercial operation in September 2015, followed by Sendai #2 two months later.[54] And in September 2016, Shikoku Electric Power's Ikata unit 3 came back onstream, as well.[55] Two other units that had obtained NRA restart approval (Takahama 3 and 4) were taken offline in early 2016, however, following brief restarts, amid anti-nuclear legal proceedings.[56]

Each of Japan's still-operational nuclear plants was stopped for extended inspection as it came to the end of its authorized period of operation, and by May 2012 all of those plants were closed. To be sure, the Oi #3 and #4 reactors near Osaka were briefly restarted between July 2012 and September 2013. Yet it was not until August 2015 that any further nuclear plants went back on line—four and a half years after Fukushima.[57]

The new aversion to nuclear power in Japan was understandable. Yet it was not without a palpable economic cost, and a deepening, unwanted Japanese hydrocarbon dependence on the broader world. As noted in Figure 7.6, Japanese energy imports began to soar in late 2011, leading to current account deficits not seen in Japan for a generation and more.

Uncertainties regarding energy supply inhibited Japanese firms from expanding Japan-based production as the yen weakened during 2013−2014, thus compounding Japan's rising trade deficits, the sharp decline in energy prices themselves notwithstanding. More than $100 billion invested in nuclear-power

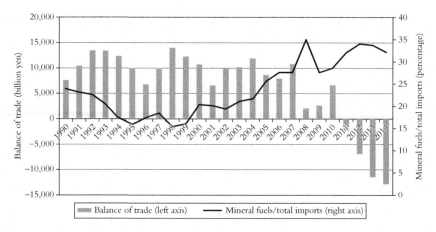

FIGURE 7.6   Impact of Fukushima on Japan's balance of trade

SOURCE: Ministry of Finance, *Trade Statistics of Japan.*

plant and equipment lay unused, despite its substantial remaining potential life, as the share of power from fossil fuel in Japan soared from 62 percent to 88 percent (in fiscal year 2010 versus fiscal year 2013).[58] Local communities hosting nuclear plants that had benefited from power-company support, and hence been key members of the energy circles of compensation, were also disadvantaged both by the post–Fukushima hiatus and a new popular aversion to nuclear power that persisted half a decade after Fukushima.

In Conclusion

From the dawn of the nuclear age, Japan has had an uneasy, paradoxical relationship with nuclear energy. Although the sole victim of the use of nuclear weapons in war, since the early 1970s Japan has become one of the most extensive users of civilian nuclear power on Earth. That paradoxical evolution is intimately bound up with the emergence of the nuclear circle of compensation, and its utility in easing Japan's profound energy insecurities in a volatile, globalizing world.

The nuclear circle of compensation is not merely a series of ad hoc compensatory gestures. To the contrary, it is an institutionalized set of routinized procedures and relationships, configured to diffuse political-economic risk, and to produce consensual outcomes with respect to potentially conflictual nuclear-plant siting decisions. The circle generates such outcomes by structuring "win-win" settlements that provide something for all relevant actors in non-crisis situations.

Three sets of pressures impelled the original emergence of Japan's nuclear circle of compensation: economic, strategic, and political. Economically, the rapidly growing demands for electric power in a crowded, rapidly growing Japanese economy devoid of fossil fuels made nuclear power compellingly attractive; the strategic imperative of autonomy from reliance on a volatile Middle East over vulnerable seven-thousand-mile sea lanes compounded this nuclear attraction. Political dynamics, including a regionalist bias under Tanaka's "Remodeling the Japanese Archipelago" plan, and the rapid mobilization of populist NGO groups, impelled grassroots compensation as a basic policy approach.

Japan's nuclear circle of compensation began emerging in the mid-1970s, shortly after the country's first nuclear plants were opened during 1970–1971, and spurred by the Oil Shock of 1973. The three electric-power-generation laws (*Dengen Sanpō*) of 1974 established the basic policy framework, and a series of nuclear accidents, including the saga of the *Mutsu* nuclear ship, intensified pressures for compensation within that context. This compensation, flowing from both government and an electric-utility sector pointedly favored by government, accelerated in times of political crisis, because stable policy parameters were needed at all costs.

Nuclear power thus became a stabilizing hallmark of the Japanese political economy for over three decades, insulating Japan from excessive hydrocarbon dependence on volatile foreign markets. It supported a modicum of energy independence for hydrocarbon-poor Japan in a globalizing world. Heavy civilian nuclear dependence continued up to the devastating Fukushima nuclear accident in the spring of 2011. With the return of conservative rule in December 2012, the prospect that nuclear power will someday continue to ease Japan's energy dependence on volatile foreign hydrocarbon supplies has risen once again, albeit tempered by cautionary memories of the recent past. For half a century, nuclear power allowed Japan to record steady economic growth while limiting energy imports—a benefit not easily discarded as the country strives to emerge from two decades of stagnation.

8

Transportation

Japan, as a casual glance at the map will reveal, is an island nation, strategically situated off the northeast coast of Asia, in one of the most rapidly growing regions on earth. It is a massive political economy, third largest in the world. It is technologically sophisticated, and heavily dependent on international trade for both commodity imports and overseas markets.

Yet the country operates within an enormous paradox. Because of deeply embedded subnational circles of compensation, Japan has a set of transportation policies that for generations have systematically impeded its globalization, as well as its international competitiveness. These circles also reduce Japan's flexibility in responding to the rapid pace of economic change sweeping the dynamic East Asian region.

Japan's "Isolationist" Transportation Bias in Comparative Perspective

Japan has massive international trade interests, and the Japanese people have become inveterate travelers. The number of foreign tourists visiting Japan has steadily increased, despite occasional setbacks, from 5.2 million in 2003 to nearly 20 million in 2015.[1] Indeed, as suggested in Figure 8.1, the growth rate of foreign visitors to Japan has been accelerating in recent years—the 2011 earthquake and Fukushima nuclear disaster notwithstanding. Japan is, furthermore, the fourth largest trader in the world, recording $1,468 billion in combined imports and exports during 2014.[2]

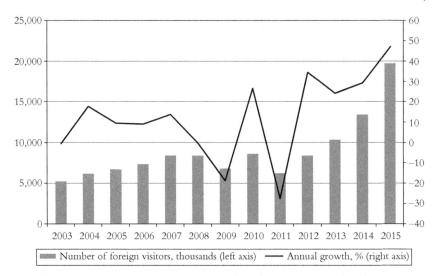

FIGURE 8.1 Japan's rising inflow of foreign visitors

SOURCE: Japan National Tourism Organization, "Kokuseki/Tsuki-betsu Hōnichi Gaikyaku-sū [Monthly Number of Foreign Visitors by Nationality] (2003–2006)," http://www.jnto.go.jp/jpn/statistics/visitor_trends/index.html.

Yet both the country's largest airports and its major seaports are curiously underdeveloped as international transportation centers. The volume of both passengers and cargo that Japanese entry ports handle, as well as the number of international destinations to which they connect, is remarkably low from a comparative standpoint, considering the huge scale of the Japanese economy, its proximity to the dynamic Asian mainland, and the affluence of Japan's people. Indeed, Japan appears to be, despite its huge economic scale, surprisingly isolated in the transport sector from the broader world, particularly compared to its dynamic neighbors. And the "connectivity gap" with competitors elsewhere in Asia seems to have widened since the 2008 Lehman Brothers shock.

Narita Airport, for example, is Japan's busiest air-freight hub, in the world's third largest economy. Yet in 2013, Narita ranked as only the tenth busiest cargo airport in the world. Hong Kong was first, with twice the volume of Narita. Nearby Shanghai Pudong in China was third, and Incheon in Korea was fourth.[3] In international passenger traffic, Narita was ranked only seventeenth in 2015. Hong Kong, by contrast, was third, again with more than twice the number of Narita. Singapore's Changi was sixth, and Incheon was eighth.[4]

The global standing of major Japanese airports has also been steadily declining—long before the tragic triple calamities of 2011 (earthquake,

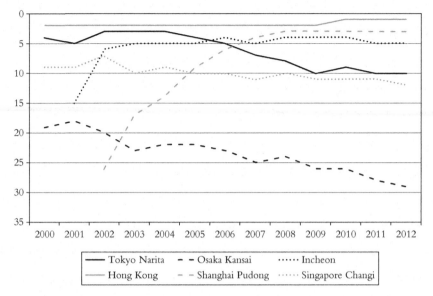

FIGURE 8.2   The declining relative position of major Japanese airports in cargo volume
(unit: ranking)

SOURCE: Airports Council International, *Annual Cargo Traffic Reports 2000–2013*, compiled by the author.
NOTE: Rankings represent an airport's position by cargo volume ("loaded and unloaded freight and mail in
metric tonnes") among all airports participating in the ACI Annual Traffic Statistics Collection.

tsunami, and nuclear crisis) made matters palpably worse. The decline of
Japan's airports as commercial centers has been especially pronounced. In 2002,
for example, Narita was the third largest airport in the world, in terms of cargo
volume, with Kansai at twentieth. By 2006, however, Narita had fallen to fifth,
with Kansai to twenty-third. And in 2013 Narita ranked even lower at tenth,
with Kansai significantly farther down, at thirtieth.[5] The trends are shown in
Figure 8.2.

For a variety of reasons, Japanese airports have not only failed to keep pace
with increases in cargo and passenger volume elsewhere, but also have failed
to become the international transportation hubs that the early development of
the Japanese economy once offered the promise of becoming. This failure is
dramatically shown, for example, in the relative importance of Narita Airport
in Tokyo and Incheon in Korea as destinations for air routes from other cities
in Japan.

Only seventeen local Japanese airports have Narita routes, while twenty-
eight, including most major cities on the Japan Sea coast, have connections to
Incheon—considerably farther away, and despite traditional Japan-Korea sociopolitical tensions.[6] Incheon is, as Figure 8.3 suggests, a principal hub linking

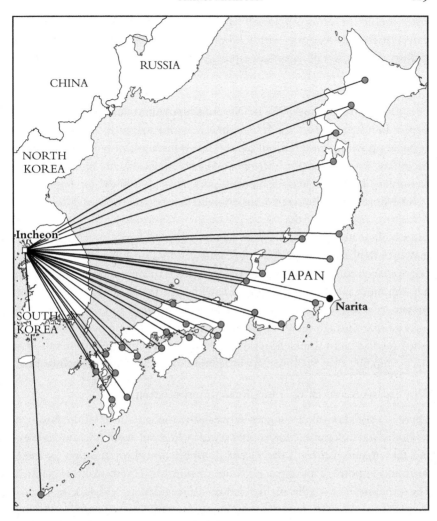

FIGURE 8.3   Incheon's importance as a hub for Japanese cities

SOURCE: Incheon Airport, "Connecting Cities—Japan."

provincial Japan to the broader world—a distinction that *no* Japanese airport can credibly claim. Ironically, parochial Japanese policies have made Incheon rather than Narita the major hub for Japanese provincial cities, as discussed later in this chapter.

Japan's largest and most traditionally international seaports, like its airports, also fail to generate the volume of traffic that one might expect to be flowing from an economy the size of Japan's. Although Japan has the third largest economy in the world, in the equation of largest global ports it has a much lower profile. In terms of tonnage handled, for example, Nagoya ranked just sixteenth globally in 2015, with Chiba next at twenty-third, and Yokohama at thirty-first.[7] Overall, Japanese seaports handle only 4 percent of the world's cargo, even though Japan's economy constitutes nearly one-twelfth of the global total.[8]

With regard to advanced sea-freight transshipment centers—the hubs of the seaport industry—Japan stands even lower, with its rivals in Asia once again dominating world standings. All the top five transshipment ports in the world are in East Asia—Singapore, Shanghai, Shenzhen, Busan, and Hong Kong, in that order.[9] No Japanese transshipment port ranks even in the top ten.

Singapore is also the second busiest container port in the world, following Shanghai, with nine of the top ten ports in Asia outside Japan. Keihin Ports ranks highest in the container port standings within Japan in 2014, but only at twentieth place in the global scales, followed by Hanshin at twenty-eighth. Nagoya failed to rank even among the top fifty.[10] Busan has become the chief transshipment port for much of Japan, with a particularly large share of the containers going to or coming from southwestern Japan and the Sea of Japan coast passing through there; fifty-two of sixty-four Japanese ports have established regular cargo shipment services with South Korea.[11] A major reason is price: Shipping costs via Busan are little more than half those through Kobe.[12]

Why Japan's Marginal Role in Global Transportation?

There is a paradoxical disconnect between the immense scale of the Japanese economy and its longtime forerunner status as an Asian economic superpower, and the anemic nature of the recent transportation flows through Japanese ports and airports. This apparent contradiction can be rationally explained. The proximate causes lie in high costs, overregulation, and lack of incentives to innovate, with the origins of those counterproductive practices deeply rooted in circles of compensation that impede Japanese access to and from the broader world.

Japan's major airports are extremely expensive to pass through, relative to their counterparts elsewhere in the world. According to Air Transport Research Society's 2015 Global Benchmark Report, it costs roughly $4,624 to land a Boeing 767-400 at Haneda Airport, whereas the peak rate to land at New York's John F. Kennedy International Airport (JFK) is $3,143. Landing charges at Haneda's Asian competitor airports are even lower—$1,843 at Singapore's Changi and $1,724 at Korea's Incheon. Although slightly lower, international landing fees at Japan's other major airports—Kansai, Chubu, and Narita—are similar to those at Haneda, and all are higher than equivalent

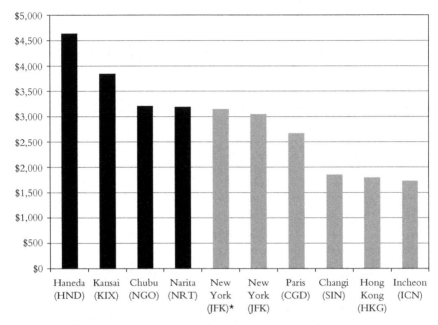

FIGURE 8.4   The high level of landing fees at Japanese airports

SOURCE: Air Transport Research Society, *2015 Global Airport Benchmarking Report.*
NOTES: 1) Landing charges are calculated for a Boeing 767–400 with a maximum take-off weight (MTOW) of 450,000 lbs. 2) The New York (JFK)* represents peak rates, while the New York (JFK) is off-peak.

charges at major airports outside Asia, such as JFK, Charles de Gaulle Airport in Paris, and Heathrow Airport in London, as indicated in Figure 8.4.

Landing fees are not the only exorbitantly high charge prevailing at Japanese international airports. There is also an unusual, and extremely heavy, government tax on aircraft fuel, totaling ¥26,000/kiloliter.[13] The United States is the only other major nation that levies such a tax at all, and the U.S. fuel tax is less than one-fifth of Japanese level.[14] Britain, Germany, and France, not to mention close-by competitor nations to Japan like Australia, Singapore, and South Korea, do not levy such a tax at all, calculating that such levies discourage international airlines from using their airports.

In addition to high landing fees and fuel surcharges imposed on the airlines directly, Japanese international airports require unusually high service facility charges and security surcharges on the tickets of travelers passing through their gates. At Tokyo's Narita Airport, for example, an adult passenger departing from Terminal 1 or Terminal 2 for international destinations must pay a ¥2,090 Passenger Service Facility Charge plus a ¥520 Passenger Security Service Charge.[15] Together, these fees and taxes made charges per passenger in Japan much higher than in Incheon, Los Angeles, Hong Kong, and San Francisco.[16]

Japan has, to be sure, developed high-quality aviation facilities and services. In the 2015 World Economic Forum Travel and Tourism Competitiveness Report, it ranked first place in treatment of customers and nineteenth place worldwide in quality of air transport infrastructure.[17] Yet it placed only 82nd with respect to ticket taxes and airport charges, not to mention 119th place globally in terms of price competitiveness—the lowest of any major Asian nation in both categories.[18]

In Narita's case, its high surcharges are moderately explicable, given the protracted history of conflict surrounding the airport's construction and operation.[19] That history of confrontation undoubtedly raised local operating costs, as did the ongoing need for compensating innately hostile local residents for aircraft noise and other inconveniences. Such heavy fees also burden the flow of international passengers between Japan and the world. They also ironically advantage other nearby competitors, such as Korea's Incheon, for international aviation status, thus impeding Japan's economic globalization.

Regulatory distortions, inspired by both bureaucratic fiat and domestic politics, also impede the emergence of Japanese airports as major international centers. At Narita Airport, for example, take-off and landing of aircrafts are in principle only allowed between 6:00 a.m. and 11:00 p.m., owing to citizen protests related to its controversial origins, themselves rooted in conservative politics during the mid-1960s.[20] Other major Asian airports, such as Incheon and Changi, typically operate around the clock, facilitating long-distance transit traffic that Narita fails to attract.

Narita has been a fully private corporation since 2004, nominally capable of concluding business deals with firms throughout the world. Haneda's terminal building facilities also are private.[21] Yet both airports pursue ambiguous policies on foreign investment in airport-related business, such as cargo storage and airline catering, inhibiting their emergence as global aviation centers still further. Their parochial orientation is intensified by the employment of numerous retired Japanese Ministry of Transportation officials at domestic firms operating in these areas.[22]

The difficulties that foreign firms have faced in entering the inefficient Japanese air-service sector are clear. In 2008, for example, an Australian investment conglomerate, the Macquarie Airports Management Ltd., increased its stake in Japan Airport Terminal (JAT, a listed company on the first section of the Tokyo Stock Exchange that owned 19.9 percent of the Haneda terminal building). The Ministry of Land, Infrastructure, Transport and Tourism

(MLIT) responded with proposed legislation to limit foreign holdings of airport operating companies to less than one-third of voting shares. The Japanese Cabinet did not endorse the proposal in the end, fearing that such restriction would discourage foreign investment. Macquarie, however, refrained from buying more shares in JAT, and instead offered to sell its stake at a loss back to the Japanese airport operator.[23]

Japan's approach to international transportation issues has also typically involved problems of *omission*, especially serious in the competitive environment surrounding globalization, which compounds the problems of *commission* outlined above. Nearby Korea, for example, has aggressively developed a state-of-the-art cargo-freight and industrial-processing complex at Incheon Airport—open twenty-four hours a day (eight hours longer than Narita) with the world's first 100 percent online clearance system (UNI-PASS), four cargo terminals, and separate areas for import, export, and transit.[24] The international delivery firm DHL, among others, has invested heavily at Incheon, and runs its Northeast Asian freight-hub operation from there.

Apart from cargo facilities, the Incheon airport complex also features a nine-story hospital, completed in 2011.[25] This facility is capable of providing medical services to thirty thousand international tourists alone every year.[26] Visitors arriving at Incheon for medical purposes are accorded special treatment in many ways; they even receive a dedicated immigration line.[27] In this way, Korea uses its airport facilities to tap strategically into the high-value-added and rapidly growing field of medical tourism,[28] in ways that Japan is just beginning to explore.[29]

The typical barriers to international commerce that distinguish Japanese airports—exorbitant user fees, high degrees of regulation, and lack of consideration for potential downstream services for foreign visitors—also characterize Japanese ports. Comparative data are scarce. One relatively recent Australian survey, however, the results of which are presented in Figure 8.5, indicated that costs incurred by a shipowner at major Japanese container shipping ports (Yokohama, Osaka, and Nagoya) were over 35 percent higher than in New York, 65 percent higher than in Melbourne, and four times or more higher than in Korea or China.[30] Container handling fees in Japan were nearly five times as high as at Busan, as also indicated in Figure 8.5.

In contrast to Japanese airports, Japanese seaports are funded largely from the national general-account budget.[31] Port administration has thus been able to finesse the airport-sector pathology of high, revenue-generating user fees, captured by special accounts, that has crippled international competitiveness there. The ports have circle of compensation–related efficiency problems of

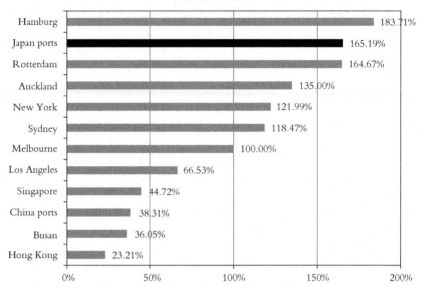

Port Price Index

FIGURE 8.5   Japan's high container seaport charges in comparative context

SOURCE: Shipping Australia Limited, *International Port Cost Comparison Project*, https://shippingaustralia.com
.au/wp-content/uploads/2012/01/L_InterPortCostCcomparison.pdf.
NOTE: The port-price index of Melbourne, Australia, has a reference value of 100 percent.

a different nature, however. These difficulties flow from their dependence on central-government subsidies,[32] and from their operational control by local authorities lacking strong incentives to reduce costs.[33] The result is inordinately high cargo-handling charges that inhibit international trade, and Japan's globalization.

During 2013 MLIT began to perceive the crippling impact of existing policies on the competitiveness of Japan's major ports. It proposed revising the Port and Harbor Law to increase national government equity participation in the strategic Keihin and Hanshin Ports, and to rationalize their management. Yet these changes, slated for fiscal 2014 (Keihin) and fiscal 2015 (Hanshin), were incremental, more limited than those undertaken at Busan a decade earlier, and slower in coming. In port management, as in many other areas, Japan is slowly globalizing, but has had trouble moving as rapidly as some of its dynamic neighbors.

As in the case of airports, Japanese seaports are also highly regulated, passive in developing downstream services, and subject to substantial, albeit nontransparent, barriers to foreign investment. Their operating hours are generally

8:30 a.m. to 4:30 p.m.—only one-third of the all-day, everyday coverage that Busan and Singapore provide.[34] Customs procedures in Japan are complex, and handling fees are traditionally high, due to limited competition and parochial local government pressure. Not surprisingly, global businesses often turn elsewhere.

Domestic Politics Trumps Global Strategy in Japanese Transportation Policy

Japan's transportation policies—high landing fees, high fuel charges, high port fees, passive approaches to downstream service, and extensive regulation—clearly inhibit Japanese private firms in their international transactions. That they constrain foreign companies conforms to the conventional wisdom that Japan is protectionist. That they hamper the global business dealings of major Japanese firms also, however, is counterintuitive, in terms of the classic argument that Japan is a strategic "developmental state." Regulatory policies in transportation appear to benefit *other* actors than airports, airlines, seaports, cargo lines, and the customers of such enterprises. What is diverting mainstream Japanese business and governmental actors from these seemingly logical strategic objectives?

The answer to this key question is complex, and is best approached indirectly, since the origins of Japan's parochial transport policies are structural, and embedded in history. Airport construction, it is important to note, constitutes only a small portion of the Japanese government's public-works budget. In fiscal 2014, for example, "improvements of harbors, airports, and railways" together constituted 7 percent of Japan's total general-account spending on public works of ¥5.97 trillion, compared to 22 percent for "road improvement works."[35] Likewise, "airport" and "harbours" only constituted 2 percent and 11 percent, respectively, of Japan's total administrative investment in industry of ¥3.9 trillion in fiscal 2011, compared to 86 percent for "national highways and prefectural roads."[36] Hong Kong and Singapore all use much larger shares of national construction funds on international transport infrastructure, especially airports.[37]

Although the Japanese national government contributes little to airport construction directly, it should be noted that construction itself is *extremely expensive*, both because land is expensive and construction itself costs atypical amounts of money in Japan. Kansai and Denver International Airports, for example were built at roughly the same time, and Denver is larger, with six runways as opposed to Kansai's one. Yet Kansai cost more than four times as much to build—both due to engineering challenges and the operation of self-serving circles of compensation.[38]

The bulk of the funds available for airport construction and maintenance in Japan traditionally came from the Airport Facilities Improvement Account (*Kūkō Seibi Kanjō*), included in the broader Infrastructure Facilities Development Special Account (IFDSA, or *Shakai Shihon Seibi Jigyō Tokubetsu Kaikei*) from 2008 to 2013. The IFDSA drew over 60 percent of its resources from precisely the heavy airport landing fees and airport fuel charges that are impeding Japan's globalization. For many years this special account structure was a major reason why landing and fuel fees were so high in the first place. Ultimately, the account's existence and operation—which epitomize the circle of compensation in Japanese transportation—were key reasons why Japan was for many years so oblivious to global competitive patterns in the aviation industry. The IFDSA was abolished and integrated into the general account after fiscal 2013, as a part of the Abe "third arrow" reforms.[39] Yet this seemingly liberal development ironically handicaps Japan's international airports once again in catching up with their rapidly growing and publically supported rivals elsewhere, in an increasingly globalized and competitive world.

The IFDSA has channeled resources not to the established international airports that are Japan's face on the broader world, but rather to the building of small and often inefficient regional airports with insufficient volume to be profitable. Such enterprises are often more regional merchandising than actual transportation centers. These diversions undermine the metropolitan airports' efforts to develop hub functions. Volume-oriented connection points like Narita, Haneda, and Kansai are Japan's best chance to be competitive in the globalizing world of airport competition, where scale, efficiency, and breadth of downstream facilities are crucial. Yet they have been crippled by their own nation's public policies.

Parochial Operation of the Airport Improvement Account

Due to the pressures of globalization and Japan's delayed response to them, the large airports of Japan, such as the two big ones serving Tokyo (Narita and Haneda), have a chronic shortage of runways. This shortage has delayed Japan's reaching Open Skies agreements with other nations, because Japan does not have sufficient departure and landing spots for negotiations. Yet the IFDSA has traditionally collected funds from such potentially promising international airports, because they are established and profitable. It then perversely redirects the money to the construction, maintenance, and operation of less-efficient regional airports, with limited potential as international connecting points, as indicated in Table 8.1.

TABLE 8.1

Flow of funds in the Airport Improvement Special Account, 2010

Airport improvement budget, FY2010 (in billions of yen)

Revenue		Expenditure	
General account	113.1	Airport improvement projects	274.5
Aviation fuel tax[a]	71.6	Haneda expansion	103.3
Other general finances	41.5	Haneda upgrade	124.2
Fiscal Investment and Loan Program (FILP)	68.7	Kansai	9.2
Airport improvement account	277.5	Other regional airports	20.3
Landing fees	81.9	General airport function improvement	17.5
Other airport usage charge	122.6	Operation maintenance fees	139.4
Miscellaneous	73.0	Others[b]	45.4
Total	**459.3**	**Total**	**459.3**

SOURCE: Ministry of Land, Infrastructure, Transport and Tourism, "Heisei 22 nendo Kōkū-kyoku Kankei Yosan Gaiyō (Aviation Bureau Related Budget Overview for FY2010)," chapter 2.

NOTES: Shaded entries indicate contributions by the aviation industry.

[a]11/13 of aviation fuel tax paid by airlines goes to Airport Improvement Account through the general account, while the rest goes to prefectural and local accounts.

[b]Including spending on aviation safety (20.2), funds for improving airport surrounding environment (6.6), subsidies for remote islands (0.6), etc.

The IFDSA has a strong political-economic bias toward building new airports in remote areas, with attached commercial facilities, because: (1) construction can be subsidized by the special account, (2) construction is attractive for local construction firms and supportive local politicians, and (3) airports enhance the value of associated commercial facilities. By Japanese practice (operative everywhere but at Narita, Kansai, and Chubu airports), these commercial facilities are owned and run separately from the runway side of the airport operation.[40]

As of 2010, the Japanese government had constructed ninety-eight airports, up from twenty-three in 1960, using funds from the Airport Improvement Account and MOF's Fiscal Investment and Loan Program, as indicated in Figure 8.6 below.[41, 42] Less than one-third of the nationally administered airports in Japan made money, not including terminal buildings. Over 30 percent of funds from the Airport Improvement Account therefore had to be devoted in 2010 to subsidizing the operations of the inefficient two-thirds.

The parochial management of Japanese airport policy is attracting rising discontent among internationalists within the Japanese government. Many of them have become alarmed by the intensifying international competition in the aviation industry, and are attempting to have expanded funds allocated to major Japanese international airports to upgrade their facilities.[43] The Abe administration announced plans to privatize all national airports by 2020,[44] starting with debt-ridden Kansai International Airport.[45] Yet real change is slow in coming, although some underutilized local airports are beginning to close as a result of cost considerations and rising national resistance to inefficient subsidies.[46]

A Perverse Circle of Compensation

As suggested in the foregoing, there is a perverse circle of compensation operating in the Japanese transportation sector. The key members of this circle in the aviation sector, which exerts an especially adverse impact on Japan's globalization, are indicated in Figure 8.6. They include transport bureaucrats, local airports and their backers, as well as (indirectly) competing foreign airports, such as Incheon in Korea.

As in so many areas of Japanese public policy, transport circles of compensation typically privilege construction interests—particularly local contractors, who have benefited greatly from the proliferation of local airports encouraged under the IFDSA system. Merchants and entrepreneurs who own and operate terminal facilities also benefit, since terminals and runways are owned

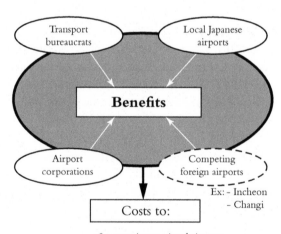

FIGURE 8.6 Circles of compensation in air transportation

SOURCE: Author's illustration.

separately, with terminals holding no responsibility for funding inefficient and unprofitable runway operations. The circle also privileges a variety of politicians, including local governors, mayors, and Diet members who initiate and support the construction of local airports, however inefficient the runways themselves may be.

Transportation-sector bureaucrats benefit from the traditional structure of airport administration in Japan in two ways. First, they gain autonomy from the intrusive and efficiency-oriented MOF through the IFDSA, which generates revenue they can then allocate independent of MOF. Second, the existing system offers lucrative postretirement employment for bureaucrats with the network of airport corporations and related businesses, both public and private, that have been steadily expanding across Japan.[47]

The airport circles of compensation also clearly disadvantage certain groups, which can be considered "outsiders." Ironically, one such outsider group is arguably the airlines that use major Japanese airports themselves. They are forced to pay high user fees, suffer from high fuel charges, and are pressed by the transportation bureaucrats to service complex, unprofitable domestic routes to the myriad local airports that have been built through political pressure and funds available through the IFDSA. Even though domestic airlines like ANA and JAL have traditionally profited from relatively high domestic airline fares,[48] the competitive advantage of these major domestic lines has been eroded in recent years by the emergence, under political pressure from MOF, of discount airlines.

It is not surprising, given the regulatory environment and lack of incentives to be globally efficient, that Japan's flag carrier, JAL, went bankrupt in early 2010.[49] Its aircraft were too large, due to slot regulation at Narita and general shortage of international airports in Japan. Its route structure was too complex and unprofitable, due to political pressure. And JAL also suffered from the high landing fees of its major home airports, described above.[50]

Historical Origins

The perverse transportation circle of compensation that prevails within Japan has defined "internationalization" in highly parochial terms, privileging inefficient local airports and seaports while handicapping the large entry ports and major airlines. They, together with cargo-handling companies, are no doubt among the Japanese aviation firms most capable of competing internationally.[51] The paradox of an allegedly strategic "developmental state" engaging in such behavior is best explained in historical terms. The institutions that create the parochial bias of Japanese transportation policy, after all, originated in a different, less global era, when domestic political considerations, rather than global competitiveness, held sway, especially in certain sheltered areas of the political economy.

Perverse Evolution of Aviation Policy

Japan's Airport Facilities Improvement Law, the legal basis of airport regulation, was promulgated in 1956, and it took little more than a decade for a parochial domestic bias, inspired by politicization, to set in.[52] In 1967, the Ministry of Transportation announced its first Airport Facilities Improvement Plan, whose main goal was to increase the number of local airports. In 1970, the critically important Airport Facilities Improvement Special Account, which introduced airport usage fees on the airlines as a means of generating income for additional airport construction, was introduced, with Tomisaburō Hashimoto, a leading figure in the Tanaka faction of the Liberal Democratic Party, serving as Minister of Transport. In the following year, boarding fees on passengers using the airports were introduced, and in 1972 a fuel tax, levied against the airlines, was added.

During the 1980s, the airport-construction process was further politicized, once again to the detriment of passengers and airlines using the large international airports. In 1986, the Fifth Airport Facilities Improvement Plan introduced the slogan of "one airport per prefecture" and proceeded to press for its realization.[53] Local prefectural capitals such as Hiroshima, Akita, and Toyama got new international airports. The next year, the Sixth Airport Facilities Improvement Plan introduced the theme of "internationalization," but employed criteria that disadvantaged Japan's large and most competitive airports. A target for total lengths of runways nationwide was introduced, with IDFSA funds used primarily to construct new runways at local airports. This practice was followed even where usage factors were low, but where construction costs were also relatively low.

It was only in the mid-1990s, two decades after globalization began transforming the world's political economy, that Japan began to change course in its airport development policies. The Seventh Airport Facilities Improvement Plan of 1996 finally established a policy goal of upgrading airports in metropolitan areas. This was followed in 2003 by the Priority Plan for Infrastructure Development (*Shakai Shihon Seibi Jūten Keikaku*). This program was created to consolidate nine development fields (roads, transportation safety infrastructure, airports, ports, parks in cities, sewerage system, flood control) and to promote more-efficient national infrastructure planning. One of the major goals was to cope with and benefit from globalization by increasing exchanges with other Asian countries.[54]

In 2010, Tokyo's large Haneda Airport, the most convenient aviation access to Japan's capital, was finally internationalized, after thirty-eight years as an almost entirely domestic facility. In the same year, Japan also finally concluded an Open Skies agreement with the United States.[55] (The U.S.-Japan Opens Skies agreement was Japan's tenth such arrangement, but the first to include Haneda and Narita.) After the agreement with the United States was concluded, Japan started negotiating with other countries and regions to include Haneda and Narita in agreements with them, as well.[56]

Open Skies agreements led to the entry of several low-cost carriers into Japan, such as AirAsia, and also to a modest expansion of international travel through major Japanese airports. AirAsia, for example, offered ¥5,000 economy tickets for travel between Haneda and Malaysia. Despite these recent developments, however, Japan continues to struggle with the parochial, and deeply embedded, transportation circle of compensation. Meanwhile, global pressures move other nearby nations, such as Korea, much more rapidly than Japan toward globalization.[57]

Dysfunctional Port Regulation

The checkered course of seaport regulation in Japan is strikingly similar to that of aviation policy. It is similarly shaped by embedded circles of compensation that merge the interests and incentives of transportation-sector bureaucrats, Diet members, local officials, and, in this case, labor unions, to the disadvantage of corporate and individual consumers. In contrast to most Japanese industries, which have enterprise unions, the seamen and port workers of Japan have an industry-wide union, the All Japan Shipping Laborers Union (*Zen Nihon Kōwan Rōdō Kumiai Rengōkai*), with unusual cohesion.

The basic framework for port regulation, established under the Law on Emergency Measures for Port Development (*Kōwan Seibi Kinkyū Sochi Hō*) of 1961, was created with heavy political input, to increase the number of ports and expand port facilities to meet growing demand.[58] As with airports, the emphasis has been on putting a heavy share of resources into local ports.[59] This parochial practice has been depriving large Japanese ports in metropolitan areas such as Yokohama and Kobe of sufficient funds to compete with global leaders like Singapore and Busan. As in aviation, this perverse "egalitarianism" has been modified in Japan since around 2004, when the "super-core ports program" was introduced by the Koizumi administration.[60] The efficiency of major Japanese ports has been gradually improving, but not enough to make a major international competitive difference as yet, especially in comparison with more rapidly globalizing players like Singapore and South Korea.

In Conclusion

Japan is the third largest economy in the world, the first non-Western industrializer, and strategically located just off the shores of rapidly growing continental Northeast Asia. It has been formidably competitive in basic and high-tech industrial sectors, and was long acclaimed as a highly successful "developmental state." Yet Japan has been strikingly and paradoxically unsuccessful in managing transportation-sector development so as to enhance global competitiveness. Indeed, its struggle with parochialism in that area appears to have impeded its globalization more generally.

Japan's lack of international competitive success in the transportation area, despite the formidable scale and basic competitiveness of its economy, are evident, first of all, in the stagnant transaction volume and declining global prominence of its airports and seaports. In 2002, for example, Narita was the third largest cargo airport in the world but by 2013 it had declined to tenth, passed by several other locations in Asia. None of Japan's seaports ranked among the top ten—in tonnage, container traffic, or transshipment volume. Their relative international standing was likewise declining.

The proximate obstacles to Japanese international competitiveness in the transportation area appear to be fourfold: (1) high user fees, (2) complex domestic regulations, (3) barriers to foreign investment, and (4) lack of proactive downstream-sector support policies. All these shortcomings have their origins in domestic political developments of the 1960s and 1970s, which gave birth to perverse regulatory structures like the Airport Facilities Improvement Special Account. These structures create intimate circles of compensation, privileging construction interests, politicians, and MOT bureaucrats.

Such circles operate to the disadvantage of Japanese international airlines, their passengers, and the bulk of the Japanese business community. With respect to seaports, local government intervention, unions, and a reliance on subsidies also undermine efficiency. Circles of compensation in both air and sea transport also impede Japan's globalization, and thus impede its long-term growth. They undermine the competitiveness of large transportation centers like Narita Airport to the advantage of foreign competitors like Incheon, even as such circles enhance the international ties of small individual communities, such as Niigata and Sapporo, on Japan's national periphery.

9

Communications

For an insular nation on the rim of a vast continent, surrounded by the seas, communications is a fundamental imperative in an economically interdependent world. Britain, in analogous geo-economic circumstances to Japan, has long felt that necessity. Many Japanese also appreciate the need for effective dialogue with the broader world, and the technical capacity to ensure it, as well.

During the 1980s, as the global information revolution was beginning to unfold, Japan stood at the forefront in communications equipment. Its switching systems were among the world's fastest and most cost effective. It was a leader in the production of fax machines, and a pioneer in cell-phone technology and commercialization, building on its earlier competitive successes in transistor radios and television. Underlying Japanese competitive strength in a broad range of communications-equipment sectors, as in consumer electronics, was one of the largest and most sophisticated semiconductor production capacities in the world.

In the softer dimensions of communications, Japan was also innovative in the early postwar years. Between 1948 and 1952, the number of universities in Japan rose from 12 to 220, while the number of junior colleges rose from 0 to 205.[1] Based on that early momentum, more than five hundred additional universities have since been established, and the share of university entrants has spiraled to over 54 percent of all Japanese in their early twenties.[2] As late as the 1980s, foreign study and new cultural-support institutions, such as the

International House of Japan, the Japan Center for International Exchange, and the Japan Foundation, were expanding vigorously.

The puzzle in Japan's patterns of both communications industry development and the evolution of communications institutions is twofold: (1) Why did the promising patterns of vigorous international exchange and global competitiveness that prevailed in the early postwar years suddenly reverse themselves, during the 1990s and thereafter; and (2) why have perverse trends in communications-hardware competitiveness, as well as software interchange with the world, covaried so ominously with one another? With respect to both puzzles, circles of compensation are central in accounting for the outcomes that we observe. There have been silver linings, including some laudable advances in domestic infrastructure and technical performance. Yet circles of compensation in the communications field have complicated and inhibited Japanese globalization.

Circles of Compensations in the Communications Industry: "Hard" Communications

Sectoral distinctions are important in operationalizing the circle-of-compensation concept. One further distinction is within the communications sphere: "hard communications," or the manufacturing side of the sector, discussed here, versus "soft communications," or the service dimension, which is considered in the latter half of this chapter. Intra-industry distinctions are also important, particularly within the "hard" industrial sphere.

In contrast to steel, electric power, shipbuilding, and banking, the hard communications industry of Japan is a relatively young sector—largely devoid of the embedded heritage of corporatist "control associations" (*tōsei kai*) that played such key roles in mobilizing Japan for World War II.[3] Much of the heavy-electrical industry had strong wartime government ties, through military procurement. Those relationships were largely dismantled after World War II, and the sector lacked a strong independent postwar industry association, in contrast to steel or banking.[4] Consumer electronics, dominated by young, aspiring entrepreneurs like Akio Morita of Sony, was even less organized as a sector than its heavy-electrical counterpart.[5]

Japan's universities and think tanks were similarly unregimented. Like consumer electronics, these institutions of soft communication lacked a prewar or wartime corporatist heritage. They were creatures of an Occupation-era liberal ethos that encouraged a much more internationalist orientation than prevailed in most of industry, or in the national bureaucracy.

Profile of Existing Circles and How They Emerged

Despite a more market-oriented historical pedigree than transportation, agriculture, or finance, the communications sector has also been a sphere— critical to Japan's ability to understand and to deal with the broader world— where Japan has had difficulty in coping with the demands of globalization. Circles of compensation, which privilege participants (mainly domestic) at the expense of outsiders, including the general public, are a central reason for this parochialism. This chapter describes key circles operating in the communications sector, explains how they came to be, and discusses their implications, for both Japanese political-economic behavior generally, and for Japan's globalization in particular.

The principal circle of compensation in the telecommunications industry, whose embedded remnants continue to influence the sector's competitive dynamics, was for many years the complex of firms surrounding Nippon Telegraph and Telephone (NTT), and popularly known as its "family." From 1950 until 2002, spanning privatization in 1985 and nominal breakup in 1999, NTT and its affiliate firms routinely bought most of their capital equipment, including switching systems and high-performance computers, as well as terminal devices like telephones, from a small, specified group of domestic Japanese suppliers, without competition. These "family" members included major suppliers such as Nippon Electric Company (NEC), Oki Electric, Hitachi, and Fujitsu, together with NTT's direct corporate affiliates, as indicated in Figure 9.1.

Within its telecommunications-equipment supplier family, NTT was at once demanding and benevolent. It did not let its suppliers devise their own products or compete against one another. NTT also insisted on precise, high-performance, and often arcane technical specifications, frequently different from those prevailing in broader global markets. In return, NTT offered a stable, guaranteed, and lucrative long-term market, insulated from outside competition by distinctive standards and protocols. At the time of its privatization in the mid-1980s, NTT enjoyed revenues of over $21 billion—more than ten times the levels of two decades previously.[6]

In the hothouse environment which the NTT family provided, participants often recorded brilliant technical achievements. NEC and Fujitsu, for example, competed head to head with Cray and IBM in building the world's fastest supercomputers.[7] Their research labs were among the best in the world, and their know-how was critical to the success of Japan's space-satellite program. For many years, before globalization and the deepening integration of Japanese and foreign telecommunications markets, all the major Japanese

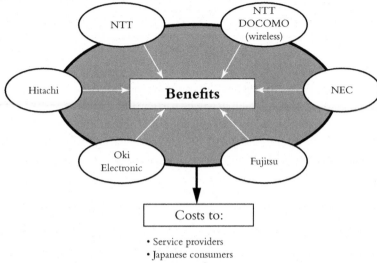

FIGURE 9.1   The NTT family

SOURCE: Author's illustration.

communications makers were consistently profitable, and mutually interdependent through cross-shareholding.[8]

High profitability, due to the NTT family system, also generated the resources for NTT to invest in high-quality infrastructure. It was a pioneer in optical-fiber transmission, and rapidly introduced optical-fiber lines and local-area networks across Japan. By the 1980s NTT and its affiliates were already laying the groundwork for one of the most advanced "information societies" in the world.[9] The emphasis, however, was on technical traits such as calculation speed and memory capacity, rather than on consumer friendliness or production cost.

The circle of compensation was also synergistic at the interpersonal level. The supplier firms got stable markets, while senior NTT officials were assured of postretirement sinecures through *amakudari* (literally, "descent from heaven"). The circle was assured of favorable regulatory treatment by the Ministry of Posts and Telecommunications, which also sent its own retired officials to member firms.

Policy Outputs and Deepening Economic Distortions

The costs of the telecommunications circle, as in so many other sectors, were externalized—to telephone users, communications-service providers, foreign

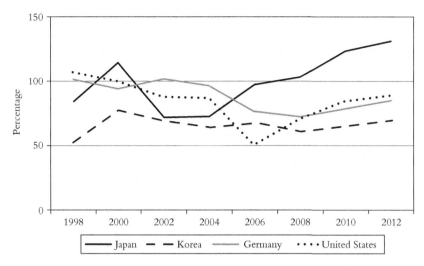

FIGURE 9.2   Japan's high level of business telephone charges

SOURCE:: OECD, Communications Outlooks 1998 (Table 7.2), 2000 (Table 7.10), 2002 (Table 6.11), 2004 (Table 6.7), 2006 (Table 7.6), 2008 (Table 7.6), 2010 (Table 7.7), and 2012 (Table 7.9), serial doi: 10.1787/19991460.

NOTE: Figures show pre-tax total charge (US$, PPP) of individual countries with respect to OECD average, i.e., OECD average = 100 percent.

equipment vendors, and the general public. Although the pace of technical innovation proved rapid in equipment and infrastructure areas of special interest to NTT, such as switching systems and optical-fiber communication networks, technical progress proved slow in service sectors such as value-added networks. Intrusive regulation of new services, restrictions on foreign participation, and the high price of telecommunications transactions all impeded service-sector innovations. As noted in Figure 9.2, business telephone charges in Japan during 2012 were nearly double those in Korea, 54 percent higher than in Germany, and 47 percent more than in the United States.[10]

The architects of the NTT family structure saw that structure—including its pricing and regulatory policies—initially as a powerful vehicle for preserving and enhancing Japan's ability to compete in a global telecom market dominated by the United States. The telecom circle of compensation encouraged domestic Japanese firms to confidently pursue sophisticated long-term research agendas, and to aggressively move into production with high-quality products. It also insulated them, by creating assured markets, from overwhelming competitive pressures exerted by global leaders in the United States and Europe. Those pressures otherwise might have destroyed a fledgling telecommunications industry like that of Japan.

Over time, however, the NTT family structure, with its closed pattern of research, development, and marketing, succeeded all too well. It encouraged Japanese firms to create their own parochial communications universe—one so distinctive, in terms of protocols, standards, and performance levels, that it effectively excluded most foreign firms. The world that the family created established stable, predictable relations among manufacturers, while limiting risks for producers.

At the same time, however, the family arrangement generated new difficulties. One drawback, emerging abruptly during the late 1990s, was that high-price telecommunications services retarded the development of the Internet, as well as the market's propensity to provide innovative telecommunications services desired by the Japanese financial, transportation, and manufacturing sectors. On several occasions in the 2000s, the telecommunications bureaucrats at what is now the Ministry of Internal Affairs and Communications,[11] acting at the instigation of NTT and affiliated politicians, rejected large-scale reductions in interconnection rates for competitors of NTT that would have encouraged expansion of the Internet.[12] Dial-up Internet access charges were kept at levels nearly three times those in the United States.[13]

Ultimately, telecommunications authorities sharply reduced access charges for digital subscriber line (DSL) broadband service, to encourage that advanced, economically productive form of Internet communication, cross-subsidizing it with higher interconnection rates on nonstrategic fixed-line phone services.[14] Yet they reduced DSL fees much later than in Korea, putting Japan at a competitive disadvantage with its proactive neighbor in the Internet area. Meanwhile, overall Japanese telecommunications charges—particularly those incurred by business—remained very high by international standards.

The trend in Japan toward distinctive technical standards—often higher performance than what prevailed globally—was a second increasingly serious problem for the Japanese telecommunications sector. Like the family structure of research and production, this pattern had its origins in parochial, circle of compensation–based decision-making that ignored emerging global realities.[15] Japan's distinctive technical standards, congenial to the family but unacceptable beyond Japanese shores, made it harder and harder for Japanese firms to compete on the world stage. Distinctive standards made their markets narrower, and their costs higher, than those of competitors from Korea, Scandinavia, and the United States.[16]

As in the Galápagos Islands, which nurture many of the strangest and most unique animals on Earth, six hundred miles from the nearest land, isolation and a benign Japanese regulatory environment encouraged the development of communications products with no clear parallels elsewhere.[17] Japan, for example, became a pioneer in cell phones. Yet it produced a distinctive variety—the "i-mode" phone—that was uniquely suited to the Japanese market, but had little attractiveness elsewhere.

Today Japan produces nearly thirty million i-mode phones annually, many of which have performed exotic, and technically advanced, functions for years. Sharp was, for example, the world's first company to add a camera to a mobile phone—in 2000.[18] By 2006—a year before Apple introduced the iPhone—Japanese consumers could watch broadcast TV in the palm of their hand. Japanese cell-phone manufacturers also pioneered with devices capable of generating digital money to make purchases; the ability to double as a monthly pass for trains and buses; and a function capable of swapping personal contact details with a push of a button.

Despite their parochial conveniences, Japanese firms sell very few i-mode phones—or any variety of cell phone—abroad.[19] In shipping three hundred million mobile phones a year, Korea's Samsung alone decisively outsells the entire Japanese industry combined.[20] Sony Ericsson, the largest Japanese producer, sells little more than one-tenth as many as Samsung.[21] Japan still dominates the cell-phone *parts* industry, with a 40–60 percent market share, including major procurement contracts from Apple, but it is losing decisively in finished systems,[22] where large firms enmeshed in parochial circles of compensation prevail. Meanwhile, the alternate iPhone technology, developed by Apple and popularized also by Samsung, has become the global standard.

The NTT family effectively dissolved in 2002, when NTT itself stopped procuring switching systems almost exclusively from its equipment-producing affiliates. Yet the family's embedded parochialism—and that of its member firms, most of whom have been vertically integrated from electronic components through finished systems—has continued to torment those companies competitively with their challenges, compounded by the emergence of global markets. During fiscal 2012 (through March 2013), major Japanese electronics firms lost $13 billion, with Panasonic alone losing $8 billion.[23] Apple, meanwhile, made $37 billion, while Korea's Samsung enjoyed profits of $28 billion.[24]

Since 2000 the five largest Japanese electronics firms, which focus heavily on communications products ranging from cell phones to personal computers and televisions, have lost nearly three-quarters of their market capitalization.[25] Japanese electronics firms in general have also lost much of their global market share, as suggested in Figure 9.3, in sectors ranging from dynamic random-access memory chips and liquid-crystal displays to solar panels and car

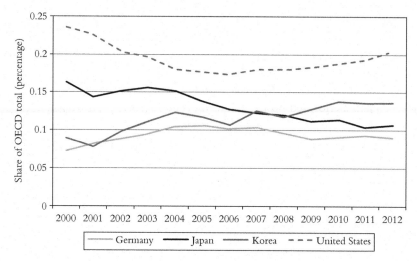

FIGURE 9.3   Japan's declining share of OECD information and communications technology exports

SOURCE: OECD, "Exports of ICT Goods: Million US dollars," *OECD Factbook 2014: Economic, Environmental and Social Statistics* (Paris: OECD Publishing), 163, doi: 10.1787/factbook-2014-en.

navigation systems.[26] Even the sharp depreciation of the yen during 2013–2014 did not decisively aid the electronics industry, which had moved much of its production capacity offshore following the yen's 50 percent appreciation during 2007–2011.[27]

Sectoral Contrasts: Telecom Versus Autos

The contrasts between perverse competitive developments in the telecommunications sector, on the one hand, and areas of Japanese global competitive success like automobiles, on the other, are striking. These contrasts illustrate the impact—largely, although not totally perverse—of circles of compensation such as the NTT family and the supportive pattern of government regulation that continued in telecom even after the family dissolved in 2002.

Telecommunications-equipment producers like NEC were driven by their NTT reliance and by lucrative price parameters provided by the NTT family to focus on areas of special interest to NTT within Japan, rather than on broader global markets. This parochial reliance led to formidable capabilities in some areas, such as optical communications, with some ultimate competitive utility in global markets.[28] Yet it also nurtured the esoteric Galápagos orientation described above.

In automobiles, by contrast, where there was no strong circle of compensation, major producers, especially the smaller ones battling for market share, focused their eyes abroad, on global competitiveness. Sensing a global market niche, they became highly competitive in compact-car production. Following the Oil Shocks of the 1970s, the auto producers pioneered globally in energy efficiency. As world environmental challenges deepened across the 1990s and 2000s, they pioneered in hybrid vehicles, such as the Toyota Prius, and in electric cars like the Nissan Leaf, as well.

Circles of Compensation in "Soft" Communications

There are fascinating parallels between developments in the sphere of knowledge creation and intellectual exchange, and the parochial patterns of the Japanese communications industry. Both have profound implications for Japan's efforts to adjust to a rapidly changing outside world. Like electronics and telecommunications firms, Japanese universities, think tanks, and mass media also tend to collaborate with one another—to stabilize group structure and maximize long-term communal benefit, even as they externalize costs, at the expense of outsiders. Circles of compensation thus appear to prevail broadly across all dimensions of Japanese communications—both internally and in dealings with the wider world. This pervasiveness of circles in the critical area of communications complicates Japan's response to globalization, although cross-cultural mediation can moderate the problems involved.

Japan has intermittently had a vigorous history of intellectual exchange with the broader world, which persisted even during its long centuries of sociopolitical isolation.[29] Yet across varied spheres of intellectual endeavor, "cartels of the mind" have also been a recurring pattern, even in democratic postwar Japan.[30] Such configurations have systematically impeded and distorted communication between Japan and the outside world, thereby delaying Japan's full globalization. Although operating in a totally different socioeconomic sphere, cartels of the mind are structurally similar to the NTT family, and appear to have surprisingly similar functional roles in slowing and limiting Japan's integration with foreign countries.

Like the NTT family, cartels of the mind include as members major actors in a specified functional area who could be potential rivals of one another. Such associations tend to inhibit competition. In the mass media area, cartels of the mind include representatives of key newspapers, such as *Yomiuri Shimbun*, *Asahi Shimbun*, and *Nihon Keizai Shimbun*, as well as radio and television networks. At the working level, typical expressions include the press clubs at

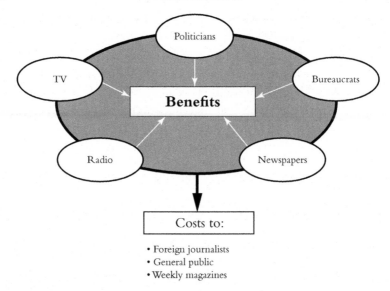

FIGURE 9.4   Traditional press clubs as circles of compensation

SOURCE: Author's illustration.

each of Japan's major ministries, and at the Prime Minister's office (*kantei*). These clubs provide arenas for periodic briefings, formal and informal, to accredited media representatives.[31] The underlying structure of the classic press-club system is presented in Figure 9.4.

Functionally, media-related cartels of the mind seek to socialize risk and internalize benefits, to the advantage of group members, much as the NTT family or the Japanese Bankers Association do in their own respective spheres. Concretely, the press clubs socialize risk by releasing sensitive government information to member organizations simultaneously, thus reducing the prospect of awkward media "scoops" that could embarrass both Japanese government authorities and journalists who are scooped. The press clubs also internalize benefits by withholding detailed information, including sensitive informal background briefings with key officials, from nonmembers of the clubs. In recent years the press clubs have gradually broadened their memberships and operating procedures—admitting selected foreign journalists, for example. Yet the embedded circle-of-compensation structure, pooling risks and rewards while externalizing costs, still persists.

Many of the service professions in Japan, like the press clubs, are also traditionally organized as cartels of the mind. Among the most organized has been the legal profession. As in the case of press clubs (or the NTT family, for that matter), associations in such areas tend to socialize risk (through collective action in dealing with challenges, ranging from financial crisis to trade liberalization). They also internalize benefits, as by standardizing professional fees at mutually comfortable levels and limiting access to membership. Traditionally, access to the Japanese legal profession is among the most restrictive in the world, with less than 3 percent of the first-time test takers passing.[32]

Universities are, by their nature, relatively liberal institutions, less amenable to collusive, cooperative action than many other service sectors. Yet in Japan they at times manifest broadly collaborative behavior, both as a class and also within individual institutions.[33] The Japan Association of National Universities, for example, has supported tuition levels and institutional rules that have allowed the number of four-year universities to grow from 507 in 1990 to 779 in 2015, in a nation whose university student base of eighteen-year-olds has simultaneously shrunk from over 2.0 million in 1990 to less than 1.2 million in 2015.[34] Some major Japanese universities have appeared hesitant about appointing tenure-track foreign faculty, even those with distinguished qualifications.[35]

Government has apparently played a role, at times, in sustaining university-related cartels of the mind. The Ministry of Education, Culture, Sports, Science and Technology, for example, has impeded competition between Japan's unwieldy private-university sector, with its 604 institutions,[36] and foreign universities, by being extremely hesitant to classify the latter as legitimate educational institutions. The Columbia University Teachers College Japan site, for example, was established in 1987, but only received permanent designation as a "foreign graduate school" by Japan's Ministry of Education in 2006.[37]

In Conclusion

Communications is a critical sector of linkage between any country and the broader world—growing increasingly important as communication costs decline and transnational socioeconomic interdependence rises. The technical quality of telecommunications is a crucial determinant—either constraint or facilitator—of a nation's ability to accommodate, and to benefit from, global change. Since the mid-1970s, as globalization has proceeded, the intellectual ability to communicate transnationally has also become a principal determinant of national economic growth potential.

Transnational communication thus has two central dimensions: the technological and the intellectual. In both respects, Japanese public policy and private practice constrain communication through circles of compensation. These circles do enhance short-term institutional stability and often profitability margins for the actors involved, particularly the domestic actors. The circles also, however, typically inhibit domestic competition, and discriminate against outside actors in ways that seriously impede Japan's globalization.

On the technical, hard side of the political economy, circles of compensation, epitomized by the NTT family in telecommunications, have encouraged the development of high-performance, high-cost devices, such as the i-mode cell phone and the vaunted supercomputers of Fujitsu and NEC, through preferential, high-margin procurement practices. Such practices successfully inhibited the penetration of foreign competition into the Japanese market for many years. Yet they also led Japanese suppliers to adopt internationally distinctive standards, in part for defensive reasons, and to focus on increasingly arcane markets of only limited interest to consumers outside Japan.

Japanese telecommunications suppliers operating within Japan, with its ubiquitous circles of compensation, have become ever more enmeshed in a "Galápagos syndrome" of exotic, if initially lucrative, high-margin production for limited domestic markets. That pattern has led to dramatic declines in global competitiveness and aggregate profitability, as well as persistent isolation from world markets. This evolution within Japan contrasts dramatically to the relative success of information-technology firms like SoftBank that have embraced and produced for global markets, often through subsidiaries and other affiliates based abroad.

On the soft side of communications, a surprisingly analogous trend is also occurring. The service professions, mass media, and intellectual life of universities outside Japan are all changing in dramatic fashion, pressured by increasingly insistent global economic and intellectual forces. Yet embedded circles of compensation, a heritage of the corporatist past, are delaying and diluting Japan's response to transnational forces in all these areas—the Abenomics reforms notwithstanding. These parochial circles facilitate stability and inhibit competition, precisely when adaptability and innovation—best fostered through competition—are needed to meet international challenges originating far beyond Japan's own shores.

10

Japan's Domestic Circles and the Broader World

In Chapters 4 through 9, we have just seen the repeated appearance of the circle-of-compensation paradigm in varied sectors of the Japanese domestic political economy. And we have observed the remarkable durability of this distinctive form of collective behavior within most of those sectors. Circles began appearing in areas ranging from agriculture to finance as early as the Meiji period, or even before. They have persisted into the twenty-first century—in the face of war, occupation, and multiple waves of political reform, including two major changes in political party leadership during the 2009–2012 period alone.

We have also seen the varied permutations in which circles of compensation appear, at the macro, meso, and micro political-economic levels. Such circles have, to be sure, had their dark sides. They have not been amenable to abstract, transcendent rules or principles, and have often pragmatically condoned discrimination and inequity. By diffusing risk, they have also at times also discouraged the impulse to innovate, and have reinforced parochialism.

As we have also observed, however, circles of compensation have at times contributed much to the remarkable economic growth, accompanied by domestic political-economic stability, that Japan experienced throughout most of its modern history, prior to the 1970s. Supported by such institutions, Japanese firms often took remarkable risks in the broader world during Japan's post–World War II years of high-speed growth. Although often discriminatory toward outsiders, including many newly arrived foreign firms, circles of compensation also often proved to be expansible, and to allow flexible entry, especially under crisis conditions, to new actors and social forces.

A Changing World and Its New Imperatives

Beginning in the 1970s, the global political economy rapidly grew far more integrated and volatile than has been true at any time since 1914, in at least five key dimensions—trade, capital, migration, knowledge, and, ultimately, politics.[1] Behind this integration were rapid advances in communications and transportation, together with growing financial market interdependence.[2] With the advent of China's Four Modernizations, India's economic reforms of the early 1990s, and the collapse of the Soviet Union at the end of 1991, an unprecedented degree of global geo-economic community began emerging, as well.[3]

Japan, with its pervasive subnational circles of compensation, which insulated its firms and general populace from external pressures for change, was slow to embrace the new, and increasingly volatile, world of globalization. A 2015 DHL worldwide survey, for example, ranked Japan only thirty-eighth in the overall global connectedness rankings, behind several similarly populated and resource endowed late developers, such as Singapore (second), Germany (seventh), and Korea (eighteenth). The United States ranked twenty-seventh. Japan also ranked behind Thailand (twenty-second), Bulgaria (thirty-second), and Vietnam (thirty-sixth), and just ahead of Saudi Arabia (thirty-ninth).[4] The analysis of previous pages suggests that pervasive subnational circles of compensation, with their parochial impact on individual incentives, are in large measure responsible for this recent Japanese hesitancy to globalize, even as more formal government constraints may have been central in isolating Japan during an earlier era.

Entrepreneurial Outliers That Suggest a Broader Conformist Pattern

To test the hypothesis that circles of compensation inhibit the willingness of Japanese firms to be proactive in the broader world, and thus to embrace the promise of globalization, it is useful to consider patterns that prevail in their absence. The automotive sector provides an important initial counterfactual that dramatizes the inhibiting role of circles of compensation on globalization in such sectors as telecommunications and air transport. Japanese communications firms, with their collusive history in the NTT family, and persisting intrasectoral links to one another, tend to suffer from a parochial "Galápagos syndrome," and have struggled to succeed in the global market, as discussed in Chapter 9.[5] In contrast, however, the auto industry, with a less cohesive set of institutional relationships and a correspondingly more vigorous pattern of intrasectoral competition, has engaged dynamically with global competitors outside Japan and become a major international force. Toyota Motor Corporation, for example, has almost continuously ranked, since 2008, as the largest auto firm in the world.[6] Together with Honda and Nissan, it accounts for over 30 percent of the automobile sales in the United States.[7]

Unlike steel, banking, and electric power—the so-called Gosanke ("honorable trio") of the Japanese big-business world, the auto industry evolved relatively late in Japan and did not develop such a powerful, well-institutionalized industry association as the other three did during the wartime mobilization of the late 1930s. That was one key factor facilitating competition and easing the path to globalization. A second key factor, synergistic with the first, was industry structure. Apart from Toyota, the auto sector featured a number of dynamic new players, especially Honda—diversifying into autos from motorcycles—that were conspicuously defiant of both the Ministry of International Trade and Industry and private-sector efforts to moderate "excessive competition."[8] Even after "orderly marketing agreements" became widespread after 1980, vigorous competition continued in knockdown system exports, as well as assembly abroad. The auto sector thus clearly appears to be an area where the absence of strong intrasectoral coordinating mechanisms, such as the circles of compensation typically provide, encourage newer and more entrepreneurial firms to compete through expanding global operations outside Japan.

The consumer-products sector, which has grown up largely since the 1950s, and never experienced the corporatist economic mobilization of the wartime era, provides additional examples, beyond autos, of Japanese global corporate success in the absence of circles of compensation. Daikin, for example, is the largest air-conditioning maker in the world, with over 60,000 global employees and 185 overseas manufacturing/sales facilities in over 70 countries. It has been in the air-conditioning business since 1951, and its overseas sales have grown steadily to over 70 percent of total net sales. In addition to more than 40 percent of market share in Japan, Daikin also has a well-established presence in China, Southeast Asia, Europe, and North America. China alone accounted for 18.5 percent of Daikin's total sales in fiscal year ended March 31, 2015.[9] Yet Daikin has no significant relationship with any major Japanese industry association to provide corporate backing.[10]

Another similarly successful Japanese global firm, which operates almost entirely without support from circles of compensation, is Unicharm, one of

Japan's largest manufacturers of personal-care products. Unicharm holds the top share of diaper sales in China and Indonesia, as well as rapidly expanding market share in India, competing head to head against Procter & Gamble, Kimberly-Clark, and a host of local players. Its overseas sales expanded from ¥137.5 billion to ¥345.9 billion between 2010 and 2014, driven by double-digit sales growth in China, Unicharm's most important market, even in the face of Sino-Japanese political tensions.[11] Like Daikin, Unicharm also lacks membership in any major Japanese domestic industry associations or industrial groupings.[12]

Daikin and Unicharm are both ranked among Japan's "best global brands" for 2015, according to a recent authoritative Tokyo marketing study.[13] According to *Harvard Business Review*, strategic approaches central to these two firms' success included the following: (1) strategic priority to middle-mass markets, (2) willingness to make deals—joint ventures and acquisitions with foreign firms, (3) strong commitment to emerging markets, and (4) localization, including product conception, production-equipment design, and sales planning.[14] None of these priorities are typically cultivated by circles of compensation within Japan.

Rakuten, Japan's emerging Internet giant, with nearly $5.9 billion in annual sales,[15] is another successful and rapidly globalizing firm with little circle-of-compensation involvement, although its president, Hiroshi Mikitani, is a former Industrial Bank of Japan alumnus.[16] It operates on a membership-system business model that connects services provided by Rakuten, including travel, telecom, and financial services, through a Rakuten Super Points reward system. Merchants from different sectors come together to form a virtual shopping mall, from which Rakuten's main profit source is fixed fees from merchants, as well as fees on various transactions that Rakuten provides through its virtual "*Rakuten Ichiba*" (Rakuten market).[17]

Like Daikin and Unicharm, Rakuten has shown a great propensity for deal making, as in its acquisition of e-commerce sites in Germany, Brazil, France, Thailand, Malaysia, Indonesia, and Taiwan.[18] Rakuten has also shown interest in emerging markets, especially in Southeast Asia. It is unusually global in its overall perspectives—since March 2010 the official language of business—even in Japan—has been English. And three of its six top executives in the engineering division do not even speak Japanese.[19]

The pattern that Daikin, Unicharm, and Rakuten epitomize—successfully globalizing Japanese firms that lack intimate relations with prominent domestic circles of compensation—appears to be generally prevalent beyond their particular industrial sectors, as well. Of the thirty firms identified as "Japan's best global brands" for 2015, for example, eight (including the top two) were in the automotive sector and four were in consumer electronics.[20] Almost all were firms that had arisen as major enterprises since World War II, in which industry associations are unimportant relative to patterns in such traditional sectors as steel, shipbuilding, finance, and electric power. Some electronics firms, especially smaller ones, outside institutionalized circles of compensation, continue to be highly competitive; many of the most important component suppliers to Apple and IBM, for example, are in Japan.

Some parts of the globalized and previously successful Japanese electronics sector have met severe recent challenges from Korea, and from entrepreneurial American firms like Apple, as noted in Chapter 9. Sony, for example, struggled during the 1980s to get its Betamax standard adopted internationally,[21] and incurred massive additional losses in fiscal years 2008 through 2014.[22] It is important to recognize, however, that Sony's recent problems appear to have been generated by closed, collaborative, bureaucratic industrial practices related to or similar to those of circles of compensation, rather than the more open, individualistic, and entrepreneurial practices of its own earlier years.[23] Sony has, for example, typically restricted access for subcontractors to its factories and been relatively closed in its relationships with prospective applications providers, in contrast to Apple and Samsung, which tend to be more open about interfaces and operating systems.[24]

Beyond autos and consumer electronics, there are also a few innovative, independent outlier firms, in sectors more generally dominated by circles of compensation, whose independence and global cosmopolitanism are exceptions that suggest the more general rule. Yamato Transport (the ubiquitous *kuroneko* or "black cat" of Japanese logistics, symbolized by its logo) has innovated many new transport services in Japan, based on the powerful networks that it laboriously created abroad, and became a global player in responding to both international and domestic business environments.[25] YKK, another individualistic, non-*keiretsu*, nongovernment-related business in a machinery sector where strong government ties are common, similarly rose through leadership vision, Industrial Bank of Japan long-term financing, and international expansion, to become the largest industrial fastener company in the world.[26] So did Suntory Beverage & Food, ranked fifth in *Fortune*'s ranking for the World's Most Admired Companies (Beverage Industry).[27] And Softbank, led by the maverick billionaire entrepreneur Masayoshi Son, has challenged and finessed circles of compensation, both inside and outside Japan, in energy, finance, and telecommunications.[28] He has not succeeded in all cases, but it has been Son's challenges to the Japanese business establishment, and his willingness to act them out on a global stage, that have fueled his dramatic economic rise since bringing the Internet portal Yahoo to Japan in 1996.

Non-circle companies vary greatly in scale and historical background, but representative firms do share important traits consistent with the circles of compensation argument, summarized in Table 10.1. As *outliers*—exceptions

TABLE 10.1

Outside the circles of compensation: Corporate characteristics of non-circle firms

Company	Industry	Founding date	*Keidanren* member	*Keiretsu* member	T10 holdings (%)
Rakuten, Inc.	e-commerce	1997	No	No	5.2 ± 5.3
Fast Retailing Co., Ltd.	Retail fashion	1963	No	No	7.2 ± 5.8
Yamato Holdings Co., Ltd.	Courier services	1919	Yes	No	3.6 ± 1.9
Unicharm Corporation	Chemicals	1961	Yes	No	5.1 ± 7.4
Toyota Motor Corporation	Automotive	1937	Yes	Limited	3.9 ± 2.7
YKK Group	Manufacturing	1934	No	No	5.9 ± 5.8
Daikin Industries, Ltd.	Electrical equipment	1924	Yes	No	2.7 ± 2.0
Kyocera Corporation	Electronics	1959	Yes	No	3.6 ± 2.5
Suntory Holdings Limited	Beverages	1899	Yes	No	7.3 ± 18.3

Financial Metrics

Company	Revenue growth (%)	Overseas sales (%)	Debt-equity ratio (%)	Return on equity (%)	Return on assets (%)
Rakuten, Inc.	17.3	—	543.1	6.7	1.0
Fast Retailing Co., Ltd.	21.3	35.9	50.2	14.2	9.5
Yamato Holdings Co., Ltd.	4.4	—	90.4	6.6	3.5
Unicharm Corporation	11.0	61.1	72.2	11.6	5.8
Toyota Motor Corporation	11.1	76.0	179.2	12.9	4.6
YKK Group	11.8	46.7	63.2	8.3	5.0
Daikin Industries, Ltd.	20.9	78.0	72.2	11.6	5.8
Kyocera Corporation	9.2	21.9	32.4	5.7	4.1
Suntory Holdings Limited	14.8	38.4	435.8	5.7	1.0

SOURCE: Annual reports and financial statements of selected companies compiled by the author.

NOTES: 1) "Revenue growth" is a company's average annual revenue growth rate since 2013; a change in accounting standards from JGAAP to IFRS by several selected companies prior to this period make longer trends difficult to calculate. 2) "Overseas sales," where available, is the percentage of a company's net sales that came from outside Japan in the most recently available source (FY2014 or FY2015). 3) "T10 holdings" contains both the mean and standard deviation of total shares outstanding held by each firm's ten largest shareholders; multiplying the mean amount by ten results in the percentage of a company's total stock that is held by this group. 4) "Debt-equity ratio," "Return on equity," and "Return on assets" are calculated using each company's annual FY2015 financial results, except in the case of Rakuten, Inc., which is for Q4 FY2015; there are occasional differences between these metrics and those reported by the company, and this is likely due to definitional differences between accounting standards. Definitions used here are as follows: Debt-equity ratio = (Total liabilities ÷ Shareholders' equity); Return on equity = (Net income ÷ Shareholders' equity); Return on assets = (Net income ÷ Total assets).

that demonstrate the general propositions at hand—they should hypotheti-cally be situated in consumer sectors, have low dependence on bank finance, and hold weak relations with *keiretsu*. Yet they should also exhibit high cor-porate sales growth, strong profitability, and competitiveness in international markets, as indicated by strong overseas sales. These outlier cases do, in fact, appear to generally manifest the empirical traits that theory would predict.

Politics in Support of Globalizing Entrepreneurs?

Innovation and *globalization* are two terms that have been in the favored lexicon of Japanese businessmen, bureaucrats, and politicians in the early twenty-first century. Yet they are also notions in tension with the operating reality that circles of compensation present. How much actual support have those liberal concepts, and the entrepreneurs who work to realize them, actually received in the domestic political process? An examination of the fate of major reform initiatives in tension with the communalist thrust of mainstream Japanese con-servative policy making is instructive in this regard.

There have been three major political reform movements with significant entrepreneurial business support since globalization pressures began deepening in the 1970s: (1) the New Liberal Club of the mid-1970s; (2) the Japan Renewal Party and Sakigake Party of the early 1990s, which banded together to elect Morihiro Hosokawa and Tsutomu Hata as Prime Ministers during 1993– 1994; and (3) the Democratic Party of Japan, which elected Yukio Hatoyama as Prime Minister in 2009, ruling Japan for three years, until losing power to the Liberal Democratic Party (LDP) in December, 2012. The first participated in reform cabinets dominated by the LDP; the second provided the core of a two coalition cabinets (Hosokawa and Hata) lasting less than a year; and the third assumed power with an overwhelming Lower House majority, only to be roundly defeated for reelection after little more than three years in office. The conservative LDP, with which virtually all circles of compensation have been affiliated, and which has nurtured them through subsidies, contracts, and supportive regulation, has, by contrast, held power for over 90 percent of the period since its foundation in 1955.

All three of these reform movements enjoyed some business support—from consumer-industry entrepreneurs like Akio Morita of Sony in the first two cases, and Kazuo Inamori of Kyocera in the case of the Democratic Party of Japan. It is noteworthy, however, that the business support was all from in-dividualistic entrepreneurs, and little came from big businesses affiliated with circles of compensation. It is also striking that the reformist coalitions did not last long in power, and could not achieve enduring institutional expression or substantial policy achievements, despite their support for causes to which large numbers of Japanese adhere.

The Japanese political economy has periodically given birth to non-party agenda-setting movements that likewise have aspirations to fundamentally change Japan. One of the most important such movements, whose evolution illustrates the dilemmas facing globalizing reformers in today's Japan, is the Japan Association of New Economy (JANE), known in Japanese as *Shin Keizai Renmei* or *Shinkeiren*. Founded by Hiroshi Mikitani in February 2010, JANE has made a series of concrete reformist proposals with strong economic logic, and broadly supported by the Japanese public, including a reduction of landing fees for Japan's major international airports; deregulation of Internet usage, and lowering of Internet fees; promotion of electronic commerce; creation of national strategic economic zones; and educational reforms to promote computer skills and English-language fluency.[29] It elected six influential politicians supporting its views in the July 2013 House of Councillors election.[30] Nevertheless, since mid-2013 JANE's supporting membership has been steadily declining, and it has failed to attract either political funds or additional Diet adherence, despite the economic rationality and the seeming political attractiveness of its reformist orientation.[31]

Cooperative Patterns Where Circles of Compensation Prevail

Although several of Japan's most successfully globalized companies have foresworn circles of compensation, with frequently positive implications for their global competitiveness, such circles are nevertheless common in the Japanese domestic political economy as a whole. What implications do their omnipresence in Japan have for that nation's relations with the broader world, including the slow and incomplete pace of its globalization? What role do circles of compensation play in the "permeable insulation" that separates Japan from the political-economic environment beyond its shores?[32] And what significance does the resultant interactive pattern—Japan's circles and the broader world—have for the international system as a whole? These are the questions of global importance which the balance of this chapter explores.

Formal Barriers and Their Support Coalitions

From the outset, it is important to make a broad, twofold distinction among the circles of compensation that we have examined: (1) those that impose *direct barriers* to Japan's interaction with the broader world, as in agriculture; and (2) those which, although not imposing explicit barriers, nevertheless generate *parochial incentives* channeling Japanese behavior away from transnational interaction, as in communications. These two patterns have contrasting internal dynamics within Japan, and different external implications for Japan's relations with other nations.

Throughout the bulk of Japan's modern history, up to the 1990s, the set of obstacles comprising direct barriers was prominent and explicit. Since the 1980s formal barriers created by domestic circles of compensation have waned in importance, in most sectors. Yet many of the parochial incentives of the past still remain. Through the "in-group" parochialism that they systematically generate, these circles simultaneously stabilize domestic transactions and complicate Japan's interdependence with the broader world.

From the case studies presented in Chapters 4 through 9, it is clear that the formal barriers to deeper Japanese interdependence with other countries are especially pronounced in agriculture and transportation. Japan continues to have tariff-rate quotas or high tariffs on a variety of commodity lines, beginning with rice.[33] Such barriers insulate inefficient Japanese agriculture, where producer supports are estimated at close to 50 percent of the value of production, from the rationalizing effect of international trade.[34] Japan's health and safety regulations also sharply constrain agricultural imports—not only of raw agricultural products but processed goods, as well.

Behind the thicket of restrictive practices, creating clear if indirect barriers to cross-border trade, lies a broad coalition of social groups. This parochial coalition includes farmers, distributors, agricultural processors, bureaucrats, and politicians of both the right and the left. Such groups make dismantling these obstacles a tortuous process at best.

The international barriers erected by circles of compensation in the transportation area are structurally different from those in agriculture, but have similarly trade-distorting effects. Landing fees at Japanese airports are among the highest in the world, while port fees at Japanese harbors are similarly exorbitant, particularly compared to those of neighbors in the East Asian region. Japanese customs and transshipment regulations are also complex, while storage and reprocessing facilities are often poor. Narita and Kansai International Airports pale in the scale of their warehouse facilities and affiliated service parks compared to counterparts in Korea or Singapore. These barriers and inefficiencies may not explicitly suppress international trade, but they demonstrably render it less economically attractive for businesses that contemplate commercial activities through, to, or from Japan.

Several other sectors of the Japanese domestic political economy not examined here exhibit similarly explicit barriers to transborder economic interaction with the broader world. The pharmaceutical sector, for example, is notable for complex health and safety regulations, including testing procedures, that separate Japanese markets from those elsewhere. Much of the Japanese telecom industry, including the huge cell-phone segment, is technically distinctive in parallel respects, due to unique standards that segment it off from global markets. Even Japanese typing paper is of an atypical width and length that complicates its use in international transactions.

Such transborder restrictions and specification differences have been a central target of continuing foreign trade liberalization efforts since the 1960s, however, and have been steadily reduced in multiple rounds of international bargaining.[35] Those incessant pressures, amplified by Japan's persistent global trade surpluses, have led to a steady reduction of formal border constraints, albeit not necessarily to flexible and unconstrained international transactions. Insulation of a sort from global incentives and pressures thus continues to prevail, although it remains permeable, in the sense that it can be penetrated with effort by determined, well-versed, or well-connected actors.

The Indirect Impact of Parochial Incentives

Across the bulk of the sectors we have considered in the foregoing chapters, the challenges to Japanese globalization and growth that are posed by circles of compensation are even more subtle and indirect, although by no means less real. Indeed, it is the subtle, indirectly parochial impact on behavior of incentives within circles of compensation—conditioning it to respond sensitively to insider concerns, while remaining unresponsive to developments outside—that is most important going forward. We have seen such a bias in sectors ranging from land policy and finance to energy, transportation, and politics. These "insider incentives" encourage private bankers to collaborate in underwriting national debt, even at below-market interest rates. They similarly encourage local communities to accept nuclear plants in their midst, or idiosyncratic standards in telecommunications that are not supported in the broader world.

Much of the pronounced Japanese parochialism in the face of global developments is ultimately rooted in the country's venerable "land-standard system" (tochi hon'isei), with its origins as far back as the eighth century. The notion that ultimate value is embodied in land has caused Japanese firms to focus on real-estate transactions, with their clear territorial focus. That notion was strongly reinforced for over a century—from mid-Meiji until the collapse of the Heisei financial bubble (roughly 1890–1990) by the "invest, then save" strategy of financing industrial development through bank lending based on steadily appreciating real-estate collateral.

This approach caused Japanese businessmen, bureaucrats, and politicians to prioritize expansionist, construction-oriented fiscal policies at the expense of broader, service-oriented global initiatives, even when real estate–based speculation opened the prospect of economic disaster, as occurred in the collapse of the Heisei financial bubble during the early 1990s. The same land-oriented incentive structures also made it difficult for Japan to recover following the bubble's collapse by writing off real-estate debts and diversifying away from land-intensive sectors, including service industries.

Japan's circles of compensation in banking and corporate finance have intensified the parochialism and rigidity implicit in the land-standard system, even as eroding border restrictions opened Japanese finance in revolutionary new ways to the broader world. These parochial circles, a veritable Bankers' Kingdom, inhibited foreclosures and radical corporate restructurings that would otherwise have forcefully reordered corporate governance in the business world, as happened in smaller industrialized states like Korea and Sweden.[36] Stakeholder dominance in the corporate-governance realm reinforced this general tendency toward rigidity, conservatism, and pervasive reliance on indirect finance, although some marginal change has been discernable since the mid-2000s.[37]

Domestic Rigidity and the Rise of the Carry Trade

Rigidity in Japanese domestic finance, intensified by circles of compensation that diffuse externally generated risk and reward, has had momentous global consequences, not all positive for Japan. Japanese financial institutions and the firms to which they lend have been saddled by unresolved debt problems, generated by serious breakdowns in the credit-monitoring system as financial liberalization proceeded in recent years.[38] As a consequence, the repeated macroeconomic stimulus packages that Japan has undertaken since the late 1990s to reflate its crippled economy have had only limited impact in sparking domestic recovery. Instead, a substantial portion of the funds they provided have been recycled out of Japan through the so-called carry trade, in large part by foreign rather than Japanese banks and hedge funds, to reflate countries as far removed from Japan as Australia and Iceland. This carry trade has often weakened the yen, affording some temporary benefit to Japanese export sectors. Yet it has also left spiraling obligations for Japanese taxpayers, despite the limited long-term benefit to domestic recovery.

Energy has been characterized by similar collaborative patterns of domestic collective action that bear mixed implications for Japan's broader global roles. Circles of compensation involving utilities, long-term credit banks, industrial bureaucrats, and politicians allowed Japan in the 1970s to forge ahead coura-geously with massive, high-risk capital investments in nuclear power. These were spread broadly across the nation, including ambitious, multibillion-dollar reprocessing facilities. Yet the same circles that diffused the risk of whole-sale investment in nuclear megafacilities also rendered Japan less responsive to broader pressures in the outside world, for adoption of smaller nuclear plants and alternative-energy technology. The circles also muted responses to sudden crises within, including the March 2011 tsunami-driven disaster, and the near nuclear-meltdown at Fukushima. Circles of compensation in energy, as else-where, are thus a double-edged sword: They reduce short-term risk to estab-lished participants, while also externalizing costs and discouraging innovation.

Even where domestic circles of compensation have not imposed direct bar-riers to trade and investment, they have subtly insulated Japan from the outside world—a form of "permeable insulation" with fateful domestic consequences when that outside world is changing and turbulent.[39] These circles have also created almost imperceptible structural rigidities, rooted in parochial incen-tives, that have slowed Japan's response to dynamic global forces, especially when the optimal international response has been risky for domestic actors. For many years, as long as the global system itself was relatively static, these subtle, circle-induced domestic rigidities did not matter much in practice. Yet their inhibiting effect on Japan's integration with the world became in-creasingly consequential from the late 1970s on,[40] as the pace of globalization worldwide began to accelerate.

The earliest changes in the international parameters within which Japan's domestic political economy operates came in the financial sphere: the break-down of the Bretton Woods system and the transition to floating currencies and freer global-capital movements. These developments began affecting Japan substantially when Tokyo fatefully revised its Foreign Exchange Law in De-cember 1979, and started to authorize freer cross-border transactions by Japa-nese banks, securities firms, and insurance companies. Capital began flowing more and more freely across Japan's borders, in response to market forces, in magnitudes that since the 1980s have reached into the trillions of U.S. dollars, as indicated in Figure 10.1.

At the same time, however, domestic rigidities in corporate governance, and in the land-standard system, inhibited Japanese domestic banks, trading companies, and manufacturers in their strategic response to deepening trans-border competition for low-cost domestic Japanese capital. Domestic rigidi-ties and bad debt within Japan, intensified by circles of compensation there, have inhibited Japanese financial institutions from seizing new opportunities

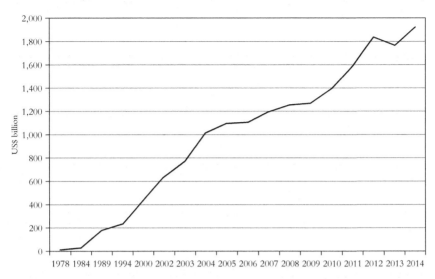

FIGURE 10.1   Total Japanese holding of U.S. Treasury securities

SOURCE: U.S. Department of Treasury, "Historical Data from the Surveys during 1974–2014," http://www
.treasury.gov/resource-center/data-chart-center/tic/Pages/fpis.aspx.

NOTES: 1) Figures before 2002 include only long-term holdings. Figures for 2002–2014 include both long-term
holdings and short-term holdings. 2) Figures for 1978–1994 reflect end of December positions, figure for 2000
reflects end of March position, and figures for 2002–2014 reflect end of June positions.

for international arbitrage. The hesitancy of Japanese firms has thus provided important new opportunities for foreign competitors, who became principal mediators of the rapidly expanding new trans-Pacific flows discussed above.[41] Continuing rigidities within Japanese domestic finance also inhibited Japanese firms from playing the dynamic and potentially important role in spearheading Japan's recovery from recession during the 1990s and 2000s that they had once played in their nation's earlier economic success. The perverse result was protracted domestic stagnation.

The pace of information flows and political interaction across national borders also began to accelerate globally across the 1980s and 1990s, especially following the collapse of the Soviet Union and the waning of the Cold War.[42] The telecommunications revolution accelerated this process, as did the rise of nonstate actors, including both multinational corporations and nongovernmental organizations. Local information cartels and rigidities in domestic politics made it difficult for Japan to respond flexibly to the revolutionary global developments, or even to fully comprehend them. These parochial rigidities impeded both globalization and Japanese economic growth.

Gaps between Japan's parochial domestic structures and developments in the broader world became increasingly crucial, and debilitating for Japan, as the pace of global change accelerated over the 1980s and 1990s. Meanwhile, structural rigidities within Japan itself, induced by the domestic circles of compensation, continued to intensify. The fact that many of Japan's increasingly competitive Asian neighbors embraced global change more rapidly than Japan itself has intensified Tokyo's challenge still further. The question now is how and indeed whether Japan will be able to respond, as the gap between a slowly changing Japan and a more rapidly evolving global system continues to widen. Nascent innovations through Abenomics during 2013–2016, such as the National Strategic Special Zones (*kokka senryaku tokku* in Japanese),[43] have only marginally begun to change this dynamic.

Fashioning an Effective Response

Human networks are growing increasingly important in international affairs, as global problems become more complex and cross-border transactions proliferate. Circles of compensation are human networks that in their domestic context have proven their ability to preserve social stability, and to diffuse economic risk. These circles can also accommodate policy innovation, provided sufficient resources are available for allocation among circle members. The problem in Japan's relations with the broader world is not circles of compensation per se, but rather the parochial bias that domestic circles almost invariably generate, through their in-group bias and the lack of institutions capable of and willing to contravene that parochial orientation.

Leadership and the Problem of Collective Action

Among the distinctive features of the Japanese political economy, from a comparative perspective, is the lack of structural catalysts for change, the rhetoric of Abenomics notwithstanding. Japan is a homogeneous society, with no salient regional divisions, in contrast to even other such homogeneous countries, including Korea and to some extent Germany. In contrast to most other Group of 7 nations, Japan has few deep socioeconomic divisions or pluralistic interests, lacking powerful labor unions, for example. Institutionally, Japan lacks a strong chief executive, in contrast to Korea or the United States, and its legislative process is highly complex, offering great scope to assorted domestic veto players. Additionally, important sectors of the political economy, including most of those considered in this volume, are highly regulated, and home to powerful embedded, status-quo-oriented interests. The patterns of differentiation suggested here are presented generally in Figure 10.2.

In sum, there are few alternative power centers in the Japanese political economy to mainstream bureaucrats and politicians that can serve as a rallying

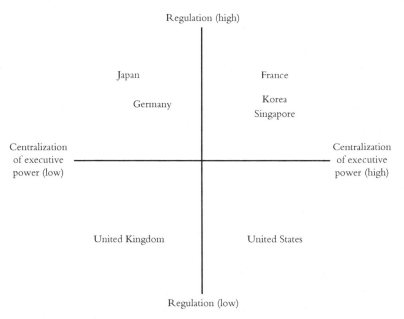

FIGURE 10.2   Regulation and centralization in comparative perspective

SOURCE: Author's illustration.

point and catalyst for major structural change. In this respect, today's Japan is in a far less dynamic situation than late-Edo Japan, when outlying regions like Choshu and Satsuma could serve as catalysts for epic change.[44] Structural-reform proposals such as the "third arrow" of Abenomics may well be able to broaden circles of compensation—as by expanding opportunity for women in the workforce. Yet these proposals lack the capacity to fundamentally transform the sociopolitical homogeneity of Japan as a whole.

Japan's convoluted social-conciliatory processes are a further barrier to innovative collective action. At the micro level, group decision-making in Japan is highly sensitive and refined, but at the national level, decision-making processes are highly complex, affording extraordinary latitude for veto players, who can obstruct decisive action and reinforce parochialism. A good example is the Japanese Diet, where short sessions, multiple chambers, complex rules on committee deliberation, and broad, ambiguous bureaucratic participation requirements make decisions difficult. They perversely handcuff the foreign-policy process, in particular, to domestic political requirements, and forestall active legislative response to globalization pressures.[45]

The consequence of Japan's monistic sociopolitical structure, its weak central institutions, and its high degree of regulation is to make decisive structural change difficult, except in a crisis. Since the late 1940s, in particular, it has been excruciatingly difficult to centralize the power to transform existing social structures through political means, even under strong, entrepreneurial leaders like Yasuhiro Nakasone, Junichirō Koizumi, and Shinzō Abe. Only market forces seem able to accomplish major transformation, as they have done in the gradual modification of the *keiretsu* structure since the 1990s.[46] Yet even market-induced structural change is not easy, owing to the pervasive risk-sharing and risk-diffusing circles of compensation.

Looking to the future, Japan has several options. One is to discard the circle-of-compensation concept itself as a paradigm for ordering public policy, and to embrace transcendent global principles, such as the notion of "a world of liberty under law."[47] While perhaps a laudable general idea, this course is in strong tension with both Japanese traditional, situationally oriented values and the deeply embedded institutions that we have reviewed in Chapters 4 through 9. There is some scope for globally oriented firms that do *not* rely on circles of compensation, especially in consumer-oriented industries. Yet their role at the heart of the Japanese political economy is inevitably limited, if only because of the deeply embedded structural heritage of history.

More Cosmopolitan Circles of Compensation?

Within the important spheres where circles of compensation inevitably remain there are also, however, two additional, potentially productive options: (1) to broaden domestic circles by introducing more international and gender-neutral viewpoints, and (2) to work at constructing international circles of compensation, transcending Japan itself. Both are consistent with Japan's traditional domestic reliance on collective sharing of risk as well as reward, and its emphasis on nurturing trustworthy human networks. Both options could also meaningfully increase consciousness of the changing world order within Japan, and likewise generate incentives for more proactive Japanese involvement in creating a new, post–Cold War world order. From a broader perspective, they could also enhance Japan's influence on the international stage, by enhancing Japanese presence in increasingly important global social, economic, and political networks.[48]

Domestic circles of compensation in Japan can be meaningfully broadened, first of all, by affording more opportunities to women. This involves not only legal protection and social support for career opportunities, but also provision of support facilities that make professional careers more attractive to the potential employees involved. The emphasis of "Abenomics 2.0" on improved childcare and social security is a small step in the right direction.[49]

Domestic circles can also be broadened by adding foreign participants, preferably those fluent in Japanese and conversant with Japanese cultural norms. They could also allow foreign members of the circles to systematically share the risks and rewards of group membership, as is commonly true in the case of Japanese members with collaborative organizations. This is already happening at the corporate level, where Kawasaki Heavy Industries cooperates with Boeing to manufacture the Boeing 777, and Japanese component producers cooperate with Apple to produce the iPhone.[50]

This pattern of transnational risk and reward sharing appears to prevail already in the life-insurance industry. More foreigners could be placed on the boards of Japanese corporations in other sectors, as well as on advisory boards of the Japanese government. There are cosmopolitan efforts in both these directions, but the pace needs to be intensified, so as to build a critical mass within Japan that is sensitive to broader global socioeconomic trends.

A second imperative is for Japan to play a more proactive role in initiating international circles of compensation within which it plays an influential role. This is more than mere lobbying—it is a matter of configuring broad multilateral groups that work, with Japanese support, to achieve ends that Japan finds congenial. A good start could be made by convening periodic international conferences in areas of special Japanese credibility, such as environmental protection or energy efficiency, and using these gatherings to develop ongoing, institutionalized transnational networks. China, Russia, and Korea have all pursued this approach through transnational networking vehicles such as the Boao Forum for Asia, the St. Petersburg International Economic Forum, the Valdai Discussion Club, and the Jeju Forum.

Cosmopolitan circles of compensation, involving a central Japanese role, complemented by meaningful foreign input, could also be created outside Japan. A dynamic new prototype is the Stanford Silicon Valley–New Japan Project, founded by the US-Asia Technology Management Center at Stanford University, which aims to "create a sustained platform for interactions between Silicon Valley and Japan."[51] New private-sector initiatives such as the Geodesic Capital Fund, involving Japanese capital support for innovative start-ups in Silicon Valley, also serve this objective.[52] Such trans-Pacific collaboration could help, in particular, to address Japan's chronic difficulties in the area of venture capital—directly related to the circles of compensation domestically within Japan.[53] An important start was made during Prime Minister Shinzō Abe's April 2015 visit to Silicon Valley.[54]

Beyond Circles Entirely?

Circles of compensation have deep roots in Japanese history, reinforced by the homogeneous nature of Japanese society, and Japanese norms of collective responsibility. They are also deeply embedded institutionally, giving rise to conservative microeconomic incentive structures. Given these realities, how likely is radical change in Japan's circle of compensation–centric resource-allocation system?

Certainly there are marginal pressures for change, driven by market forces, outside pressures, and technological changes, such as the emergence of the Internet. Yet the pace of *structural* change in Japan—beyond broadening circles of compensation—will inevitably be slow, given the institutional strength of existing circles, the conservative bias which their internal incentives impart, and the complexity of the central Japanese decision-making that would be needed to transform them. Only externally induced shocks or suasion—the Meiji Restoration or the post–World War II Allied Occupation—have historically proved capable of provoking wholesale reforms in Japan's decision-making system as a whole.

The body politic of Japan may thus be saddled with circles of compensation for some time. Yet small, explicitly liberalized parts of the country could be an exception. Prime Minister Abe has stressed the concept of special economic zones in his Abenomics program, and this may well be the most viable element in his "third arrow" package of structural reforms. Although special economic zones in previous policy incarnations have not proved capable of inducing fluid, Western-style individualistic competitive behavior, they may have better prospects over the coming decade, particularly in the Tokyo area, as Japan and the world prepare for the 2020 Olympics, and as incentives for foreign investment into Japan improve.

In Conclusion

Across a century of rapid economic growth and intermittent international crisis, from the Meiji Restoration until the collapse of the Heisei financial bubble in the early 1990s, Japan was well served domestically by circles of compensation. Those circles allowed Japanese private and public decision-makers to cope with risk and uncertainty, while pursuing aggressive, often innovative strategies that fueled economic growth, especially in capital-intensive sectors such as steel, shipbuilding, petrochemicals, and electric power. Such configurations were the envy of many across the world. There were, of course, costs, but those were externalized to nonmembers of the circles and the wider world.

In a static international system, within which Japan was not called upon to innovate or lead, and where it lacked nearby economic rivals, circles of compensation within Japan caused few complications for the country's international role. America was the pioneer, and Japan could be content as an imitative pursuer, leveraged in its ability to imitate, especially in capital-intensive sectors, by the cohesiveness of human ties among its corporate leaders, bureaucrats, and politicians. The world was still willing to countenance explicit barriers that Japan's domestic circles created, in sectors such as agriculture or transportation. And the domestic constraints on Japanese innovation and activism, due to the land-standard system and stakeholder-dominant corporate-governance system, had little consequence for either international affairs or for Japan domestically.

In the era of globalization that began dawning during the late 1970s, the adverse consequences of Japan's domestic circles of compensation—in their nature parochial—have begun to multiply. The circles can meaningfully diffuse microeconomic risk, to be sure. Yet they simultaneously increase prices and inhibit innovation.

The pace of change in the global system is clearly accelerating—in finance, in information flow, and in international political-economic association. Meanwhile, Japan, to the extent that circles of compensation prevail, is continuing to resist structural change, and remaining ambivalent toward external stimuli, filtered as they are through a risk-diffusing lens. Countervailing forces to this inertia, including national leadership, lack the institutional strength to easily overcome the parochial tendencies induced by the circles and reinforced by culture, especially when national political leadership is unstable and rapidly changing. Domestic circles are both impeding the process of domestic restructuring, on problems like bad debt, and inhibiting a proactive Japanese international leadership role. That leadership role is much needed today, due to Japan's massive international economic scale, which is of particular geostrategic importance in the Pacific as China rises.

One potential response for Japan to rapidly deepening globalization could be to actively embrace abstract global norms, and the idealistic vision of a "world of liberty under law." That would be difficult in practice, given both Japan's situational values and deeply embedded corporatist institutions. There are niche areas where circles of compensation do not prevail, but most of those do not lie at the heart of the Japanese system. National Strategic Special Zones, being actively promoted since 2014, could provide marginally more leeway for entrepreneurship and free competition to develop.

More realistic for the political economy as a whole is to adapt the circles of compensation concept itself to the realities of a global world. More foreigners knowledgeable about Japan, as well as more Japanese women, could be involved in Japanese domestic circles of compensation, such as boards of directors and government advisory committees. Another approach would be a more proactive Japanese role in creating new transnational networks and circles of compensation within which Japan plays a leading role, akin to the positions that China, Russia, and Korea are playing as hosts to their own international forums. Cosmopolitan circles of compensation outside Japan, such as trans-Pacific innovation funds based in Silicon Valley, could be another possibility.

Models for the Future

As has been suggested throughout this volume, the prevalent political-economic model in Japan since the 1930s has privileged and maximized stability as well as harmony, often thereby constraining the operation of market forces in some sectors while enhancing predictability across the political economy as a whole. This communalistic pattern, epitomized in circles of compensation, many of which feature banks as connectors, is inherently conservative. It internalizes benefits to group members while externalizing costs. The pattern has generally prevailed at both the national and sectoral levels, in Japan and a small number of other late-developing political economies, principally those that have experienced capital-intensive industrialization. Although disrupted by transnational forces in such heavily traded sectors as the automotive industry and consumer electronics, this configuration has been especially salient in traditionally nontraded sectors of the Japanese political economy, such as finance, agriculture, transportation, and communications. Although particularly prominent in Japan, it represents a social-science construct of significant relevance to the broader world.

Since the late 1970s, and especially since the collapse of the Soviet bloc in the early 1990s, all the major nations of the world have been forced to interact with an increasingly global political economy. Circles of compensation, which gained currency and utility as risk-diffusing mechanisms during the high-growth 1960s, have had particular trouble in adapting to this new paradigm. Privileging their long-standing members, and prioritizing group stability, the circles have been a profoundly conservative and parochial force, inhibiting the adaptability of domestic systems to the strong pressures for political-economic change that are often provoked by globalization.

This problem of subnational parochialism has been especially serious in nations like Japan, where circles of compensation are especially prominent, due to the intimacy of government–business relations forced by the exigencies of capital-intensive industrialization, and one-party conservative political dominance. During the 1990s, such parochialism generated serious trade frictions and exacerbated financial crises, resulting in liberalizing changes at the macro level, such as relaxation of capital-export restraints. Macro changes, such as relaxation of foreign-exchange controls, in turn made modifying changes at the micro level—including transformation of the circles of compensation—increasingly urgent. Yet the circles themselves have been intrinsically resistant to change.

How can Japan escape the inhibiting influence of circles of compensation on its response to globalization, and at the same time capture the positive implications of such circles for domestic stability, as for social harmony? And what relation has Japan's own experience to trends in the broader world? These are the vexing, complex, and increasingly urgent questions addressed in this chapter. We approach the problem of improving on the rapidly eroding status quo by presenting alternative models in use elsewhere that address the key external challenges that Japan itself confronts, but nevertheless do so with more efficiency than the traditional Japanese modus operandi can provide.

Parameters for Comparison

To assure that alternative models are as relevant as possible in gauging the response of a given nation to the stresses of globalization, it seems important that the nations whose responses are being compared confront parallel external stimuli. Challenges from abroad appear to be especially intense in the case of Japan. First, Japan has one of the highest population densities of any nation in the world, with over 120 million inhabitants living in a highly mountainous archipelago no larger than California. The challenge of global adaptation is compounded secondly, by Japan's high geographical concentration of economic activity—the country is not only as small as California, but also concentrates nearly one-twelfth of global gross domestic product (GDP) within that limited space.

Japan's third distinctive challenge relates to energy. The country has a huge industrial base, with numerous energy-intensive manufacturing sectors, like steel and shipbuilding. The country is also home to over 120 million affluent consumers, who drive cars, enjoy air conditioning, and run a wide variety of home appliances. Yet despite its massive energy demand, Japan has almost no domestic oil and gas reserves;[1] indeed, it imports 94 percent of its total hydrocarbon requirements, with over 82 percent of that total, in the case of oil, flowing from the Persian Gulf. In contrast, imports only count for 14 percent of U.S. total energy need, about a quarter of which is imported from the Gulf region.[2]

Japan's fourth and final challenge, going forward, is institutional reform. Its bureaucracy, politics, and business structures were configured for a catch-up, late-developer world in which high financial leverage, patient capital, and trade protection presented competitive advantages. In the world of the twenty-first century, however, more cosmopolitan and market-oriented structures that nevertheless support stable growth are urgently needed.

America's creative, dynamic responses to globalization have provided a stimulating and often inspirational benchmark for much of the world. Yet precisely due to its contrasting economic profile (copious energy reserves, service-oriented economic structure, low population density, and Anglo-Saxon "first-mover" embedded institutions), the United States may not be the most appropriate prism through which to view Japan, or to use as a reference point in generating prescriptions for Japan's future. In this chapter, we present policy paradigms from Germany, Singapore, and South Korea—late developers that all suggest instructive models of potential relevance for Japan's own future, particularly in the areas of globalization and growth.

These three alternative cases are good benchmarks for comparison with Japan, because they confront the same four critical challenges that necessarily condition Japan's own response to a changing world. As noted in Table 11.1, all three countries have high population densities. All are late developers. All three have a high concentration of economic activity in a limited geographical space. And all three depend heavily on energy imports, with the volatile Middle East looming large as a major supplier, particularly for Singapore and South Korea.

As suggested in Table 11.1, Japan, Korea, Germany, and Singapore, despite their geographical and cultural heterogeneity, all confront basically similar geo-economic challenges in world affairs. As Table 11.1 also indicates, however, the United States—a nation of plenty—is a clear outlier with respect to these environmental variables. Its anomalous standing reinforces the proposed approach of benchmarking three reference cases in order to generate useful recommendations for future Japanese public policy.

There is also an important historical-institutional dimension that must not be forgotten. The three reference cases, together with Japan, are all

TABLE 11.1

Limited resources and challenging external environments:
Japan in comparative perspective

Country	Population density (millions/km²)	Concentration of economic activity (US$)	Energy imports (%)	Gulf dependence (%)	Late developer?
Japan	348.25	11,310,230.44	93.85	82.65	Yes
South Korea	519.33	14,136,961.69	83.47	85.94	Yes
Singapore	7,828.86	414,058,426.50	97.53	> 66.67	Yes
Germany	233.58	9,628,084.09	62.10	4.22	Yes
Austria	104.34	4,532,307.52	63.53	17.47	Yes
Switzerland	209.71	16,821,984.60	51.54	0.00	Yes
United States	35.14	1,961,973.54	14.04	25.82	No

SOURCES: World Bank, "Population density (people per sq. km of land area)," *World Development Indicators*. [Data for 2015]; World Bank, "GDP (current US$)," *World Development Indicators*. [Data for 2015]; World Bank, "Land area (sq. km)," *World Development Indicators*. [Data for 2015]; World Bank, "Energy imports, net (% of energy use)," *World Development Indicators*. [Data for 2013]; IEA, *Oil Information 2015* (Paris: OECD Publishing, 2015), doi: 10.1787/oil-2015-en. [Data for 2013]; U.S. Energy Information Administration, "Singapore," http://www.eia.gov/beta/international/analysis.cfm?iso=SGP.

NOTES: 1) "Concentration of economic activity" is defined here as nominal GDP per square kilometer of land area. 2) "Gulf dependence" is defined here as the share of total crude oil imports from the Middle East. Data compiled by the author. IEA's Oil Information does not include country profile of Singapore. According to the EIA, in 2014 Singapore imported more than two-thirds of its total crude oil imports from the UAE, Saudi Arabia, and Qatar. See U.S. Energy Information Administration, "Singapore," http://www.eia.gov/beta/international/analysis.cfm?iso=SGP.

late-developer, coordinated market economies (CMEs). All four struggled historically to compete with the Anglo-Saxon early developers, or liberal market economies (LMEs), and created institutions enabling them to do so effectively.[3] All four thus prioritized rapid growth and political stability, while being distinctively tolerant of developmental and corporatist ideologies. The four thus bear important institutional and ideological similarities to one another—not shared with the LMEs—that make comparison among them especially appropriate.

Japan's Deepening Challenge

Seen from a comparative standpoint, with other late-developing CMEs as a benchmark, Japan has had mixed success at economic globalization. It has risen slowly, if at all, in the highly regarded KOF Index of Globalization, from 64th of 141 countries included in 1970, to 48th of 207 in 2016.[4] Yet it remains decisively behind pace-setting CMEs, actually declining in its relative standing against them in economic globalization since the early 1990s, as suggested in Figure 11.1.

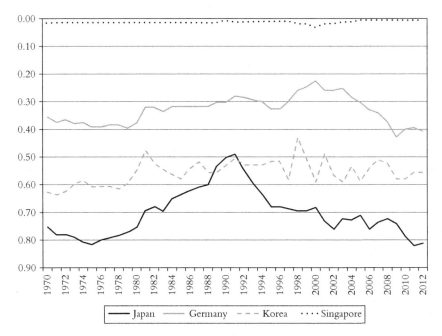

FIGURE 11.1   KOF Index of Economic Globalization, 1970–2012

SOURCE: KOF Swiss Economic Institute, *KOF Index of Globalization* (March 5, 2015 Version), http://globaliza tion.kof.ethz.ch/. Originally published as Axel Dreher, "Does Globalization Affect Growth? Evidence from a New Index of Globalization," *Applied Economics* 38, no. 10 (2006), 1091–1110.

NOTE: Rankings have been adjusted to a relative scale of 0–1, where approaching 0 indicates an increase in position, to compensate for the inclusion of more countries over time.

Disaggregated data on economic globalization suggest that mean tariff rates in all four CME nations under consideration (Japan, Korea, Germany, and Singapore) have declined throughout the 1970–2012 period. Japan appears to diverge from the three other late developers most strongly with regard to economic globalization indicators, such as foreign direct investment stocks and portfolio investment. Japan also declined, together with Korea, during the latter half of the 2000s decade, on the restrictions to international trade and capital flows.[5]

Lessons for Japan

The three reference cases are relevant to this research along two distinct dimensions:

1. How they help to modify and correct the defects of the circle-of-compensation model, whose functioning, conservative character

and deeply embedded standing in Japan have been presented in the
foregoing pages; and

2. How their example can help improve the general functioning of the
    political-economic sectors that are highlighted in the foregoing analy-
    sis. In this chapter, we address both questions with special precedence
    to how circles of compensation can be rendered less pernicious and
    more efficacious in supporting national goals.

Circles of compensation are slowly eroding in several sectors of the Japanese
political economy, such as finance, agriculture, and real estate, as the sector-
specific chapters have shown. Yet such circles are likely to persist for some time
as central features of the Japanese political economy, for three reasons. First,
the prevailing incentive structures of the circles themselves, which internalize
benefits and externalize costs, are by definition resistant to change. Second,
the political institutions of Japan, particularly the byzantine legislative structure, make change difficult except in a political or economic crisis.[6] Third,
the homogeneous character of the Japanese political economy, characterized
by an absence of major ethnic cleavages, powerful antiestablishment interest groups, or competitive opposition parties, makes sweeping institutional
change extremely difficult.

Given the embedded influence and likely durability of circles of compensation in most areas, as evidenced in the limited success of Prime Minister Shinzō
Abe's "third-arrow" program of structural reform,[7] the focus of cross-national
comparison needs to lie on ways to remedy defects that circles of compensation manifest in a twenty-first-century world of deepening globalization.
These defects lie in three functional areas:

1. *External monitoring and strategic support.* Traditionally, long-term
    credit banks, industrial groups, and government institutions provided
    political-economic support for patient capital, with intrusive moni-
    toring and administrative guidance mitigating potential dangers of
    moral hazard. The finance-centric mechanism broke down in the late
    1990s, and has not been fully reconstituted and reconfigured for a
    globalized world.

2. *Innovation.* Circles of compensation tend to be risk-diffusing and risk-
    reducing, which reduces incentives for circle participants to innovate
    in complex, unfamiliar areas. While the circles actually encourage
    collective risk-taking in familiar circumstances, as well as incremental
    modifications of an existing paradigm, where the prognosis is clear,
    as in building new steel mills or engineering more precise electronic

circuitry, they appear to inhibit attempts at radical innovation (like the Apple iPhone, for example).[8]

3. *Global connectivity.* Traditional circles of compensation, owing to their cost-externalizing structure, have a parochial cast. They tend to privilege long-standing partners—mainly domestic—and discriminate against new entrants—mainly foreign. How circles of compensation can accommodate outsiders is a critical underlying challenge.

Modernizing Collective Action: Lessons from Abroad

All of our three reference cases, as noted above, are late-developing nations that face similar challenges to Japan's: growth, stability, and response to global rivals. In none of the three, however, are circles of compensation nearly as salient as in Japan itself.[9] These cases—so comparable to Japan on other grounds—thus can provide particularly useful insights into how the specific perversities in Japan's patterns of collective action can be overcome.

(a) *External monitoring and strategic support.* Throughout the high-growth years, a classical triumvirate of long-term credit banks, *keiretsu*, and government institutions (preeminently MITI and MOF) provided a potent, synergistic combination of strategic guarantees and intrusive monitoring, based on high-leverage, "invest, then save" financial policies. Those policies supported explosive, investment-driven growth, at the same time minimizing the moral hazard implicit in such guarantees.[10] The classical Japanese system was critically compromised by the removal of capital-export controls after 1980; the increasing subsequent volatility of domestic financial parameters; the collapse of the long-term credit banks in the late 1990s; and the erosion of the *keiretsu* over the subsequent decade.

Since the mid-2000s, Japan has been striving to reconfigure its financial paradigm, to cope with the demise of traditional monitoring institutions and the declining institutional power of MOF. The basic circle-of-compensation structure remains embedded, but foreign paradigms for monitoring and strategy are increasingly relevant. Bank hesitancy in Japan at project finance, leading to periodic credit crunches, has made reforms increasingly urgent. Germany's Federal Financial Supervisory Authority (the BaFin)—independent regulatory apparatus, supervisory board mechanism, and external audit system—together with the credit-information index systems of Singapore and Korea, seem especially relevant. The World Bank notes that Korean and Singaporean credit-evaluation systems have two important traits that their counterparts in Japan lack: (1) broad distribution of credit-information indices to both firms and individuals, and (2) provision of credit scores as value-added services for banks and other financial institutions.[11]

(b) *Innovation.* Circles of compensation may diffuse project-specific risk, but they also tend to inhibit disruptive innovation, especially in sectors where future competitive prospects are ill-defined. Circles also tend to inhibit independent small-business start-ups. Such constraints prevail in none of the reference countries, since circles of compensation are either nonexistent, or much less salient there.

World Bank's Doing Business project provides some interesting comparative insights that suggest both the challenge Japan confronts in the area of innovation, relative to the reference countries, and how their approach might inform its future policies.[12] First, regarding the rule of law, in the area of enforcing commercial contracts efficiently—a fundamental issue for aspiring start-ups—Japan ranked fifty-first, while Singapore, Korea, and Germany were first, second, and twelfth, respectively, as noted in Table 11.2. As a consequence of more favorable start-up policies in Korea, and contrasting problems with monitoring and strategic support in Japan, as also suggested in Table 11.2, Korea's ratio of venture-capital investment to GDP is nearly twice as high as Japan's.[13]

German small-business development also provides a useful benchmark for Japan, with respect to innovation, albeit one advantaging established small proprietors rather than outside investors, as suggested in Table 11.2. The German pattern, it should be noted, is more conservative, more discriminatory toward newcomers, and closer to the Japanese paradigm than the other reference cases, probably due to the parallel importance of bank finance in Germany and Japan. Bank finance appears to both inhibit start-up-based innovation and discriminate against outsiders, just as circles of compensation do. Japan, to

TABLE 11.2

Japanese innovation-related practices in comparative context
(unit: ranking)

Practices	Japan	Singapore	Republic of Korea	Germany
Enforcing contracts	51	1	2	12
Protecting minority investors	36	1	8	49
Getting credit	79	19	42	28
Starting a business	81	10	23	107
Overall (ease of doing business)	32	1	4	15

SOURCE: World Bank, "Economy Rankings," *Doing Business: Measuring Business Regulations,* June 2015, http://www.doingbusiness.org/rankings.

be sure, has well-developed small-business policies, including substantial government financial support enabling small firms to purchase robots and other forms of productivity-increasing investment. Most productive Japanese small businesses in manufacturing, however, are subcontractors within larger conglomerates, and the support they receive is limited to domestic operations.

Germany, by contrast, has a large and vigorous community of highly innovative yet independent small proprietors; in total, small business—known as the Mittelstand—generates 56 percent of Germany's economic output, and provides nearly 60 percent of all jobs.[14] This community is also decidedly international in its operations. German small and medium-sized enterprises (SMEs) pursue an innovative long-term human resources policy of vocational education that enhances their ability to become innovation leaders, and that is discussed later in this chapter. Germany ranked fourth among the twenty-eight EU nations on the European Commission's Innovation Scoreboard for 2015, with high scores for "SMEs with product/process innovations" and "SMEs with marketing/organisational innovations."[15]

Germany pursues a number of policies in support of its Mittelstand small-business community that could be of special utility in Japan, including the following: (1) The EXIST program of start-up grants for high-tech spin-offs from academia. This has recently been opened to foreign start-up teams that want help from EXIST as they set up a business in Germany. A pilot project with Israel, for example, was launched during the summer of 2015.[16] (2) The German Accelerator program, supporting German tech start-up efforts to enter the U.S. market, including New York, Silicon Valley, and San Francisco. This provides support for start-ups in the energy, ICT, and cleantech sectors, giving young German firms the chance to gain experience in the U.S. market, and to build professional networks. In late 2015, the Boston life-science sector was included in the program.[17] (3) The Central Innovation Program for SMEs (ZIM), founded in 2008. This supports small-business research and development projects, with a special focus on cross-border cooperation. Companies aligning with international partners receive a funding bonus of up to 10 percent.[18]

Singapore also has a variety of programs that support start-ups at various stages of growth, including: (1) The Business Angel Scheme provides innovative young Singapore-based companies that have obtained investment commitment from preapproved business angel investors with a matching dollar-for-dollar investment for up to S$2 million. (2) The SPRING Startup Enterprise Development Scheme provides innovative young Singapore-based companies with an equity-based co-financing option for up to S$2 million plus an additional S$1 million maximum investment depending on the company's specific progress. (3) The Sector Specific Accelerator Programme has committed $70 million to encourage the formation and growth of start-ups in medical and clean technology. (4) The Technology Enterprise Commercialisation Scheme provides proof-of-concept or proof-of-value funding for innovative technology ideas.[19]

The Singapore government places strong emphasis on *translating basic research into commercial products*. This was a function that the long-term credit banks, the general trading companies, and the *keiretsu* traditionally performed in Japan. It has been compromised since around 2000, however, by the collapse of the long-term credit banks and most of the *keiretsu*, as well as erosion of the traditional informal credit-evaluation functions that these institutions traditionally performed.

(c) *Global connectivity*. Japanese circles of compensation have been structurally biased against transnational ties—cross-border corporate alliances and networks, which the German government has been trying explicitly to foster. That is to some extent changing, especially since the advent of Prime Minister Abe, who visited Silicon Valley during April 2015 in an attempt to begin building innovative transnational business networks. Japan's active membership in various international trade agreements will help enhance global connectivity in coming years, just as Germany's central role in the European Union has done since the late 1950s.

Connectivity nevertheless needs to be an even more consistent priority for Japan, given the typical structural bias of the circles of compensation against outsiders. At the general policy level, one useful paradigm is Korea's national *Segyehwa* (globalization) policy, adopted by President Kim Young-sam in 1993, sought at an early stage to create a bilingual workforce capable of serving the needs of an increasingly global market.[20] The interaction of public and private efforts produced a foreign-language frenzy that now provokes Koreans to spend $17 billion a year on English proficiency alone, to hire thirty thousand native English speakers as tutors, and to send more than three times as many foreign students to the United States as Japan does, even though South Korea has less than half the population.[21, 22]

Singapore, one of the most cosmopolitan business and educational environments in the world, also provides important reference points for Japan with respect to global connectivity. In the intellectual sphere, its National Research Foundation strategically invests massive sums in partnerships between local Singapore institutions of higher education and research leaders worldwide, including MIT, Oxford, University of California, Berkeley, and Tsinghua

University. It also creates research parks where both universities and corporations from throughout the world can directly interact, and works to set up concrete partnerships through its Economic Planning Board.[23]

Singapore's efforts at global connectivity also have a more tangible physical expression—systematic efforts to convert itself into a global logistics, trading, and general business hub, through a combination of world-class infrastructure and targeted free-trade policies. Singapore boasts the world's most highly rated airport in Changi, and a container port that handles one-seventh of the world's transshipment throughput.[24] It seeks "global-hub" synergies to this state-of-the-art infrastructure, through establishment of a special economic zone, extensive storage facilities, and low corporate tax rates.

Singapore, Germany, and Korea also promote global connectivity by fostering international sociopolitical networks between their citizens and the broader world in ways that Japan could reference with profit. All these countries have extensive, government-supported, foreign scholarship and personnel exchange programs. Each also strategically sponsors large numbers of international conferences, often with government support. Japan, to be sure, will be hosting the G7 Summit in 2016, and the Olympic Games in 2020. Korea, however, has already hosted the G20 Summit (2010) and the Nuclear Security Summit (2012), the first nation in Asia to do so. It has also hosted the annual Jeju Forum since 2001. Singapore is continually hosting a multitude of international events, both at the technical and the political levels, with its attractiveness leveraged by a variety of first-class infrastructure, including the world's most highly regarded airport,.[25]

In the realm of global connectivity, our reference cases also suggest ways in which Japan's circles of compensation can be broadened to make them more cosmopolitan, even if it is unrealistic to dismantle them. One approach, for example, could be through a more substantial role for both foreign investment and for individual foreign businesspeople as advisers in the corporate world, particularly in banking, and even in government-related institutions. In Singapore, for example, Robert Zoellick, former U.S. Trade Representative and President of the World Bank, serves on the board of the Temasek, Singapore's sovereign wealth fund.[26] In Korea, two of the country's seven nationwide banks are foreign.[27] In Germany, foreign firms also have a central presence, and a foreigner, John Cryan, serves as Chief Executive Officer of Deutsche Bank, Germany's largest.[28]

Overall, foreign assets comprise a much larger share of total bank assets in our three reference cases than in Japan. In Germany, for example, the foreign share is roughly 12 percent (data for 2013), versus 1 percent in Japan

(2008), 6 percent in Singapore (2010), and 7 percent in Korea (2013).[29] Admitting more foreigners to existing circles of compensation—corporate boards, government advisory committees, and so on, as a start—including those in finance, a crucial potential driver of economic reform—would help significantly to enhance the global connectivity needed to reduce the parochialism embedded in Japanese circles of compensation.

Recommendations on Best Practice from Abroad for Key Sectors

There are two dimensions to Japan's challenge of learning from overseas. The first is the challenge of modifying the perverse effects of existing circles of compensation as globalization proceeds. The second is sector specific: upgrading the industries and people at the interface between Japan and the broader world, who are concentrated in the sectors described earlier in this book. Here we present thirteen suggestions, drawn from the three successfully globalizing reference nations whose experience, structure, and physical endowments most closely parallel Japan's own.

(1) Circles of compensation fill some positive functions in political-economic life, including risk diffusion, broadened participation in group decision-making, and enhanced collective solidarity.

Each of the three reference countries employs such circles effectively in some dimensions. Germany, for example, employs the executive board system of corporate governance, in accordance with which labor and management hold seats on corporate boards of directors. Such boards exhibit some characteristics of circles of compensation, and seem to generally enhance corporate cohesion and industrial efficiency. Korea also has German-style corporatist institutions for labor-management consultation. In both Korea and Germany, agricultural cooperatives also have roles in public policy, as in Japan. In Singapore, unions cooperate with professional management in operating the taxi system. Meanwhile, government-linked companies, ranging from urban development (Singbridge)[30] to aviation (Singapore Airlines), also operate in market-oriented fashion, responsive to broad public priorities.[31]

(2) Nations need a holistic set of policies, oriented toward the global.

One of the hallmarks of Japanese economic policies since the Meiji Restoration has been their holistic character—a propensity to link efforts in many sectors to a single goal—in this case national economic development. Until the gradual abolition of the unequal treaties during the two decades before World War I,[32] national policies were necessarily focused on the global. Japan lacked tariff autonomy, and was much more exposed to international economic forces than great empires like the United Kingdom or France, not to mention continental economies such as the United States. Yet as Japan regained sovereignty over its finances, mobilized for war, and embarked on heavy industrialization early in the twentieth century, a parochial preoccupation with risk reduction through domestic collaborative action began to override the earlier global concerns.

Particularly from the 1930s on, Japan developed a segmented, inward-looking dual political economy with formidable competitiveness in its traded sectors. The major concern of that system, however, was domestic stability rather than responsiveness to the world outside. This parochial bias was deepened, especially on the nontraded side of the political economy, by the democratic political pressures and the one-party conservative dominance that arose and deepened from the mid-1950s on. The Japanese political economy gradually became a holistic risk-reduction mechanism—reducing domestic risk through both circles of compensation and protectionism—that consequently lost its focus on and consciousness of the global in many areas. The problem was especially intense in nontraded sectors such as transportation, communications, and agriculture, whose development was subordinated to domestic political considerations, without regard to their potential international impact.

The situation was somewhat different in our three reference economies. Singapore, an island state totally exposed to the vagaries of international markets, was unavoidably globally oriented, from its very beginnings. Germany—economically competitive and lying at the center of Europe, was similarly cosmopolitan in most respects, from the time of the Federal Republic's entry into the European Economic Community in 1958. South Korea moved more diffidently, but also began progressing toward globalization with the *Segyehwa* policies of the mid-1990s,[33] followed by the brutal yet galvanizing shock of the 1997–1998 Asian financial crisis, and a dramatic recovery thereafter.

By the dawn of the twenty-first century, a sharp divergence was thus emerging between our three reference economies, on the one hand, and Japan, on the other. In Japan, a pronounced dichotomy between traded and nontraded sectors prevailed, with efficiency, cost reduction, and market orientation the order of the day on the traded side, yet with parochial domestic political concerns prevailing elsewhere in the system. Policy sectors such as communications and energy, as well as policy areas like agriculture and construction that are related to land—the overriding preoccupation of the Japanese political system—were dominated by parochial political concerns, crippling their ability to respond to the deepening imperatives of globalization.

(3) *Financial systems need to both encourage innovation and nurture patient capital, consistent with an inevitably substantial degree of global interdependence.*

Japan's central political-economic difficulty of the past generation, we have found, has been reconfiguring a highly leveraged Bankers' Kingdom for an era of globalization. Monitoring, moral hazard, and corporate governance challenges have been monumental for all four late-developing nations considered here; they are pivotal in shaping the micro-level incentives that catalyze constructive change. The three challenges have been especially acute in Japan, as it has, however, pursued an unusual combination of bank-centric finance and one-party dominance that has led to unusually tight relations between politics and finance. All the reference cases have addressed those challenges in different ways than has Japan, but all nevertheless provide useful insights in support of Japan's future globalization, in such technical areas as creation of global hubs, through the synergistic integration of infrastructure and taxation policies.

(4) *Transportation is a critical sector in determining successful globalization, and in successfully promoting globally oriented economic development. Transportation centers with potential to be globally competitive must be market oriented, but also need strategic government resource commitments.*

In all three reference countries considered, major international airports are considered as key drivers of national economic growth. They are supported actively by both government and private-sector programs, in contrast to Japan's stronger emphasis on local-airport development, and heavy taxation of international airports to support these smaller local airports. National policy in the reference countries treats national airports as a key national infrastructure whose facilities should be high quality, efficient in operation, and provided to customers at low cost.

The two Asian reference countries have been especially zealous in modernizing and improving their largest airports: Incheon in Korea and Changi in Singapore. As a result of these efforts, Changi and Incheon were recently ranked by Skytrax, in its annual survey of world airports, as the two best airports in the world.[34] As indicated in Table 11.3, these two airports ranked among the top three worldwide every year from 2008–2015. Significantly, the runner-up to these two in 2015 was Munich, in Germany. The highest-ranking Japanese airport in 2016 was fourth—still lower than the others, although an improvement from previous years.[35]

TABLE 11.3

The top twelve airports worldwide

Airport	2015	2014	2013	2012	2011	2010	2009	2008
Singapore Changi	1	1	1	2	2	1	3	2
Incheon Int'l	2	2	2	1	3	2	1	3
Munich	3	3	6	6	4	4	5	5
Hong Kong Int'l	4	4	4	3	1	3	2	1
Tokyo Int'l (Haneda)	5	6	9	14	17	—	—	—
Zurich	6	8	7	7	7	6	4	8
Central Japan Int'l	7	12	13	10	11	—	9	12
London Heathrow	8	10	10	11	16	—	—	—
Amsterdam Schiphol	9	5	3	4	6	7	8	11
Beijing Capital Int'l	10	7	5	5	5	8	17	—
Vancouver Int'l	11	9	8	9	12	—	—	—
Kansai Int'l	12	14	18	19	14	—	6	6

SOURCE: Skytrax World Airport Awards, historical records compiled by the author.

The East Asia and Pacific region, according to the World Bank, generated one-third of world total passenger air traffic in 2015.[36] This massive market, much of it transit related, no doubt provides part of the incentive for Incheon and Changi—and for that matter Hong Kong International Airport—to be innovative, efficient, and to supply excellent transit facilities.[37] The growing Asian consumer aviation market also provides incentives to supply low-cost, volume-oriented travel services, as market share can have important implications for long-term market dominance. Unfortunately, however, the prospects of rapidly expanding regional passenger and cargo markets, and the consequent strategic importance of battling for international market share, appears to have been lost on the Japanese bureaucrats and politicians who make airport policy.

Changi and Incheon exhibit several common features that make them preeminent in global airport rankings, which could be usefully emulated in Japan. Their salient traits include:

(a) *Provision of leisure amenities.* Changi ranked tops worldwide in this category in 2015, with its cultural facilities including seven playgrounds; a multimedia entertainment center; three movie theaters, including a 4D theater; cultural activities, including an opportunity to do artwork with wood blocks; gambling and a gaming club; pools, showers, a fitness center, and a spa; and a music bar lounge. Longer-term transit passengers can also take a free Singapore tour—over one million passengers have availed themselves of this service over the years.[38]

Incheon's approach is parallel to that of Changi, although more directly tailored to enhance understanding of local culture. High-quality Korean handicrafts are available duty-free at an Incheon arts center inside the airport, which also offers passengers the opportunity to practice calligraphy through brush writing, or to make designs using Korean woodblock printing. Roving musicians and actors wearing traditional garb also bring the arts of Korea's classical past back to life.[39]

(b) *Free Internet and communications facilities.* Changi has over five hundred Internet stations available at all terminals, as well as a free high-speed wireless network. Incheon has three free Wi-Fi areas sponsored by Naver that require no registration, and that provide computers for personal use, as well as the general Wi-Fi access that is common at Western airports.

(c) *Shopping.* Changi and Incheon, together with European centers like London's Heathrow, provide some of the best duty-free shopping in the world. In 2011, Changi recorded over $1 billion in retail sales, through facilities with 750,000 square feet of concession space—about the size of a small suburban shopping mall.[40] This constituted fully 50 percent of the airport's revenue, helping to pay for the generous amenities, while also keeping down costs to the airlines. Elaborate shopping facilities were thus one major reason that Changi, like Incheon, has been able to avoid the high landing fees that are crippling the ability of Narita and Kansai Airports to compete on the world stage.

In order to promote the shopping that is so central to Changi's ability to maintain its global competitiveness, the airport is continually engaged in passenger-oriented promotions encouraging transit visitors to spend. Launched in 2010, for example, the anchor promotion was "Be a Changi Millionaire," where passengers and visitors spending S$30 or more in a single receipt would be eligible for entering a drawing to win S$1 million, attracted nearly 2 million lucky drawers from 229 nationalities globally.[41] Together with loyalty programs and a Christmas campaign, these promotions led to over S$2 billion retail sales and a 7 percent year-to-year increase in Changi's concessions and rental income despite a more challenging operating environment faced by the industry as a whole.[42]

(d) *Volume-oriented strategies.* The rapid growth of aviation traffic in the Asia-Pacific region naturally gives Changi and Incheon a strategic opportunity. Yet these dynamic hub airports have both taken unusually astute advantage of that opportunity, not only through their excellent facilities and passenger orientation, but also through the sort of international air-traffic patterns that they have promoted.

Both Changi and Incheon have consciously sought to become transnational air-traffic hubs, for the Southeast and Northeast Asian regions, respectively, thus stimulating airport traffic volume. To achieve their goal, these airports have encouraged long-haul, point-to-point traffic. Changi, for example, has taken advantage of its tropical location and excellent shopping to forge extensive airline connections with an increasingly affluent Russia, whose wealthy elite lack both warm weather and high-quality shopping. In July 2011, Singapore Airlines and Transaero Airlines, the second-largest passenger airline in Russia, reached codeshare agreement, adding Moscow, Ekaterinburg, Novosibirsk, Samara, and St. Petersburg to its service destinations.[43] The following year, the number of Russian visitors Singapore received expanded by 16.1 percent, with a 19.6 percent further expansion in 2013, and 10.4 percent in 2014.[44] Similarly, Incheon also serves as a key hub for Vladivostok and other points in the Russia Far East, as well as Moscow and St. Petersburg, though a network of point-to-point flights. Incheon, too, is becoming a luxury-goods shopping center for reasons similar to those perceived in Changi.

Volume-oriented and profit-maximizing strategies involve appealing to both upscale and downscale markets. To develop the upscale market, Changi lured in a range of international full-service carriers, such as Turkish Airlines, Finnair, Lufthansa, and Air France. It did so by creating the world's busiest multicarrier Airbus A380 hub, and providing amenities attractive to affluent, cosmopolitan travelers. On average, recent research indicates that fliers through Changi earn six times their respective home country's average income.[45] .

To lure more numerous budget travelers as well, the Singapore government encouraged creation of Scoot—a low-cost subsidiary of Singapore Airlines. It also built a separate charter terminal, which many migrant workers use. That terminal provides both convenient service and separation from the upscale traffic at the other Changi facilities.

(e) *The "air city" concept.* Both Incheon and Changi sense the potential role of international airports as locales for a broad range of services beyond air travel. They see airports as not only transportation centers, but also broad-gauge human communities. Incheon is developing an 809-acre super-resort modeled after Singapore's Resorts World Sentosa.[46] Apart from recreation, passengers can avail themselves of a wide range of services, such as medical checkups. Changi, similarly, has five clinics and seven pharmacies.[47] Incheon features a whole complex of medical facilities close to the airport itself, as well as extensive product-assembly facilities. In all, around forty thousand people work in the Incheon airport complex.

(f) *Exporting local-airport expertise.* Both Incheon and Changi see exporting their award-winning capabilities and investing in other airports elsewhere in the world as high priorities. Incheon, for example, played a two-year consulting role in the preparation of Erbil International Airport in Iraqi Kurdistan, which opened in March 2011.[48] Incheon has also taken an equity stake in the Khabarovsk airport in the Russia Far East.

Changi has been even more ambitious. Its wholly owned subsidiary, Changi Airports International (CAI), offers airport consultancy with regard to master planning, capacity enhancement, airport management, and commercial development. It holds equity interests in India's first privately managed airport, the Durgapur Aerotropolis in West Bengal, as well as Brazil's Tom Jobim International Airport, the main international gateway to Rio de Janeiro. In addition, CAI formed a joint venture with Russian investors in June 2012 to develop four airports—Sochi, Krasnodar, Anapa, and Gelendzhik—in Russia's Krasnodar region.[49] CAI has also engaged in airport renovation projects in China's Beijing Capital International, Italy's Rome Fiumicino, and UK's London Luton Airport.[50]

(5) *Communications is another strategic sector, where a hybrid mixture of market orientation and state support for basic infrastructure is also needed.*

The optimal equation is illustrated clearly in all of the three reference countries. Singapore is the most straightforward: a variety of multinational telecommunications companies are welcomed, with tariffs on value-added services determined by market forces. At the same time, however, the Singapore government, through its Temasek holding company, retains dominant shares in *two competing* government-linked companies (Singtel and StarHub). The state also played the central role in planning and implementing the Next Generation Nationwide Broadband Network project launched in 2006, which aims at providing high-quality telecommunications infrastructure at reasonable cost to both business and individual consumers, at both indoor and outdoor locations.[51]

Communications policy in Korea, given that country's larger economy and aspiring electronics industry, has historically been a more complex proposition. Access for foreign firms has not been as open as in Singapore, and the government has played a larger role in setting telecommunications tariffs. Yet in sharp contrast to Japan, the Korean telecommunications and telecomservices markets have not been dominated by a single, domestically oriented producer. Regulation has been less clientelized, more market oriented, and in many ways more globally conscious than in its larger neighbor.[52]

Korea has no domestic analogue to the NTT family, a huge, long-public firm that was for many years a heavily regulated and quasi-monopolistic provider of telecommunications services in Japan. NTT's demanding, parochial requirements forced its equipment suppliers into specialized production that was largely irrelevant for broader global markets, especially those of the developing world.[53] Korea's lack of an elaborate telecom-sector circle of compensation, for years a seeming drawback, has conversely freed Korean firms to orient themselves to global markets, including rapidly growing developing nations, rather than tying them to a demanding domestic supplier with parochial requirements. As Japan's NTT, together with domestic regulators, forced suppliers to develop arcane "i-mode" applications and to pursue incremental innovation through stability-oriented circles of compensation within Japan, Korean cell-phone and consumer electronics producers like Samsung pursued strategic alliances and promising technology abroad. The Koreans also aggressively developed growing markets in developing nations, as well as new digital technologies in which Japan initially showed little interest.[54]

Samsung, in particular, has made important corporate strategic innovations since the 1990s, under CEO Lee Kun-hee. These changes have enabled it to dramatically upstage Japanese firms that had previously dominated the global electronics industry. On the Japanese side, the NTT family and its related circle of compensation introduced a conservative bias that inhibited Japanese responses to changing technology, and to globalization, as has been noted.

Samsung moved into the gap opened by the conservatism of Japanese firms with powerful new innovations in marketing, research and development, and design, while at the same time building on their traditional strengths in quality control and continuous operational improvements.[55] Samsung hired ethnic Korean engineers away from Intel, IBM, and Bell Labs. It also systematically pursued the implications of the digital revolution while the Japanese were inhibited by their lead in analog electronics from doing so. It established a regional specialist program giving its executives third-world expertise, and plunged into aggressive market development in developing nations. And it created the Samsung Art and Design Institute, to leverage its strategic interest in product design.

The success of Samsung's strategy is evidenced by its dramatic recent success in global electronics markets, which Japanese firms have traditionally dominated. In the third quarter of 2013, Samsung was the largest smartphone vendor in the world, with a 31.4 percent market share—substantially greater than all the Japanese smartphone makers combined.[56] In 2015, Samsung continued to dominate the global TV market, the tenth straight year since it beat Sony in 2006.[57] In 2015, Samsung also led the dynamic random-access memory sector with 45.3 percent global market share and the NAND flash market with 39.1 percent share globally.[58] Around 90 percent of its sales came from overseas, a larger share than typical of most Japanese producers.[59]

Korean public policy toward the communications sector, particularly Internet development, provides additional comparative reference points of relevance in evaluating Japanese approaches. In the depths of the 1997–1998 Asian financial crisis, Korea decisively embraced informatics policy as a key tool to lead the country out of the crisis, and developed a series of plans to transform Korea into a dynamic information society. These included Cyber Korea 21 (1999–2002); e-Korea Vision 2006 (2002–2006); and the U-Korea Master Plan (2006–2015).[60]

Soon after adoption of the Cyber Korea 21 program in 1999, Korea put strong emphasis on development of broadband Internet. It did so through a combination of infrastructural improvements supported by the government and pricing policies that made advanced Internet communications affordable. By 2002, as indicated in Figure 11.2, around 25 percent of all Korean

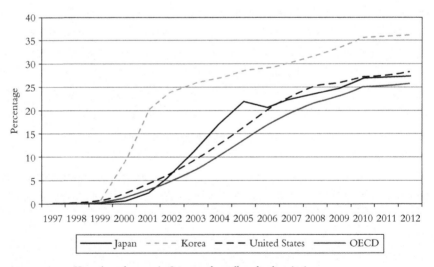

FIGURE 11.2   Korea's early start in Internet broadband subscriptions

SOURCE: OECD, "Table 4.11. Total fixed broadband subscriptions per 100 inhabitants in the OECD area," *OECD Communications Outlook 2013* (Paris: OECD Publishing, 2013), 129, doi: 10.1787/comms_outlook-2013-en.

households had broadband subscriptions, compared to just over 5 percent in Japan and the United States. Korea continued to maintain its lead, ranking fourth within the OECD in broadband diffusion by June 2012, while the United States and Japan ranked fifteenth and seventeenth, respectively.[61]

Korea developed and sustained its lead in high-speed Internet by offering high-performance services at reasonable prices. As indicated in Figure 11.3, in 2014 Korean broadband prices were only 4 percent of those in the United States, or less than one-tenth those in Japan. In first quarter 2016, Korea continued to top globally with an average connection speed of 29.0 megabits per second (Mbps), compared to 18.2 Mbps for Japan and 15.3 Mbps for the United States.[62]

As Korea has moved deeper and deeper into the information age, it has embraced the concept of the independent telecommunications regulator, in contrast to Japan. In February 2008, the Korea Communications Commission (KCC) was established, merging regulatory functions of the Ministry of Information and Communication (MIC) and the Korean Broadcasting Commission (KBC). The KCC administers Korea's broadband plan—the "u-Korea Master Plan"—which MIC adopted in 2006, with the goal of providing every household in Korea with access to high-speed Internet. The KCC has been working with operators to establish a new regulatory framework designed for

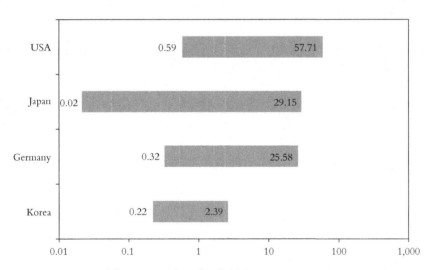

FIGURE 11.3   Korea's low Internet broadband pricing

SOURCE: OECD, "Figure 2.37 Fixed broadband prices per megabit per second of advertised speed, September 2014, USD PPP," OECD Digital Economy Outlook 2015 (Paris: OECD Publishing, 2015), 119, doi: 10.1787/9789264232440-en.

an all-Internet-protocol era, and on improving the openness of fixed line and wireless networks.[63]

Germany is the reference country, of the three we consider, that has been the least innovative and responsive to globalization in telecommunications—for reasons similar to those prevailing in Japan. The Germans entered the information age, as Japan did, with a massive state telecommunications monopoly—the Deutsche Bundespost, which in 1985 employed over five hundred thousand people.[64] That massive public firm was split into three divisions in 1989, as Japan's NTT was in 1999, with these divisions being privatized in 1995, as also happened in Japan a decade earlier (1985).[65] Yet the German government retained a significant equity stake in the successor firms, and thus placed a premium on its profitability, as its Japanese counterpart did with NTT. Deutsche Telekom was the monopoly Internet service provider until 1995, and continues to adopt a high-tariff strategy that maximizes short-term revenue, as opposed to growth and innovation.

To the extent that Germany can serve as a model for Japan's future in the communications field, its relevance lies in the approach of Deutsche Telekom and its siblings, Deutsche Post and Deutsche Postbank, to corporate strategy, rather than toward the information revolution or globalization. Management has, in each case, maintained cooperative relations with labor, which supported the firm's privatization, and has prospered since. Japanese Prime Minister Koizumi, as he was considering Japan Post's privatization in the mid-2000s, was himself impressed by the cooperative relations that German labor and management were able to maintain during the privatization process.[66] Deutsche Post also efficiently plowed a substantial share of the large profits it generated from its postal business into diversification, including acquisition of the DHL express-mail firm during 1998–2002.[67]

(6) *Education*

All three of our reference cases suggest important modifications of Japan's circles-of-compensation approach. Collectively, they do *not*, it is important to note, repudiate the value of collaborative, group-oriented approaches per se. Close links among educational researchers, educators, and policy implementers, for example, are fundamental to Singapore's approach to educational innovation and best-practice dissemination.[68] Yet the approach of the reference countries to collaboration appears strikingly more global, more decentralized, less parochial, less status-quo oriented, and less bureaucracy-centric than in Japan. It also seems to produce more creative and globally oriented students, as well as a more intense interaction with the world beyond the nation itself.

Germany's globally relevant contributions are concentrated in three areas: decentralization, vocational education, and international policy dialogue. In conformity with its post–World War II political structure, education policy is decentralized to the level of the *Lander*, or provinces, allowing for more pluralism, policy borrowing, and adjustment to local conditions than in a more centralized system.[69] In the sphere of vocational education that integrates experiences in the school and the workplace, Germany is a world leader, thanks to the active, systematic involvement of business organizations in practical curriculum development and job placement, with the bureaucratic role marginalized.[70] German education systematically engages an institutional self-reflection, through a well-respected, independent federal research institute (the Federal Institute for Vocational Education and Training) and a national network of smaller research centers that study different aspects of the vocational employment system.[71] Thanks to this feedback-oriented approach, students are well prepared for available jobs, and youth unemployment is the lowest among the thirty OECD advanced industrial nations.[72]

Germany also engages in extensive international educational dialogue, focused on vocational education. The Federal Ministry of Education and Research (BMBF) has vigorous bilateral exchange programs for vocational trainees with France and Israel. The BMBF also maintains close cooperation in the area of vocational training with a broad range of developing countries, including China, India, Russia, and Turkey. The BMBF supports German service providers in their efforts to promote vocational training as an export industry for Germany, as well.[73]

The educational efforts of Korea and Singapore are more oriented toward promoting international educational exchange, and to absorbing lessons from abroad, than they are toward educational exports per se. Yet both countries are similar to Germany in their global and innovative orientation. Both countries are obtaining outstanding results that validate their approach, such as Singapore's preeminent standing both on international standardized mathematics and science exams, as well as in world studies of how educational systems can serve the needs of an internationally competitive economy.[74] Korea, meanwhile, has for the past decade and more ranked consistently among the top five Programme for International Student Assessment (PISA) competing countries in math, science, and reading—an achievement matched only by Singapore and Finland.[75]

For both Korea and Singapore, encouraging two-way educational exchange with major global centers of excellence is fundamental. Singapore, for example, offers full-tuition scholarship opportunities (both graduate and undergraduate) at the best foreign universities to its brightest students, as identified on competitive national exams. It also encourages them to capitalize on the scholarship programs of other nations. Further, it offers over two thousand scholarships annually to foreign students studying in Singapore—so many as to provoke a parliamentary investigation by more parochial members of parliament in 2012.[76] In 2014, there were about seventy-five thousand foreign students are enrolled in Singaporean universities, constituting about 18 percent of Singapore's entire university student population.[77]

Systematic international benchmarking is a hallmark of Singapore's education policies, which contributes to their success, and to the vitality of Singapore's education interaction with the broader world. Ministry of Education staff travel the world in search of best practices, culminating in successes such as Singapore's acclaimed elementary and secondary school mathematics program, which has resulted in top scores for Singapore schools on international standardized tests.[78] Singapore has also put substantial effort into multilingual education, both to deepen national consciousness, in that multi-ethnic society, and to enhance global competitiveness.[79]

Like Singapore, Korea has adopted a broad range of policies to promote international educational exchange, with similarly positive results. English is compulsory from the third grade of elementary school through high school, with emphasis on both oral skills and reading.[80] The English-language ratio of courses in Korean universities is now remarkably high, averaging well over 20 percent at most major schools.[81] Internationalization, and educational enhancement more generally at higher levels, are promoted by Brain Korea 21, a high-quality human resource nurturing program designed to aid candidates for both master's and doctoral degrees, as well as advanced-level researchers.[82]

As a consequence of their own globalization policies and the persistence of parochial circles of compensation in Japan, Korean universities are now significantly more internationalized than their Japanese counterparts. Seoul National University, for example, was rated more than three times higher in "foreign instructors" and "foreign exchange students" than the University of Tokyo in 2012. Moreover, Seoul National University was rated over four times higher than Tokyo in "sending students abroad."[83]

More generally, at the national level, globally oriented domestic programs have allowed Korea to both send a large number of its students overseas and attract a rising number of foreign students to study at Korean universities. The OECD survey found that, in 2011, 139,000 Korean students were enrolled full time at foreign universities. Japan, by contrast, only had 39,000. In addition, between 2000 and 2011, the number of foreign students in Korea increased over seventeenfold.[84] The Korean government also generously sponsors overseas internships, distinctive internationally, that send thousands of young Koreans, typically university students, annually into work-study programs worldwide.[85] Japan, in cooperation with foreign partners, has begun encouraging overseas work experience, as through its "working holiday" visa arrangements with Australia. Its government programs of this sort remain much less extensive than those of Korea, however.

(7) *Housing requires a heavier dose of welfare-oriented government involvement, with less of a construction-sector bias, than has been common in Japan.*

Land policy that systematically inflated the price of land in Japan was central to Japan's unorthodox "invest, then save" growth policies of the 1950s, 1960s, and 1970s, and was supported by the prevailing circles of compensation. Such an approach complicated the supply of affordable housing for the general public, and introduced a construction-oriented bias that especially discouraged markets for used housing. In the low-growth environment of the twenty-first century, there is a pressing need for new, more consumer-oriented approaches to housing in Japan, for which our three advanced but densely populated reference countries provide excellent models for emulation.

Singapore, of our reference cases, represents the clearest contrast to Japan in housing-policy terms, presenting alternatives that many would consider attractive, and others debatable. The Housing & Development Board (HDB) provides homes—from basic flats catering to everyday needs, to five-room luxury apartments—for over 80 percent of Singapore's residents, of which 90 percent own their home.[86] The Singapore government provides attractive financing options, especially for first-home buyers, to make sure quality housing is affordable to the Singaporean people.[87]

Singapore's government also relates housing policy strategically to broader social goals. The HDB, responsible for virtually all of the island-country's housing, builds environmentally friendly housing that both conserves energy and lowers operating costs. Solar photovoltaic systems have been installed in hundreds of blocks with the aim of achieving net-zero energy for common services. And "green roofs" of vegetation have been planted since the 1990s to provide recreational spaces as well as help cool the surrounding temperature.[88]

Singapore's government uses housing policy as a vehicle for promoting both political stability—by giving young people a Lockean "stake in society"—and ethnic integration. It seeks to achieve the latter through ethnic quotas within public housing. Prospective housing applicants can only buy into a given housing complex when space for their ethnic group is available in accordance with preestablished quotas.[89]

Korea's distinctive housing-policy contributions are threefold: (a) greenbelts, (b) extensive use of eminent domain, and (c) government housing expansion drives, focusing on apartment construction.[90] In 1971–1972, the government set aside over four hundred square kilometers (4 percent of Korea's total landmass) as greenbelts around Seoul and thirteen other major cities. In 1981, it passed the sweeping Housing Site Development Promotion Act, to forcefully increase the supply of urban land, under eminent domain, if the government designated a certain area as a development district. Beginning in the late 1980s, just as democratization was occurring, the government also inaugurated large-scale housing construction drives, promising to build two million housing units during President Roh Tae-woo's tenure (1988–1993). Many new apartment complexes were built by Korea's massive chaebol, suffering from a decline during this period in Middle East contracts, with strong support from the Korea Land Corporation and the Korea Housing Corporation.[91] Between 1990 and 1997, about 650,000 new housing units per year were supplied to the market, of which over 75 percent were high-rise multifamily "aparts." At the same time, the jeonse home-rental system also provides a unique way of financing personal housing, even of older housing stock, which is discriminated against in Japan.

The housing policies of Singapore and Korea are the most relevant to Japan, among our three reference cases. Yet Germany provides important insights into means of enhancing housing affordability and access—critically important issues in Japan. Germany addresses these issues through an emphasis on regulated mortgage availability, secure rental tenancy, and flexible, responsive housing supply, even at the cost of meager incentives (in contrast to Japan) for new housing construction.[92] Germany also engages in extensive land-use planning and incentives for "green" infrastructure (green roofs, green facades, and permeable pavements), which reduce urban heat, improve air quality, and manage storm-water problems.[93]

(8) _The land-standard system_ (tochi hon'isei) _is an outmoded one, which none of the other three countries pursues. Broader forms of collateral, together_

with more sophisticated and transparent risk evaluation, are clearly needed in Japan.

The land-standard system encourages steady increases in land prices, particularly under conditions of high economic growth in nations with limited supply of commercially salable land, for housing, commercial, or industrial purposes. It also tends to inhibit investments in firms underendowed with land assets, especially start-ups and service-sector enterprises. The system can also encourage land-price and stock-market speculation, as occurred in Japan during the late 1980s. Our three reference countries, with more diversified collateral requirements, have been largely able to avoid the overexpansion and bad-debt problems associated with real-estate expansion in Japan, although Korea—with a collateral system closest to Japan's, and likewise privileging real estate as a collateral asset—has suffered the most severely of the three. Japan is converging with the reference countries, as well as with global standards with regard to variety of collateral and transparency of evaluation; this trend should be encouraged.[94]

(9) *Budgetary special accounts* (tokubetsu kaikei) *are subversive of the general interest, and should be avoided.*

These accounts create privileged pools of capital, not subject to general allocation principles, that accord preferential benefits, without competition, to predetermined sectors of the political economy. Due to a lack of transparency and intersectoral competition, they can easily breed "iron triangles" among bureaucracy, business, and politics. Special accounts are less common in the three reference countries than in Japan, although their incidence, and countermeasures to control them, vary cross-nationally.

Korea's budgetary system appears closest to the Japanese paradigm, with eighteen special accounts, which accounted for 14 percent of total central government expenditures in 2014.[95] Like Japan's, they were concentrated in the agricultural, energy, transportation, and communications sectors, albeit with less parochial impact on national response to globalization. The degree of particularism in Korean budgeting has declined sharply, however, with the number of special accounts declining from twenty-nine in 1970, and the share of government funds that they absorb also declining greatly, especially since the 1997–1998 Asian financial crisis.[96]

The most creative response among our reference countries to the particularistic bias implicit in special accounts comes from Singapore. Singapore does allow multiple special investment funds, including endowment funds, where are often nontransparent. It does not, however, operate special accounts Japanese style, with protected revenue sources, other than the Central Provident Fund, which supports personal housing retirement and medical savings. Singapore fights "iron-triangle" particularism and ministerial empire-building through its innovative Reinvestment Fund, drawn since 2004 from mandatory annual extractions from ministerial budgets, equal to the *annual* rate of labor-productivity increase in the private sector. The funds thus amassed are real-located among ministries on a competitive basis, with special preference to projects involving cooperation among ministries.[97]

(10) *Finance. Bankers' Kingdoms socialize risk, but invite serious moral hazard when the political-economic influence of financial institutions over government grows too strong, and independent credit-monitoring capabilities decline.*

Japan's banks have had formidable embedded strengths dating back to their reconstruction in the 1920s, 1930s, and 1940s, which contributed to the capital-intensive, expansionary bias of Japanese growth across most of the succeeding years. The institutional strengths of Japanese bankers were measurably enhanced during the high-growth period, when industrial financing was in short supply, in relation to private firms, to financial regulators, and even to the political world. The unique political-economic combination of bank-centered finance and the dominance of a single conservative party, strongly supported by the banks, embedded deep, sustaining networks that continue to influence policy to this day, even as society and economy continue to change.

The embedded influence of the banking community allowed it to both to over-lend during the 1980s economic bubble, creating a major moral hazard which MOF and the Bank of Japan could not control, and then to resist regulatory pressures to write off bad debt during the 1990s. These actions prolonged the "lost decade" economic stagnation that has to some extent persists. The political-economic strength of Japanese banks thus helps account for the explosive high growth of the 1950s and 1960s, on the one hand, and the persistent stagnation that has prevailed since the early 1990s, on the other.

Financial structure has been decidedly different in our three reference countries, although they differ among themselves in structural characteristics. Most similar is Germany, with its powerful universal banks. Those banks, however, have been juxtaposed with a powerful and conservative regulator—the Bundesbank—and lack a direct analogue to the deep, expansion-oriented political involvement of the Japanese Bankers Association (*Zenginkyō*). So the German banks never engaged in the overexpansion and moral-hazard difficulties of their Japanese counterparts, partly because they had not so fully coopted the public sector. Distinctive German external audit mechanisms also helped to provide rigorous monitoring.

Korea and Singapore avoided the perils of the Bankers' Kingdom and the "lost decade" for different reasons than did Germany. Their banks did at times promote overexpansion, but were too weak to impede the process of rationalization once their respective bubbles collapsed. The international orientation of their financial system also helped. They suffered a traumatic adjustment in the Asian financial crisis, to be sure. Yet that critical juncture rationalized their lending portfolios, forced market-oriented changes in corporate governance, and gave the domestic financial system a global orientation, through expanded foreign investment. Those structural changes have been clearly beneficial to the real economies of Korea and Singapore in recent years.

(11) *Energy. Alternative energy deserves consideration, but cannot be a full alternative to nuclear power. For at least the next generation, nuclear power needs to have a significant role, within a more competitive energy-supply regime.*

One of our reference countries, Germany, sharply renounced nuclear power in the wake of Fukushima, vowing to close all its existing nuclear plants by 2022.[98] Germany is not, however, a realistic model for Japan in the energy sphere, as it can flexibly rely on electric-power imports from surrounding nations, such as France, while Japan is a more isolated island nation.

Korea and Singapore, both lacking in domestic energy supplies and largely devoid of readily accessible alternatives, are the best reference cases for Japan. Korea has embraced nuclear power, and is relying on technical innovation, such as pyroprocessing, to provide safer and smaller-scale nuclear plants. To the extent that Japan continues with nuclear power beyond the useful life of existing nuclear facilities, which need to come back on stream to sustain Japanese economic life, it might consider the power of technology to make nuclear energy more plausible, as Korea seems to be doing.

With respect to hydrocarbons, both Korea and Singapore are pursuing an option that Japan might also consider—increasing domestic energy security through downstream expansion. Neither Korea nor Singapore has domestic hydrocarbon reserves. Yet both sharply expanded their oil-refining sectors in the wake of the Oil Shocks of the 1970s, and became exporters of such refined products as aviation fuel to rising new importers such as China. Recently both have also been actively promoting liquefied natural gas (LNG) use, attempting to deregulate LNG imports, and beginning to explore the possibility of becoming LNG trading centers, as spot markets in that strategic fuel begin to rapidly expand.[99]

Japan, together with all of our reference nations, is encouraging the development of alternatives to both nuclear power and hydrocarbons. Its new feed-in tariff system, which guarantees benchmark prices for alternative energy, is one powerful mechanism for encouraging this transition, although it is criticized by power companies as inefficient. Korea and Singapore, however, are pioneering with respect to pilot projects such as wind, solar, and tidal, research and development centers, competitive renewable energy project funding, and promotion of International Green Energy Expos in ways that Japan might profitably consider.

(12) *Agriculture. Collectives may be useful in facilitating transition— they played a constructive role in restructuring the shipbuilding industry during the 1970s. But they must not be given veto power on change.*

Agriculture is a sector where circles of compensation are strong in Japan, and also where Japanese policies have been strongly parochial. Since Japan has a large market for agricultural goods, which is one of the last bastions of protectionism in a political economy that in other areas is increasingly open, concessions on agriculture are of considerable importance to Japan's trading partners in both bilateral and multilateral negotiations. Japan's political difficulties in providing those concessions, due to the strength of agricultural circles of compensation, have been a major stumbling block in its inability to conclude bilateral free-trade agreements with any of its major trading partners, including the United States, the European Union, China, and South Korea. These failures are significantly inhibiting Japan's globalization, serious efforts in connection with the ironically abortive 2015 TPP agreement notwithstanding.

Each of our three reference countries has been more flexible about agricultural liberalization than Japan, and has consequently found it easier to conclude strategic free-trade agreements with other major nations. Korea, most importantly, has weaker national agricultural federations than Japan, which are far less powerful politically, and more reliant on state support. The Korean executive branch, conversely, is stronger than in Japan, and has actively overridden agricultural NGOs, which lack the broad coalitional support of Japan's agricultural circles of compensation, in order to secure recent free-trade agreements with the United States, the European Union, and ASEAN, as well.

The contrasts to our three reference countries are striking. Germany, with a significant agricultural sector, has liberalized in the context of the European Union, providing major subsidies to its own and its partners' farmers in compensation. Singapore is an open economy with no domestic agriculture to speak of, which has helped it to become a strongly globalized free trader. Korea is the most similar to Japan politically and economically. It revised its farmland legislation three times (1992, 2002, and 2006), in response to OECD recommendations to promote larger farms that could benefit from economies of scale.[100] These Korean changes were more substantial than early Japanese reforms, and helped support Korea's ambitious and ultimately successful free-trade agreement initiatives. Japan has begun to emulate this pattern.[101]

(13) *Macropolitical profile—crucial to successful reform.*

Circles of compensation create a strong stability bias within the Japanese domestic political economy at the subnational, and especially the intrasectoral, levels. Individual firms and even individual policy makers find it easier to cope with the challenges of uncertainty risk and conflict management through pooling risks and rewards, rather than confronting the excruciating process of handling these challenges through case-by-case allocation. Decision-makers thus systematically undervalue transcendent national considerations in favor of uncertainty avoidance.

National leadership could potentially override this subnational bias toward risk aversion, which prevails so strikingly in Japan, but the political system in Japan is not well equipped to override the embedded anti-risk institutional bias, for several reasons. First, in contrast to Korea, France, or the United States, Japan lacks a strong executive capable of countervailing circles of compensation. Instead it has a parliamentary system, with the prime minister subject to deposition at any time by a Diet that is replete with "veto players" capable of blocking legislation at any turn.[102] Diet processes, which severely limit session length and time available for deliberation, compound the leverage that veto players enjoy in legislative processes, and the corresponding challenges that leaders confront in overriding circles of compensation.[103]

The homogeneous nature of the Japanese political economy, and the dearth of political players, outside the circles of compensation, who enjoy political leverage against the Japanese state, compounds the problem of overriding the circles, with all their subnational influence and broad range of contacts. Japan is ethnically homogeneous, and exhibits few of the deep regional divisions that prevail in Korea or Germany. It also lacks the sociopolitical pressure groups, such as powerful labor movements, that operate in the reference cases to exert populist claims against the state. The highly regulated nature of the Japanese system, and the power of its entrenched bureaucracy, also make it difficult for strong nationwide protest to gain headway. So neither national leaders nor nationwide interest groups or regional interests normally have the power to override circles of compensation in non-crisis situations. This is a weakness of the Japanese system that can only be corrected through major structural reform.

Our three reference cases suggest the sort of reforms which might be in order, so as to countervail the power of circles of compensation and channel their manifest positive traits, such as the ability to neutralize risk and encourage cooperation in constructive directions. Most important, our three reference cases suggest the importance of *predictable national leadership*, capable of overriding particularistic interests, as a countervailing force. In Korea, presidents are elected for a single five-year term, independent of a unicameral National Assembly. In Germany, chancellors are similarly powerful, and elected for a finite term. In Singapore, there is no independent chief executive, and prime ministers are subject to parliamentary approval. Yet the ruling People's Action Party is so entrenched that such approval is a formality, and national leaders continue predictably for many years. Predictable leadership, in each case, allows national authority to suppress particularistic interests to a degree that has been difficult so far to achieve in Japan.

Strengthening the prime minister's office, by increasing staff, expanding prerogatives, and improving information flow, is a clear imperative for Japan. Reforming Diet procedures, to reduce the leverage of parochial veto players, and to allow legislators to more directly engage with the broader world is also greatly needed. Only if Japanese politicians can engage more closely with the world, to fully grasp its rapid pace of transformation, and then centralize more authority at home to implement needed structural reforms, can Japan fully assume the respected place in world affairs that its substantial scale, and the formidable industry of its people, entitle that remarkable nation.

In Conclusion

We have pointed out throughout this volume the difficulties in responding decisively to broad national interests, and to the deepening requirements of globalization, which are posed acutely in Japan by circles of compensation. Since the 1990s, what were once highly functional supports for Japan's high-speed growth process have been transformed into regressive barriers to the restructuring needed to escape from the "lost decade" of stagnation. The question arises: Isn't there an alternative?

We have striven to answer that question through broad international comparative analysis, albeit not through the conventional, ethnocentric comparisons with Anglo-American best practice. As benchmarks of comparison, we have relied instead on best practices out of nations with a similar late-developer historical-institutional character that are more structurally similar to Japan than are Britain and the United States: Germany, South Korea, and Singapore. All three are densely populated, as is Japan, and also energy deficient. We have sought ways that these countries can address deficiencies that circles of compensation create in Japan. We have also sought useful policy benchmarks for Japan, addressing problems illuminated in the cases reviewed in previous chapters.

Transportation, education, and telecommunications are three areas, in particular, where Japan has much to learn from the reference countries, as those sectors are central to a nation's ability to globalize. The basic insight is the importance of privileging cosmopolitan impulses over the parochial concerns of local interest groups. Incheon, Changi, and Munich International Airports, for example, are all more welcoming, easier to use, and less expensive than Narita, Haneda, or Kansai. These cross-national differences have major implications—that could be corrected—for Japan's ability to deal more effectively with the world.

The broad picture we have drawn regarding Japan is of a system that functioned smoothly during the high-growth period, but which has since become increasingly set in comfortable yet parochial ways that ultimately induce stagnation. A volatile, changing world demands quick responses that parochial, risk-averse Japanese circles of compensation cannot easily generate. The most effective antidote to this situation—so deeply subversive of Japan's ability to globalize and grow—is national leadership capable of and willing to countervail parochial circles of compensation by focusing on structural reform. Germany, Korea, and Singapore have all had this sort of transformational leadership at critical junctures in their globalization process, and Japan needs it, as well.

Japan's problem is that it has powerful circles of compensation, and no coherent central authority to control them, so they are autonomous, and prone to impose their perverse features on society. *Japan's problem is thus a combination of no central authority, homogeneous society, and high regulation*—traits which in combination inhibit opposition to the state, so that Stigler's corruption of power through regulatory capture can easily occur. The circles are not intrinsically bad, and play important social functions in generating stability. They become dysfunctional only with the passage of time, when the mechanisms for controlling their predatory or rent-seeking dimensions prove inadequate, thus frustrating or delaying needed agricultural, financial, or communications reform.

Conclusion
Unraveling the Paradox

In the preceding chapters, we constructed an analytical paradigm—the circle of compensation. We also identified its central features, and documented its pervasive and persistent presence in the Japanese political economy of the past and current century. We noted that circles of compensation exist at various levels of analysis, including national, sectoral, local, and even intracorporate. These circles are not unique to Japan, being prevalent also in the small democratic corporatist nations of northwestern Europe, in the heavy-industrial sectors of many coordinated market economies (CMEs) globally, and occasionally even in the United States.

In addition to identifying such configurations in various parts of the world, especially Japan, we also ventured explanatory hypotheses linking such circles and a variety of counterintuitive outcomes that we also observed in comparative political economy. They correlate with rapid economic growth, including the explosive "invest, then save" variety, for which they provide critical risk diffusion. Circles of compensation, however, also invite moral hazard, financial bubbles, and extended resultant intervals of stagnation.

Circles of compensation, we found, also enhance our theoretical understanding of cooperative market capitalism. They help us refine the exaggerated dichotomy between markets and hierarchy. They enrich our insights into subgovernments that stand between individuals and the state, as well as prevailing incentive structures. They help us grasp contrasting patterns of response to globalization across human society and the efficacy of domestic pressures for economic reform.

The Problem for Analysis

As we noted at the outset of this volume, Japan outpaced the world in economic growth for the better part of a century, from the 1880s until the collapse of its bubble economy after 1990. It often proved remarkably adaptable in confronting its challenges, especially during the early post–World War II period, and in political-economic crises across the ensuing forty years. Yet since the collapse of the Heisei bubble in the early 1990s, Japan has neither grown much economically nor proven notably adaptable in meeting domestic and international challenges, even as the pace of global economic change and structural transformation beyond its shores has markedly accelerated.

This chapter returns to the problems for analysis that we originally raised, centering on the paradox of Japan's checkered recent political-economic performance against the formidable achievements of that country's more distant past. We noted two central puzzles to be unraveled: (1) a *paradox of growth*, centering on the protracted stagnation which the Japanese political economy has experienced since 1990, following rapid and sustained expansion—among the most rapid in the world—for most of the preceding century; and (2) *incongruous contours of policy*, in sectors ranging from finance and transportation to agriculture. These we attributed to a proliferation of private, non-union sociopolitical organizations with public functions that skew the incentives of policy makers toward stability and away from innovation or response to outside stimuli, including globalization.

We examined the Japan-specific anomalies of our study with respect to growth and public policy against the backdrop of broader social theory. In this connection, we asked: (1) Why do collective-action groups emerge in such profusion, and prove so active in Japan, despite the fragile incentives for substantive participation that Mancur Olson contends should prevail?[1] (2) What functional role do organized private bodies, intermediate between state and society, actually play in economic life?[2] Are they "distributional coalitions" disruptive to economic growth, as Olson suggests?

We hypothesized that circles of compensation influence political-economic behavior in four specific ways, summarized in Table CON.1 below, with concrete implications for both growth and globalization. We tested this supposition in six sectors where global pressures for domestic structural change within Japan appear to be particularly intense, and yet where circles of compensation nevertheless continue to prevail. These sectors of strategic inquiry included finance, land policy, agriculture, energy, transportation, and communications. We contrasted policy and corporate decision-making in those areas to other related sectors where circles of compensation are weak or absent, such as automobiles and consumer electronics, and investigated the impact of circles at both the sectoral and corporate levels. Through this classic methodological approach, testing for outcomes alternatively in the presence and absence of a key intermediate variable, we were able to more rigorously test the hypothesis that circles of compensation decisively shape patterns of corporate and bureaucratic decision, slowing adaptation within Japan to the forces of globalization, and perpetuating post-bubble economic stagnation.

Methods of Exploration

In exploring the response of Japanese firms and individuals to pressures from the broader world, and the role of an intermediate structural variable—circles of compensation—in conditioning that response, we made an important assumption that should be rendered explicit. We assumed that individuals are the appropriate unit of decision-making analysis, and that they respond rationally to the menu of incentives which directly confront them. We consequently postulate that firms will respond differently where circles of compensation exist and where they do not exist, provided that the intermediate structural variable that circles constitute influences the internal cost-benefit calculations of such firms.

Research Findings

In our review of modern Japanese economic history, we found private-sector vehicles for collective action—industrial associations, civic associations, neighborhood associations, chambers of commerce, political support groups, and cartels (both formal and informal), to name just a few—to be both ubiquitous and consequential, although less salient in consumer-oriented sectors than elsewhere. Some such collective-action bodies, including neighborhood associations, are of venerable provenance, dating from the Edo period or even before. Many, such as the early chambers of commerce, were established and supported by the Meiji government in an effort to co-opt the new social forces arising out of Japan's early modernization. Still others, especially industry associations for sectors like steel and shipbuilding, arose out of Japan's mobilization for the Pacific War. Some, such as the modern agricultural cooperatives, either originated or at least came to fruition during the early days of postwar democracy.

Whatever their origin, Japan's voluntary organizations have generally fallen into intimate regulatory relationships with the state. Once incorporated, such bodies have typically grown conservative in their basic political-economic orientation. They also typically exhibit a stability bias, both in membership and in policy orientation.

Such institutional continuity is rooted in the distinctive microeconomic returns to the established iterative relationships that typically prevail in circles of compensation. These returns flow from both regulatory and distributive benefits conferred by governmental participants in the circles, as well as private-sector accommodations. The circles diffuse risk, since other group members are available to share risk, and provide support in case of emergency.

Because most circles exist in regulated contexts, as in finance, transportation, or telecommunications, and because regulatory capture has been typical in Japan, with its extended periods of one-party dominance, circles of compensation commonly generate attractive economic rents for participants, causing members to support perpetuation of the circles themselves. For bureaucratic overseers, circles of compensation have the attraction of simplifying and stabilizing government–business relations within the regulatory process. Circles also exploit the desire of private firms for a stable, profitable environment, in order to elicit their cooperation with broader bureaucratic objectives.

We identified many instances of positive social benefits accruing to circles of compensation—particularly during the high-growth period of Japanese economic development. The circles encouraged high rates of capital investment, especially in capital-intensive sectors like steel and shipbuilding, based on high debt-equity ratios that would have been unsustainable without the sort of collective-support structure that circles of compensation provided. In times of adversity, as following the Oil Shocks of the 1970s, circles also facilitated coordinated capacity reduction, as in shipbuilding, special steel, and coal mining. Similarly, the circles also at times promoted healthy mutual specialization—as in the development of VLSI electronic circuitry in the 1980s, or in the robotics industry of the same decade—that would have otherwise proven impossible. Circles of compensation have thus been far more than simple vested interests.

Yet circles of compensation also have often had perverse implications. They inhibit individual risk taking, externalize costs, and discriminate against outsiders. Along these lines, they resemble Olson's perverse "distributional coalitions."[3] Those drawbacks have become more serious as the pace of global innovation has accelerated, and where markets have grown increasingly complex, protean, and global. Through their inhibiting impact on risk taking, as well as outreach to nonmembers, circles of compensation indirectly tend to impede Japanese interaction with the broader world, as well as responsiveness to developments beyond Japanese shores.

Telecommunications is a case in point. Japan's i-mode cell-phone technology, for example, evolved steadily across the 1990s and 2000s, but in directions at sharp variance from developments overseas, driven by the parochial concerns of the "NTT family" circle of compensation, and its defensive side-stepping of the risks of international competition. A "Galápagos syndrome" set in, by which cooperative yet parochial interactions among Japanese firms and the local regulatory authorities produced high-performance products attractive to many Japanese, but with only a limited market outside Japan itself. Since around 2010, this Galápagos dynamic, induced by parochial circles of compensation limited to Japanese firms, has rendered Japanese electronics manufacturers uncompetitive with Apple's iPhone or Samsung's Android-based technology, generating a crisis for the Japanese producers. This pattern has prevailed in other sectors, also.

Transportation is a parallel case. High landing fees at Japan's largest airports, raised in a political effort to generate funds that could cross-subsidize smaller domestic airports, make international centers like Narita increasingly unattractive as regional hubs. As a result, Narita declined steadily, from third largest airport in the world to fourteenth in international cargo volume between 2002 and 2015, passed by several other Asian locations, such as Shanghai and Incheon.[4]

Although circles of compensation do often appear to perversely affect Japan's responsiveness to global trends, there has been remarkably little debate regarding how circles affect Japan's globalization, or even regarding the pros and cons of globalization at all. Indeed, the concept of globalization itself—dramatically highlighted in Korea by creation of the *Segyehwa* concept in the mid-1990, does not even have a well-articulated translation in Japanese.[5] This absence of debate regarding globalization, or even a clear popular consciousness of its revolutionary potential, is one of our most striking political findings. Even entrepreneurs with strong stakes in its advancement, such as the founders of *Shinkeiren* in the 2010s, were unable to leverage their articulate stress on the merits of globalization with demonstrable impact on policy or politics. No doubt this absence of a vigorous, policy-related globalization debate in Japan, despite the costs to competitiveness of not so engaging, is related both to values (priority to self-reliance) and the parochial incentives typically embedded in circles of compensation themselves. The parochial pull of domestic incentives, in short, obscures the importance of a cosmopolitan response.

There are a few exceptions to this pattern. *Shinkeiren*, a principal business advocate of globalization, has had some limited success in agenda setting, as in promoting the concept of National Strategic Special Zones to the Cabinet

Office of Prime Minister Shinzō Abe. It has, however, lacked the funding or institutional cohesion of established organizations like *Keidanren*, the six-hundred-member Japan Business Federation, and suffered from declining membership after a dynamic start-up in 2010−2012.

Circles of compensation impede Japanese domestic structural change in response to global forces for several reasons. First, they induce a parochial bias that makes member firms more responsive to internal group pressures than to incentives from the outside. Even where circle members can see the value of responding to outside forces, they often fail to do so, due to the attractive economic rents, including administered prices higher than market levels, that accrue to group membership. Such rents are frequently sustained by supportive government regulation, including favorable government procurement pricing; attractive pricing of production inputs, such as electric power or telecommunications services; and outright trade protection, as in some of Japanese agriculture. Such direct protection significantly impedes response to globalization, although it is waning outside a small number of agricultural sectors.

Circles of compensation within Japan can also, secondly, inhibit inquisitive search processes, especially by outsiders lacking basic context to engage in informed debate. Circles thus reduce a competition of ideas that would otherwise encourage globalization. Education and telecommunications are sectors where this tendency appears to prevail.

The land-standard system of Japan (*tochi hon'isei*), itself a figurative circle of compensation linking conservative politicians, big business, banks, farmers, and real-estate interests, introduces a third impediment to globalization. Since loans are traditionally secured by land collateral, this embedded system, which prompted banks to over-lend in the bubble years, ultimately generating bad debt when land prices collapsed, has rendered many Japanese banks and firms hesitant in their lending and borrowing behavior, at precisely the point when their proactive response was needed to energize the globalization process. The collapse of the entrepreneurial long-term credit banks in the late 1990s compounded this hesitancy.

Since the beginning of the 1990s, the land standard has also impeded expansionary behavior by Japanese corporations, both at home and abroad, since the price of critically important land collateral has been generally declining or stagnant. This inhibiting impact on firm-level investment has also been a powerful contributor to Japanese stagnation at the macro level, as well. New types of equity-oriented corporate innovators, such as Kazuo Inamori of Kyocera, Hiroshi Mikitani of Rakuten, and Masayoshi Son of SoftBank, have begun to emerge, but their most dynamic contributions have been outside rather than inside Japan.

Circles of compensation typically internalize benefits and externalize costs. Generally costs are externalized to parties outside Japan, but frequently those costs entail negative consequences for some domestic groups, as well. Thus they might be assumed to stir domestic as well as foreign opposition. Yet we have found that they tend not to do so. One reason for this lack of domestic resistance to the negative externalities of protection is that circles of compensation often include both producer and consumer interests—agriculture, for example, where *nōkyō* and *seikyō* combine to oppose the use of genetically modified organisms and many specialized foreign agricultural chemicals.

The pace of change in the relative salience and political-economic importance of circles of compensation appears to vary from sector to sector. Land-policy circles seem to have declined in influence since the early 1990s, as land prices stagnated and public-works construction declined, although the land-lending linkage continues to inhibit many Japanese banks, and to slow Japanese economic transformation as a whole. Agricultural circles, however, maintained formidable defensive influence in the face of pressures for trade liberalization. This embedded influence helped delay Japanese domestic assent to the abortive TPP agreement until October 2015,[6] although the prerogatives of agricultural cooperatives outside finance were critically curtailed;[7] no doubt circles will continue to impede Japanese trade liberalization even more strongly, given TPP's early 2017 rejection by the United States. Telecommunications circles are likewise declining in coherence, but not fast enough to inspire dynamic corporate response, within Japan itself, to explosive global developments in mobile telephony, or to the rise of the Internet. The signature initiatives of new, entrepreneurial Japanese firms like SoftBank and Rakuten are increasingly outside Japan, even though Japan is their homeland and logical base of operations.

Public manipulation of asset prices through circles of compensation, in cases ranging from the sale of bonds to the pricing of land, is a venerable tradition in Japan. Especially pronounced, for many years, were public policies encouraging high and rising real-estate prices, as discussed in the land, finance, and agricultural-policy chapters. Foreign-exchange controls until late 1979 constrained capital outflows that might have otherwise been attracted to alternative investments abroad.

With the December 1979 revision of the Foreign Exchange and Foreign Trade Control Law, as well as subsequent relaxation of administrative constraints on foreign investment by Japanese institutional investors, such as life insurance companies, Japanese corporate investment horizons began to broaden dramatically. Yet circles of compensation within Japan inhibited responsive changes in domestic regulatory structures, rendering domestic rates of return in many sectors less favorable than those overseas. Capital began to flow outward from Japan in large amounts for the first time since World War II.

This new combination of capital mobility and domestic rigidity led to rising international capital flows, by both Japanese financial institutions and foreign actors, including hedge funds. These actors exploited the domestic rigidities within Japan, and used Japan's persistent reflation packages over the lost decade of the 1990s to swap funds abroad through an expanding, and highly lucrative, "carry trade." The perverse combination of rigidifying circles of compensation within Japan and capital mobility outward from Japan thus played a fundamental role in Japan's enduring economic stagnation since 1990.

Prime Minister Abe came to power at the end of 2012 intent on reviving Japan after two decades of low growth. The first two arrows of his economic program—monetary reflation and fiscal stimulus—achieved dramatic short-term results during 2013, boosting the Tokyo Stock Exchange Nikkei index by nearly 57 percent, its biggest annual rise in over forty years.[8] Yet the "third arrow" of Abenomics—structural reform—proved difficult to implement, and growth thereafter began to slow.[9] Given the pervasiveness of circles of compensation, and the stability bias that they generate, it remains an open question how far structural changes that dismantle the circles can proceed—or whether they can be broadened to induce new economic dynamism. Structural biases against globalization within Japan, which also perpetuate stagnant growth, remain to be overcome.

In Chapter 3, we hypothesized that circles of compensation would have four concrete implications for political-economic behavior: They would (1) internalize collective rewards, and externalize risk, (2) impart a parochial policy bias, (3) bias incentives away from innovation, and (4) impede responsiveness to global and other transnational forces. In the intervening chapters, we tested these four hypotheses in six Japanese policy sectors where circles of compensation prevail, and examined nine counterfactual corporate and two sectoral cases, where circles are less salient. Our empirical findings and assessment of these results are summarized in Table CON.1.

As is clear from Table CON.1, the postulated traits associated with circles of compensation do *not* prevail in the control cases, where circles do not exist. They *are*, however, pervasive to varying degrees in the six sectors where circles of compensation exist. Most strikingly, all four postulated traits are clearly

TABLE CON. I

Circles of compensation and their impact on the Japanese political economy

Circle function	Internal reward, external risk	Parochial policy bias	Incentive restructuring	Globalization
Finance	Systemic	Extensive	Moderate	Moderate
	• Bankers' Kingdom promotes land-based borrowing at the expense of small businesses and consumers	• Revision of Banking Ordinance (1893) • National Finance Control Association under the National Mobilization Law • Zenginkyō and the Industrial Capital Subcommittee (1962–1964)	• Marginal role for foreign capital and investment • Prevention of Green Card system in the late 1980s	• Revision of Foreign Exchange and Foreign Trade Law (1980)
Land and housing	Systemic	Systemic	Extensive	—
	• Construction and bureaucratic interests align to inflate the price of land at the expense of home buyers	• The Land and House Lease Law • Inheritance and Property Tax System • Production Greening Law (1974) and Price Reduction Ordinance (1976)	• Housing Construction Planning Law (1966) and the Housing Loan Corporation • Recent increase in land taxation	
Food policy	Systemic	Systemic	Systemic	Limited
	• Agricultural and political interests align to inflate food commodity prices, while excluding foreign producers, at the expense of consumers	• Food Control Law (1942) • Agricultural Cooperatives Law (1947)	• Sheer dominance of JA Group, such as Zen-Noh's percentage share in pesticides and machinery • Financing and insurance options though the Norinchukin Bank and Zenkyoren, respectively	• Aversion to the Trans-Pacific Partnership, although recent restructuring attempts under the Abe Administration

(continued)

TABLE CON. I (*continued*)

Circle function	Internal reward, external risk	Parochial policy bias	Incentive restructuring	Globalization
Energy	Moderate • Local political and residential interests align under a central government-backed strategy to develop the nuclear sector at the expense of citizens and potential accident victims	Extensive • *Dengen Sanpō* under Prime Minister Tanaka Kakuei (1974)	Extensive/moderate • Crisis-driven change following Fukushima	Moderate • International cooperation on decommissioning • Post-Fukushima LNG sourcing
Transportation	Moderate • Airport/port companies and bureaucratic interests align to build local airports and increase fees at the expense of passengers and domestic airlines	Moderate • Airport Facilities Improvement Special Account (1970–2013) • Airport Facilities Improvement Plan beginning from 1976 • Connection to land price and the land-standard system	Moderate • Crisis-driven JAL restructuring	Limited • Open Skies agreement with the U.S. (2010) and slot negotiations at Haneda Int'l Airport (2016)
Communications	Extensive • Manufacturing and political interest align to promote significant R&D at the expense of domestic consumers and foreign producers	Extensive • NTT family until 1980s • Slow deregulation/privatization/standards policy change	Extensive • Development of i-mode phones and Japan-specific technical standards • Rejection of large-scale reduction of interconnection rates in the 2000s	Limited • Galápagos syndrome persists
Outlier firms	Limited	Absent	Limited	Extensive

SOURCE: Author's illustration.

NOTES: The characteristics of a sector in each of the four selected areas is ranked on a five-level scale, where *Systemic* > *Extensive* > *Moderate* > *Limited* > *Absent*. Decisions regarding the classification of outlier firms are made using the observations detailed in Table 10.1.

present in the land and agricultural sectors, although reform is beginning to occur in the countryside, as indicated in the land and food-policy chapters.

Finance, as is evident from Table CON.1, is a mixed and highly strategic case. The Bankers' Kingdom, linking financiers with industrialists and the conservative political world, lay at the core of the high-growth Japanese political economy of the early postwar period. Strong ties linking finance, politics, and industry remain embedded at the heart of the Japanese political economy and impedes full-scale restructuring. Japanese finance has been changing, however, with the collapse of the long-term credit banks in the late 1990s, and the rising role of direct finance since around 2005. Since revision of the Foreign Exchange and Foreign Trade Control Law in 1980, cross-border capital flows have also been exerting pressure for change, both in finance itself and in asset pricing throughout the Japanese political economy.

Policy Prescriptions

The hypotheses presented in Chapter 3 suggested that circles of compensation should be profoundly conservative and parochial, due to the way that they internalize benefits and externalize costs. The ensuing empirical presentation uncovered some positive implications for economic growth not considered in Mancur Olson's formulation, particularly relating to risk diffusion under the "invest, then save" pattern of high-leverage industrialization. Yet circles of compensation clearly do have perverse macrosocial implications that raise the important issue of how they might be either dismantled or transformed.

"Deregulation doesn't help much." Deregulation has often been prescribed as a remedy for parochialism and stagnation induced by organized interests, and was for many years a central element of U.S. trade policy toward Japan. The research presented here suggests that too much confidence has been placed in such a priority. Subnational private-sector institutions larger than the firm, such as industry associations, together with their extended sociopolitical networks, are indeed pervasive across much of the Japanese political economy, and they are often collusive in nature. To the extent that such associations are sustained and supported by state regulation, as through circles of compensation, and cannot exist without it, deregulation may intensify competitive forces and promote globalization. Yet converse cases are numerous, as well. On balance, recent history has shown deregulation to be a futile trade strategy for economic partners of Japan.

"Political change is not a panacea." For many years it was also fashionable to contend that political change could transform the Japanese political economy and its constituent parts. Canadian, Australian, and sometimes U.S. government

officials, especially those interested in agricultural access, subscribed to this
view. Recent history, and the analysis provided here, suggests against overreli-
ance on party-political change as a driver of economic liberalization. This research suggests strongly, from the experience of both the Democratic Party of
Japan government of 2009–2012, and the return to Liberal Democratic Party
rule thereafter, that political parties cannot easily serve as agents of transformation in the deeply rooted subnational circles of compensation that prevail in
Japan. Even the forceful efforts of Shinzō Abe, like those of Junichirō Koizumi
and Yasuhiro Nakasone before him, have had only limited impact in achieving
structural change. The most realistic initiatives involve broadening the circles,
to expand the diversity of viewpoints they represent, rather than disrupting
their fundamental, deeply embedded mode of operating, which so profoundly
influences underlying incentive structures.

A more nuanced political argument has maintained that changes in electoral
rules, such as the 1994 transition from multi-member to single-member rep-
resentation in the Japanese Diet, should provoke significant structural change,
not only in Japanese politics, but also in the Japanese political economy more
generally. This argument is based on a set of rational-choice assumptions about
the determinants of human behavior that this volume broadly accepts. The
argument does, however, neglect the role of intermediate institutions and networks, such as circles of compensation, in shaping individual choice, so tends
to generate overly optimistic predictions about the ability of political reform
to achieve economic revitalization, at least in the short run.

If deregulation, party-political transition, and the adjustment of electoral
rules cannot meaningfully loosen the hold of circles of compensation, what
are the prospects for transforming them in a more felicitous and cosmopolitan direction? Five alternatives suggest themselves: (1) demographic attrition,
(2) foreign pressure, (3) emulating best practices from abroad, (4) initiatives
from political leadership, and (5) enlargement of the circles themselves. All of
these are synergistic with a final important, and catalytic, variable: enlightened
domestic leadership.

"Demography has some impact." Attrition is gradually changing the profile of
the Japanese political economy: the average farmer in Japan is now sixty-seven
years old, and the average small shopkeeper is his contemporary. Japan as a
whole has a population older than that of Florida, the very symbol of geron-
tocracy in the United States; Japan's population has been steadily declining
since 2012. Indeed, in Japan today, around 26 percent of the population is over
sixty-five, compared to just 19 percent in Florida, America's most geriatric
state.[10] Demography is quietly transforming some important sectors, such as

agriculture and distribution, reducing the centrality of circles there, and opening broader room for market forces, but it is doing so very slowly.

"Foreign pressure in special circumstances has utility." This research suggests that foreign pressure is creating some momentum for change, and it does offer hope for a "reactive" Japanese response under certain limited circumstances. The utility of *gaiatsu* (foreign pressure) is, however, diluted by the underlying structural realities that: (1) circles of compensation are subnational, and thus not directly amenable to outside pressure; and (2) circles share risk and reward, rendering them formidably stable, and thus defusing the transformational impact of foreign pressures. *Gaiatsu* can nevertheless have some indirect utility, as was clear during the Structural Impediments Initiative (SII) distribution-sector talks of the early 1990s, when it was clearly aligned with domestic economic forces, and well coordinated with domestic actors having access to relevant circles of compensation.[11] Foreign pressure under the multilateral TPP initiative was beginning to have this sort of effect, until it was fatefully diluted by the rejection of the final agreement by the United States in early 2017.

Although the Japanese people were once responsive to foreign pressure, especially from the United States, that propensity is waning. A new generation that feels less beholden to the West than their Occupation-era forebears, and also less economically dependent on their country's Group of 7 partners, is less inclined to concede to demands they often find unreasonable. That said, the efficacy of combined pressure and introduction of foreign best practices, especially in consumer-related matters, may be growing more effective.

"The financial sector is a potential driver for long-term change." We have noted repeatedly the Japanese malaise of being overly introverted and failing to globalize. While the core of these dual challenges is the incentive structure created by circles of compensation, the perversions of the financial structure since the collapse of "strategic capitalism" during the 1990s have blinded the ability of finance to send incentive signals, and thus gravely compromised Japan's difficulties. The collapse of long-term banking and the salience of political influence in finance, together with struggles of alternate credit analysis and regulatory structures to emerge, have prevented the financial system from adequately perceiving, evaluating, and responding to the revolutionary changes in technology and the broader world that have occurred.

Financial transformation, of course, is a delicate and time-consuming task. Two large changes are in order, however, that could make an important long-term difference. Most important, much of the Japanese business world needs corporate-governance changes. Stakeholder dominance facilitates the easy, stability-oriented trade-offs (often blind to profit, globalization, and even growth) that are implicit in circles of compensation. Shareholder dominance has perversities of its own, including short-term horizons and resource allocations toward private rather than collective goods. So some middle way is needed. Indirect efforts to change market signals, through steps like establishment of the Nikkei 400 index, identifying firms with positive corporate-governance practices; and government pension-fund purchases that accord with such positive criteria, would be preferable to abrupt and sweeping regulatory changes.

Second, Japanese finance needs better risk analysis and credit assessment. The long-term credit banks, and to some extent the main banks of the *keiretsu* in their heyday, filled this function for many years, albeit in a somewhat subterranean fashion, and in a more stable political-economic environment than prevails today. Their calculations were distorted in the 1980s, however, by the intrusion of politics, financial deregulation, and the distortions introduced by the land-standard system. Constructing an alternate, more transparent system nevertheless sensitive to the underlying coordinated market economy character of the Japanese political economy involves complex yet interrelated legal, accounting, and regulatory changes, and will take considerable time to emerge.

Over time, changes in corporate governance, coupled with development of a more transparent regulatory and accounting structure, should lead to the development of expanded equity markets. That could in turn lead to less reliance on indirect finance, and new incentives for equity-driven venture-capital development. Yet the embedded influence of long-established institutions and practices will be difficult to dislodge.

"Enlarge and diversify the circles." If circles of compensation will continue to be a salient presence for the foreseeable future, the most effective way to liberalize, and also globalize, Japan may well be to enlarge and diversify the circles themselves. More women clearly need to join the top ranks of bureaucracy and corporate boards, and more foreigners, as well.[12] A start has been made in this direction: The share of women in middle-senior management positions with private corporations rose from 6.5 percent in 2009 to 8.3 percent in 2014.[13] Japan has started a promising dialogue with Silicon Valley, in multiple dimensions. Yet much more needs to be done.

"Proactive national leadership is crucial." The most important positive prescription suggested by this research is fostering proactive national leadership that sees globalization as a priority, appreciates the importance of structural change, and is sensitive to and knowledgeable about subnational realities that impede the process of change. The Japanese political economy, as we have come to

understand it here, is dominated by complex and pervasive strata of subnational organizations, which extract economic rents that frequently have perverse broader economic consequences. There are few potential countervailing forces to these circles in the short run other than strong national leadership.

Given that Japan is a parliamentary democracy, without powerful, institutionally independent executive-leadership structures, decisive change is more difficult than in presidential systems like Korea, France, or the United States. Strong leaders like Junichirō Koizumi and Yasuhiro Nakasone have shown, however, that such change is to some extent possible, if leadership priorities are sharply focused. Shinzō Abe has made an important start, with his Abenomics program, but needs to develop a more credible "third arrow" program, and to resist political pressures to inhibit change, as he failed to do during 2013–2014, in limiting online pharmaceutical sales.[14] Abenomics 2.0, announced in September 2015, provided some useful supplementary proposals regarding childcare and social security that could support structural change. Yet it did not create any major new incentives for such transformation.

One promising future option for finessing the circles of compensation could be expansion, using the opportunity that the 2020 Tokyo Olympic Games preparations will provide, of the National Strategic Special Zones that Prime Minister Abe has already begun to introduce.[15] Implementing the Japan Stewardship Code of February 2014, and the Corporate Governance Code of June 2015, both proposed by Prime Minister Abe, should also be helpful.[16] So could innovations in electronic governance, which can link citizens more directly with the state, thereby bypassing the intermediate bodies on which the circles so heavily rely.

Both Nakasone and Koizumi promoted privatization (national railways and postal savings) that represented important structural change, in both economic and political dimensions. Abe's massive ¥1.4 trillion ($11.6 billion) Japan Post initial public offering (IPO) of November 2015, the largest Japanese government asset sale since 1987, should be helpful.[17] Even more extensive structural change at the subnational level is clearly needed in Japan, however—the encouragement of more-dynamic venture-capital markets, and of the Internet economy, through clearer and more liberal regulatory policies in sectors free of embedded circles of compensation. Apart from such structural change, this research suggests that new forms of social capital investment—in hospitals and forward-looking mobile communications, for example—are also critically needed, although they have not heretofore been supported by the highly conservative circles of compensation.

Issues for Future Research

Most research on the Japanese political economy thus far has focused on national governmental institutions, such as METI, MOF, and the office of the Prime Minister. This book suggests, however, that more attention needs to be directed to the *subnational*—toward public–private partnerships, with demonstrably collective functions, embedded deeply in the structure of the Japanese political economy. Industry associations like the Japanese Bankers Association and the Federation of Electric Power Companies, not to mention Japan's Central Union of Agricultural Co-operatives (JA-Zenchu), definitely need to be understood better. So do cross-sectoral linkages, such as those among the Bankers' Kingdom, politicians, and the land-policy process.

The contention of this book—that subnational institutions are key determinants of policy outcomes, and their incentive structures need to be better understood—should also serve as catalyst for new forms of policy research. How to make the *financial sector* more responsive to the dual imperatives of innovation and globalization, through stronger incentives for venture capital and corporate-governance reform, should be top research priorities. Mechanisms for improving the chances that international trade agreements will effect meaningful structural change in Japan need more attention, as do the role of banks and their networks in shaping the Japanese political economy. Such issues need to be seen in the context of the incentive structures and patterns of transformation at the banks, the agricultural cooperatives, real-estate firms, and other such communal institutions. So far, however, little micro-level work has been done on any of the foregoing topics.

One central theoretical contribution of this research is that it challenges the classical dichotomy in institutional economics between "markets" and "hierarchies."[18] It suggests, based on the detailed empirical work presented in this book, that the relationship between those classic variables should instead be presented as a continuum.[19] Between markets and hierarchies stand a variety of subgovernments, with diverse functional roles, that reduce transaction costs, constrain free riders, and radically shift levels of effective decision. Subgovernments—public–private partnerships with clearly public functions—deserve more extended examination, and more systematic cross-national comparison.[20] Circles of compensation are one important variant, the study of which deepens our understanding of how subgovernments perform these diverse functions. Special attention should be given to circles in the financial area, as banks have central embedded roles as connectors across the political economy as a whole.

At the macro level, the influential distinction made in the "varieties of capitalism" literature between liberal market economies and CMEs certainly seems valid. Yet this research suggests that many details, especially at the micro- and cross-sectoral levels, remain to be clarified.[21] Only one chapter of the pathbreaking Hall and Soskice volume, *Varieties of Capitalism*, dealt in detail with Japan, and the analytical concern there was reinterpreting the welfare state in CMEs generally.[22] In particular, the role of nonfinancial service sectors and interpersonal networks in CME capitalism, as well as the relationship between land policy and economic growth, all need more precise specification. This volume begins that task, but additional cross-national research, especially on European versus East Asian CME comparisons, is clearly needed.

Corporate governance also deserves more systematic study in the context of its considerable systemic implications for collective action. Stakeholder dominance appears to be an important support for stable subgovernments, including circles of compensation, owing to the ways that it simplifies corporate decision-making and limits pressure to maximize profits. The impact of governance changes on the functioning of subgovernments, including circles of compensation, remains to be explored systematically, however.

The systemic implications of domestic circles of compensation within Japan, on the one hand, and international capital mobility between Japan and the broader world, on the other, also urgently need deeper analysis. Circles of compensation tend to slow Japanese domestic policy and corporate responses to global trends because of their risk-diffusion effects, which increase incentives to free ride, as Olson might predict.[23] Before Japanese financial liberalization, such rigidity had only a limited impact on the supply of capital to domestic firms, since virtually all capital supply was domestic, and constrained by foreign-exchange controls from considering investment options abroad. Since the early 1980s, however, this situation has dramatically changed, and rigidities within the domestic system, as well as the traditional bias of the banks toward land-based investment, are increasingly penalized by capital outflows, which reduce demand for domestic assets. Capital outflows from Japan have thus played an important indirect role in the collapse of land-based domestic assets, and to Japan's economic frustrations since the early 1990s.

The circle-of-compensation concept, as we have insisted from the beginning, is an abstract formulation. The idea has powerful heuristic value, however, in enhancing scholarly understanding of the Japanese political economy and its challenges, in both their domestic and international contexts. That heuristic value—the ability to help us achieve new insights—is no doubt the most powerful argument for promoting the concept; it does a parsimonious job of explaining stability at the micro level in the face of pressures for change.

Yet the circle-of-compensation concept should be relevant elsewhere in the world, as well. It should be especially relevant in other CMEs, where political structure, socioeconomic heritage, and linkages to the global political economy approximate those of Japan. Smaller European social democracies with a corporatist heritage, such as Switzerland and Austria, or late-developing industrial democracies, such as Italy, Turkey, and South Korea, where capital-intensive industrialization has occurred, and cooperative-capitalist risk-diffusion mechanisms are consequently needed, could be particularly promising cases for cross-national comparison involving circles of compensation.

Students of Japan have imported many concepts from the broader field of comparative analysis to aid them in understanding Japan. The time has come for the intellectual flow to reverse itself. How national governments and civil societies respond to the pressures of growth and globalization are questions of increasing importance. And the circles-of-compensation concept can help clarify and explain those responses—not only in Japan but across the wider world, as well.

Notes

INTRODUCTION

1. Alexander Gerschenkron, *Economic Backwardness in Historical Perspective* (Cambridge, MA: Harvard University Press, 1962).

2. Samuel Huntington, *Political Order in Changing Societies* (New Haven, CT: Yale University Press, 1968).

3. See, for example, Stephan Haggard, Wonhyuk Lim, and Euysung Kim, eds., *Economic Crisis and Corporate Restructuring in Korea: Reforming the Chaebol* (Cambridge: Cambridge University Press, 2003); T. J. Pempel, ed., *The Politics of the Asian Economic Crisis* (Ithaca, NY: Cornell University Press, 1999); and Joseph E. Stiglitz, *Globalization and Its Discontents* (New York: W. W. Norton, 2002).

4. See, for example, Chalmers Johnson, *MITI and the Japanese Miracle: The Growth of Industrial Policy, 1925–1975* (Stanford, CA: Stanford University Press, 1982); Peter Evans, *Embedded Autonomy: States and Industrial Transformation* (Princeton, NJ: Princeton University Press, 1995); Meredith Woo-Cumings, ed., *The Developmental State* (Ithaca, NY: Cornell University Press, 1999); and Atul Kohli, *State-Directed Development: Political Power and Industrialization in the Global Periphery* (Cambridge, UK: Cambridge University Press, 2004).

5. Rajat Ganguly and Ian Macduff, eds., *Ethnic Conflict and Secessionism in South and Southeast Asia: Causes, Dynamics, Solutions* (New Delhi: Sage Publications, 2003).

6. See Robert Putnam, "Diplomacy and Domestic Politics: The Logic of Two-Level Games," *International Organization* 42, no. 3 (Summer 1988): 427–460, www.jstor.org/stable/2706785.

7. On the scope of these changes, see Jeffry A. Frieden, *Global Capitalism: Its Fall and Rise in the Twentieth Century* (New York: W. W. Norton, 2006), 363–472.

8. This series of six scholarly conferences, convened at Hakone, in the shadow of Mount Fuji, beginning in late August 1960, brought together academics from major Japanese and American universities to discuss the concept of modernization and its applications in Japan. For a description, see Sebastian Conrad, "'The Colonial Ties Are Liquidated':

Modernization Theory, Post-War Japan and the Global Cold War," *Past and Present*, no. 216 (August 2012): 181–214. doi:10.1093/pastj/gts007.

9. By "globalization" we mean the process of transregional international integration arising from the interchange of products, ideas, and other aspects of culture. Advances in transportation and telecommunications infrastructure, including development of the Internet, are major factors in globalization, generating further interdependence of economic and cultural activities.

10. World Bank, "Merchandise exports (current US$)," *World Development Indicators*, 2015, http://data.worldbank.org/indicator/TX.VAL.MRCH.CD.WT; and World Bank, "GDP (current US$)," *World Development Indicators*, 2015, http://data.worldbank.org/indicator/NY.GDP.MKTP.CD.

11. For trade patterns of Japan, Korea, and China in 2014, see A. J. G. Simoes and C. A. Hidalgo, *The Economic Complexity Observatory: An Analytical Tool for Understanding the Dynamics of Economic Development* (Workshops at the Twenty-Fifth AAAI Conference on Artificial Intelligence, 2011).

12. United Nations Conference on Trade and Development (UNCTAD), "Annex table 1. FDI flows, by region and economy, 2009–2014," *World Investment Report 2015*, A3–A6, http://unctad.org/en/PublicationsLibrary/wir2015_en.pdf.

13. Ibid. Japan's FDI outflow in 2014 was $113.6 billion. Korea's FDI outflow in 2014 was $30.6 billion, and China's FDI outflow in the same year was $116.0 billion.

14. Japan's FDI stock in Africa totaled $6.9 billion in 2012, which was 0.66 percent of Japan's total FDI stock abroad. In contrast, China's FDI stock in Africa in the same year was as high was $21.7 billion, equal to 4.10 percent of its total FDI stock abroad. See UNCTAD, *Bilateral FDI Statistics 2014*, http://unctad.org/en/Pages/DIAE/FDI%20Statistics/FDI-Statistics-Bilateral.aspx.

15. Korea's FDI inflow in 2014 was $9.9 billion and China's FDI inflow in the same year was $128.5 billion. See *World Investment Report 2015*.

16. World Bank, "Foreign direct investment, net inflows (% of GDP)," *World Development Indicators*, 2014, http://data.worldbank.org/indicator/NY.GDP.MKTP.CD. According to World Bank, net FDI inflows to Japan equaled 0.2 percent of Japanese GDP in 2014, while net FDI inflows to the United States equaled 0.8 percent of U.S. GDP in the same year.

17. Japan's FDI inflow was $11.9 billion in 2009, declining to $2.1 billion in 2014. See *World Investment Report 2015*.

18. The notion of deepened interdependence with the world is typically expressed as *kokusaika* ("internationalization"), or occasionally *gurōbaruka* (transliteration of the English expression), and there is no clear analytical distinction between deepened ties with neighboring countries and recognition of a broader, integrated new global reality.

CHAPTER ONE

1. Author's calculation based on World Bank, "GDP growth (annual %)," *World Development Indicators*, 1990–2015, http://data.worldbank.org/indicator/NY.GDP.MKTP.KD.ZG.

2. Ibid.

3. Author's calculation based on Ministry of Internal Affairs and Communications Statistics Bureau, "3–1 Gross Domestic Expenditure (At Constant Prices)—68SNA, Benchmark year = 1990 (C.Y.1955–1998)," *Historical Statistics of Japan*.

4. In 1990 Japan ranked twelfth place globally in GDP per capita at current prices in U.S. dollars, compared to thirteenth place for the United States. By 2015 Japan had fallen to twenty-third by the same measure, whereas the United States had risen into the top ten. See World Bank, "GDP per capita (current US$)," *World Development Indicators*, 2015, http://data.worldbank.org/indicator/NY.GDP.PCAP.CD.

5. International Monetary Fund, "General government gross debt (Percent of GDP)," *World Economic Outlook*, October 2016.

6. The stimulus measures came in three huge packages: ¥3.12 trillion in October 1985; ¥3.63 trillion in September 1986; and ¥6.00 trillion in May 1987, which included a mix of public works and tax reductions. For example, the 1987 package included ¥5.00 trillion of public works and ¥1.00 trillion of tax reductions. Japan's *Diplomatic Bluebook 1988* described the implementation of the stimulus package as an achievement in redressing Japan's huge external imbalance and turning Japan's economic structure into one that is "in more harmony with the economies of other countries." See Michio Muramatsu and Wataru Kitamura, "Zaisei-akaji no Seijigaku: Seiji no Fuanteisei, Keizai-baburu, Saishutsu-akaji [The Political Science of Budget Deficit: Political Uncertainty, Economic Bubbles, and Government Spending Deficits]," in *Kōzōmondai to Kiseikanwa [Structural Problems and Deregulation]*, ed. Jūrō Teranishi (Tokyo: Keio University Press, 2010), 175, under Cabinet Office Economic and Social Research Institute, www.esri.go.jp/jp/others/kanko_sbubble/analysis_07.html; "Japanese Optimistic on Economic Growth," *Journal of Commerce*, June 21, 1987, www.joc.com/maritime-news/japanese-optimistic-economic-growth_19870621.html-0; and Ministry of Foreign Affairs, *Diplomatic Bluebook 1988*, www.mofa.go.jp/policy/other/bluebook/1988/1988-contents.htm.

7. Takao Komine and Keiko Okada, "Baburu-hōkai to Furyōsaiken Taisaku [Countermeasures to Bubble Collapse and Non-performing Loans]," in *Nihonkeizai no Kiroku: Dai-2-ji Sekiyukiki e no Taiō kara Baburu-hōkai made [Records of Japanese Economics: From Countermeasures to the Second Oil Crisis to the Bubble Collapse]*, ed. Takao Komine (Tokyo: Cabinet Office Economic and Social Research Institute, 2011), 419, www.esri.go.jp/jp/prj/sbubble/history/history_01/history_01.html.

8. This included ¥23.9 trillion announced in November 1998 and ¥18 trillion in November 1999. See Muramatsu and Kitamura.

9. On Japan's coordinated government-business effort to develop VLSI memory chips, see Kent E. Calder and Roy Hofheinz, Jr., *The Eastasia Edge* (New York: Basic Books, 1982), 154–157.

10. The Nikkei 225 reached a high of 38,957.44 on December 29, 1989. See Nikkei Indexes, "Historical Data (Nikkei 225)," http://indexes.nikkei.co.jp/en/nkave/archives/data.

11. Ibid. The high price of Nikkei 225 on December 9, 2016, was 19,042.48. Despite a major stimulus from Abenomics, it had recovered to only 49 percent of its 1989 level.

12. Ministry of Finance, "Table 6s-a-1 Current account (seasonally adjusted) (Quarterly Figures)," *Balance of Payments (Historical Data)* and Cabinet Office, "Annualized rate of changes from the previous quarter (at current prices: seasonally adjusted series)," *Quarterly Estimates of GDP Jan.–Mar. 2016 (The 2nd preliminary)*.

13. On this rapidly emerging global opportunity and challenge, see Yves Tiberghien, *Entrepreneurial States: Reforming Corporate Governance in France, Japan, and Korea* (Ithaca, NY: Cornell University Press, 2007).

14. "Globalization" in this volume refers to the process or processes of international integration, occurring principally along four dimensions: trade, capital flows, migration,

and dissemination of knowledge. It involves the reduction and removal of barriers across national borders to facilitate the flow of goods, capital, services, and labor.

15. See, for example, Kent E. Calder, "Japanese Foreign Economic Policy Formation: Explaining the Reactive State," *World Politics* 40, no. 4 (July 1988): 517–541, www.jstor .org/stable/2010317; Leonard J. Schoppa, *Bargaining with Japan: What American Pressure Can and Cannot Do* (New York: Columbia University Press, 1997); and Ulrike Schaede and William Grimes, ed., *Japan's Managed Globalization: Adapting to the Twenty-First Century* (Armonk, New York: M. E. Sharpe, 2003).

16. See, for example, Frances McCall Rosenbluth and Michael F. Thies, *Japan Transformed: Political Change and Economic Restructuring* (Princeton, NJ: Princeton University Press, 2010).

17. On the methods of difference and similarity, see John Stuart Mill, *A System of Logic, Ratiocinative and Inductive: Being a Connected View of the Principles of Evidence, and Methods of Scientific Investigation* (London: J. W. Parker, 1843).

18. See, for example Thomas C. Schelling, *The Strategy of Conflict* (Cambridge, MA: Harvard University Press, 1960); and Kenneth Arrow, *The Limits of Organization* (New York: Norton, 1974), 15–29.

19. Robert Axelrod, *The Evolution of Cooperation* (New York: Basic Books, 1984), 145–191; and George Tsebelis, *Nested Games: Rational Choice in Comparative Politics* (Berkeley: University of California Press, 1990).

20. Mancur Olson, *The Logic of Collective Action: Public Goods and the Theory of Groups* (Cambridge, MA: Harvard University Press, 1965).

21. See Oliver E. Williamson, *The Economic Institutions of Capitalism: Firms, Markets, Relational Contracting* (New York: The Free Press, 1985); Oliver E. Williamson, *The Mechanisms of Governance* (New York: Oxford University Press, 1996); Douglass C. North, *Institutions, Institutional Change and Economic Performance* (Cambridge: Cambridge University Press, 1990); George J. Stigler, "The Economics of Information," *Journal of Political Economy* 69, no. 3 (June 1961): 213–225, www.jstor.org/stable/1829263; George J. Stigler, "The Theory of Economic Regulation," *Bell Journal of Economics and Management Science* 2, no. 1 (Spring 1971): 3–21, www.jstor.org/stable/3003160; Elinor Ostrom, *Governing the Commons: The Evolution of Institutions for Collective Action* (Cambridge: Cambridge University Press, 1990); and Daron Acemoglu and James A. Robinson, *Why Nations Fail: The Origins of Power, Prosperity and Poverty* (London: Profile Books, 2012).

22. Olson argued that the longer a society enjoys political stability, the more likely it is to develop special-interest lobbies ("distributional coalitions") that make it less efficient economically. See Mancur Olson, *The Rise and Decline of Nations: Economic Growth, Stagflation, and Social Rigidities* (New Haven, CT: Yale University Press, 1982).

23. Jeffrey Pfeffer and Gerald R. Salancik, *The External Control of Organizations: A Resource Dependence Perspective* (New York: Harper & Row, 1978) and Neil Fligstein, *The Architecture of Markets: An Economic Sociology of Twenty-First-Century Capitalist Societies* (Princeton, NJ: Princeton University Press, 2001).

24. T. J. Pempel and Keiichi Tsunekawa, "Corporatism without Labor? The Japanese Anomaly," in *Trends toward Corporatist Intermediation*, eds. Philippe C. Schmitter and Gerhard (Beverly Hills, CA: Sage Publications, 1979), 231–270.

25. See, for example, Howard J. Wiarda, *Corporatism and Comparative Politics: The Other Great "Ism"* (Armonk, NY: M. E. Sharpe, 1997).

26. On the distinctions between late-developing cooperative market systems and the liberal market economies, see Peter A. Hall and David Soskice, eds., *Varieties of Capital-*

ism: The Institutional Foundations of Comparative Advantage (Oxford, UK: Oxford University Press, 2001).

27. One pioneering work, grounded in broader theory yet focusing empirically on Japan, and sharing a common philosophical conviction with this work of the importance of individual incentives as a key to understanding broader social outcomes, is Ronald Dore, *British Factory, Japanese Factory: The Origins of National Diversity in Industrial Relations* (Berkeley: University of California Press, 1973). A later, more formalized, and highly innovative work in this area is J. Mark Ramseyer and Frances McCall Rosenbluth, *Japan's Political Marketplace* (Cambridge, MA: Harvard University Press, 1993).

28. Kazushi Ohkawa and Henry Rosovsky, *Japanese Economic Growth: Trend Acceleration in the Twentieth Century* (Stanford, CA: Stanford University Press, 1973).

29. Chalmers Johnson, *MITI and the Japanese Miracle: The Growth of Industrial Policy, 1925–1973* (Stanford, CA: Stanford University Press, 1982).

30. Johnson, 18–21.

31. In this volume both "MITI" and "METI" are used, applied to essentially the same organization, which was reorganized, with expanded functions, in 2001. "Ministry of International Trade and Industry (MITI)" refers to the entity before reorganization. "Ministry of Economy, Trade and Industry (METI)" refers to the post-reorganization entity, with functions previously performed by the defunct Economic Planning Agency added.

32. Ulrike Schaede, *Choose and Focus: Japanese Business for the 21st Century* (Ithaca, NY: Cornell University Press, 2008).

33. See Kent E. Calder, *Crisis and Compensation: Public Policy and Political Stability in Japan, 1946–1986* (Princeton, NJ: Princeton University Press, 1988) and Kent E. Calder, *Strategic Capitalism: Private Business and Public Purpose in Japanese Industrial Finance* (Princeton, NJ: Princeton University Press, 1993).

34. See Daniel Okimoto, *Between MITI and the Market: Japanese Industrial Policy for High Technology* (Stanford, CA: Stanford University Press, 1989); Richard J. Samuels, *The Business of the Japanese State: Energy Markets in Comparative and Historical Perspective* (Ithaca, NY: Cornell University Press, 1987); and T. J. Pempel, *Regime Shift: Comparative Dynamics of the Japanese Political Economy* (Ithaca, NY: Cornell University Press, 1998).

35. Steven K. Vogel, *Japan Remodeled: How Government and Industry Are Reforming Japanese Capitalism* (Ithaca, NY: Cornell University Press, 2006), 4.

36. Edward J. Lincoln, *Arthritic Japan: The Slow Pace of Economic Reform* (Washington, DC: Brookings Institution Press, 2001), 94–120.

37. Richard Katz, *Japan, the System That Soured: The Rise and Fall of the Japanese Economic Miracle* (Armonk, NY: M. E. Sharpe, 1998) and Richard Katz, *Japanese Phoenix: The Long Road to Economic Revival* (Armonk, NY: M. E. Sharpe, 2003).

38. Tiberghien, 104–155.

39. Frances McCall Rosenbluth and Michael F. Thies, *Japan Transformed: Political Change and Economic Restructuring* (Princeton, NJ: Princeton University Press, 2010); and Margarita Estevez-Abe, *Welfare and Capitalism in Postwar Japan* (Cambridge: Cambridge University Press, 2008).

40. Ulrike Schaede, *Cooperative Capitalism: Self-Regulation, Trade Associations, and the Antimonopoly Law in Japan* (Oxford, U.K.: Oxford University Press, 2000).

41. Schaede, *Choose and Focus*.

42. Schaede and Grimes, eds., 6–9.

43. Rosenbluth and Thies and Estevez-Abe stress the importance of the 1994 electoral reforms in transforming voter and candidate incentive structures.

44. On the emergence of a truly global political economy, see Jeffry A. Frieden, *Global Capitalism: Its Fall and Rise in the Twentieth Century* (New York: W. W. Norton, 2006) and Niall Ferguson et al., eds., *The Shock of the Global: The 1970s in Perspective* (Cambridge, MA: Harvard University Press, 2011).

45. Olson, *The Rise and Decline of Nations.*

46. See, for example, Lincoln, *Arthritic Japan.*

47. During 1979–1980, for example, Japan successfully cut shipbuilding capacity by 35 percent, through a program devised by two private industry associations, and operationalized through government subsidies. See "The Shipping Industry in the 1970s," GlobalSecurity.org, globalsecurity.org/military/world/japan/industry-shipbuilding-1970s.htm.

48. Perry's "black ships" appeared off the entrance to Tokyo Bay in July 1853. After a firepower demonstration, Perry was allowed to land on July 14, 1853, to present a letter demanding commercial rights. He returned to sign the Convention of Kanagawa, opening Japan, in March 1854.

49. Kent E. Calder, "The Turbulent Path to Social Science: Japanese Political Analysis in the 1990s," in *The Postwar Development of Japanese Studies in the United States,* ed. Helen Hardacre (Boston: Brill, 1998), 336–353.

CHAPTER TWO

1. Some landmarks in this evolution include Samuel P. Huntington, *Political Order in Changing Societies* (New Haven, CT: Yale University Press, 1968); Philippe C. Schmitter and Gerhard Lehmbruch, eds., *Trends Toward Corporatist Intermediation* (Beverly Hills, CA: Sage Publications, 1979); Stephan Haggard, *Pathways from the Periphery: The Politics of Growth in the Newly Industrializing Countries* (Ithaca, NY: Cornell University Press, 1990); and Arend Lijphart, *Patterns of Democracy: Government Forms and Performance in Thirty-Six Countries* (New Haven, CT: Yale University Press, 1999); as well as Daron Acemoglu and James A. Robinson, *Why Nations Fail: The Origins of Power, Prosperity, and Poverty* (London: Profile Books, 2012).

2. Among the few has been Chalmers Johnson's notion of the developmental state, invoked particularly to elucidate political-economic developments in Korea. See Meredith Woo-Cumings, ed., *The Developmental State* (Ithaca, NY: Cornell University Press, 1999).

3. For an overview of efforts at developing abstract concepts inductively from Japanese experience that have broader applicability, see Kent E. Calder, "The Turbulent Path to Social Science: Japanese Political Analysis in the 1990s," in *The Postwar Development of Japanese Studies in the United States,* ed. Helen Hardacre (Boston: Brill, 1998), 336–353.

4. Kent E. Calder, *Crisis and Compensation: Public Policy and Political Stability in Japan, 1946–1986* (Princeton, NJ: Princeton University Press, 1988), 160.

5. This adopts the definition I originally set out in *Crisis and Compensation.* See Calder, *Crisis and Compensation,* 160.

6. On the concept of iteration and its implications for incentive structure, see George Tsebelis, *Nested Games: Rational Choice in Comparative Politics* (Berkeley: University of California Press, 1990), 72–78, and Robert Axelrod, *The Evolution of Cooperation* (New York: Basic Books, 1984), 73–87. Axelrod notes, for example, that small units that faced each other in trench warfare during World War I for extended periods would often develop ritualized forms of warfare like the British "evening gun," fired at predictable times, that demonstrated both potential for aggressiveness and willful restraint, subject to reciprocity by the enemy.

7. On the operation of *dangō* in the Japanese construction industry, see Brian Woodall, *Japan under Construction: Corruption, Politics, and Public Works* (Berkeley: University of California Press, 1996), 27–28.

8. On this distinction, see John Shuhe Li, "Relation-based versus Rule-based Governance: An Explanation of the East Asian Miracle and Asian Crisis," *Review of International Economics* 11, no. 4 (September 2003): 651–673, http://ssrn.com/abstract=450973.

9. Hall and Soskice note that this bias toward incremental rather than radical innovation is common to CMEs more generally. See Peter A. Hall and David Soskice, "An Introduction to Varieties of Capitalism," in *Varieties of Capitalism: The Institutional Foundations of Comparative Advantage*, eds. Peter A. Hall and David Soskice (Oxford, UK: Oxford University Press, 2001), 44.

10. On these concepts, which have recognized legitimacy in the Japanese industrial policy process, see Robert M. Uriu, *Troubled Industries: Confronting Economic Change in Japan* (Ithaca, NY: Cornell University Press, 1996) and Iyori Hiroshi, "Antitrust and Industrial Policy in Japan: Competition and Cooperation," in *Law and Trade Issues of the Japanese Economy: American and Japanese Perspectives*, ed. Gary R. Saxonhouse and Kozo Yamamura (Seattle: University of Washington Press, 1996), 79–81.

11. Japan's cooperative project among MITI and several private firms, to develop and operationalize VLSI, is a case in point. See Roy Hofheinz, Jr. and Kent E. Calder, *The Eastasia Edge* (New York: Basic Books, 1982).

12. Ralf Dahrendorf, *Society and Democracy in Germany* (Garden City, NY: Doubleday, 1967), 267. Dahrendorf noted that "a genuine sense of development starts with domesticating conflict by recognizing and regulating it, rather than suppressing or laying it aside."

13. On industry associations in the United States and Japan, see Leonard H. Lynn and Timothy J. McKeown, *Organizing Business: Trade Associations in America and Japan* (Washington, DC: American Enterprise Institute for Public Policy Research, 1988).

14. Hofheinz and Calder, 154–157.

15. Kent E. Calder, *Strategic Capitalism: Private Business and Public Purpose in Japanese Industrial Finance* (Princeton, NJ: Princeton University Press, 1993), 29–30, 164–167, and 214–218.

16. Patricia A. O'Brien, "Industry Structure as a Competitive Advantage: The History of Japan's Post-war Steel Industry," *Business History* 34, no. 1 (1992): 128–159 and 145–149, doi: 10.1080/00076799200000006.

17. Japan, for example, as of fiscal 2015 has established fourteen special accounts with a total budget of ¥403.55 trillion, well over four times that of the general account. See Ministry of Internal Affairs and Communications Statistics Bureau, *Statistical Handbook of Japan 2015*, 35–36, www.stat.go.jp/english/data/handbook/pdf/2015all.pdf.

18. Peter J. Katzenstein, *Small States in World Markets: Industrial Policy in Europe* (Ithaca, NY: Cornell University Press, 1985); as well as Peter J. Katzenstein, *Corporatism and Change: Austria, Switzerland, and the Politics of Industry* (Ithaca, NY: Cornell University Press, 1984), 198–238.

19. John Sutton, *Sunk Costs and Market Structure: Price Competition, Advertising, and the Evolution of Concentration* (Cambridge, MA: MIT Press, 1991), and John Sutton, *Technology and Market Structure: Theory and History* (Cambridge, MA: MIT Press, 1998).

20. Taekyoon Kim, "Variants of Corporatist Governance: Differences in the Korean and Japanese Approaches in Dealing with Labor," *Yale Journal of International Affairs* 3, no. 1 (Winter 2008): 78–94, http://yalejournal.org/wp-content/uploads/2011/01/083106kim.pdf.

21. See Kent E. Calder, "The Japanese Model of Industrial Policy," presented at the Beijing Forum 2007.

22. See Schmitter and Lehmbruch.

23. Timothy J. Power and Mahrukh Doctor, "Another Century of Corporatism? Continuity and Change in Brazil's Corporatist Structures," in *Authoritarianism and Corporatism in Latin America—Revisited*, ed. Howard J. Wiarda (Gainesville: University Press of Florida, 2004), 218–241.

24. Guilds, cartels, and various experiments with corporatism have a venerable pedigree in Europe and Latin America, in particular, but Japanese government–business relations have had a corporatist cast since the Meiji era. See Schmitter and Lehmbruch.

25. On transnational emulation of the Japanese socioeconomic model, see, for example, Byung-Kook Kim and Ezra F. Vogel, ed., *The Park Chung Hee Era: The Transformation of South Korea* (Cambridge, MA: Harvard University Press, 2011) and Ezra F. Vogel, *Deng Xiaoping and the Transformation of China* (Cambridge, MA: Harvard University Press, 2011), 291–310.

26. See, for example, Chitoshi Yanaga, *Big Business in Japanese Politics* (New Haven, CT: Yale University Press, 1968); Ira C. Magaziner and Thomas M. Hout, *Japanese Industrial Policy: A Descriptive Account of Postwar Developments with Case Studies of Selected Industries* (London: Policy Studies Institute, 1980); as well as Takashi Inoguchi and Tomoaki Iwai, *Zoku Giin no Kenkyū: Jimintō Seiken wo Gyūjiru Shuyakutachi [A Study on "Tribal Dietmen": The Leading Players Who Manipulate the LDP Government]* (Tokyo: Nikkei Inc., 1987).

27. In 2015, exports of goods and services valued 17.9 percent of Japan's GDP, versus 45.9 percent for South Korea. See World Bank, "Export of goods and services (% of GDP)," *World Development Indicators*, 2015, http://data.worldbank.org/indicator/NE.EXP .GNFS.ZS.

28. Robert Gilpin, *The Political Economy of International Relations* (Princeton, NJ: Princeton University Press, 1987).

29. Mancur Olson, *The Rise and Decline of Nations: Economic Growth, Stagflation, and Social Rigidities* (New Haven, CT: Yale University Press, 1982).

30. On recent patterns of industry or trade association activity, see Ulrike Schaede, *Cooperative Capitalism: Self-Regulation, Trade Associations, and the Antimonopoly Law in Japan* (Oxford, UK: Oxford University Press, 2000).

31. On trade associations, and their role in muting uncertainties in the corporate political-economic environment, see Schaede, *Cooperative Capitalism*, 30–68.

32. The Chamber of Commerce Ordinance (1890), for example, mandated creation of and membership in business organizations, while the Agrarian Association Law (1899) similarly precipitated the emergence of *nokai* (agricultural associations), as well as compulsory membership in them. See T. J. Pempel and Keiichi Tsunekawa, "Corporatism without Labor? The Japanese Anomaly," in *Trends toward Corporatist Intermediation*, eds. Philippe C. Schmitter and Gerhard Lehmbruch (Beverly Hills, CA: Sage Publications, 1979), 249.

33. On *keiretsu* structure and risk-diffusion mechanisms, see Michael L. Gerlach, *Alliance Capitalism: The Social Organization of Japanese Business* (Berkeley: University of California Press, 1997). For a skeptical view, see Yoshiro Miwa and J. Mark Ramseyer, *The Fable of the Keiretsu: Urban Legends of the Japanese Economy* (Chicago: University of Chicago Press, 2006).

34. See Calder, *Strategic Capitalism*, 29–30, 164–167, and 214–218.

35. On the dissolution process, see Masahiro Hosoya, "Senryō-ki Nihon (1945–1952 nen) ni okeru Keizai Minshuka to Gyaku Kōsu [Economic Democratization and the 'Reverse Course' during the Allied Occupation of Japan, 1945–1952]," *Sophia Institute of International Relations Journal of International Studies*, no. 11 (July 1983): 59–104.

36. Yukio Noguchi, *1940-nen Taisei: Saraba Senji Keizai [The 1940 System: Farewell to Wartime Economy]* (Tokyo: Toyo Keizai Inc., 1995).

37. On the details, see Calder, *Strategic Capitalism*, 151–161, and Schmitter and Lehmbruch, 231–270.

38. For an influential view of Japanese associations that equates them with vested interests, and fails to note these broader functions, see Edward J. Lincoln, *Arthritic Japan: The Slow Pace of Economic Reform* (Washington, DC: Brookings Institution Press, 2001), 94–120.

39. See Uriu, *Troubled Industries*.

40. On this point, see Kent E. Calder, *Japan's Stealth Reform: The Key Role of Political Process*, The Edwin O. Reischauer Center for East Asian Studies Asia-Pacific Policy Papers Series (Washington, DC: Johns Hopkins University, 2005).

41. On the veto-player concept, see George Tsebelis, *Veto Players: How Political Institutions Work* (Princeton, NJ: Princeton University Press, 2002).

42. For a survey of Japan's civil society in comparative perspective, see Frank J. Schwartz and Susan J. Pharr, eds., *The State of Civil Society in Japan* (Cambridge: Cambridge University Press, 2003).

43. As Schaede and Grimes point out, contemporary Japan is characterized by "permeable insulation" from the broader world. The above sectors are fertile fields to study where and how that insulation is being breached. See Ulrike Schaede and William Grimes, "Introduction: The Emergence of Permeable Insulation," in *Japan's Managed Globalization: Adapting to the Twenty-First Century*, eds. Ulrike Schaede and William Grimes (Armonk, NY: M. E. Sharpe, 2003), 3–16.

44. On innovative Japanese firms operating in the changing business environment of the early twenty-first century, see Ulrike Schaede, *Choose and Focus: Japanese Business for the 21st Century* (Ithaca, NY: Cornell University Press, 2008).

CHAPTER THREE

1. On the centrality of finance to an understanding of political-economic evolution, see Thomas Piketty, *Capital in the Twenty-First Century*, trans. Arthur Goldhammer (Cambridge, MA: Harvard University Press, 2014).

2. On the "invest, then save" bias, see Mark Metzler, *Capital as Will and Imagination: Schumpeter's Guide to the Postwar Japanese Miracle* (Ithaca, NY: Cornell University Press, 2013).

3. See, for example, James C. Abegglen, *The Japanese Factory: Aspects of Its Social Organization* (Glencoe, IL: Free Press, 1958); Masahiko Aoki, *Information, Incentives, and Bargaining in the Japanese Economy* (Cambridge: Cambridge University Press, 1988); Kent E. Calder, *Crisis and Compensation: Public Policy and Political Stability in Japan, 1949–1986* (Princeton, NJ: Princeton University Press, 1988); Kent E. Calder, *Strategic Capitalism: Private Business and Public Purpose in Japanese Industrial Finance* (Princeton, NJ: Princeton University Press, 1993); Ronald Dore, *Flexible Rigidities: Industrial Policy and Structural Adjustment in the Japanese Economy 1970–80* (London: Athlone Press, 1986); Daniel I. Okimoto, *Between MITI and the Market: Japanese Industrial Policy for High Technology* (Stanford, CA: Stanford University Press, 1989); Richard J. Samuels, *The Business of the Japanese State: Energy Markets in Comparative and Historical Perspective* (Ithaca, NY: Cornell University Press, 1987); and Ulrike Schaede, *Cooperative Capitalism: Self-Regulation, Trade Associations, and the Antimonopoly Law in Japan* (Oxford, UK: Oxford University Press, 2000).

4. See, for example, Chalmers Johnson, "The Reemployment of Retired Government Bureaucrats in Japanese Big Business," *Asian Survey* 14, no. 11 (November 1974):

953–956, www.jstor.org/stable/2643506; Kent E. Calder, "Elites in an Equalizing Role: Ex-Bureaucrats as Coordinators and Intermediaries in the Japanese Government-Business Relationship," *Comparative Politics* 21, no. 4 (July 1989): 379–403, www.jstor.org/stable/422004; and Ulrike Schaede, "The 'Old Boy' Network and Government-Business Relationships in Japan," *Journal of Japanese Studies* 21, no.2 (Summer 1995): 293–317, www.jstor.org/stable/133010.

5. Douglass C. North, *Institutions, Institutional Change, and Economic Performance* (Cambridge: Cambridge University Press, 1990) and Oliver E. Williamson, *The Economic Institutions of Capitalism: Firms, Markets, Relational Contracting* (New York: Free Press, 1985).

6. Douglass C. North, "Privatization, Incentives, and Economic Performance," 1, http://econwpa.repec.org/eps/eh/papers/9411/9411002.pdf.

7. Burke asserted that "to be attached to the subdivision, to love the little platoon we belong to in society, is the first principle . . . of public affections. It is the first link in the series by which we proceed towards a love to our country, and to mankind." See Edmund Burke, *Reflections on the French Revolution and Other Essays*, Everyman edition (London: J. M. Dent & Sons, 1955), 44.

CHAPTER FOUR

1. On the recent manifestations of these vested interests in the Japanese political economy, see Edward J. Lincoln, *Arthritic Japan: The Slow Pace of Economic Reform* (Washington, DC: Brookings Institution Press, 2001).

2. Kent E. Calder, *Strategic Capitalism: Private Business and Public Purpose in Japanese Industrial Finance* (Princeton, NJ: Princeton University Press, 1993), 235–237.

3. Ibid.

4. "City banks" in the traditional Japanese system that prevailed from the 1920s until the 1990s were the thirteen largest commercial banks in the country, which were the most substantial lenders to large manufacturing firms, such as those of the Mitsubishi, Mitsui, and Sumitomo groups.

5. For an articulate contrast between this classic system and the subsequent evolution of credit review processes in Japanese corporate finance, see Ulrike Schaede, "The Strategic Logic of Japanese *Keiretsu*, Main Banks and Cross-Shareholdings, Revisited" (working paper no. 247, Working Paper Series, Center on Japanese Economy and Business, Columbia Business School, October 2006), www8.gsb.columbia.edu/rtfiles/japan/WP%20247.pdf.

6. Akiyoshi Horiuchi, "Financial Fragility and Recent Developments in the Japanese Safety Net," *Social Science Japan Journal* 2, no. 1 (April 1999): 23–43; and Yoshinori Shimizu, "Convoy Regulation, Bank Management, and the Financial Crisis in Japan," in *Japan's Financial Crisis and Its Parallels to the U.S. Experience*, eds. Ryoichi Mikitani and Adam S. Posen (Washington, DC: Institute for International Economics, 2000), 57–99.

7. See Calder, *Strategic Capitalism*, 134–210.

8. On the operation of Japanese bond-underwriting syndicates, see Masaru Konishi, "Bond Underwriting Syndicates Organized by Commercial Banks: Evidence from Prewar Japan," *Journal of the Japanese and International Economies* 19, no. 3 (September 2005): 303–321, doi:10.1016/j.jjie.2004.05.004; Abe de Jong, Peter Roosenboom, and Willem Schramade, "Bond Underwriting Fees and Keiretsu Affiliation in Japan," *Pacific-Basin Fi-*

nance Journal 14, no. 5 (November 2006): 522–545, doi:10.1016/j.pacfin.2006.03.003; as well as Yasushi Hamao and Narasimhan Jegadeesh, "An Analysis of Bidding in the Japanese Government Bond Auctions," *Journal of Finance* 53, no. 2 (April 1998): 755–772, www .jstor.org/stable/117369.

9. On the late-developer pattern and its implications for government business relations generally, see Alexander Gerschenkron, *Economic Backwardness in Historical Perspective* (Cambridge, MA: Harvard University Press, 1962).

10. See Thomas C. Smith, *Political Change and Industrial Development in Japan: Government Enterprise, 1868–1880* (Stanford, CA: Stanford University Press, 1955) and W. E. Lockwood, *The State and Economic Enterprise in Japan: Essays in Political Economy* (Princeton, NJ: Princeton University Press, 1965).

11. See Yutaka Kosai and Yoshitaro Ogino, *The Contemporary Japanese Economy* (Armonk, NY: M. E. Sharpe, 1984), 93–105.

12. For a comprehensive view of the early modern Japanese financial system that illustrates this point, see Kōkichi Asakura, *Meiji-zenki Nihon Kinyū Kōzō Shi [History of Financial Structure of Japan in Early Meiji]* (Tokyo: Iwanami Shoten, Publishers, 1961).

13. Chalmers Johnson, *MITI and the Japanese Miracle: The Growth of Industrial Policy, 1925–1975* (Stanford, CA: Stanford University Press, 1982), 236–237.

14. See Calder, *Strategic Capitalism*, 23–44.

15. On the early history of the *Takuzen Kai*, see Ginkō Kyōkai 20-nen Shi Hensanshitsu, ed. *Ginkō Kyōkai 20-nen Shi [A Twenty-year History of the Japanese Bankers Association]* (Tokyo: Zenkoku Ginkō Kyōkai Rengōkai, 1965), 3–5.

16. On the various institutional permutations of banking regulations, after the Banking Bureau's establishment in 1881, see Mondo Ōkura, *Ōkura-shō Ginkō-kyoku [The Ministry of Finance Banking Bureau]* (Tokyo: Paru Shuppan, 1985), 242.

17. Yoshikazu Miyazaki, "Rapid Economic Growth in Post-war Japan: With Special References to 'Excessive Competition' and the Formation of 'Keiretsu,'" *Developing Economies* 5, no. 2 (June 1967): 329–350.

18. The National Mobilization Law marked a major expansion of MOF administrative guidance, but by no means its beginning. In 1911, as Yabushita and Inoue pointed out, the MOF gave its local directors their first official notice to encourage mergers among small banks operating in their areas; in 1923 MOF began, in response to the 1922 financial crisis, to propose bank control measures, such as suspension of charters to new banks, restriction on new branches, promotion of bank mergers, and restriction on mortgage loans. See Shiro Yabushita and Atsushi Inoue, "The Stability of the Japanese Banking System: A Historical Perspective," *Journal of the Japanese and International Economies* 7, no. 4 (December 1993): 387–407, doi:10.1006/jjie.1993.1023.

19. Richard Rice, "Economic Mobilization in Wartime Japan: Business, Bureaucracy, and Military in Conflict," *Journal of Asian Studies* 38, no. 4 (August 1979): 689–706, doi:10.2307/2053908.

20. On the control associations, see Takafusa Nakamura, *Nihon no Keizai Tōsei: Senji, Sengo no Keiken to Kyōkun [Japan's Economic Controls: Prewar and Postwar Experiences and Lessons]* (Tokyo: Nikkei Inc., 1974); as well as Takafusa Nakamura and Konosuke Odaka, eds., Noah S. Brannen, trans., *The Economic History of Japan, 1600–1990*, Vol. 3: *Economic History of Japan, 1914–1955: A Dual Structure* (Oxford, UK: Oxford University Press, 2003).

21. *Ginkō Kyōkai 20-nen Shi*, 7.

22. The Wartime Finance Corporation was established in February 1942 to offer government-backed bonds to firms in priority sectors that could not easily qualify for regular loans. See Akira Hara, "Wartime Controls," in Takafusa Nakamura and Konosuke Odaka, eds., Noah S. Brannen, trans., *The Economic History of Japan, 1600–1990*, Vol. 3: *Economic History of Japan, 1914–1955: A Dual Structure* (Oxford, UK: Oxford University Press, 2003), 247–286.

23. Miyazaki, 329–350.

24. Miyazaki, 332–333.

25. Miyazaki, 333.

26. MacArthur's first wife's stepfather, Edward Stotesbury, was wealthy, and did withdraw substantial funds safely during the Great Depression, but he also incurred significant losses on Wall Street in 1929. On his financial history, see "Banking: Wealth and Folly and More," *Philadelphia Business Journal*, January 10, 2000, www.bizjournals.com/philadelphia/stories/2000/01/10/story6.html.

27. See Takeshi Matsuura, *Tokubetsu Kaikei e no Michiannai [A Guide to Special Accounts]* (Tokyo: Sougei Press, 2008), 65, and newspaper accounts.

28. In fiscal 2015, Japan's general account of national government expenditure was about ¥96.34 trillion, while special accounts expenditures totaled over ¥403.55 trillion. See Ministry of Internal Affairs and Communications Statistics Bureau, "National Government Finance," *Statistical Handbook of Japan 2015*, www.stat.go.jp/english/data/handbook/c0117.htm#c04.

29. See Japanese Bankers Association, "Principal Financial Institutions," http://www.zenginkyo.or.jp/en/banks/principal/ and Japanese Bankers Association, "Changing Banking Industry," www.zenginkyo.or.jp/en/banks/changing/.

30. *Ginkō Kyōkai 20-nen Shi*, 133.

31. For details, see Calder, *Strategic Capitalism*, 64–65.

32. See Johnson, *MITI and the Japanese Miracle;* John Zysman, *Government, Markets, and Growth: Financial Systems and the Politics of Industrial Change* (Ithaca, NY: Cornell University Press, 1983); and Peter J. Katzenstein, ed., *Between Power and Plenty: Foreign Economic Policies of Advanced Industrial States* (Madison: University of Wisconsin Press, 1978).

33. See Yoshirō Tsutsui, *Kinyū Shijō to Ginkōgyō [The Financial Market and the Banking Industry]* (Tokyo: Toyo Keizai Inc., 1988), 106–131, on the regulatory dynamics of the banking industry.

34. For more details, see Tsutsui, 331–366.

35. See Zenkoku Ginkō Kyōkai Rengōkai, *The Banking System in Japan* (Tokyo: Japanese Bankers Association, 2001), 1–51.

36. Interviews with *Zenginkyō* member bank executives and *Zenginkyō* officials from the 1955–1975 period, July–August 1987.

37. The *Besshitsu* consisted of about twenty capable employees from the *Zenginkyō* chairman's bank. On this body and its lobbying activities, see Asahi Shimbun staff, "'Kan-min Ison' Handan kuruwasu, Kaikaku wa Rigai Chōsei de [Reforms Derailed by 'Public-Private Co-dependence']," September 18, 1999.

38. On the Koizumi reforms, see Jennifer A. Amyx, *Japan's Financial Crisis: Institutional Rigidity and Reluctant Change* (Princeton, NJ: Princeton University Press, 2004), 280–284.

39. The *Besshitsu, Zenginkyō*'s powerful lobbying department, was abolished in 1998.

40. On the multiple functions of the long-term credit banks in Japanese corporate finance, see Frank Packer, "The Role of Long-Term Credit Banks Within the Main Bank System," in *The Japanese Main Bank System: Its Relevance for Developing and Transforming Economies*, eds. Masahiko Aoki and Hugh Patrick (Oxford, UK: Oxford University Press, 1994), 142–187.

41. On the history and functional role of the Industrial Bank of Japan, see Nihon Kōgyō Ginkō Nenshi Hensan Iinkai, ed., *Nihon Kōgyō Ginkō 75-nen Shi [A Seventy-Five Year History of the Industrial Bank of Japan]* (Tokyo: Industrial Bank of Japan, 1982); Nihon Kōgyō Ginkō Nenshi Hensan Iinkai, ed., *Nihon Kōgyō Ginkō 50-nen Shi [A Fifty Year History of the Industrial Bank of Japan]* (Tokyo: Nihon Kōgyō Ginkō Rinji Shiryōshitsu, 1957); and Calder, *Strategic Capitalism*, 134–173.

42. In 1902 the Treasury's share of total stock outstanding was 21.2 percent, which rose to 23.7 percent in 1930. By 1939 its share had fallen to only 2.3 percent, with most of the balance having gone to local governments, to encourage their participation in the war effort. See *Nihon Kōgyō Ginkō 50-nen Shi*.

43. Calder, *Strategic Capitalism*, 159.

44. "Long-Term Credit Bank of Japan, Ltd.," in *International Directory of Company Histories*, ed. Lisa Mirabile, vol. 2 (Chicago: St. James Press, 1990), 310–311, http://go.galegroup.com/ps/i.do?id=GALE%7CCX2840600118&v=2.1&u=balt85423&it=r&p=GVRL&sw=w&asid=783dd2ce74bca0e62e8c35292ee8c051.

45. Shinichi Fukuda and Satoshi Koibuchi, "The Impacts of Shock Therapy under a Banking Crisis: Experiences from Three Large Bank Failures in Japan," *Japanese Economic Review* 57, no. 2 (June 2006): 232–256, doi:10.1111/j.1468–5876.2006.00375.x.

46. See Calder. *Strategic Capitalism*, 160–161.

47. The IBJ credit department had been in operation since 1929, and the industrial research department since 1955. See Calder, *Strategic Capitalism*, 161.

48. Gerald L. Curtis, *The Japanese Way of Politics* (New York: Columbia University Press, 1988), 183–184.

49. For an in-depth, micro-level profile of such a firm and its incentives, see Albert J. Alletzhauser, *The House of Nomura: The Inside Story of the Legendary Japanese Financial Dynasty* (New York: Arcade Publishing, 1990).

50. On the operation of these bodies, see Calder, *Strategic Capitalism*, 29–30, 164–167, and 214–218.

51. Frances McCall Rosenbluth, *Financial Politics in Contemporary Japan* (Ithaca, NY: Cornell University Press, 1989), 167–230.

52. The original law, promulgated in 1949, regulated international trade and financial transactions between Japan and the broader world. It was superseded by the even more liberal Foreign Exchange and Foreign Trade Law, which came into effect on April 1, 1998.

53. Japanese institutional investors, such as banks and insurance companies, joined individual savers in this transition, although their overseas investment was moderated by expended additional investment in Japanese government securities.

54. Calder, *Strategic Capitalism*, 134–173.

55. "The Industrial Bank of Japan, Ltd.," in *International Directory of Company Histories*, ed. Lisa Mirabile, vol. 2 (Chicago: St. James Press, 1990), 300–301, http://go.galegroup.com/ps/i.do?id=GALE%7CCX2840600114&v=2.1&u=balt85423&it=r&p=GVRL&sw=w&asid=3471d008fdfbcd6f55cf4ea4c606fdof.

56. Ibid.

57. On the details, see Packer.

58. On the perverse environmental pressures weighing on the long-term credit banks in the 1990s, including *zaitech* (financial technology), see Kent E. Calder, "Assault on the Bankers' Kingdom: Politics, Markets, and the Liberalization of Japanese Industrial Finance," in *Capital Ungoverned: Liberalizing Finance in Interventionist States*, Michael Loriaux, et al. (Ithaca, NY: Cornell University Press, 1997), 17–56.

59. On the nationalization of the LTCB, see Prime Minister's Office, trans., "Statement by Prime Minister Obuchi on the Temporary Nationalization of the Long-Term Credit Bank of Japan, Ltd.," October 23, 1998, http://japan.kantei.go.jp/souri/981023thogin.html; Jathon Sapsford, "Long-Term Credit Bank Is Judged to Be Insolvent after Nationalization," *Wall Street Journal*, October 26, 1998, www.wsj.com/articles/SB909348043163614500; and "End of the Road for LTCB," *BBC*, October 23, 1998, http://news.bbc.co.uk/2/hi/business/199409.stm.

60. On the conditions behind nationalization of NCB, see Bank of Japan, trans., "Statement by the Governor Concerning the Temporary Nationalization of the Nippon Credit Bank," December 18, 1998, www.boj.or.jp/en/announcements/press/danwa/dan9812a.htm/.

61. On the Long-Term Credit Bank case, see Gillian Tett, *Saving the Sun: A Wall Street Gamble to Rescue Japan from Its Trillion-Dollar Meltdown* (New York: Harper Business, 2003).

62. See "Saberasu, Aozora-gin no Zen-kabushiki Baikyaku: Bakureizu-shōken ni [Cerberus sells all shares of Aozora Bank to Barclays]," *Nikkei*, August 6, 2013, www.nikkei.com/article/DGXNASGC06011_W3A800C1EE8000/.

63. At the end of the first quarter of fiscal year 2015, the Mizuho Financial Group had total assets of around $1.5 trillion, and was the seventeenth largest bank in the world in total assets. See Mizuho Financial Group, Inc., "Consolidated Financial Statements for the First Quarter of Fiscal 2015," July 31, 2015, www.mizuho-fg.co.jp/english/investors/financial/fin_statements/data15_1q/pdf/1q.pdf. On the rankings, see "Top Banks in the world," *Banks Around the World*, www.relbanks.com/worlds-top-banks/assets.

64. On the new entrepreneurs, see Ulrike Schaede, *Choose and Focus: Japanese Business Strategies for the 21st Century* (Ithaca, NY: Cornell University Press, 2008), 226–252.

65. On Horie's background, see "Business Profile: Anti-Hero Flies into Gathering Storm," *The Telegraph*, January 19, 2006, www.telegraph.co.uk/finance/2930416/Business-profile-Anti-hero-flies-into-gathering-storm.html.

CHAPTER FIVE

1. As of 2015, Bangladesh had 1,237 people per square kilometer, followed by Lebanon (572), South Korea (519), the Netherlands (503), Rwanda (471), India (441), Haiti (389), Israel (387), Belgium (373), and Japan (348). See World Bank, "Population density (people per square kilometer of land area)," *World Development Indicators*, 2015, http://data.worldbank.org/indicator/EN.POP.DNST. This list does not include city-states or small island states.

2. Kokudo Chō [National Land Agency], *Kokudo Riyō Hakusho, Shōwa 58-nen [National Land Use White Paper, 1983]* (Tokyo: Ministry of Finance Printing Bureau, 1983).

3. The land-standard system is said to have originated in the Konden Eidai Shiyūrei (the notion that land reclaimed or cultivated by an individual is perpetually owned by them) in 743. Private ownership of land was first permitted as an incentive for the large investments required to make wild land suitable for paddy irrigation. On this system, see Edwin O. Reischauer and Marius B. Jansen, *The Japanese Today: Change and Continuity* (Cambridge, MA: Harvard University Press, 1995), 49.

4. Osamu Saito, "Land, Labour and Market Forces in Tokugawa Japan," *Continuity and Change* 24, no. 1 (May 2009): 169–196, doi:10.1017/S0268416009007061.

5. Yukio Noguchi, "1% Kazei de Chika wa 20% mo Teirakusuru: Yuganda Keizai-kōzō wo Ippensuru Shin-tochihoyūzei [1% Tax would Reduce Land Prices by 20%: New Land

Holding Tax Will Completely Change the Distorted Economic Structure]," *Ekonomisuto,* October 16, 1990, 24.

6. Shigeto Tsuru, *Japan's Capitalism: Creative Defeat and Beyond* (Cambridge, UK: Cambridge University Press, 1993), 160.

7. Ibid.

8. Richard A. Werner, *Princes of the Yen: Japan's Central Bankers and the Transformation of the Economy* (Armonk, NY: M. E. Sharpe, 2003), 89.

9. Across most of the high-growth period, Japanese public works spending averaged four times the share of GDP that prevailed in the United States, and double the share prevailing in France. In 1984, for example, Japanese government capital formation (predominantly public works) was 5 percent of GNP, compared with 1983 figures of 3.1 percent in France, 2.5 percent in West Germany, 1.9 percent in Britain, and 1.5 percent in the United States. See Ōkura-shō Shukei-kyoku Chōsa-ka [Ministry of Finance Budget Bureau Research Section], *Zaisei Tōkei Shōwa 61-nendo [Financial Statistics 1986]* (Tokyo: Ōkura-shō Insatsu-kyoku, 1986), 13.

10. In the early 1990s, a 1.0 percent increase in the price of rice led on average to an approximate 2.1 percent increase in the shadow value of farmland in Tohoku. See Yoshimi Kuroda, "Price-Support Programs and Land Movement in Japanese Rice Production," in *Land Issues in Japan: A Policy Failure?* eds. John O. Haley and Kozo Yamamura (Seattle, WA: Society for Japanese Studies, University of Washington, 1992), 235.

11. The LTCB Law required that land be presented as collateral for all loans of over six months' duration. See the full text of the Long-Term Credit Law at Chōki Shinyō Ginkō Hō, Shōwa 27-nen 6-gatsu 12-nichi Hōritsu dai-187-go [Long-Term Credit Bank Law, June 12, 1952, no. 187] http://law.e-gov.go.jp/htmldata/S27/S27Ho187.html.

12. Tsuru, 164.

13. Yukio Noguchi, "Land Prices and House Prices in Japan," in *Housing Markets in the United States and Japan,* eds. Yukio Noguchi and James M. Poterba (Chicago: University of Chicago Press, 1994), 24–25.

14. In 1986, for example, real-estate tax revenue constituted only 2.1 percent of national income in Japan, compared to 3.3 percent in the United, and 5.8 percent in the United Kingdom. See Yukio Noguchi, "Land Problems and Policies in Japan: Structural Aspects," in *Land Issues in Japan: A Policy Failure?* eds. John O. Haley and Kozo Yamamura (Seattle, WA: Society for Japanese Studies, University of Washington, 1992), 20.

15. Tsuru, 161.

16. Yōnosuke Inamoto, Shunichirō Koyanagi, and Toshikazu Sutō, *Nihon no Tochihō: Rekishi to Genjō [Japan's Land Law: History and Current Situation],* 2nd ed. (Tokyo: Seibundoh, 2009), 65.

17. Nobuyuki Kabeya and Yoshio Itaba, "Tochi Zeisei to Chihō Zaisei Shūnyū: Nōchi ni taisuru Yūgūzeisei wo megutte [Land Taxation and Local Public Finance Income: Farmland Tax Breaks]," *Kaikei Kensa Kenkyū* 40 (September 2009): 80.

18. Ibid., 82.

19. Ibid., 82.

20. Ibid., 85.

21. Shigeki Morinobu, "The rise and fall of the land myth in Japan—some implications for Chinese land taxation," *PRI Discussion Paper Series No. 06A-08* (Tokyo: Ministry of Finance Policy Research Institute, March 2006), 11; and Ministry of Finance Tax Bureau, *Comprehensive Handbook of Japanese Taxes 2010* (Tokyo: Ministry of Finance Tax Bureau),

144, www.mof.go.jp/english/tax_policy/publication/taxes2010e/taxes2010e.pdf. The land-value tax was suspended in 1998.

22. Mark Metzler, *Capital as Will and Imagination: Schumpeter's Guide to the Postwar Japanese Miracle* (Ithaca, NY: Cornell University Press, 2013), 220. Also, see Metzler's discussion of the thinking of Ichiro Nakayama and Saburō Ōkita, who developed the "invest, then save" concept more explicitly, on pages 61 and 190.

23. For a narrower view, see Chalmers Johnson, *MITI and the Japanese Miracle: The Growth of Industrial Policy, 1925–1975* (Stanford, CA: Stanford University Press, 1982).

24. Capital investment averaged 3.08 percent of nominal GDP between 1961 and 1965, while commercial land prices rose at an average annual rate during this period of 21.00 percent. Author's calculation based on Ministry of Internal Affairs and Communications Statistics Bureau, "22–20 Urban Land Price Index—All Urban Land, 6 Major Cities and excluding 6 Large Cities (1955–2005)," *Historical Statistics of Japan*; Ministry of Finance Policy Research Institute, "Investment in plant and equipment and inventories," *Financial Statements Statistics of Corporations by Industry, Quarterly*; and Ministry of Internal Affairs and Communications Statistics Bureau, "3–1 Gross Domestic Expenditure (At Current Prices, At Constant Prices, Deflators)-68SNA, Benchmark year=1990 (C.Y. 1955–1998, F.Y. 1955–1998)," *Historical Statistics of Japan*.

25. From 1965 to 1974, the heart of Japan's high-growth period, Japan was never dependent on foreign markets for over 3 percent of its total supply of funds through financial markets. See Yoshio Suzuki, ed., *The Japanese Financial System* (Oxford, UK: Oxford University Press, 1987), 32. In Korea, by contrast, during the same high-growth period foreign debt/GNP rose from under 4 percent in 1961 to over 56 percent in 1985. See Susan M. Collins and Won-Am Park, "An Overview of Korea's External Debt," *Developing Country Debt and Economic Performance, Volume 3: Country Studies—Indonesia, Korea, Philippines, Turkey*, eds. Jeffrey D. Sachs and Susan M. Collins (Chicago: University of Chicago Press, 1989), 171.

26. World Bank, "GDP growth (annual %)," *World Development Indicators*, 1980–2015, http://data.worldbank.org/indicator/NY.GDP.MKTP.KD.ZG.

27. On the career of Kakuei Tanaka, and particularly on how institutional changes in early postwar Japan accelerated his rise, see Kent E. Calder, "*Kanryo vs. Shomin*: The Dynamics of Conservative Leadership in Postwar Japan," in *Political Leadership in Contemporary Japan*, ed. Terry Edward MacDougall, Michigan Papers in Japanese Studies, vol. 1 (Ann Arbor: University of Michigan, 1982), 1–31.

28. Hara profited, both politically and no doubt to some extent personally, by engineering the construction of railway lines in localities where he or counterparts held real-estate interests. On Hara's real-estate politics, see Tetsuo Najita, *Hara Kei in the Politics of Compromise, 1905–1915* (Cambridge, MA: Harvard University Press, 1967).

29. On broader global trends of this period, see Niall Ferguson, et al., eds., *The Shock of the Global: The 1970s in Perspective* (Cambridge, MA: Harvard University Press, 2010).

30. On these real-estate interests, see Brian Woodall, *Japan under Construction: Corruption, Politics, and Public Works* (Berkeley: University of California Press, 1996), 25–50.

31. On Tsutsumi's career, see Lesley Downer, *The Brothers: The Hidden World of Japan's Richest Family* (New York: Random House, 1994), 386–391.

32. On Keita Gotō, see Satoru Sakanishi, *Tōkyū: Gotō Keita no Keiei Senryaku [Tokyu: The Management Strategy of Goto Keita]* (Tokyo: Bungeisha, 2001).

33. On Kenji Osano, see Ryūzō Saki, *Seishō Osano Kenji [Osano Kenji, the Political Merchant]* (Tokyo: Tokuma Shoten Publishing Co., Ltd., 1986).

34. For more information about these complexes, see Shiodome City Center, www
.shiodome-cc.com/english/, Roppongi Hills, www.roppongihills.com.e.nt.hp.transer
.com/, Tokyo Midtown, www.tokyo-midtown.com/en/; and Toranomon Hills, http://
toranomonhills.com/en/.

35. Itochu operates through Itochu Property Development, Ltd., and Marubeni
through Marubeni Real Estate Management. Mitsubishi Corporation also established an
in-house Real Estate Investment and Management Group on October 1, 2010.

36. The Netherlands, for example, spent over four times the share of its national budget
on housing (8.0 percent vs. 1.8 percent) than Japan did in 1982. See footnote 5 in Chapter 9 of Kent E. Calder, *Crisis and Compensation: Public Policy and Political Stability in Japan*
(Princeton, NJ: Princeton University Press, 1988), 380.

37. Democratic Party of Japan, *Manifesto 2009*, www.dpj.or.jp/policies/manifesto2009.

38. Shiro Sugai, *Kokudo Keikaku no Keika to Kadai [The Progress and Problems regarding
National Land-Use Planning]* (Tokyo: Taimeidō, 1975), 128, and Calder, *Crisis and Compensation*, 388. Land for the construction of Shōwa Dōri, obtained by extensive rezoning within
the earthquake-hit area that compelled virtually all landowners within the impacted area to
give up 10 percent of their land without compensation, amassed nearly one-half of the total
land devoted to roads in midtown Tokyo today.

39. On the details of these systematic wartime land-use planning efforts, see Calder,
Crisis and Compensation, 394–395.

40. For a description of these important pieces of legislation, see Tokyo Metropolitan
Government Bureau of Urban Development, "Transition of Tokyo's Urban Planning,"
www.toshiseibi.metro.tokyo.jp/eng/pdf/index_01.pdf?1503.

41. See Calder, *Crisis and Compensation*, 389–390.

42. Shigezō Hayasaka, "Tanaka Kakuei Mumei no 10-nen [Tanaka Kakuei's Anony-
mous Decade]," *Chūō Kōron* (November 1986): 381–382.

43. On the 1951 Public Housing Law, see Yoshihito Honma, *Naimushō Jūtaku Seisaku
no Kyōkun: Kōkyō Jūtaku Ron Josetsu [Lessons from Housing Policy of the Home Ministry: An
Introduction to the Theory of Public Housing]* (Tokyo: Ochanomizu Shobo, 1988).

44. The Housing Construction Planning Law (*Jūtaku Kensetsu Keikaku Hō*) was enacted
in June 1951, and abolished in June 2006. See National Diet Library, *Japan Laws and Regulations Index*.

45. Yōsuke Hirayama, *Jūtaku Seisaku no Doko ga Mondai ka? [Where is the Problem in
Housing Policy?]* (Tokyo: Kobunsha, 2009), 26.

46. Calder, *Crisis and Compensation*, 399–400.

47. On the Plan for Remodeling the Japanese Archipelago, see Kakuei Tanaka, *Build-
ing A New Japan: A Plan for Remodeling the Japanese Archipelago* (Tokyo: Simul Press, 1973);
John Sargent, "Remodeling the Japanese Archipelago: The Tanaka Plan," *The Geographical
Journal* 139, no. 3 (October 1973): 426–435, www.jstor.org/stable/1795023; and Calder,
Crisis and Compensation, 400–402.

48. Economic growth during the 1950s and 1960s, it should be noted, was sharply
higher than in prewar years: 10.72 percent (1956–1962) and 11.91 percent (1962–
1969) versus 5.71 percent during the fastest period of growth (1931–1937) between
1897 and 1945. See Kazushi Ohkawa and Henry Rosovsky, *Japanese Economic Growth:
Trend Acceleration in the Twentieth Century* (Stanford, CA: Stanford University Press,
1973), 25.

49. Japan Statistical Association, ed., *Nihon Chōki Tōkei Sōran Dai-3-kan [Overview of
Long-term Statistics of Japan]* (Tokyo: Japan Statistical Association, 1988), 374.

50. The price of urban residential land in Japan rose twenty-five-fold between 1955 and the Oil Shock of 1973, and nearly seventyfold between 1955 and its high point in 1991. Author's calculation based on Ministry of Internal Affairs and Communications Statistics Bureau, "22–20 Urban Land Price Index—All Urban Land, 6 Major Cities and excluding 6 Large Cities (1955–2005)," *Historical Statistics of Japan*.

51. Housing finance, for example, rose from 13.9 percent of Japanese government lending in 1965, and 18.1 percent in 1973, to 30.3 percent in 1990. See Ōkura-shō Shukei-kyoku Chōsa-ka [Ministry of Finance Budget Bureau Research Section], *Zaisei Tōkei Heisei 2-nendo [Financial Statistics 1990]* (Tokyo: Ōkura-shō Insatsu-kyoku, 1990), 41.

52. On Tanaka's political ascent, and its relationship to his land-policy initiatives, see Calder, "Kanryo vs. Shomin." Tanaka also served as head of the LDP's Urban Policy Research Committee (1967–1968) and chairman of the LDP's Rice Price Committee (1968–1972), thus playing a central role in many of the policy sectors where new circles of compensation formed in the post–World War II period.

53. A prime example was the Plan for Remodeling the Japanese Archipelago (*Nihon Rettō Kaizō Ron*) of the early 1970s, initiated by then MITI Minister Kakuei Tanaka. On Tanaka's comprehensive political-economic strategies, see Shigezō Hayasaka, *Hayasaka Shigezō no Tanaka Kakuei Kaisōroku [Memoires of Tanaka Kakuei by Shigezō Hayasaka]* (Tokyo: Shogakukan, 1987).

54. On the National Land Planning Ordinance, see Calder, *Crisis and Compensation*, 388–389.

55. Calder, *Crisis and Compensation*, 395, and Yuzuru Hanayama, "The Housing Land Shortage in Japan—A Myth," *Japanese Economic Studies* 11, no. 3 (1983): 29–31, doi:10.2753/JES1097-203X11033.

56. Local government land-use planning in such urban centers as Sapporo, Nagano, and Kobe is a partial exception to this general pattern. But much of this planning, especially in Sapporo, has prewar origins; hence it confirms the general argument here.

57. As a result of these policies, Tokyo, for example, is self-sufficient in onions, and an exporter to Japan as a whole. See Takashi Tachibana, *Nōkyō [The Agricultural Cooperatives]* (Tokyo: Asahi Shimbun Publications Inc., 1980), 34–35.

58. The preferential tax ratios are 2.1:1 for rice land vs. housing in urban areas, and 5.7:1 for land used for vegetable cultivation, in the Capital, Kinki, and Chubu designated urban areas of Japan. See Ministry of Internal Affairs and Communications Statistics Bureau, *Heisei 20-nendo Koteishisan no Kakaku-nado no Gaiyō Chōsho [Outline Report of Fixed Asset Prices 2008]*, www.soumu.go.jp/main_sosiki/jichi_zeisei/czaisei/czaisei_seido/ichiran08_8.html.

59. "Japanese Agriculture: Government Weighs Higher Tax on Idle Farms," *Nikkei Asian Review*, November 11, 2015, http://asia.nikkei.com/Politics-Economy/Policy-Politics/Government-weighs-higher-tax-on-idle-farms.

60. Calder, *Crisis and Compensation*, 401–402, and Marc-Andre Pigeoon, "'It' Happened, but Not Again: A Minskian Analysis of Japan's Lost Decade" (Jerome Levy Economics Institute Working Paper No. 303, June 2000), 6, http://dx.doi.org/10.2139/ssrn.240286.

61. Although the Japan Housing Loan Corporation was founded in 1950, it was largely dormant until the early 1970s. Between 1973 and 1985, however, after long years of delay in coping with the Japanese living environment, its lending grew eighteen-fold between 1973 and 1985. See Kent E. Calder, *Strategic Capitalism: Private Business and Public Purpose in Japanese Industrial Finance* (Princeton, NJ: Princeton University Press, 1993), 61.

62. Subsidized government loans are available through the Housing Loan Corporation to finance purchase of newly constructed housing, and through the Public Housing Corporation (*Nihon Jūtaku Kōdan*) to finance apartments for salaried workers. See Hiroshi Murakami, "Nihon no Toshi Seisaku: Hatten no Tokuchō to Seiji Gyōseikatei [Japan's Urban Policy: Characteristics of Development and Administrative Progress]," *Ritsumeikan Hōgaku,* no. 3 and 4 (2000): 943, www.ritsumei.ac.jp/acd/cg/law/lex/00-34/murakami.htm.

63. According to the Japanese Ministry of Construction, tax expenditures for housing in Japan under the 1984 budget were only ¥82 billion. This compared to 3.4 times the Japanese amount in Britain, 7.6 times in Germany, 20.3 times in France, and 40.4 times in the United States. See Tetsu Naito, "Jitsugen Dekiru ka? Shotokuzei Genzei, Jūtaku Genzei? [Can a Reduction in Income and Housing Taxes be Realized?]," *Shūkan Tōyō Keizai,* June 15, 1985, 76. This pattern continued for nearly three decades, but began to be marginally changed in 2014, when the Ministry of Land, Infrastructure, Transport and Tourism introduced a system to provide long-term superior home certification to secondhand homes that had been renovated to meet current earthquake-resistance and energy-efficiency standards. See Asahi Shimbun staff, "Chūkojūtaku mo Yūryō-seido, Taishin, Shō-ene no Rifōmu Jōken: Kokkosho, Rainen kara" [Ministry of Land, Infrastructure, Transport and Tourism: Excellent Long-term Housing Certification to Include Used Houses from Next Year with Earthquake Resistance and Energy-saving Performance Conditions], *Kikuzō II Visual,* December 13, 2016.

CHAPTER SIX

1. Only 3.4 percent of Japan's labor force worked in agriculture and forestry (2013 data) and only 1.2 percent of Japan's GDP was generated from agriculture, forestry, and fishing activities (2012 data). See Ministry of Internal Affairs and Communications Statistics Bureau, "16-3 Employed Persons By Industry" and "3-8 Gross Domestic Product Classified by Economic Activities (at Current Prices)," *Japan Statistical Yearbook 2015.*

2. Organisation for Economic Co-operation and Development (OECD), *Agricultural Policies in OECD Countries 2003: Monitoring and Evaluation* (Paris: OECD Publishing, 2003), 169, doi:

10.1787/agr_oecd-2003-en.

3. *Nōhonshugi* (in Japanese), or *nongben zhuyi* (in Chinese), was also, for example, a central element of Chinese classical thinking. The concept was that government itself depended on surplus food-grain production, without which no armies could be raised and no ruling elite had the leisure to pursue education and politics. From this rationale, a unique tradition of pro-agricultural statecraft emerged—a tradition that still survives in the government–rural alliances that dominate most of East Asia. China, for example, still pays $165 billion annually in agricultural subsidies, versus $65 billion in Japan—a remarkable amount, given China's relatively low overall income level. See Roy Hofheinz, Jr. and Kent E. Calder, *The Eastasia Edge* (New York: Basic Books, 1982), 90; Thomas R. H. Havens, "Kato Kanji (1884–1965) and the Spirit of Agriculture in Modern Japan," *Monumenta Nipponica* 25, no. 3/4 (1970): 249–266, www.jstor.org/stable/2383537; Kyōgi Takeda, *Nihon Nōhonshugi no Kōzō [The Structure of Japanese Agriculturism]* (Tokyo: Soufusha, 1999); and Grant Potter, "Agricultural Subsidies Remain a Staple in the Industrial World," *Worldwatch Institute,* March 12, 2014, www.worldwatch.org/agricultural-subsidies-remain-staple-industrial-world-1.

4. Chalmers Johnson, *MITI and the Japanese Miracle: The Growth of industrial Policy, 1925–1975* (Stanford, CA: Stanford University Press, 1982), 86–99. Between 1881 and 1925, agriculture and industry were administered together by the Ministry of Agriculture and Commerce. It was the imperial agricultural cooperatives, rather than the industrialists, who ultimately pushed for a separation of agricultural and industrial administration.

5. On Meiji corporatist innovations in the agricultural area, see Robert Bullock, "*Nokyo:* A Short Cultural History" (Japan Policy Research Institute Working Paper No. 41, Oakland, CA, December 1997), www.jpri.org/publications/workingpapers/wp41.html; Robert Bullock, "Redefining the Conservative Coalition: Agriculture and Small Business in 1990s Japan," in *The State of Civil Society in Japan,* eds. Frank J. Schwartz and Susan J. Pharr (Cambridge: Cambridge University Press, 2003), 175–194; James I. Nakamura, *Agricultural Production and the Economic Development of Japan, 1873–1922* (Princeton, NJ: Princeton University Press, 1966); and T. J. Pempel and Keiichi Tsunekawa, "Corporatism without Labor? The Japanese Anomaly," in *Trends Toward Corporatist Intermediation,* eds. Philippe C. Schmitter and Gerhand Lehmbruch (Beverly Hills, CA: Sage Publications, 1979), 231–270.

6. On Kagawa's role in *Seikyō's* development, see Takeshi Suzuki, ed. and trans., *A Brief Chronicle of the Modern Japanese Consumer Cooperative Movement* (Tokyo: Japanese Consumers' Co-operative Union, June, 2010), 18–20, http://jccu.coop/eng/aboutus/pdf/a_brief_chronicle.pdf.

7. Sheldon Garon, *Molding Japanese Minds: The State in Everyday Life* (Princeton, NJ: Princeton University Press, 1997), 166.

8. The *Seiyūkai,* Japan's most powerful early political party, dominated the Lower House of the Diet during most of the period from its foundation in 1900 until the assassination of Prime Minister Tsuyoshi Inukai in 1932. It typically promoted big business and large public-works spending, especially in the countryside. See Tetsuo Najita, *Hara Kei and the Politics of Compromise, 1905–1915* (Cambridge, MA: Harvard University Press, 1967); and Peter Duus, *Party Rivalry and Political Change in Taishō Japan* (Cambridge, MA: Harvard University Press, 1968).

9. On the comparison, see Barrington Moore, Jr., *Social Origins of Dictatorship and Democracy: Lord and Peasant in the Making of the Modern World* (Boston: Beacon Press, 1966).

10. On the alliance of "steel and rice," together with the political imperatives behind this counterintuitive coalition, see Frances McCall Rosenbluth and Michael F. Thies, *Japan Transformed: Political Change and Economic Restructuring* (Princeton, NJ: Princeton University Press, 2010), 77–78; and Calder, *Crisis and Compensation,* 133–137.

11. Communist strength in the Diet soared from four seats in 1947 to thirty-five in the January 1949 election, and the Communist share of the popular vote to 9.7 percent—a level not even approached again for over two decades. See Calder, *Crisis and Compensation: Public Policy and Political Stability in Japan, 1949–1986* (Princeton, NJ: Princeton University Press, 1988), 77–82. Yoshida came back to power, following a social-democratic interlude, in October 1948, but it was only following a decisive electoral victory in January 1949 that he really consolidated his authority.

12. Bullock, "*Nokyo,*" 1.

13. On this process, initiated under Minister of Agriculture Kōzen Hirokawa, see Calder, *Crisis and Compensation,* 260–264. Hirokawa, a prewar labor-union activist in Tokyo who organized strikes as president of the City Streetcar Factories League (*Shiden Kōjō Rengōkai*) before aligning with the conservatives, and ultimately becoming Secretary

General of the early postwar Liberal Party, and then Minister of Agriculture in the third Yoshida cabinet, epitomized the undifferentiated urban/rural populism that has helped give Japanese agriculture and distribution policy a unified, broadly protectionist cast. On Hirokawa, see Mainichi Shimbun, *Nihon Jinbutsu Jiten [An Encyclopedia of Japanese Personages]* (Tokyo: Mainichi Shimbun, 1952), 302.

14. Calder, *Crisis and Compensation,* 260.

15. See Calder, *Crisis and Compensation,* 250–273.

16. Steven K. Vogel, *Japan Remodeled: How Government and Industry Are Reforming Japanese Capitalism* (Ithaca, NY: Cornell University Press, 2006), 53.

17. See Ellis S. Krauss, *Broadcasting Politics in Japan: NHK and Television News* (Ithaca, NY: Cornell University Press, 2000).

18. See Kent E. Calder, *Japan's Stealth Reform: The Key Role of Political Process,* The Edwin O. Reischauer Center for East Asian Studies Asia-Pacific Policy Papers Series (Washington, DC: Johns Hopkins University, 2005).

19. Calder, *Crisis and Compensation,* 77–86.

20. Robert Bullock, *"Nokyo,"* 3.

21. These services fall into four categories: (1) farming and marketing support, (2) financial services, (3) insurance services, and (4) welfare services, such as medical support and home nursing. JA has a large share in marketing major domestic agricultural products (90 percent in chemical fertilizer; 63 percent in beef; 60 percent in pesticides; 55 percent in farm machinery; 54 percent in vegetables; and 50 percent in rice, for example. Nearly two-thirds of its business profits, however, come from credit and insurance services. See OECD, *Evaluation of Agricultural Policy Reforms in Japan* (Paris: OECD Publishing, 2009), 65, doi: 10.1787/9789264061545-en.

22. See Takashi Tachibana, *Nōkyō [The Agricultural Cooperatives]* (Tokyo: Asahi Shimbun Publications Inc., 1980).

23. The number of part-time farmers rose from 32 percent of Japan's total farming population in 1960, to nearly 62 percent in 2005, and to 71 percent in 2013. See Kazuhito Yamashita, "High Rice Prices Feed Japan's Farming Woes," *Asia Times,* February 19, 2010, www.atimes.com/atimes/Japan/LB19Dho1.html, and Ministry of Internal Affairs and Communications Statistics Bureau, "7–2 Farm Households by Degree of Engagement and Size of Operating Cultivated Land," *Japan Statistical Yearbook 2015.*

24. Figures are as of March 31, 2016. See The Norinchukin Bank, "Corporate Outline," www.nochubank.or.jp/en/about/profile.html.

25. Over one-quarter of the former bureaucrats in the Diet (27/98, or 27.6 percent in 2014) are former MOF officials—many of them representing agricultural communities. See Seikanyōran-sha, *Seikan Yoran* (Spring 2014).

26. OECD, *Evaluation of Agricultural Policy Reforms in Japan,* 65, and Zen-Noh, "About the Livestock Production (Feed) Business," www.zennoh.or.jp/about/english/business/livestock_production.html.

27. In fiscal year 2013, MAFF had 17,055 employees, while METI had 4,557. See Ministry of Internal Affairs and Communications Statistics Bureau, "27–2 National Government Employees by Agency," *Japan Statistical Yearbook 2016.*

28. On MAFF's administrative responsibilities, see Aurelia George-Mulgan, *Japan's Interventionist State: The Role of the MAFF* (New York: Routledge, 2005), 45–126.

29. For a list of MAFF's semigovernmental affiliates, see Mulgan, 216–220.

30. Mulgan, 142–143.

31. Under this system officials "descend" from the "heaven" of bureaucratic employment upon retirement into senior posts with private firms and semipublic corporations. On *amakudari,* see Richard A. Colignon and Chikako Usui, *Amakudari: The Hidden Fabric of Japan's Economy* (Ithaca, NY: Cornell University Press, 2003) and Kent E. Calder, "Elites in an Equalizing Role: Ex-Bureaucrats as Coordinators and Intermediaries in the Japanese Government-Business Relationship," *Comparative Politics* 21, no. 4 (July 1989): 379–403, www.jstor.org/stable/422004.

32. *Seikyō* provides a broad range of services to members, including, of course, raw and processed food, but also insurance, nonedible household goods, and even funeral support.

33. Japan ranked with Norway, Switzerland, and Korea as a nation where support policies generated more than half of gross farm receipts. See OECD, *Agricultural Policy Monitoring and Evaluation 2014: OECD Countries* (Paris: OECD Publishing, 2014), 29, doi: 10.1787/agr_pol-2014-en.

34. Mulgan, 168–211.

35. This basic principle was modified by the New Food Law, implemented in November 1995, offering farmers marginally greater choice in marketing routes. Japan also moved internationally in the late 1990s from a quota to a tariff system of border controls as a result of the Uruguay Round negotiations. Yet these liberalizing developments were only marginal changes, with the fundamentally control-oriented and protectionist structure of rice distribution, leading to domestic prices many times international levels, being essentially preserved. See Mulgan, 168–176.

36. In 2013, rice constituted 31.2 percent of crops output in Japan. See Ministry of Internal Affairs and Communications Statistics Bureau, "Table 5.1 Agricultural, Forestry and Fisheries Output," *Statistical Handbook of Japan 2015,* www.stat.go.jp/english/data/handbook/c0117.htm#c05.

37. Yūjirō Hayami and Masayoshi Honma, *Kokusai Hikaku kara mita Nihon Nōgyō no Hogo Suijun [Japan's Agricultural Protection Levels in International Comparative Perspective]* (Tokyo: The Forum for Policy Innovation, 1983), 20. European figures considered by the authors were a weighted average of France, West Germany, Italy, and the Netherlands.

38. See Christina Davis and Jennifer Oh, "Repeal of the Rice Laws in Japan: The Role of International Pressure to Overcome Vested Interests," *Comparative Politics* 40, no. 1 (October 2007): 21–40, www.jstor.org/stable/20434062.

39. 2012 subsidies paid by MAFF were 29.6 percent of the 2012 national budget. See MAFF, "2012 Budget," on the MAFF website, at www.maff.go.jp.

40. In 2010, Japan's Producer Support was estimated at $56.7 billion, about 54 percent of the $105.4 billion subsidies made by the EU-28. See OECD, *Agricultural Support Estimates,* ed. 2015, doi: 10.1787/data-00737-en.

41. According to the OECD, in 2006 Japan spent nearly ¥5 trillion yen for agricultural protection, while its total agricultural GDP in the same year was ¥4.7 trillion. See Yamashita.

42. Ministry of International Affairs and Communications Statistics Bureau, "Table 5.4 Commercial Farm Households and Commercial Farmers," *Statistical Handbook of Japan 2015,* www.maff.go.jp/j/tokei/syohi/rokuji/index.html.

43. The total number of farm households in Japan declined from over 6.0 million in 1950, and nearly 4.0 million in 1990, to just 1.6 million in 2010. See Ministry of Internal Affairs and Communication Statistics Bureau, "7–1 Farm Households by Degree of Engagement and Size of Operating Cultivated Land," *Japan Statistical Yearbook 2011.*

44. Ibid.

45. The Food Control Law, cornerstone of Japan's rice-price support system, involved government purchase of rise via *nōkyō* at highly inflated prices, and sale at lower prices to consumers through licensed vendors. The post-1995 system opened the market to limited rice imports, partially liberalized retail licensing, and permitted farmers to sell a portion of their produce directly to vendors and consumers. See Davis and Oh, 21–40.

46. One example of Abe's ambitious agricultural reform policy is to phase out the *gentan* rice production control system by 2018. See "Rice Farming in Japan: Political Staple," *The Economist,* November 30, 2013.

47. Designed to consolidate small and scattered plots of farmland, these banks were authorized by the Diet in December 2013, together with a fiscal-year 2013 funding authorization of ¥45.3 billion to support them. See "Diet Enacts Law to Consolidate the Nation's Farmland," *The Japan Times,* December 6, 2013, www.japantimes.co.jp/news/2013/12/06/national/politics-diplomacy/diet-enacts-law-to-consolidate-the-nations-farmland/#.V32Yg_krKUk; and "'Farmland Bank' Program off to a Slow Start," *The Japan Times,* August 6, 2015, www.japantimes.co.jp/news/2015/08/06/business/farmland-bank-program-off-slow-start/#.V32ag_krKUl.

48. The "sixth industrialization" (*rokuji sangyōka*) policy supports farms and local co-ops in their efforts at not only primary-sector production, but also secondary-sector manufacturing (processing), and tertiary-sector services (agritourism and marketing). Thus, 1x2x3=6. For more information, see information published under MAFF, "Nōringyogyō no 6-ji Sangyōka [The 6th Industrialization of Agricultural, Forestry, and Fisheries Industries]," www.maff.go.jp/j/tokei/syohi/rokuji/index.html.

49. Mina Pollmann, "Agricultural Reforms in Japan Pave the Way for TPP," *The Diplomat,* February 12, 2015, http://thediplomat.com/2015/02/agricultural-reforms-in-japan-pave-the-way-for-tpp/. TPP was ratified in Japan during late 2016, although rejected in the United States during early 2017 by the incoming Trump administration.

50. For schedule of implementation, as well as details of the legislation, see Ministry of Agriculture, Forestry and Fisheries, "Nōkyōhō Kaisei ni tsuite [About Agricultural Cooperative Law Reform]," January 2016, www.maff.go.jp/j/keiei/sosiki/kyosoka/k_kenkyu/pdf/1_nokyohou_kaisei.pdf.

51. Fully 163 of the 294 Liberal Democratic Party Diet members who won seats in the December 2012 Lower House election, for example, had the formal backing of *Zenkoku Nōseiren* (the All-Japan Agricultural Policy League), the vote-mobilizing arm of *nōkyō*. See Ryūnosuke Uchida, "TPP-kōshō to Nōsei-kaikaku: Seikenfukki-go ni Okeru Nōrin-zoku Giin no Kōdō Henka [TPP Negotiations and Agricultural Policy Reforms: Agricultural Tribal Men of the Second Abe Administration]," *Journal of Policy Studies* 9 (March 2015): 235.

52. For example, only 4.9 percent of targeted small and scattered farmland was successfully consolidated under the "farmland bank" program and only 18.0 percent of funds appropriated to support the program were used in fiscal 2014. See "'Farmland Bank' Program off to a Slow Start."

CHAPTER SEVEN

1. On the details, see Kent E. Calder, "Japan's Energy Angst: Asia's Changing Energy Prospects and the View from Tokyo," *Strategic Analysis* 32, no. 1 (2008): 123–129, doi: 10.1080/09700160701559359.

2. Daniel Yergin, *The Prize: The Epic Quest for Oil, Money, and Power* (New York: Simon and Schuster, 1991), 305–327.

3. On the speech, and the origins of U.S.-Japan nuclear cooperation, see Peter Kuznick, "Japan's Nuclear History in Perspective: Eisenhower and Atoms for War and Peace," *Bulletin of the Atomic Scientists*, April 13, 2011, http://thebulletin.org/japans-nuclear-history -perspective-eisenhower-and-atoms-war-and-peace-0.

4. Ibid.

5. Ibid.

6. Ibid.

7. Ibid.

8. Tetsuo Arima, *Genpatsu, Shōriki, CIA: Kimitsubunsho de Yomu Showa Rimenshi [Nuclear Power, Matsutarō Shōriki, and the CIA: Decipher Hidden History of Showa with Confidential Documents]* (Tokyo: Shinchosha, 2008), 43–47.

9. 1956 was the year that Japan decided to purchase the British reactor. The U.K.-Japan agreement for cooperation in the peaceful uses of atomic energy was signed in 1958, with the formal purchase made in 1959, and with construction starting in 1960. See Arima, 235 and 254.

10. Kuznick.

11. Yukawa received the Nobel Prize in Physics in 1949, with his prize greatly increasing awareness of the peaceful uses of nuclear energy among the Japanese people, in no small measure due to Matsutarō Shōriki's efforts to use Yukawa's celebrity to promote nuclear policies. Shōriki's paper, *The Yomiuri Shimbun*, established a Yukawa Hideki Scholarship in 1950, soon after the Nobel award. That and other publicity helped precipitate a "Yukawa Boom" that involved both personal acclaim for Yukawa and enhanced popular support for nuclear power, particularly during the five years between Yukawa's prize award and the *Daigo Fukuryū Maru* incident of March 1954. Ironically, Yukawa himself was ambivalent about Japan's own nuclear power development policy. He preferred a more cautious pace and more autonomous process of introducing nuclear power into Japan than the government proposed, and resigned from the Atomic Energy Commission in 1957 to protest the U.S.-Japan nuclear power agreement. See Arima, 47, and Tatsuo Tabata, "Hideki Yukawa's Words about Nuclear Power Development-1-," *IDEA & ISAAC: Femto-Essays* (Blog), June 11, 2011, http://ideaisaac.blogspot.com/2011/06/hideki-yukawas-words-about-nuclear .html.

12. Kuznick.

13. Ibid.

14. See International Atomic Energy Agency (IAEA), "Country Statistics—Japan," *Power Reactor Information System (PRIS)*, www.iaea.org/PRIS/CountryStatistics/Country Details.aspx?current=JP.

15. As of April 2016, sixteen of these sixty had been shut down permanently (including all six reactors at the Fukushima Daiichi plant), and one (Monju) was under long-term shutdown. The current number of operational reactors in Japan was thus forty-three, with two additional new reactors under construction. See IAEA, *PRIS*.

16. Japan in 2010 relied on nuclear power for 26.0 percent of its electricity. Only France (75.9 percent) and Korea (29.9 percent), among major industrialized nations, had a higher reliance on civilian nuclear power than Japan.

17. Figure for 2013. World Bank, "Energy imports, net (% of energy use)," *World Development Indicators*, 2013, http://data.worldbank.org/indicator/EG.IMP.CONS.ZS.

18. In 2013, 82.65 percent of the crude oil Japan imported came from the Middle East. Author's calculation based on IEA, *Oil Information 2015* (Paris: 2015), III.339, doi: 10.1787/ oil-2015-en.

19. Malcolm Grimston, "The Importance of Politics to Nuclear New Build," Energy, Environment and Development Program (London: Chatham House, December 2005), 34, www.chathamhouse.org/sites/files/chathamhouse/public/Research/Energy,%20Environ ment%20and%20Development/deco5nuclear.pdf; and John E. Parsons, and Yangbo Du, "Update on the Cost of Nuclear Power" (working paper, 2009), http://hdl.handle.net/ 1721.1/45666.

20. Georgia Power, for example, concluded a contract agreement for two AP1000 reactors in 2008, at an estimated final cost of $13 billion, plus $3 billion for necessary transmission upgrades. The reported cost for the first AP1000 units under construction in China was $8 billion in 2007. See Terry Macalister, "Westinghouse Wins First US Nuclear Deal in 30 Years," *The Guardian*, April 9, 2008, www.theguardian.com/world/2008/apr/10/ nuclear.nuclearpower.

21. International Energy Agency (IEA) and OECD Nuclear Energy Agency, "Table 3.9: Levelised cost of electricity for natural gas plants" and "Table 3.11: Levelised cost of electricity for nuclear plants," in *Projected Costs of Generating Electricity 2015* (Paris: OECD Publishing, 2015), 48–49, doi: 10.1787/cost_electricity-2015-en.

22. IEA, *PRIS*.

23. Ibid.

24. Ibid.

25. See Peter Navarro, "The Japanese Electric Utility Industry," in *International Comparisons of Electricity Regulation*, eds. Richard J. Gilbert and Edward P. Kahn (Cambridge, UK: Cambridge University Press, 1966), 258.

26. Japanese nuclear power plants are said to be amortized in around twenty-one years. After that, tax deductions are limited to property tax, fuel expenses, and operating costs only. See Denki Jigyō Rengōkai, "Moderu-shisan ni yoru Kaku-dengen no Hatsuden-kosuto Hikaku [Simulation of Comparative Power Generation Costs]," *Ministry of Economy, Trade and Industry*, January 2004, www.meti.go.jp/policy/electricpower_partialliberalization/ costdiscuss/siryou/4.pdf.

27. IEA, *PRIS*.

28. Kent E. Calder, *Crisis and Compensation: Public Policy and Political Stability in Japan, 1949–1986* (Princeton, NJ: Princeton University Press, 1988), 103–109.

29. On Tanaka's role in the conceptualization and passage of the three electric-power generation Laws, see Tōru Takeda, "Han-genpatsu to Suishin Ha: Nikōtairitsu ga Unda Kyodai Risuku [The Anti-Reactor and Pro-Reactor Factions: The Huge Risk that their Opposition Generated]," *Nikkei Business Online*, March 30, 2011, http://business.nikkeibp .co.jp/article/life/20110328/219175/?P=1&rt=nocnt.

30. Federation of Electric Power Companies of Japan (*Denjiren*), "Dengen Sanpō Seido [The Three Electric-Power Laws System]," http://www.fepc.or.jp/nuclear/policy/ houritsu/dengensanpou/index.html.

31. The nuclear ship *Mutsu* experienced a radiation leak in the reactor shield to its pressurized-water reactor on its first experimental voyage, in September 1974, just as the reactor was being powered. Its home port of Ohminato, Aomori Prefecture, concerned about dangers to the community and its substantial fishing industry, refused to let the ship return to harbor. For details, see Masayuki Nakao, "Radiation Leaks from Nuclear Power Ship 'Mutsu,'" *Failure Knowledge Database / 100 Selected Cases*, www.sozogaku.com/fkd/ en/hfen/HA1000615.pdf.

32. For *Mutsu* and Japan's anti-nuclear-power movements in the 1970s, see Hiroshi Honda, "Nihon no Genshiryoku Seiji Katei (3): Rengō Keisei to Funsō Kanri [Nuclear

Energy Politics in Japan (3): Coalition Formation and Conflict Management]," *Hokudai Hōgaku Ronshū* 54, no. 3 (August 2003): 220–160, http://hdl.handle.net/2115/15222.

33. See "Nihonjin no Anzenkan [Safety Perceptions of the Japanese People]" (report, Genshiryoku Anzen Kiban Chōsa Kenkyū [Research on the Foundations of Nuclear Safety], FY2012–2014), Chapter 3, http://nakamuraisao.a.la9.jp/anzenkan.htm.

34. At the Tomari nuclear plant in February 2001, for example, Hokkaido Electric Power Company provided ¥4.2 billion to the local fishing cooperative as insurance payment. See Nikkei Sangyō Shimbun staff, "Hokuden: 4 Gyokyō ni 42-oku-en no Hoshōkin, Tomari-genpatsu 3-gō-ki Kensetsu de [Hokkaido Electric Power: ¥4.2 billion Compensation to Four Fishery Cooperatives for Construction of Tomari Unit 3]," *Nikkei Sangyō Shimbun*, February 26, 2001.

35. In Mihama, for example, between 1,600 and 2,600 people, equal to one-third to one-half of the local workforce, are employed at the local power plant or related businesses, with the number going up during periodic inspections. Around the Fukushima nuclear plant, 20–30 percent of local workers were traditionally employed at the power plant or in related services, until the March 2011 disaster. See Nihon Keizai Shimbun staff, "Genpatsu 40-nen-chō Jidai Kanden Mihama Enchōunden e (Ge): Kōkeiki Kensetsu, Jimoto ga Unagasu [Kansai Electric Power's Mihama Nuclear Power Plant to Enter the 40th year of Operation: Local Communities Urge for Construction of Replacements]," *Nihon Keizai Shimbun*, November 26, 2010, and "Genshiryoku-hatsuden, Saikō 3 [Reconsidering Nuclear Power Generation, Part 3]," *Shūkan Daiyamondo*, April 16, 2011, 54.

36. "Genshiryoku-hatsuden, Saikō 3 [Reconsidering Nuclear Power Generation, Part 3]," 54.

37. In 1977, the year that the Mihama nuclear reactor #3 came into operation, 82 percent of local tax revenues came from Kansai Electric Power. Even in 2009, more than three decades later, 50 percent of local tax revenues still came from Kansai Electric Power. The bigger the nuclear plant, the more tax revenue a town typically receives. See "Genpatsu 40-nen-chō Jidai Kanden Mihama Enchōunden e (Ge): Kōkeiki Kensetsu, Jimoto ga Unagasu [Kansai Electric Power's Mihama Nuclear Power Plant to Enter the 40th year of Operation: Local Communities Urge for Construction of Replacements]." Also, National Citizens Ombudsman Liaison Conference, "Genpatsu Rieki Yūdō ni Yotte Yugamemareta Chihō Zaisei (Local Finances Distorted by Nuclear Power Generation Interests), August 20, 2011, www.ombudsman.jp/nuclear/yugami.pdf.

38. Figure 3-2 in "Genshiryoku-hatsuden, Saikō 3 [Reconsidering Nuclear Power Generation, Part 3]," 53.

39. The Japan Development Bank, for example, strongly supported Japan's large nuclear-power expansion of the 1970s. See Kent E. Calder, *Strategic Capitalism: Private Business and Public Purpose in Japanese Industrial Finance* (Princeton, NJ: Princeton University Press, 1993), 255.

40. For more information about the NRA and Japan's post-Fukushima regulatory reforms, see NRA profile leaflet "Nuclear Regulation Authority, Japan," www.nsr.go.jp/english/e_nra/nsr_leaflet_English.pdf.

41. In January 2011, for example, Tōru Ishida, former Commissioner of METI's Agency for Natural Resources and Energy, became an advisor to Tokyo Electric Power Company, and was expected to be elevated to Executive Vice President. Ishida resigned, however, following the Fukushima accident in March 2011. See "Ishida, Moto-Enechō Chōkan, Tōden Komon Jinin he: 'Isshinjō no Tsugō' [Ishida, Former Commissioner of Agency

of Natural Resources and Energy, Resigns from TEPCO 'for Personal Reasons']," *Asahi Shimbun*, April 18, 2011, www.asahi.com/special/10005/TKY201104180500.html. In total, between March 11, 2011, and March 31, 2015, there were a total of seventeen former METI officials became hired by the electric-power industry, as well as seven from MEXT, three from MOF, two from the Ministry of the Environment, and three from the Ministry of Land, Infrastructure, Transport and Tourism. See "Denryoku Kanren ni 71-nin Amakudari, Genpatsujiko-go, Keisanshō Saita 17-nin [71 Amakudari to Power Companies after Fukushima Incident, with 17 from METI]," *Tokyo Shimbun*, October 4, 2015, www.tokyo -np.co.jp/article/national/list/201510/CK2015100402000159.html.

42. The Rokkasho Reprocessing Plant, with an annual MOX fuel reprocessing capacity of eight hundred tons, is undergoing final commissioning tests as of 2016, but commercial operation has been delayed to 2018. Since commencement of construction in 1993, an estimated $25 billion has been invested in the plant. In addition to the Reprocessing Plant, the Rokkasho complex also has a MOX Fuel Fabrication Plant, a Uranium Enrichment Plant, a Low-Level Radioactive Waste Disposal Center, and a Vitrified Waste Storage Center. Construction of the MOX Fuel Fabrication Plant started in late 2010 and is scheduled to be complete in 2019. See Japan Nuclear Fuel Limited, "Our Business," www.jnfl.co.jp/en/business/, and Stephen Stapczynski, "Japan's $25 Billion Nuclear Recycling Quest Enters 28th Year," *Bloomberg*, January 5, 2016, www.bloomberg.com/ news/articles/2016−01−04/japan-s-25-billion-nuclear-recycling-quest-enters-28th-year. Rokkasho's small and more experimental predecessor, the Tokai reprocessing plant, entered full operation in 1981 but has stood idle since 2006. See "Tokai Reprocessing Plant to Shut," *World Nuclear News*, September 29, 2014, www.world-nuclear-news.org/W R-Tokai-reprocessing-plant-to-shut-2909144.html.

43. "Japan to Drop Troubled Fast Breeder Reactor from Energy Plan," *Nikkei Asian Review*, February 7, 2014, http://asia.nikkei.com/Politics-Economy/Policy-Politics/ Japan-to-drop-troubled-fast-breeder-reactor-from-energy-plan; Mizuho Aoki, "Fate of Troubled Monju Reactor Hangs in the Balance," *The Japan Times*, November 23, 2015, www.japantimes.co.jp/news/2015/11/23/reference/fate-of-troubled-monju-reactor -hangs-in-the-balance/#.V3_Ne_krKUk; and Ryoko Takeishi, "Plug pulled on costly Monju fast-breeder reactor project," *The Asahi Shimbun*, December 21, 2016.

44. Takeishi, "Plug pulled," www.asahi.com/ajw/articles/AJ201612210059.html.

45. See Hikaru Hiranuma, "Japan's Energy Policy in a Post-3/11 World: Juggling Safety, Sustainability and Economics," *Tokyo Foundation*, October 15, 2014, www.tokyofounda tion.org/en/articles/2014/energy-policy-in-post-3−11-world.

46. For the three objectives and implementation schedule of Japan's electricity-system reform, see Ministry of Economy, Trade and Industry, "Electricity System Reform: Outline," December 7, 2015, www.meti.go.jp/english/policy/energy_environment/electri city_system_reform/outline.html.

47. "Japan Passes Major Reforms to Electricity, Gas Sectors," *The Japan Times*, June 17, 2015, www.japantimes.co.jp/news/2015/06/17/business/japan-passes-major -reforms-electricity-gas-sectors/#.V3_QN_krKUk.

48. Hiranuma.

49. See "Genpatsu Baishō, Denryoku 10-sha ga Futankin Kyoshutsu: Tōden Shien Wakugumi Kettei [Ten Electric Power Companies to Pay for Nuclear Power Plant Incident Compensation: Decisions Made on TEPCO Support Framework]," *Asahi Shimbun*, May 13, 2011, www.asahi.com/special/10005/TKY201105130140.html.

50. "Genshiryoku-hatsuden, Saikō 3 [Reconsidering Nuclear Power Generation, Part 3]," 53.

51. Since September 2012, the NRA, an external affiliate of the Ministry of the Environment, has supervised safety issues with respect to the nuclear plants.

52. "Nuclear Remains Cheapest Power Source Despite Fukushima Meltdowns: Government," *The Japan Times*, May 11, 2015, www.japantimes.co.jp/news/2015/05/11/business/ nuclear-remains-cheapest-power-source-despite-fukushima-meltdowns-government/# .V3_XHPkrKUk.

53. Linda Sieg, "Japan PM Abe's Support Slips, Majority Oppose Nuclear Restart," *Reuters*, August 10, 2015, www.reuters.com/article/us-japan-abe-support-idUSKC N0QF0A820150810.

54. Osamu Tsukimori and Kentaro Hamada, "Japan Restarts Second Reactor at Sendai Nuclear Plant," *Reuters*, October 14, 2015, www.reuters.com/article/us-japan-nuclear -restarts-idUSKCN0S90872015101 5.

55. See "Ikata 3 back in commercial operation," *World Nuclear News*, September 7, 2016, www.world-nuclear-news.org/C-Ikata-3-back-in-commercial-operation-0709165.html.

56. See "Injunction halts operation of Takahama units," *World Nuclear News*, March 9, 2016, www.world-nuclear-news.org/RS-Injunction-halts-operation-of-Takahama-units -0903165.html.

57. For more on the post-Fukushima nuclear reactors shutdown and restart, see "Nuclear Power in Japan," *World Nuclear Association*, www.world-nuclear.org/information -library/country-profiles/countries-g-n/japan-nuclear-power.aspx.

58. At the same time, average electricity expenses per household increased 25.2 percent between fiscal years 2010 and 2014. See Ministry of Economy, Trade and Industry Agency for Natural Resources and Energy, *Energy White Paper 2015 (Japanese edition)*, 71 and 73.

CHAPTER EIGHT

1. The number of tourists entering Japan fell from 8.6 million in 2010 to 6.2 million in 2011, due to the Tōhoku earthquake and tsunami, but their number rebounded to 10.3 million in 2013, to 13.4 million in 2014, and to 19.7 million in 2015. See Japan National Tourism Organization and Figure 8.1.

2. For Japan's international trade pattern, see A. J. G Simoes and C. A. Hidalgo, *The Economic Complexity Observatory: An Analytical Tool for Understanding the Dynamics of Economic Development* (Workshops at the Twenty-Fifth AAAI Conference on Artificial Intelligence, 2011).

3. Rankings are based on cargo volume, as measured by "loaded and unloaded freight and mail in metric tonnes." Airports Council International, "Cargo Traffic 2013 FINAL (Annual)," updated December 22, 2014, www.aci.aero/Data-Centre/Annual-Traffic -Data/Cargo/2013-final.

4. Rankings based on the number of international passengers. Airports Council International, "International Passenger Traffic for Past 12 Months (ENDING DEC 2015)," updated April 11, 2016, www.aci.aero/Data-Centre/Monthly-Traffic-Data/International -Passenger-Rankings/12-months.

5. Airports Council International, "Cargo Traffic 2002 FINAL," updated July 2004, www.aci.aero/Data-Centre/Annual-Traffic-Data/Cargo/2003-final; "Cargo Traffic 2006 FINAL," updated July 18, 2007, www.aci.aero/Data-Centre/Annual-Traffic-Data/ Cargo/2006-final; and "Cargo Traffic 2013 FINAL (Annual)."

6. Information as of July 2016. See official websites of the two airports.

7. In 2014, Nagoya handled 208 million freight tons of cargo. In comparison, Singapore handled 581 million freight tons. See American Association of Port Authorities, "World Port Rankings 2014."

8. In 2014, Japan's liner exports totaled 5.28 million TEUs (twenty-foot equivalent unit shipping containers). Although ranked the fourth largest exporter of containerized cargo in absolute terms, Japan shared only 4.1 percent of global liner exports. Similarly, although Japan ranked the third largest importer of containerized cargo in 2014, its share of global liner imports was only 5.1 percent (6.55 out of 127.60 million TEUs). See World Shipping Council, "Top 20 Exporters of Containerized Cargo—2010, 2013 & 2014" and "Top 20 Importers of Containerized Cargo—2010, 2013 & 2014," www.worldshipping.org/about -the-industry/global-trade/trade-statistics.

9. "In Pictures: Top 5 Transshipment Hubs," *Port Technology,* February 25, 2015, www .porttechnology.org/news/in_pictures_top_5_transhipment_hubs.

10. Keihin Ports is Japan's superport hub on Tokyo Bay, and includes Yokohama, Kawasaki, and Tokyo. Hanshin Ports is Japan's superport hub on Osaka Bay, and includes Kobe, Osaka, Sakai-Semboku, and Amagasaki-Nishinomiya-Ashiya. For Journal of Commerce's Top 50 World Container Ports 2014 rankings, see: Marsha Salisbury, "Shanghai Strengthens Its Grip on Port Rankings." *Journal of Commerce* 16, no. 17 (2015): 25–34.

11. Nihon Keizai Shimbun staff, "Kontena Senryaku Kōwan ni Keihin, Hanshin— 'Pusan kara Dakkan' Michi Kewashiku [Keihin and Hanshin Chosen as Strategic Container Ports: Steep Path toward Reclaiming Market from Busan]," *Nihon Keizai Shimbun,* August 27, 2010, and Ministry of Land, Infrastructure, Transport and Tourism Ports and Harbors Bureau, "Wagakuni Kōwan he no Gaibō Teiki Kontena Kōro Binsū [Weekly International Container Shipment Services in Japan]," April 1, 2015, www.mlit.go.jp/ common/000228238.pdf.

12. Data for 2006. "Kontena Senryakukō ni Kei-Hin to Han-Shin: Ajia Kyotenkō he Michi Kewashi [Keihin and Hanshin Picked as Strategic Container Ports: Rocky Road to Hub Port of Asia]," *Nikkei,* August 6, 2010, www.nikkei.com/article/DGXNASFS0602Z _W0A800C1EE2000/.

13. This tax prevails only in the case of airplanes leaving one airport in Japan for another Japanese airport. That tax does, however, inhibit the potential role of Japanese airports as hubs to Japanese cities, relative to Incheon. See Ministry of Environment, "Environment-Related Tax System in Japan," August 14, 2012, www.env.go.jp/en/policy/tax/ env-tax/20120814a_ertj.pdf.

14. The United States charges $0.218/gallon general aviation fuel tax on jet fuel. See Federal Aviation Administration, "Current Aviation Excise Tax Structure," January 2013, www.faa.gov/about/office_org/headquarters_offices/apl/aatf/media/Excise_Tax _Structure_Calendar_2013.pdf.

15. See National International Airport official website, "Travel Support—Frequently Asked Questions (FAQ)—Passenger Service Facility Charge (PSFC) and Passenger Security Service Charge (PSSC)," www.narita-airport.jp/en/travel/faq_ask/psfc/after.html.

16. See Figures 9–16 in Leigh Fisher, "Aeronautical Charges Benchmarking: Final Report," prepared for Auckland International Airport, April 11, 2013.

17. Hassan Al Ibrahim et al., "Index of Country/Economy Profiles—Japan," The Travel & Tourism Competitiveness Report 2015 (Geneva: World Economic Forum, 2015), 193, www3.weforum.org/docs/TT15/WEF_Global_Travel&Tourism_Report_2015.pdf.

18. Korea, by comparison, ranked 23rd in ticket taxes and airport charges, and 109th in price competitiveness. See Ibid, 201.

19. On this issue, see David E. Apter and Nagayo Sawa, *Against the State: Politics and Social Protest in Japan* (Cambridge, MA: Harvard University Press, 1984).

20. On Narita's operating hours, see Narita International Airport Corporation, "Narita International Airport Service Regulations (Provisional Translation)," www.naa.jp/en/airport/pdf/kitei_kyoyou.pdf.

21. The Haneda Airport, apart from the terminal building, is still owned by MLIT and administered by the Ministry's Tokyo Regional Civil Aviation Bureau.

22. Among 38 private companies that operate terminal buildings at 26 government-administered airports, 11 out of 205 board members came from MLIT. See "11-nin ga Kokkōshō kara Amakudari: Kuni-Kanri Kūkō no Minkan Gyōsha [11 Descended from the Heaven of MLIT: Survey of Private Enterprises Operating Government-Administered Airports]," *47 News*, November 10, 2009.

23. See Hiroko Nakata, "Cap on Foreign Holdings in Airports to be Dropped," *The Japan Times*, February 29, 2008, www.japantimes.co.jp/news/2008/02/29/business/cap-on-foreign-holdings-in-airports-to-be-dropped/#.V4JoVvkrKUk; and Jonathan Soble and Peter Smith, "Macquarie to Sell Stake in Airport Group," *Financial Times*, May 20, 2009, https://next.ft.com/content/1269f8c4-455b-11de-b6c8-00144feabdco.

24. See Incheon Airport, "Cargo Services."

25. The Yeongjong Medical Center is a collaborative effort between the Incheon International Airport Corporation and the Inha University Hospital. See Korean Hospital Association, "Inha University Hospital," *Medical Institutions & Location Information*, www.hospitalmaps.or.kr/frHospital/hospital_view_1.jsp?s_hosp_code=400130&s_mid=&s_tab=01.

26. See "Airport Hospital Planned to Attract Foreign Patients," *The Chosun Ilbo*, January 10, 2008, http://english.chosun.com/site/data/html_dir/2008/01/10/2008011061012.html.

27. For more on medical services provided at Incheon Airport, see Incheon Airport, "Medical Transit Tour Program," www.airport.kr/pa/en/d/2/3/5/index.jsp?tabIndex=4. For more on Korea's medical tourism visa, see "South Korea: Medical Tourism Boosted by Changes in Regulation," *International Medical Travel Journal*, August 12, 2009, www.imtj.com/news/south-korea-medical-tourism-boosted-changes-regulation/.

28. For more on Korea's medical tourism programs, browse the official website Visit Medical Korea, http://english.visitmedicalkorea.com/english/pt/index.do.

29. In October 2010, for example, the Shin-Urayasu Toranomon Clinic, in Urayasu near Narita International Airport, began to offer a comprehensive checkup program (*ningen dokku*) specially oriented toward Chinese tourists, but this had no direct relationship to Narita Airport itself. See Iryōhōjinshadan Shin-Toranomon Kai and Kabushikigaisha KIT, "Rainichi Chūgokujin Kankōkyaku Taishō no 'Inbaundo Iryōkankō' Sabisu Kaishi ['Inbound Medical Tourism' Targeting Chinese Tourists Kicked Off]," *atpress*, October 22, 2010, www.atpress.ne.jp/news/17335.

30. Costs included pilotage, towage, and linesman costs, including wharfage on full and empty containers, but excluded charges such as stevedoring and miscellaneous utility charges. See Shipping Australia Limited, *International Port Cost Comparison Project*, https://shippingaustralia.com.au/wp-content/uploads/2012/01/L_InterPortCostCcomparison.pdf.

31. For example, the Infrastructure Development Special Account Harbour Account budget for 2009 was ¥302.7 billion, including ¥212.6 billion general account support. The numbers were down to ¥210.6 billion and ¥160.0 billion, respectively, in 2010. Details of the Infrastructure Development Special Account can be found at Ministry of Land, Infrastructure, Transport and Tourism, "Tokubetsu Kaikei ni Kansuru Jōhō Kaiji [Explication of Special Accounts]," www.mlit.go.jp/page/kanbo01_hy_000162.html.

32. Provided under the Port Facilities Emergency Measures Law of 1961, originally intended to expand port facilities to meet demand during the high-growth era.

33. Nobuo Akai, *Kōtsū Infura to Gabanansu no Keizaigaku: Kūkō, Kōwan, Chihō Yūryōdōro no Zaiseibunseki [The Economics of Transportation Infrastructure: Financial Analysis of Airports, Seaports and Local Toll Roads]* (Tokyo: Yuhikaku Publishing Co., Ltd., 2010), 88.

34. Akai, 132.

35. See Ministry of Internal Affairs and Communications Statistics Bureau, "5 – 4 General Accounts B Expenditure Budget by Principal Item," *Japan Statistical Yearbook 2015*.

36. See Ministry of Internal Affairs and Communications Statistics Bureau, "5 – 19 Administrative Investment A Investment by Work Purpose and Burden Share," *Japan Statistical Yearbook 2015*.

37. Hong Kong's fiscal year 2015 – 2016 budget, for example, provides 17.3 percent of total expenditures for public works, including development of a three-runway system at the Hong Kong International Airport on Lantau Island that is expected to cost HK$141.5 billion. See "The 2015 – 16 Budget-Highlights," February 25, 2015, www.budget.gov .hk/2015/eng/highlights.html, and Hong Kong International Airport, "Cost & Financial Arrangements: Estimated Cost for Building the 3RS," www.threerunwaysystem.com/en/ Overview/Cost_and_Funding_Arrangement.aspx. Singapore also spends heavily on transport development—S$554.9 million, or 27 percent of total government economic development expenditures in 2013, more than twice the comparable expenditure one decade ago. See Department of Statistics Singapore, "M130581—Government Operating Expenditure, Annual."

38. Kansai International Airport reportedly cost ¥1.46 trillion to build, of which two-thirds was the real-estate cost, and Denver the equivalent of ¥320 billion, of which only one-third was land cost. See Kazuki Sugiura, "Habu-Kūkō-ka wo Habamu 'Chōkō' Chakurikuryō ['Super High' Landing Fees that Impede the Hubization of Airports]," *Ekonomisuto* 80, no. 40 (September 24, 2002): 91 – 93.

39. See Ministry of Finance, "Japanese Public Finance Fact Sheet 2014," 66, www.mof .go.jp/english/budget/budget/fy2014/factsheet2014.pdf.

40. Akai, 33 and 57.

41. "Kūkō-sū no Suii [Number of Airports]," *Shakai Jijō Deta Suroku*, www2.ttcn .ne.jp/honkawa/6882.html.

42. On the Fiscal Investment and Loans Program (FILP), see Ministry of Finance Financial Bureau, "FILP Report 2015," www.mof.go.jp/english/filp/filp_report/zaito2015/ pdf/filp2015_eng.pdf.

43. At Narita, for example, the number of passport control counters in Terminal 2 was doubled at busy hours. See "Narita Airport to Open more Passport Control Counters at Busy Times," *The Japan Times*, April 1, 2015, www.japantimes.co.jp/news/2015/04/01/ national/narita-airport-open-passport-control-counters-busy-times/#.V4ZLvvkrKUk. The airport also added fifty-one SIM-card vending machines to encourage international travelers. See Kazuaki Nagata, "Narita Airport to Get SIM Card Vending Machines," *The*

Japan Times, July 15, 2015, www.japantimes.co.jp/news/2015/07/17/business/tech/narita -airport-get-sim-card-vending-machines/#.V4ZL6PkrKUk. Haneda expanded its landing slots and gave additional emphasis to new slots for mainland China flights. See Takeshi Shiraishi, "Haneda Expanding China Flights to Handle Influx," *Nikkei Asian Review,* October 24, 2015, http://asia.nikkei.com/Business/Trends/Haneda-expanding-China-flights -to-handle-influx.

44. CAPA Centre for Aviation, "Kansai and Osaka Itami Lead Japan's Ambitious Airport Privatisation Programme—with 2020 the Target," September 7, 2014, http://centre foraviation.com/analysis/kansai-and-osaka-itami-lead-japans-ambitious-airport-privati sation-moves—with-2020-the-target-185261.

45. Orix and France's Vinci SA jointly won operating right for Kanai in early 2015, although their partnership was the only bidder. See Junko Fujita, "Sinking under Debt, Kansai Airport Privatization Presents Test for Abe," *Reuters,* March 13, 2015, www.reuters .com/article/us-japan-airport-idUSKBN0M90P320150313.

46. "Chihō-kūkō, Ryokaku Nobinai nara Haishi mo Ketsudan wo [Local Airports with Low Passenger Traffic might be Closed]," *Asahi Shimbun,* March 11, 2011.

47. The MLIT Administrative Vice-Minister Masahiko Kurono, for example, was appointed president of Narita International Airport Corporation, when this operator of Japan's main gateway airport was privatized, and served in that capacity until 2011. Similarly, MLIT bureaucrats served as president of the Kansai International Airport Corporation from its foundation until 2003, with Kiyoyasu Mikanagi, former Director of MOF's Ports and Harbours Bureau, serving as president from 1996 until 2003.

48. Seasonal fluctuations in fares are substantial and discount options are emerging. These nuances make it difficult to calculate Japanese domestic fares precisely, but by almost all qualitative accounts, they are high in comparative perspective.

49. Mariko Sanchanta and Yoshio Takahashi, "JAL Bankruptcy Shakes Up Japan Inc.," *Wall Street Journal,* January 20, 2010, www.wsj.com/articles/SB1000142405274870383700 4575012323580338724.

50. On JAL's structural problems and their relation to public policy, see Kazuhiko Toyama, "The Real Story of the Problems at Japan Airlines," *Global Asia* 5, no.2 (Summer, 2010).

51. Cargo-handling companies such as Yamato Transport are illustrative. See Yamato Holdings Co. Ltd., "Annual Report 2015," www.yamato-hd.co.jp/investors/library/ annualreport/pdf/2015/ar2015_00.pdf.

52. On the chronology of airport policy development, see Akai, 16–19.

53. See Akai, 17.

54. A report regarding the 2003 Cabinet approval of the Priority Plan for the Development of Social Capital Facilities is available at www.nilim.go.ūp/lab/bcg/siryou/tnn/ tnn0533pdf/ks053309.pdf.

55. Under the terms of this Open Skies agreement, the U.S. and Japanese governments decided the number of departure and landing spots between them, but private airlines and airport owners were allowed to make decisions on participating airlines, routes, the number of flights, and air fares.

56. "Haneda, Narita: Ajia-bin Jiyūka, Kakuyasukōkū Sannyū ni Hazumi [Liberalization of Lines between Haneda/Narita and Asia: Competition to Rise with Entry of LCCs]," *Nikkei,* October 25, 2010.

57. Incheon, for example, already handled nearly forty-one million passengers in 2013, but is investing $5 billion more to build a second terminal for completion in late 2017,

in preparation for the 2018 Pyeongchang Winter Olympics. See William Dennis, "South Korea Builds Smart Terminal to Expand Airport," *Engineering and Technology Magazine*, January 22, 2014, https://eandt.theiet.org/content/articles/2014/01/south-korea-builds -smart-terminal-to-expand-airport/.

58. This law regulated Japanese ports, and also stipulated broader objectives for ports policy, including the need to increase the number of ports, to expand port facilities to meet growing economic demand, and to reduce economic imbalances between metropolitan areas and other parts of Japan.

59. There were 997 actual ports in Japan as of 2010, including 126 that were registered as "important ports." See Akai, 79.

60. See Akai, 93–95.

CHAPTER NINE

1. Ministry of Internal Affairs and Communications Statistics Bureau, "25-1 Schools by Founder and Kind of School (1947–2005)," *Historical Statistics of Japan*, April 2012, www .stat.go.jp/english/data/chouki/25.htm.

2. As of May 2015, Japan had 779 universities (86 national, 89 public, and 604 private). Of the March 2015 upper secondary school graduates, 54.6 percent went straight on to enter a university or junior college. See Ministry of Internal Affairs and Communications Statistics Bureau, "Chapter 16 Education and Culture," *Statistical Handbook of Japan 2016*, 172–173, www.stat.go.jp/english/data/handbook/pdf/2016all .pdf#page=187.

3. On these "control associations," see Jerome B. Cohen, *Japan's Economy in War and Reconstruction* (Minneapolis: University of Minnesota Press, 1949), 32 and 60; Takafusa Nakamura, *Economic Growth in Prewar Japan*, trans. Robert A. Feldman (New Haven, CT: Yale University Press, 1983); as well as Takafusa Nakamura and Konosuke Odaka, eds., Noah S. Brannen, trans., *The Economic History of Japan, 1600–1990*, Vol. 3: *Economic History of Japan, 1914–1955: A Dual Structure* (Oxford, UK: Oxford University Press, 2003).

4. There was the Electric Machinery Control Association, established in January 1942, and succeeded by the Japan Electric Machinery Association. The cited source used Japan Electric Machinery Association founded in 1946. Yet neither was well developed institutionally. See Tetsuji Okazaki, "The Government-Firm Relationship in Postwar Japan: The Success and Failure of Bureau Pluralism," in *Rethinking the East Asia Miracle*, eds. Joseph E. Stiglitz and Shahid Yusuf (New York: Oxford University Press, 2001), 329.

5. On Sony's evolution, stressing the unregimented character of its early years, see Akio Morita, Edwin M. Reingold, and Mitsuko Shimomura, *Made in Japan: Akio Morita and Sony* (New York: Dutton, 1986).

6. In 1967 NTT's revenues were ¥700.5 billion ($1.93 billion). They rose to ¥5.09 trillion ($21.33 billion) by 1985. See Marie Anchordoguy, "Nippon Telegraph and Telephone Company (NTT) and the Building of a Telecommunications Industry in Japan," *The Business History Review* 75, no. 3 (Autumn 2001): 507–541, www.jstor.org/stable/3116385.

7. "Japanese Manufacturing: From Summit to Plummet," *The Economist*, February 18, 2012, www.economist.com/node/21547815.

8. In 2012, for example, NEC held ¥2.6 billion in NTT shares. See Ibid.

9. See Marie Anchordoguy, "Whatever Happened to the Japanese Miracle?" (JPRI Working Paper No. 80, September 2001), www.jpri.org/publications/workingpapers/ wp80.html.

10. Japan ranked sixth in the entire Organisation for Economic Co-operation and Development (OECD) in its level of business telephone charges in 2012 with $55.78 per 100 calls, PPP and value-added tax excluded. In comparison, the United States ranked in twenty-first place ($37.90), twenty-fifth for Germany ($36.23), and thirty-first for Korea ($29.27). See OECD Communications Outlook 2013, "Table 7.9. OECD basket of business telephone charges, 100 calls, VAT excluded, August 2012," in *OECD Communications Outlook 2013* (Paris: OECD Publishing, 2013), 236, doi: 10.1787/comms_outlook-2013-en.

11. From 1949 until 2001, the Japanese telecommunications sector was administered by the Ministry of Posts and Telecommunications. From 2001 to 2004, the same function was discharged by the Ministry of Public Management, Home Affairs, Posts, and Telecommunications. Since 2004 telecommunications has been overseen by the Ministry of Internal Affairs and Communications.

12. Mark Tilton, "Nonliberal Capitalism in the Information Age: Japan and the Politics of Telecommunications Reform" (JPRI Working Paper No. 98, February 2004), www.jpri.org/publications/workingpapers/wp98.html.

13. In 2000 it cost $78 in Japan to use the Internet for forty hours and $23 in the United States. See Ibid.

14. Ibid.

15. Japan, for example, tried to sell its distinctive 2G personal digital cellular technology standards to Asian neighbors in the early 1990s, but those standards were rejected in favor of European standards, owing to the latter's superior international-roaming services. See Tomoo Marukawa and Masanori Yasumoto, *Keitaidenwa Sangyō no Shinka Purosesu: Nihon wa Naze Koritsushita no ka [The Advancement Process of the Cell Phone Industry: Why Japan Got Isolated]* (Tokyo: Yuhikaku Publishing Co., Ltd., 2010), 25–26 and 29–30.

16. Due to more complex features and insufficient economies of scale, Japanese cellphone production costs were reportedly ¥20,000 (around US$250) higher per unit than Samsung by 2011. See "Sumātohon no Kōbō: Sekai 4-oku-dai Shijō e Kōbō [Smartphones: Attack on a 400 Million Unit Global Market]," *Nikkei Sangyō Shimbun*, June 27, 2011.

17. The analogy between the biological peculiarities of the Galápagos Islands, first noted by Charles Darwin in the late nineteenth century, and the esoteric tendencies of Japanese industry in recent years, was first popularly emphasized by Nomura Research Institute analysts. See Naohiro Yoshikawa, *Garapagosu-ka-suru Nihon [The Japan That Is Being Galápagosized]* (Tokyo: Kodansha, 2010).

18. Daisuke Wakabayashi, "Japan's Dimwitted Smartphones," *Wall Street Journal*, August 16, 2012, www.wsj.com/articles/SB100008723963900443517104577574470875390872.

19. Ibid.

20. Brian X. Chen, "BlackBerry under Siege in Europe," *The New York Times*, January 29, 2012, www.nytimes.com/2012/01/30/technology/blackberry-under-siege-in-europe-from-rivals.html.

21. Sony Ericsson, the largest Japanese producer, sold 34.4 million handsets in 2011, compared to 300.0 million for Samsung. See Sony Ericsson, "Press Release: Sony Ericsson Reports Fourth Quarter and Full Year 2011 Results," January 19, 2012, www.sony.net/SonyInfo/IR/library/semc/pdf/q411.pdf.

22. Among the component areas Japan dominates are electromagnetic wave-shield films (Tatsuta Densen) and electronic compasses (Asahi Kasei). See "Sumātohon no Kōbō: Sekai 4-oku-dai Shijō e Kōbō [Smartphones: Attack on a 400 Million Unit Global Market]," *Nikkei Sangyō Shimbun*, June 27, 2011.

23. Data from company annual reports for Panasonic, NEC, Fujitsu, Sony, and Sharp.

24. Data from company annual reports. For a comparison showing the rising profitability of Apple and Samsung, contrasting the continuing difficulties of the Japanese electronics firms, see "Japanese Manufacturing: From Summit to Plummet," *The Economist*.

25. According to data accessed via the Bloomberg terminal, the total market capitalization of five large Japanese electronics firms (Panasonic, NEC, Sharp, Sony, and Fujitsu) in fiscal year 2015 was only 26.9 percent of the equivalent level in 2000. For an analysis covering the period prior to 2012, see "Japanese Manufacturing: From Summit to Plummet," *The Economist*.

26. Kōichi Ogawa, "From Product Innovation to Business Model Innovation: Architecture-based Proposal for Japanese Innovation System (1)" (IAM Discussion Paper Series # 001, Intellectual Asset-Based Management Endorsed Chair, University of Tokyo, December, 2008), http://pari.u-tokyo.ac.jp/unit/iam/outcomes/pdf/papers_090105.pdf.

27. By 2014 Toshiba was relying on overseas factories to produce all of its televisions, and 96 percent of its home appliances. Similarly, Kenwood was producing 90 percent of its car-navigation systems abroad, while Bridgestone was making 70 percent of its tires overseas. See Takashi Nakamichi, "Japan's 'Hollowing-Out' Means Weaker Yen Not Helping Much," *The Wall Street Journal*, February 4, 2014, http://blogs.wsj.com/japanrealtime/2014/02/04/japans-hollowing-out-means-weaker-yen-not-helping-much/.

28. Ministry of Internal Affairs and Communications, "Information and Communications in Japan 2003," 10.

29. On this long history of transnational cultural exchange, see, for example, Ronald P. Toby, *State and Diplomacy in Early Modern Japan: Asia in the Development of the Tokugawa Bakufu* (Princeton, NJ: Princeton University Press, 1984); Marius B. Jansen, *Japan and its World: Two Centuries of Change* (Princeton, NJ: Princeton University Press, 1980); Marius B. Jansen, *The Making of Modern Japan* (Cambridge, MA: Harvard University Press, 2000); and Michael R. Auslin, *Pacific Cosmopolitans: A Cultural History of U.S.-Japan Relations* (Cambridge, MA: Harvard University Press, 2011).

30. For an introduction to these patterns, see Ivan P. Hall, *Cartels of the Mind: Japan's Intellectual Closed Shop* (New York: W. W. Norton, 1998). Also, Gregory J. Kasza, *The State and the Mass Media in Japan, 1918–1945* (Berkeley: University of California Press, 1988).

31. On the classical press club system, see Ofer Feldman, *Politics and the News Media in Japan* (Ann Arbor: University of Michigan Press, 1993) and Hall, 48–55.

32. Since 2004 competition at any one point has been eased by introduction of a "law-school system," requiring a graduate J.D. course, followed by a new bar exam, which 25–50 percent of graduates typically pass, and a subsequent apprenticeship. Yet admission to the bar is still highly restrictive, in international comparative terms. See Miki Tanikawa, "A Japanese Legal Exam that Sets the Bar High," *The New York Times*, July 11, 2011, www.nytimes.com/2011/07/11/world/asia/11iht-educLede11.html.

33. See T. J. Pempel, "The Politics of Enrollment Expansion in Japanese Universities," *The Journal of Asian Studies* 33, no. 1 (November 1973): 67–86, www.jstor.org/stable/2052886.

34. Ministry of Internal Affairs and Communications Statistics Bureau, "25-1 Schools by Founder and Kind of School (1947–2005)," *Historical Statistics of Japan*, April 2012, www.stat.go.jp/english/data/chouki/25.htm; "Chapter 16 Education and Culture," *Statistical Handbook of Japan 2016*, 172–173, www.stat.go.jp/english/data/handbook/

pdf/2016all.pdf#page=187; "2-2 Population by Single Years of Age and Sex (1884–2005)," *Historical Statistics of Japan*, April 2012, www.stat.go.jp/english/data/chouki/02.htm; and "2-5 Population by Age," *Japan Statistical Yearbook 2017*, www.stat.go.jp/english/data/nenkan/66nenkan/1431-02.htm.

35. Hall, 80–122.

36. Ministry of Internal Affairs and Communications Statistics Bureau, "Chapter 16 Education and Culture," *Statistical Handbook of Japan 2016*, 172–173, www.stat.go.jp/english/data/handbook/pdf/2016all.pdf#page=187.

37. See Columbia University Teachers College, "Coming of Age in Japan," October 27, 2006, www.tc.columbia.edu/articles/2006/october/coming-of-age-in-japan/.

CHAPTER TEN

1. Jeffry A. Frieden, *Global Capitalism: Its Fall and Rise in the Twentieth Century* (New York: W. W. Norton, 2006).

2. World exports, for example, grew from 13.4 percent of global product in 1970 to 25.5 percent by 2001, and 29.1 percent in 2015, with capital flows growing much faster than trade. Foreign exchange turnover relative to merchandise trade rose from a ratio of 50:1 during the 1980s to 100:1 by the 2000s. By 2012, transborder flows of goods, services, and financial products constituted 36 percent of global GDP, or 50 percent more than the ratio in 1990. See World Bank, "Exports of goods and services (% of GDP)," World Development Indicators, 1970–2015, http://data.worldbank.org/indicator/NE.EXP.GNFS.ZS; United Nations Conference on Trade and Development (UNCTAD), *Development and Globalization: Facts and Figures, 2012* (United Nations Publication, April 2012), 16–17, http://unctad.org/en/PublicationsLibrary/webgdsdsi2012d2_en.pdf; and James Manyika, Jacques Bughin, Susan Lund, Olivia Nottebohm, David Poulter, Sebastian Jauch, and Sree Ramaswamy, "Global flows in a digital age," *McKinsey Global Institute Report*, April 2014, www.mckinsey.com/business-functions/strategy-and-corporate-finance/our-insights/global-flows-in-a-digital-age.

3. On these critical junctures in China, India, and the Soviet Union that contributed so substantially to global transformation, see Kent E. Calder, *The New Continentalism: Energy and Twenty-First Century Eurasian Geopolitics* (New Haven, CT: Yale University Press, 2012), 47–99.

4. Pankaj Ghemawat and Steven A. Altman, "DHL Global Connectedness Index 2016: The State of Globalization in an Age of Ambiguity," *Deutsche Post DHL Group*, October 2016, 30, www.dhl.com/content/dam/downloads/go/about_us/logistics_insights/gci_2016/DHL_GCI_2016_full_study.pdf.

5. Hiroko Tabuchi, "Why Japan's Cellphones Haven't Gone Global," *The New York Times*, June 19, 2009, www.nytimes.com/2009/07/20/technology/20cell.html?_r=0.

6. Toyota's preeminence began in 2008, the year of the Lehman Brothers financial crisis, which impacted General Motors more severely. See Kendra Marr, "Toyota Passes GM as World's Largest Automaker," *The Washington Post*, January 22, 2009, www.washingtonpost.com/wp-dyn/content/article/2009/01/21/AR2009012101216.html. Toyota claimed to be the world's largest automaker all years from 2008 to 2015, except in 2011, the year of the Tōhoku earthquake. See Bertel Schmitt, "Nice Try VW: Toyota Again World's Largest Automaker," *Forbes*, January 27, 2016, www.forbes.com/sites/bertelschmitt/2016/01/27/nice-try-vw-toyota-again-worlds-largest-automaker/#523e1f4f2b65.

7. Toyota (13.1), Honda (9.2), and Nissan (9.3) together held 31.6 percent of the U.S. market as of June 2016. See Wall Street Journal, "Sales and Share of Total Market by Manufacturer," *Market Data Center: Auto Sales.*

8. Phyllis A. Genther, *A History of Japan's Government-Business Relationship: The Passenger Car Industry* (Ann Arbor: University of Michigan Center for Japanese Studies, 1990), 154–155.

9. See Daikin's "Corporate Data," www.daikin.com/about/corporate/corporate_data/index.html; "Global Locations," www.daikin.com/locations/group/europe/index.html; "FAQ-Corporate Information," www.daikin.com/faq/faq_corporate/index.html; and "Annual Report 2015," www.daikin.com/investor/library/pdf/2015/ar_15.pdf.

10. Daikin's industrial affiliations are with the Japan Refrigeration and Air Conditioning Industry Association and the Japan Society of Industrial Machinery Manufacturers, neither of which has a major role in the broader Japanese political economy, or substantial funds or staff at its disposal.

11. See Unicharm's "Integrated Report 2015," www.unicharm.co.jp/english/ir/library/annual/__icsFiles/afieldfile/2015/07/23/1_All_E_2015.pdf.

12. Unicharm is a member only of the Japan Hygiene Products]Industry Association and the Japan Pet Products Manufacturers Association.

13. Daikin was ranked No. 21 and Unicharm No. 23 in Japan's Top 30 Global Brands. Toyota was No.1. Virtually all top brands were located in sectors where circles of compensation are relatively unimportant, e.g., automotive and consumer electronics. See Interbrand, "Japan's Best Global/Domestic Brands 2015," http://interbrand.com/wp-content/uploads/2015/08/Interbrand-Best-Japanese-Brands-2015-English.pdf.

14. Shigeki Ishii, Susumu Hattori, and David Michael, "How to Win in Emerging Markets: Lessons from Japan," *Harvard Business Review*, May 2012, https://hbr.org/2012/05/how-to-win-in-emerging-markets-lessons-from-japan.

15. Rakuten's consolidated revenue in 2015 was nearly $5.9 billion. See Rakuten's "Annual Report FY2015," available for download at http://global.rakuten.com/corp/investors/documents/annual.html.

16. The Industrial Bank of Japan was the most entrepreneurial of Japan's large financial institutions, and its executives nurtured several innovative and global firms, such as YKK.

17. See the Rakuten website, http://global.rakuten.com/corp/about/.

18. Omar Akhar, "Rakuten: The Biggest E-Commerce Site You Haven't Heard Of," *Fortune*, March 22, 2013, http://fortune.com/2013/03/22/rakuten-the-biggest-e-commerce-site-you-havent-heard-of/.

19. Tsedal Neeley, "Global Business Speaks English," *Harvard Business Review*, May 2012, https://hbr.org/2012/05/global-business-speaks-english.

20. See Interbrand, "Japan's Best Global/Domestic Brands 2015." Interbrand categorized Canon and Konica Minolta in "computer hardware" and Fujitsu in "computer services." These three may also be categorized as electronics.

21. See Paula Vasan, "Sony's Betamax, Long Thought Dead, Officially Gets Last Nail in Its Coffin," *CNET*, November 10, 2015, www.cnet.com/news/sony-says-it-will-stop-producing-its-betamax-tapes-in-march/.

22. Sony reported net income of ¥369.4 billion in fiscal year 2007 and has since reported net losses. It reported net loss of ¥98.9 billion in fiscal 2008, ¥40.8 billion in 2009, ¥259.6 billion in 2010, ¥456.7 billion in 2011, ¥43.0 billion in 2012, ¥68.8 billion in 2013, and ¥9.0 billion in 2014. See Sony's Annual Reports 2009–2013 at www.sony.net/Sony

Info/IR/library/ar/Archive.html. Sony stopped producing annual reports from 2014. Financial data for fiscal years 2013 and 2014 are obtained from Sony, "Investor Relations—IR Library—Historical Data," www.sony.net/SonyInfo/IR/library/historical/.

23. On the earlier years, before Sony became as bureaucratized and interdependent with government as during the 1990s and 2000s, see Akio Morita, Edwin M. Reingold, and Mitsuko Shimomura, *Made in Japan: Akio Morita and Sony* (New York: Dutton, 1986).

24. Samsung, for example, claims that being "open" gives it the flexibility to shift gears if a given operating system (such as Google's Android, on which it has been recently dependent) falls out of favor. See Michael Lev-Ram, "Samsung's Road to Global Domination," *Fortune*, January 22, 2013, http://fortune.com/2013/01/22/samsungs-road-to-global-domination/.

25. On Yamato's innovation within Japan, see Patrick Reinmoeller, "Service Innovation: Towards Designing New Business Models for Aging Societies," in *The Silver Market Phenomenon: Marketing and Innovation in the Aging Society*, 2nd ed., eds. Florian Kohlbacher and Cornelius Herstatt (Berlin: Springer, 2011), 133–146. On Yamato's expanding global operations, see Yamato's "Annual Report 2015," www.yamato-hd.co.jp/investors/library/annualreport/pdf/2015/ar2015_00.pdf.

26. For more on YKK's success and corporate governance, see Benjamin Fulford, "Zipping Up the World," *Forbes*, November 24, 2003, www.forbes.com/global/2003/1124/089.html, and Sugio Baba, "Senryaku-keiei ni Kansuru Jirei Kenkyū (7): YKK Kabushikigaisha, Kyanon Kabushikigaisha [Case Studies on Strategic Management (7): YKK Corporation and Canon Inc.]," *Business Review of the Senshu University*, no. 98 (2014): 5–19.

27. See Suntory, "Annual Report 2015," www.suntory.com/softdrink/ir/library/pdf/2015_00_Full.pdf, and "Suntory Holdings Limited Ranked No.5 in the World's Most Admired Companies (Beverage Industry) by American Business Magazine FORTUNE," February 23, 2016, www.suntory.com/news/article/12593E.html.

28. Son was reputedly, in 2016, the second richest person in Japan, with personal assets of around $7.2 billion. In finance, he co-founded the promising but ultimately abortive Nasdaq Japan securities exchange in 1999. In energy, he pioneered in developing megasolar power within Japan after the Fukushima earthquake of 2011. And in telecommunications, his area of greatest success, Son introduced the Apple iPhone to Japan in 2008, after having brought in Silicon Valley start-ups Yahoo, Cisco, and E★TRADE, as well. Son also made lucrative, far-sighted investments in Chinese e-commerce giant-to-be Alibaba, later becoming majority owner of U.S. wireless operator Sprint, and co-founding a $100 billion technology-related venture fund, jointly with Saudi Arabia. See Mitsuru Obe, "First the iPhone. Now Renewables," *The Wall Street Journal*, June 18, 2012, www.wsj.com/articles/SB10001424052702304371504577404343259051300; Kana Inagaki, Leo Lewis, and Arash Massoudi, "Masayoshi Son: The unrepentant visionary," *Financial Times*, July 22, 2016, www.ft.com/content/7b2da318-4f2d-11e6-8172-e39ecd3b86fc; and Michael J. de la Merced, "After Meeting Trump, Japanese Mogul Pledges $50 Billion Investment in the U.S.," *The New York Times*, December 6, 2016, www.nytimes.com/2016/12/06/business/dealbook/donald-trump-mayayoshi-son-softbank.html.

29. See Japan Association of New Economy (JANE), "Japan Ahead," May 14, 2015, http://jane.or.jp/pdf/20150514.pdf.

30. JANE recommended eight candidates for the July 2013 House of Councillors election, of which six were elected. These included Hiroshige Sekō, Deputy Chief Cabinet Secretary in the Abe Cabinet; Yoshimasa Hayashi, Agriculture Minister; Shingo Miyake,

LDP; Ichita Yamamoto, Minister of State for Science and Technology Policy; Masamune Wada, Your Party; and Yoshio Kimura, LDP. See JANE, "7.21 San'insen Suisen Kōhosha Happyō Kishakaiken wo Kaisaishimashita [JANE Revealed Upper House Election Candidates Recommendations at Press Conference]," http://jane.or.jp/topic/detail?topic_ id=178, and The National Diet of Japan House of Councillors, "List of the Members," www.sangiin.go.jp/japanese/joho1/kousei/eng/members/index.htm.

31. In May 2013 JANE had 476 sponsoring members, but by March 2016 this had fallen to only 193. General membership remained more stable: 311 in May 2013 versus 299 in April 2015, and 324 in March 2016. See JANE, "Member List." Past membership information obtained through the Internet Archive's Wayback Machine.

32. On the concept of "permeable insulation," see Ulrike Schaede and William W. Grimes, "Introduction: The Emergence of Permeable Insulation," in *Japan's Managed Globalization: Adapting to the Twenty-First Century*, eds. Ulrike Schaede and Willam W. Grimes (Armonk, NY: M. E. Sharpe, 2003), 6–9.

33. On Japan's agricultural-sector supports and their trade implications, see United States Department of Agriculture Economic Research Service, "Japan—Issues & Analysis," www.ers.usda.gov/topics/international-markets-trade/countries-regions/japan/issues -analysis.aspx.

34. The Organisation for Economic Co-operation and Development (OECD) estimated that in 2014 Japan's agricultural-producer supports was about 49 percent of the cost of production, compared to 18 percent for the European Union, 17 percent for the OECD average, and less than 10 percent for the United States. See Figure 6.2, as well as OECD, *Agricultural Policy Monitoring and Evaluation 2015* (Paris: OECD Publishing, 2015), doi: 10.1787/agr_pol-2015-en.

35. The Market-Oriented Sector-Selective (MOSS) talks, Structural Impediments Initiative, and Framework for a New Economic Partnership negotiations between the United States and Japan, for example, made some headway in dismantling some transborder restrictions, although their net impact on the salience of circles of compensation within Japan itself has been limited. See Yumiko Mikanagi, *Japan's Trade Policy: Action or Reaction?* (London: Routledge, 1996) and Leonard J. Schoppa, *Bargaining with Japan: What American Pressure Can and Cannot Do* (New York: Columbia University Press, 1997).

36. On corporate governance in Korea and Sweden, see Peter A. Gourevitch and James Shinn, *Political Power and Corporate Control: The New Global Politics of Corporate Governance* (Princeton, NJ: Princeton University Press, 2005), 123–131 and 140–146.

37. For examples, see Ulrike Schaede, *Choose and Focus: Japanese Business Strategies for the 21st Century* (Ithaca, NY: Cornell University Press, 2008).

38. On this problem, see Yasushi Suzuki, *Japan's Financial Slump: Collapse of the Monitoring System under Institutional and Transition Failures* (Basingstoke, UK: Palgrave Macmillan, 2011), 77–117.

39. On "permeable insulation," see Schaede and Grimes, *Japan's Managed Globalization*.

40. On the details of this transformation, see, for example, Niall Ferguson et al., eds., *The Shock of the Global: The 1970s in Perspective* (Cambridge, MA: Harvard University Press, 2010).

41. See, for example, Richard Katz, *Japanese Phoenix: The Long Road to Economic Revival* (Armonk, NY: M. E. Sharpe, 2003), 165–176, and Gillian Tett, *Saving the Sun: A Wall Street Gamble to Rescue Japan from Its Trillion-Dollar Meltdown* (New York: Harper Business, 2003).

42. Ferguson et al.

43. Prime Minister Abe designated ten National Strategic Special Zones across Japan. These special zones are in the Tokyo metropolitan area (international business and innovation hub), the Kansai area (center for innovation in medical care and entrepreneurial support), Niigata city of Niigata prefecture (center for agricultural reform in large-scale farming), Yabu city of Hyogo prefecture (center for agricultural reform in hilly and mountainous areas), Fukuoka city and Kitakyushu city of Fukuoka prefecture (center for employment system reform for business creation), Okinawa prefecture (center for international tourism), Semboku city of Akita prefecture (center for the reform for agriculture and forestry/international exchange of medical treatment), Sendai city of Miyagi prefecture (center for the reform for women's active social participation and start-ups), Aichi prefecture (center for the general reform for education, employment, agriculture for fostering industry leaders), and Hiroshima prefecture and Imabari city of Ehime prefecture (special zone for international exchange and utilization of big data). See slide 14 of Government of Japan, "Abenomics of Progressing: Toward the Reinvigoration of the Japanese Economy," July 2016, www.japan.go.jp/_userdata/abenomics/pdf/160712_abenomics.pdf.

44. See, for example, Albert M. Craig, *Chōshū in the Meiji Restoration* (Cambridge, MA: Harvard University Press, 1961).

45. On these problems, including the leverage that complex legislative structures give to veto players, see Kent E. Calder, *Japan's Stealth Reform: The Key Role of Political Process*, The Edwin O. Reischauer Center for East Asian Studies Asia-Pacific Policy Papers Series (Washington, DC: Johns Hopkins University, 2005).

46. Schaede, *Choose and Focus*, 254–255 and Steven K. Vogel, *Japan Remodeled: How Government and Industry Are Reforming Japanese Capitalism* (Ithaca, NY: Cornell University Press, 2006), 218–220.

47. See John Ikenberry and Anne-Marie Slaughter, "Forging a World of Liberty Under Law: U.S. National Security in the 21st Century" (Final Paper of the Princeton Project on National Security, The Woodrow Wilson School of Public and International Affairs, Princeton University, September 27, 2006), www.world-governance.org/IMG/pdf_080_Forging_a_world_of_liberty_under_law.pdf.

48. On the rising international importance of such networks, which lie at the heart of globalization itself, see David Singh Grewal, *Network Power: The Social Dynamics of Globalization* (New Haven, CT: Yale University Press, 2008), 17–43.

49. Anthony Fensom, "Abenomics 2.0: A Reform Reboot for Japan?" *The Diplomat*, September 30, 2015, http://thediplomat.com/2015/09/abenomics-2-0-a-reform-reboot-for-japan/.

50. Kana Inagaki, "Japan's Toray signs $8.6bn Boeing deal," *Financial Times*, November 17, 2014, www.ft.com/content/7c8811b0-6e26-11e4-bffb-00144feabdco.

51. On the details of the Stanford Silicon Valley–New Japan Project, see its website, www.stanford-svnj.org/overview.

52. See "Geodesic Capital Launches a $335 Million Growth Fund to Bridge Silicon Valley, Japan, and Asia," *PR Newswire*, May 17, 2016, http://prnewswire.com/news/geodesic+capital.

53. In 2014, around *fifty times* as much venture capital was raised in the United States as in Japan—$48 billion versus $940 million. See Alexander Martin, "Japan's Top University Embraces Silicon Valley Spirit," *Wall Street Journal*, August 27, 2015, www.wsj.com/articles/silicon-valley-ethos-prestigious-japan-school-ventures-into-entrepreneurship-1440704144.

54. See Nathan Layne, "Abe, Seeking New Spark for Japan High-Tech, Meets Silicon Valley Chiefs," *Reuters*, May 1, 2015, www.reuters.com/article/us-usa-japan-abe-idUSKB N0NL0A420150501.

CHAPTER ELEVEN

1. In 2013, Japan is the third largest oil consumer in the world, with negligible proved crude oil reserves. See U.S. Energy Information Administration, "Total Petroleum Consumption 2014," *International Energy Statistics*.

2. See Table 11.1.

3. On this distinction, see Peter A. Hall and David Soskice, *Varieties of Capitalism: The Institutional Foundations of Comparative Advantage* (Oxford, UK: Oxford University Press, 2001).

4. The KOF Index of Globalization is an unusually comprehensive indicator, comprised of three separate dimensions: economic globalization, social globalization, and political globalization. It is available on an extended 1970–2016 time series, longer than alternate measures such as the Maastricht Globalization Index. For an in-depth technical comparison of common globalization indices and the accompanying methodologies, which prompted the selection of KOF here, see Axel Dreher, Noel Gaston, and Pim Martens, *Measuring Globalisation: Gauging its Consequences* (New York: Springer, 2008). On rankings from 1970 to 2016, see KOF Index of Globalization, http://globalization.kof.ethz.ch/.

5. See Fraser Institute, "2015 Dataset," *Economic Freedom of the World Annual Report*, 2015 edition.

6. On the institutionally rooted stability bias of Japanese policy making, and its propensity toward policy change in a crisis, see Kent E. Calder, *Crisis and Compensation: Public Policy and Political Stability in Japan, 1946–1986* (Princeton, NJ: Princeton University Press, 1988) as well as Kent E. Calder, *Japan's Stealth Reform: The Key Role of Political Process*, The Edwin O. Reischauer Center for East Asian Studies Asia-Pacific Policy Papers Series (Washington, DC: Johns Hopkins University, 2005).

7. The "third arrow" of Abenomics (structural reform) was proposed in 2013, as a complement to expansionary programs for monetary and fiscal policy (first and second arrows). On recent "third arrow" developments, see Government of Japan, "Abenomics is Progressing: Towards the Reinvigoration of the Japanese Economy," July 2016, www.japan .go.jp/_userdata/abenomics/pdf/160712_abenomics.pdf.

8. Circles of compensation follow the bias toward incremental as opposed to radical innovation that Hall and Soskice ascribe to CMEs more generally. See Hall and Soskice, 44.

9. Korea has *chaebol* (industrial groups), Germany has universal banking, and Singapore has a multifaceted Economic Planning Board. All these late developers have collectivist qualities, but broader patterns of sociopolitical organization are by no means as pronounced as in Japan.

10. Kent E. Calder, *Strategic Capitalism: Private Business and Public Purpose in Japanese Industrial Finance* (Princeton, NJ: Princeton University Press, 1993) and Mark Metzler, *Capital as Will and Imagination: Schumpeter's Guide to the Postwar Japanese Miracle* (Ithaca, NY: Cornell University Press, 2013).

11. For Singapore, see World Bank, "Doing Business 2016: Measuring Regulatory Quality and Efficiency—Singapore," *Doing Business 2016* (Washington, DC: World Bank Group, 2016), 55–60, http://documents.worldbank.org/curated/en/366741467999718929/

Doing-business-2016-measuring-regulatory-quality-and-efficiency-Singapore. For Korea, see World Bank, "Doing Business 2016: Measuring Regulatory Quality and Efficiency—Korea, Republic of," *Doing Business 2016* (Washington, DC: World Bank Group, 2016), 57–62, http://documents.worldbank.org/curated/en/756121468184736025/Doing-business-2016-measuring-regulatory-quality-and-efficiency-Korea-Republic-of.

12. On *Doing Business* project, see World Bank, "About Doing Business," *Doing Business*, www.doingbusiness.org/about-us; on rankings, see Table 11.2 and World Bank, "Economy Rankings," *Doing Business*, www.doingbusiness.org/rankings.

13. See OCED, "Figure 7.1. Venture capital investments as a percentage of GDP," *Entrepreneurship at a Glance 2015*, 103, doi: 10.1787/entrepreneur_aag-2015-en.

14. Federal Ministry of Economic Affairs and Energy (BMWi), "'Future of the German Mittelstand' Action Programme," July 2015, 2, www.bmwi.de/English/Redaktion/Pdf/future-of-the-german-mittelstand,property=pdf,bereich=bmwi2012,sprache=en,rwb=true.pdf. In Japan, similarly, SMEs generate 50 percent of GDP and employ 70 percent of the Japanese labor force. See OECD, *OECD Economic Surveys: Japan 2015* (Paris: OECD Publishing, 2015), 92, doi: 10.1787/eco_surveys-jpn-2015-en.

15. See Hugo Hollanders, Nordine Es-Sadki, and Minna Kanerva, "Innovation Union Scoreboard 2015," European Innovation Scoreboards project for the European Commission, 2015.

16. On EXIST, see BMWi, "EXIST—University-Based Business Start-Ups," www.exist.de/EN/Programme/About-EXIST/content.html; on the Israel program, see BMWi, "EXIST Start-up Germany," www.exist.de/EN/Network/EXIST-Start-up-Germany/content.html;jsessionid=8F1D92ECA225572C367881A245711326.

17. On the German Accelerator Program, see BMWi, "German Accelerator," www.exist.de/EN/Network/German-Accelerator/content.html and the program's official website, http://germanaccelerator.com/.

18. On ZIM, see BMWi, "The Central Innovation Programme for SMEs," www.zim-bmwi.de/zim-overview.

19. On Singapore's policies in support of entrepreneurship, see Singapore Government, "Nurturing Start-Ups," *SPRING Singapore*, www.spring.gov.sg/Nurturing-Startups/Pages/nurturing-startups-overview.aspx.

20. Kim Young-sam's globalization vision was announced at the November 1994 Asia-Pacific Economic Cooperation meeting in Sydney, Australia. He established an elaborate Globalization Promotion Committee with subcommittees on policy planning, administrative reform, and educational reform, as well as science and technology. He also reached out extensively to Korea's overseas diaspora, with festivals, scholarships, and dedicated foundations, to serve the over 150,000 Koreans residing abroad. Foreign investment, both outbound and inbound, was also strongly promoted. See C. S. Eliot Kang, "*Segyehwa* Reform of the South Korean Developmental State," in *Korea's Globalization*, ed. Samuel S. Kim (Cambridge, UK: Cambridge University Press, 2000), 88.

21. On Korea's English fever, see "The Future of English in Korea," *The Diplomat*, June 29, 2014, http://thediplomat.com/2014/06/the-future-of-english-in-korea/, and "English Education in Korea: Unrealistic Expectations," *The Diplomat*, October 18, 2014, http://thediplomat.com/2014/10/english-education-in-korea-unrealistic-expectations/.

22. During the 2014–2015 academic year, for example, 63,710 Korean students were enrolled in American schools, compared to 19,064 Japanese. See Institute of International Education, "Top 25 Places of Origin of International Students, 2013/14–2014/15," *Open*

Doors Report on International Educational Exchange, www.iie.org/Research-and-Publications/Open-Doors/Data/International-Students/Leading-Places-of-Origin/2013−15.

23. On the role of Singapore as a global policy laboratory, see Kent E. Calder, *Singapore: Smart City, Smart State* (Washington, DC: Brookings Institution Press, 2016).

24. See Economic Development Board, "Logistics and Supply-Chain Management," www.edb.gov.sg/content/edb/en/industries/industries/logistics-and-supply-chain-man agement.html.

25. Singapore, for example, has hosted the Shangri-La Pacific Security Dialogue annually since 2002, International Water Week annually since 2008, and the World Cities Summit biennially since 2008.

26. See Temasek, "Board of Directors," www.temasek.com.sg/abouttemasek/boardofdirectors#s14.

27. The two foreign banks that operate nationwide in Korea are Citibank Korea and Standard Chartered Korea.

28. Cryan also served previously as president for Europe at Singapore's Temasek. See Deutsche Bank, "Management Board," www.db.com/company/en/management-board.htm.

29. See "Percentage of Foreign Bank Assets Among Total Bank Assets" for individual countries compiled by the Federal Reserve Bank of St. Louis.

30. "Singbridge Unveils Plans to be Global 'Master Developer,'" *Singapore Government News*, July 9, 2010, http://search.proquest.com/docview/596971697?accountid=11752.

31. Carlos D. Ramírez and Ling Hui Tan, "Singapore, Inc. Versus the Private Sector: Are Government-Linked Companies Different?" (IMF Working Paper, WP/03/156, IMF Institute, July 2003), www.imf.org/external/pubs/ft/wp/2003/wp03156.pdf.

32. The Anglo-Japanese Treaty revision of 1911 finally achieved the almost complete eradication of what had remained of "unequal treaties" with Britain, including tariffs imposed by those treaties, and other major powers soon followed. On the details of unequal-treaty revision, see Michael R. Auslin, *Negotiating with Imperialism: The Unequal Treaties and the Culture of Japanese Diplomacy* (Cambridge, MA: Harvard University Press, 2004), 118−145.

33. Korea, for example, joined the OECD in December 1996, liberalized restrictions on transnational capital flows, increased overseas development assistance, and accelerated the promotion of Korean Studies abroad. On *Segyehwa*, and subsequent Korean globalization, see Gi-Wook Shin, "The Paradox of Korean Globalization" (working paper, Asia-Pacific Research Center, Stanford University, January 2003); as well as Philipp Olbrich and David Shim, "South Korea's Quest for Global Influence," *Global Asia* 7, no. 3 (Fall, 2012): 100−107, www.globalasia.org/wp-content/uploads/2012/09/95.pdf.

34. The Skytrax survey, which has taken place annually since 1999, ranks the top one hundred airports worldwide. It evaluates them in terms of thirty-nine airport services, related to accessibility, comfort, speed of transit, shopping facilities, and quality of services, from check-in through departure at the gate. For the most recent Skytrax World Airport Awards results, see Skytrax, "World Airport Awards," at http://www.worldairportawards.com/.

35. It is noteworthy that, although Japan's largest airports have not traditionally been highly ranked overall, they have ranked well in certain specialized categories, testifying to an organizational efficiency in Japan that contrasts strongly to the politically inspired inefficiencies noted above. Haneda was, for example, ranked in 2015 as the best domestic airport in the world, the world's second cleanest airport, as well the airport with the best airport

security. See Skytrax, "The World's Best Airports in 2015," www.worldairportawards.com/ Awards/airport_award_winners_2015.html.

36. World Bank, "Air transport, passengers carried," *World Development Indicators*, 2015, http://data.worldbank.org/indicator/IS.AIR.PSGR.

37. Incheon and Changi ranked in 2015 as best and second best international transit airports—interestingly, the reversal of their rankings in overall quality. See Skytrax, "The World's Best Airports for Transit Passengers," www.worldairportawards.com/Awards/ worlds_best_transit_airports.html.

38. See Changi Airport Singapore, "Facilities & Services," www.changiairport.com/en/ airport-experience/attractions-and-services.html, and "Things to Do," www.changiairport .com/en/airport-experience/explore-changi.html.

39. See VisitKorea, "Incheon Airport Korea Traditional Culture Center," http://en glish.visitkorea.or.kr/enu/ATR/SI_EN_3_1_1_1.jsp?cid=609933.

40. Scott McCartney, "The World's Best Airport?" *Wall Street Journal*, December 1, 2011, www.wsj.com/articles/SB10001424052970204397704577070502443425304.

41. See Dermot Davitt, "'Changi Millionaire' is Crowned as Promotion Attracts Two Million Entries," *The Moodie Davitt Report*, January 24, 2016, www.moodiedavitt report.com/changi-millionaire-is-crowned-as-promotion-attracts-two-million-entries/. The minimum entry spending has been raised to S$50 for 2016.

42. See Changi Airport Group, "Annual Report 2014/15," 32, www.changiairport .com/content/dam/cacorp/publications/Annual%20Reports/2015/Changi_Airport_ Group_Annual_Report_2015_Full-Report.pdf.

43. Singapore Airlines, "Singapore Airlines And Transaero Airlines Sign Codeshare Agreement," July 18, 2011, www.singaporeair.com/en_UK/us/media-centre/press -release/article/?q=en_UK/2011/July-September/18Ju12011–1658.

44. Singapore Tourism Board, "Visitor Arrivals Statistics 2012," updated December 10, 2013, "International Visitor Arrivals Statistics," updated June 2, 2014; and "Visitor Arrival Statistics 2015," updated October 2015.

45. JCDecaux Airport Singapore, "Changi Airport: The World Class Airport Media Brand, 2014 Media Kit," 19, www.jcdecaux.com.sg/wp-content/uploads/2014/05/2014 -CAG-MEDIA-OFFER_23.5.14.pdf.

46. Kyunghee Park, "South Korea's Incheon Airport to Woo Chinese With Resort," *Bloomberg*, February 10, 2015, www.bloomberg.com/news/articles/2015–02–10/korea -s-incheon-airport-to-emulate-singapore-s-integrated-resort.

47. See Changi Airport Singapore, "Clinics and Pharmacies," www.changiairport .com/en/airport-experience/attractions-and-services/clinics-and-pharmacies.html.

48. "Incheon International Airport Extends Wings Abroad," *Korean.net*, December 8, 2011, www.korea.net/NewsFocus/Business/view?articleId=90241.

49. See Changi Airports International, "Current Investments," www.cai.sg/invest ments/current-investments/.

50. See Changi Airports International, "Realised Investments," www.cai.sg/invest ments/realised-investments/.

51. See Infocomm Development Authority of Singapore, "Building Singapore's Next Generation Nationwide Broadband Network," www.itu.int/net/wsis/stocktaking/docs/ activities/1291981845/Towards%20a%20Next%20Generation%20Connected%20Nation_ Singapore.pdf.

52. For a broadly parallel comparative assessment of the Japanese and Korean informa- tion and communications industries, see Steven K. Vogel, "Japan's Information Technology

Challenge," in *The Third Globalization: Can Wealthy Nations Stay Rich in the Twenty-First Century?* eds. Dan Breznitz and John Zysman (Oxford, UK: Oxford University Press, 2013), doi:10.1093/acprof:oso/9780199917822.003.0016.

53. Failure to orient toward rapidly expanding developing markets has been one of the classic recent mistakes of many Japanese multinationals. See Shigeki Ishii, Susumu Hattori, and David Michael, "How to Win in Emerging Markets: Lessons from Japan," *Harvard Business Review*, May 2012, https://hbr.org/2012/05/how-to-win-in-emerging-markets -lessons-from-japan.

54. See Tarun Khanna, Jaeyong Song, and Kyungmook Lee, "The Globe: The Paradox of Samsung's Rise," *Harvard Business Review*, July-August 2011, https://hbr.org/2011/07/ the-globe-the-paradox-of-samsungs-rise; John A. Quelch and Anna Harrington, "Samsung Electronics Company: Global Marketing Operations" (Harvard Business School Case 504–051, March 2004), revised January 2008; and James Mawson, "Samsung's Corporate Venturing Strategy," *Harvard Business Review*, October 10, 2011, https://hbr.org/2011/10/ corporate-venturing-rhymes-wit. Samsung apparently monitors promising foreign technology developments in part through its role in the Samsung Venture Investment Corporation, in partnership with other members of the Samsung Group.

55. Khanna, Song, and Lee, "The Globe."

56. International Data Corporation, *Worldwide Quarterly Mobile Phone Tracker*.

57. According to IHS Research, Samsung held a 21.0 percent market share in terms of sold units in 2015. LG Corporation was second place with a 12.6 percent share, and Sony, Hisense, and TCL Corporation won third to fifth places. See Rasmus Larsen, "Samsung Dominates Global TV Market for 10th Straight Year," *flatpanelshd*, March 15, 2016, www .flatpanelshd.com/news.php?subaction=showfull&id=1458017308.

58. See Samsung Electronics, "Samsung Sustainability Report 2016," www.sam sung.com/us/aboutsamsung/sustainability/sustainabilityreports/download/2016/2016 -samsung-sustainability-report-eng.pdf.

59. Ibid.

60. See Ovum Consulting, "Broadband Policy Development in the Republic of Korea," A Report for the Global Information and Communications Technologies Department of the World Bank, October 2009, www.infodev.org/infodev-files/resource/Infodev Documents_934.pdf.

61. OECD, "Table 4.11. Total fixed broadband subscriptions per 100 inhabitants in the OECD area," *OECD Communications Outlook 2013* (Paris: OECD Publishing, 2013), 129, doi: 10.1787/comms_outlook-2013-en.

62. See Akamai, "State of the Internet Q1 2016 Report," www.akamai.com/es/ es/multimedia/documents/state-of-the-internet/akamai-state-of-the-internet-report -q1-2016.pdf.

63. Federal Communications Commission, "International Broadband Data Report (Second)," May 20, 2011, 46–47, https://apps.fcc.gov/edocs_public/attachmatch/DA-11 -732A1.pdf.

64. Der Präsident des Bundesrechnungshofes als Bundesbeauftragter für Wirtschaftlichkeit in der Verwaltung [The President of the Federal Court of Auditors as Federal Commissioner for Efficiency in Administration], *Die Postreform in Deutschland: Eine Rückschau [The Post Reform in Germany: A Review]* (Rheinbreitbach, Germany: Kohlhammer, 2009) 87, www.bundesrechnungshof.de/de/veroeffentlichungen/gutachten-berichte -bwv/berichte/langfassungen/2008-bwv-bericht-die-postreform-in-deutschland-eine -rueckschau.

65. The sequence of privatization and segmentation was different in the two cases: The NTT was first privatized in 1985, then split into smaller divisions in 1991; whereas the Deutsche Bundespost was first split into postal, telecommunications, and financial services, then privatized. On NTT, see Kenji Kushida, "The Politics of Restructuring NTT: Historically Rooted Trajectories from the Actors, Institutions and Interests," Summer 2005, http://web.stanford.edu/group/sjeaa/journal52/japan1.pdf; on Deutsche Bundespost, see OECD, OECD, "Regulatory and Competition Issues in Key Sectors: Telecommunications," in *OECD Reviews of Regulatory Reform: Germany 2004: Consolidating Economic and Social Renewal* (Paris: OECD Publishing, 2004), http://dx.doi.org/10.1787/9789264107861 -8-en.

66. Author's personal recollections from Japan's postal privatization conference, chaired by Prime Minister Junichirō Koizumi, on January 18, 2005. For further details on the conference, see, for example, "Koizumi May Send Observers to Private German Postal Firm," *The Japan Times*, May 21, 2002, www.japantimes.co.jp/news/2002/05/21/business/koizumi-may-send-observers-to-private-german-postal-firm/#.V4Q5h_krKUk.

67. See Deutsche Post DHL Group, "History—2002 Deutsche Post acquires DHL," www.dpdhl.com/en/about_us/history/history_without_flash.html.

68. The Singapore government, for example, supports an elaborate National Institute of Education to train educators, and finances a long-term Centre for Research in Pedagogy and Practice within it, which interacts intensely with both teachers and the Ministry of Education. On the details of these trilateral interactions, see OECD, "Singapore: Rapid Improvement Followed by Strong Performance," *Lessons from PISA for the United States* (Paris: OECD Publishing, 2011), 166, doi: 10.1787/9789264096660-en.

69. See Peter J. Katzenstein, *Policy and Politics in West Germany: The Growth of a Semisovereign State* (Philadelphia: Temple University Press, 1987).

70. For example, dual school-workplace vocational educational programs are offered in over 340 trades in Germany, and can take between two and three-and-a-half years, with major input from local economic chambers. For an overview of the Germany's VET system, see Kathrin Hoeckel and Robert Schwartz, *OECD Reviews of Vocational Education and Training: A Learning for Jobs Review of Germany 2010* (Paris: OECD Publishing, 2010), 10–13, doi: 10.1787/9789264113800-en.

71. On strengths of the German system, see Ibid., 13–14.

72. Ibid., 14 and 64. Germany's "ratio of the unemployment rate of 20–24 year-olds to those of adults" was less than 1.5 percent in 2009, even amid the Lehman Brothers shock recession.

73. For an overview of Germany's bilateral vocational training programs, see Federal Ministry of Education and Research (BMBF), "Report on Vocational Education and Training 2015," 122–124, www.bmbf.de/pub/BBB_2015_eng.pdf.

74. On the 2012 PISA tests of fifteen-year-olds, for example, Singapore ranked first among nation states, following only limited samples from Shanghai and Hong Kong. Singapore was also rated as one of the best-performing educational systems in a 2007 McKinsey study of teachers, and rated first in the 2007 IMD World Competitiveness Yearbook for having an educational system that best meets the needs of a competitive economy. See OECD, *PISA 2012 Results: What Students Know and Can Do*, vol. 1, revised edition (Paris: OECD Publishing, 2014), 19, doi: 10.1787/9789264208780-en, and OECD, *Lessons from PISA for the United States*, 160.

75. In math, for example, Korea placed only after Singapore, Hong Kong, and Taiwan in 2012, with Japan two places farther behind. The United States was thirty-fifth. See

OECD, "PISA: Programme for International Student Assessment," *OECD Education Statistics* database, doi: 10.1787/data-00365-en.

76. See Seah Chiang Nee, "Talent Buy becomes Sore Point," *The Star Online*, March 24, 2012, www.thestar.com.my/opinion/columnists/insight-down-south/2012/03/24/talent-buy-becomes-sore-point/.

77. Sandra Davie, "Singapore May Rue Fall in Foreign Student Numbers," *The Strait Times*, October 2, 2014, www.straitstimes.com/opinion/singapore-may-rue-fall-in-foreign-student-numbers.

78. See OECD, *Lessons from PISA for the United States*, 171.

79. Singapore has four official languages—Malay (in which the national anthem is written), English, Mandarin, and Tamil. While promoting those, the government discourages patois and dialects conflicting with them, such as Singlish and Chinese dialects like Hokkien and Teochow, by restricting their use in the media. As a result, only 20 percent of Singaporeans now speak non-Mandarin Chinese dialects at home, versus almost 80 percent thirty years ago. See "Singapore: The Language Holding Malays, Tamils and Chinese Together," *The Economist*, January, 28, 2011, www.economist.com/blogs/johnson/2011/01/singapore.

80. For more on English education in Korea, see Bok-Myung Chang, "Korea's English Education Policy Innovations to Lead the Nation into the Globalized World," *Journal of Pan-Pacific Association of Applied Linguistics* 13, no.1 (2009): 83–97, http://files.eric.ed.gov/fulltext/EJ921027.pdf.

81. At Korea University, for example, 40 percent of courses were taught in English in 2010: at Sungkyunkwan 35.7, at Kyunghee 34.2, at Yonsei 28.5, and at Seoul National University 15.0 percent. See Sang-hoon Tak, "Heundeulli neun Daehak Yeong'eo Gang'ui Shiltae neun? [The Shaking Truth of University English Education]," *Chosun Ilbo*, February 23, 2011, http://news.chosun.com/site/data/html_dir/2011/02/23/2011022300159.html.

82. On the Brain Korea 21 program, see Jung Cheol Shin, "Building World-Class Research University: The Brain Korea 21 Project," *Higher Education* 58, no. 5 (November, 2009): 669–688, http://dx.doi.org/10.1007/s10734–009–9219–8.

83. Data from QS Intelligence Unit, see Soo-hye Kim, Yeon-joo Kim, and Hyun-jeong Shim, "2012 Asia Daehak Pyeong'ga: Seoul-Dae Dokyo-Dae Jechin geon Gukjaehwa deokbun [2012 Asian University Rankings: Seoul National Surpassed University of Tokyo Thanks to Globalization]," *Chosun Ilbo*, May, 29, 2012, http://news.chosun.com/site/data/html_dir/2012/05/28/2012052801942.html.

84. See OECD, "How Is International Student Mobility Shaping Up?" *Education Indicators in Focus*, no. 14 (July 2013), doi: 10.1787/5k43k8r4k821-en.

85. One of the largest work-study programs, the U.S.-Korea WEST (Work, English Study, Travel) program, for example, sponsors about four hundred overseas internships annually. The program lasts a maximum of eighteen months and participants receive 2.1–14.63 million won stipends depending on the lengths of their internships. See Hyun-woo Kang, "Jeongbu Jiwon Haehoe Inteon Olhae 3000-myung Bbomneunda [Government-sponsored Overseas Internships will Select 3000 This Year]," *The Korea Economic Daily*, January 10, 2012, www.hankyung.com/news/app/newsview.php?aid=2012011006691.

86. See Housing & Development Board, "Public Housing—A Singapore Icon," www.hdb.gov.sg/cs/infoweb/about-us/our-role/public-housing-a-singapore-icon.

87. One example of Singapore's home ownership scheme is that all Singaporeans are entitled to access their compulsory Central Provident Fund (CPF) savings for down payments

on housing, with the CPF also offering attractive mortgage rates. In 2006, the Additional CPF Housing Grant Scheme was introduced to help low-income families purchase their first apartment. For more on Singapore's affordable homes policy, see Ibid.

88. See Ibid.

89. For example, since 2010, the Singaporean Permanent Resident (SPR) quota has specified a maximum proportion of non-Malaysian SPR households within a block or neighborhood. See Ibid.

90. See Sun-woong Kim, "Korea Exports Knowhow on Housing Urban Mass," *The Korea Times*, June 25, 2010, www.koreatimes.co.kr/www/news/biz/2016/04/291_68295 .html.

91. The Korea Land Corporation and Korea Housing Corporation merged into the Korea Land and Housing Corporation in 2009 under Lee Myung-Bak administration.

92. "How Germany Achieved Stable and Affordable Housing," *Macro Business*, June 22, 2011.

93. See Ralph Buehler, et al., "How Germany Became Europe's Green Leader: A Look at Four Decades of Sustainable Policymaking," *Solutions Journal* 2, no. 5 (October, 2011), www.thesolutionsjournal.com/node/981.

94. See assessments by Bank for International Settlements, "Central Bank Collateral Frameworks and Practices," March 2013, www.bis.org/publ/mktc06.pdf.

95. Based on total spending of the 2014 budget, the Korean central government spent 355.8 trillion won in 2014, and the eighteen special accounts spent 49.2 trillion won in total in the same year. See Ministry of Strategy and Finance, "The Budget System of Korea," March 2014, http://english.mosf.go.kr/upload/pdf/TheBudgetSystemofKorea.pdf.

96. Special accounts share of total central government expenditures peaked in 1999 at 32.9 percent. The share has declined steadily since. See Changhoon Jung and Cal Clark, "The Impact of the Asian Financial Crisis on Budget Politics in South Korea," *Asian Affairs: An American Review* 37, no. 1 (2010): 41–42, doi: 10.1080/00927671003591391.

97. See Jón R. Blöndal, "Budgeting in Singapore," *OECD Journal on Budgeting* 6, no. 1 (October 2006): 45–85, doi: 10.1787/budget-v6-art3-en.

98. See "Germany: Nuclear Power Plants to Close by 2022," *BBC*, May 30, 2011, www.bbc.com/news/world-europe-13592208.

99. Singapore launched its first liquefied natural gas terminal with throughout capacity of six million tons per annum in May 2013 and has revealed plans for a second terminal. See Energy Market Authority, "Singapore's First LNG Terminal Launched," April 2014, www.ema.gov.sg/cmsmedia/Newsletter/2014/04/spotlight-on/singapores-first-lng -terminal-launched.html. On Korea's LNG market deregulation, see "S Korea to Revive Parliamentary Bid to Deregulate LNG Imports, Domestic Sales," *Platts*, July 10, 2012, www.platts.com/latest-news/natural-gas/seoul/s-korea-to-revive-parliamentary-bid-to -deregulate-7845794. On Singapore's plans for regional LNG trading hub, see Tim Daiss, "Singapore's LNG Trading Hub Ambitions Press Forward," *Forbes*, March 21, 2016, www .forbes.com/sites/timdaiss/2016/03/21/singapores-lng-trading-hub-ambitions-press -forward/#261b37a873f8.

100. OECD, "Evaluation of Agricultural Policy Reforms in Korea," 2008, 70, www .oecd.org/tad/agricultural-policies/40383978.pdf.

101. In 2009, for example, the Revised Agricultural Land Act aimed to restructure the leasing of farmland, while in 2014 a Farmland Intermediary Administration Organiza- tion was created to "increase production by consolidating farmland." See Jennifer Clever,

Midori Iijima, and Benjamin Petlock, "Agricultural Cooperations Help Revitalize Japan's Farm Sector" (USDA Foreign Agricultural Service Global Agricultural Information Network (GAIN) Report No. JA4019, 2014).

102. On veto players, see George Tsebelis, *Veto Players: How Political Institutions Work* (Princeton: Princeton University Press, 2002). On the role of veto players in Japanese policy making specifically, see Calder, *Japan's Stealth Reform.*

103. See Calder, *Japan's Stealth Reform.*

CONCLUSION

1. Mancur Olson, "A Taxonomy of Groups," in *The Logic of Collective Action: Public Goods and the Theory of Groups* (Cambridge, MA: Harvard University Press, 1965), 43–52.

2. See Olson's observations on special-interest organizations. Mancur Olson, *The Rise and Decline of Nations: Economic Growth, Stagflation, and Social Rigidities* (New Haven, CT: Yale University Press, 1982), 41–57.

3. Olson, *The Rise and Decline of Nations*, 58–61. Many Japanese circles of compensation, however, diffused risk for their members without exacting oligopolistic rents—a pattern divergent from common practice among Olson's "distributional coalitions."

4. See Figure 8.2.

5. Globalization tends to be equated with internationalization (*kokusaika*), which need not have the holistic, transregional connotation that globalization has in English.

6. Aurelia George Mulgan, "Why the US Struggles against Japan in TPP negotiations," *East Asia Forum*, August 27, 2014, www.eastasiaforum.org/2014/08/27/why-the-us-struggles-against-japan-in-tpp-negotiations/, and Jackie Calmes, "Trans-Pacific Partnership is Reached, but Faces Scrutiny in Congress," *The New York Times*, October 6, 2015, www.nytimes.com/2015/10/06/business/trans-pacific-partnership-trade-deal-is-reached.html.

7. In February 2015, JA-Zenchu and the Liberal Democratic Party reached agreement on an agricultural law revision that sharply reduced the JA-Zenchu's power over local farmers, while preserving its role in finance. See Ministry of Agriculture, Forestry and Fisheries, "Nōkyōhō Kaisei ni Tsuite [About Agricultural Cooperative Law Reform]," January 2016, www.maff.go.jp/j/keiei/sosiki/kyosoka/k_kenkyu/pdf/1_nokyohou_kaisei.pdf, and Aya Takada, "Japan's Farm Lobby Concedes to Abe's Agricultural Reform Plans," *Bloomberg*, February 9, 2015, www.bloomberg.com/news/articles/2015–02–10/japan-s-farm-lobby-concedes-to-abe-s-agriculture-reform-plans.

8. Alanna Petroff, "Japan Index Posts Crazy 57% Rise in 2013," *CNN Money*, December 31, 2013, http://money.cnn.com/2013/12/31/investing/japan-nikkei-stocks/.

9. During the second quarter of 2014, Japanese real gross domestic product growth fell 2.0 percent, compared to the previous quarter's positive growth of over 1.0 percent. During the succeeding four quarters, it averaged only 0.18 percent. See Cabinet Office, "Changes from the previous quarter (at chained (2005) prices: seasonally adjusted series)," *Quarterly Estimates of GDP, Jan.-Mar. 2016 (The 2nd preliminary).*

10. For Japan, see World Bank, "Population ages 65 and above (% of total)," *World Development Indicators*, 2015, http://data.worldbank.org/indicator/SP.POP.65UP.TO.ZS. For Florida, see United States Census Bureau, "QuickFacts—Florida." Data for 2015.

11. The Structural Impediments Initiative (SII) talks were sector-specific U.S.-Japan bilateral negotiations undertaken during the early 1990s, and designed to exert pressure

for structural change in the Japanese domestic political economy. For details, see Leonard J. Schoppa, *Bargaining with Japan: What American Pressure Can and Cannot Do* (New York: Columbia University Press, 1997).

12. Only 8.0 percent of Japanese parliamentarians after Lower House elections in December 2012 and 1.1 percent of corporate board directors in 2013 were female. See Kathy Matsui et al., "Womenomics 4.0: Time to Walk the Talk," Goldman Sachs Portfolio Strategy Research, May 30, 2014, www.goldmansachs.com/our-thinking/outlook/womenomics4-folder/womenomics4-time-to-walk-the-talk.pdf.

13. Gender Equality Bureau Cabinet Office, "Numerical Targets and Updated Figures of the Third Basic Plan for Gender Equality," www.gender.go.jp/about_danjo/seika_shihyo/pdf/numerical_targets_2015.pdf.

14. See Toko Sekiguchi, "Japan Limits Scope of Online Pharmaceutical Sales," *The Wall Street Journal*, November 6, 2013, www.wsj.com/articles/SB10001424052702303936904579180572851628610.

15. On the National Strategic Special Zones and other recent policy innovations related to Abenomics, see The Government of Japan, "Abenomics is Progressing: Towards the Reinvigoration of the Japanese Economy," July 2016, www.japan.go.jp/abenomics/html/.

16. See "Almost 130 Institutional Investors Adopt Japan Shareholder Code," *Reuters*, June 10, 2014, www.reuters.com/article/japan-stocks-stewardshipcode-idUSL4N0OR2CC20140610, and "Japan Steps Up Corporate Governance Code," *World Finance*, July 16, 2015, www.worldfinance.com/strategy/japan-steps-up-corporate-governance-code.

17. The November 2015 Japan Post IPO, involving around 10 percent of each of Japan Post's shares, reportedly raised ¥1.44 trillion ($12 billion)—the largest IPO in two decades. NTT DoCoMo raised ¥2.1 trillion when it went public in 1998, while NTT raised ¥2.4 trillion in 1987. See Takahiro Hyuga, "Japan Post Shares Surge 26% in the Biggest IPO of 2015," *Bloomberg*, November 3, 2015, www.bloomberg.com/news/articles/2015-11-04/japan-post-poised-to-jump-on-debut-after-year-s-biggest-ipo, and Atsuko Fukase, "Japan Post Targets $11.6 Billion with IPO," *The Wall Street Journal*, September 10, 2015, www.wsj.com/articles/japan-post-set-for-major-ipo-1441873250.

18. Oliver E. Williamson, *Markets and Hierarchies: Analysis and Antitrust Implications: A Study in the Economics of Internal Organization* (New York: Free Press, 1975).

19. For support in the business-history literature for this concept, see Naomi R. Lamoreaux, Daniel M. G. Raff, and Peter Temin, "Beyond Markets and Hierarchies: Toward a New Synthesis of American Business History," *American Historical Review* 108, no. 2 (April 2003): 404–433. doi: 10.3386/w9029.

20. Previous work in this area includes Frank R. Baumgartner and Beth L. Leech, *Basic Interest: The Importance of Groups in Politics and in Political Science* (Princeton, NJ: Princeton University Press, 1998) and Jeffrey M. Berry, "Sub-governments, Issue Networks, and Political Conflict," in *Remaking American Politics*, eds. Richard A. Harris and Sidney M. Milkis (Boulder, CO: Westview Press, 1989), 239–260.

21. For a comprehensive introduction to the basic varieties of capitalism, see Peter A. Hall and David Soskice, ed., *Varieties of Capitalism: The Institutional Foundations of Comparative Advantage* (Oxford, UK: Oxford University Press, 2001), 1–70.

22. See Margarita Estevez-Abe, Torben Iversen, and David Soskice, "Social Protection and the Formation of Skills: A Reinterpretation of the Welfare State," in *Varieties of Capitalism*, eds. Hall and Soskice, 145–183.

23. Olson, *The Logic of Collective Action*, 5–52.

Bibliography

Abegglen, James C. *The Japanese Factory: Aspects of Its Social Organization*. Glencoe, IL: Free Press, 1958.

Acemoglu, Daron, and James A. Robinson. *Why Nations Fail: The Origins of Power, Prosperity, and Poverty*. London: Profile Books, 2012.

Akai, Nobuo. *Kōtsū Infura to Gabanansu no Keizaikaku: Kūkō, Kōwan, Chihō Yūryōdōro no Zaiseibunseki [The Economics of Transportation Infrastructure: Financial Analysis of Airports, Seaports and Local Toll Roads]*. Tokyo: Yuhikaku Publishing Co., Ltd., 2010.

Aldrich, Daniel P. *Site Fights: Divisive Facilities and Civil Society in Japan and the West*. Ithaca, NY: Cornell University Press, 2008.

Alletzhauser, Albert J. *The House of Nomura: The Inside Story of the Legendary Japanese Financial Dynasty*. New York: Arcade Publishing, 1990.

Amyx, Jennifer A. *Japan's Financial Crisis: Institutional Rigidity and Reluctant Change*. Princeton, NJ: Princeton University Press, 2004.

Anchordoguy, Marie. *Reprogramming Japan: The High Tech Crisis under Communitarian Capitalism*. Ithaca, NY: Cornell University Press, 2005.

Aoki, Masahiko. *Information, Incentives, and Bargaining in the Japanese Economy*. Cambridge, UK: Cambridge University Press, 1988.

Aoki, Masahiko, and Ronald Dore, eds. *The Japanese Firm: The Sources of Competitive Strength*. Oxford, UK: The Clarendon Press, 1994.

Aoki, Masahiko, and Hugh Patrick, eds. *The Japanese Main Bank System: Its Relevance for Developing and Transforming Economies*. Oxford, UK: Oxford University Press, 1994.

Aoki, Masahiko, Gregory Jackson, and Hideaki Miyajima, eds. *Corporate Governance in Japan: Institutional Change and Organizational Diversity*. Oxford, UK: Oxford University Press, 2007.

Asakura, Kōkichi. *Meiji-zenki Nihon Kinyū Kōzō Shi [History of Financial Structure of Japan in Early Meiji]*. Tokyo: Iwanami Shoten, Publishers, 1961.

Auslin, Michael R. *Negotiating with Imperialism: The Unequal Treaties and the Culture of Japanese Diplomacy*. Cambridge, MA: Harvard University Press, 2004.

Axelrod, Robert. *The Evolution of Cooperation*. New York: Basic Books, 1984.

Ballon, Robert J., and Keikichi Honda. *Stakeholding: The Japanese Bottom Line*. Tokyo: The Japan Times, 2000.

Baumgartner, Frank R., and Beth L. Leech. *Basic Interest: The Importance of Groups in Politics and in Political Science*. Princeton, NJ: Princeton University Press, 1998.

Berry, Jeffrey M. "Sub-governments, Issue Networks, and Political Conflict." In *Remaking American Politics*, edited by Richard A. Harris and Sidney M. Milkis, 239–260. Boulder, CO: Westview Press, 1989.

Bordo, Michael D., Alan M. Taylor, and Jeffrey G. Williamson, eds. *Globalization in Historical Perspective*. Chicago: University of Chicago Press, 2003.

Bullock, Robert. "*Nōkyō:* A Short Cultural History." Japan Policy Research Institute Working Paper No. 41, Oakland, CA, December, 1997.

———. "Redefining the Conservative Coalition: Agriculture and Small Business in 1990s Japan." In *The State of Civil Society in Japan*, edited by Frank J. Schwartz and Susan J. Pharr, 175–194. Cambridge, UK: Cambridge University Press, 2003.

Burke, Edmund. *Reflections on the French Revolution and Other Essays*. London: J. M. Dent & Sons, 1955.

Calder, Kent E. "Assault on the Bankers' Kingdom: Politics, Markets, and the Liberalization of Japanese Industrial Finance." In *Capital Ungoverned: Liberalizing Finance in Interventionist States*, Michael Loriaux, et al., eds., 17–56. Ithaca, NY: Cornell University Press, 1997.

———. "Circles of Compensation and the Politics of Late Development." Presented at the 2005 Annual Meeting of the American Political Science Association, Washington, DC, September 2005.

———. *Crisis and Compensation: Public Policy and Political Stability in Japan, 1949–1986*. Princeton, NJ: Princeton University Press, 1988.

———. "Elites in an Equalizing Role: Ex-Bureaucrats as Coordinators and Intermediaries in the Japanese Government-Business Relationship." *Comparative Politics* 21, no. 4 (July 1989): 379–403. www.jstor.org/stable/422004.

———. *Japan's Stealth Reform: The Key Role of Political Process*. The Edwin O. Reischauer Center for East Asian Studies Asia-Pacific Policy Papers Series, Washington, DC: Johns Hopkins University, 2005.

———. "Japanese Foreign Economic Policy Formation: Explaining the Reactive State." *World Politics* 40, no. 4 (July 1988): 517–541. www.jstor.org/stable/2010317.

———. "*Kanryo vs. Shomin*: The Dynamics of Conservative Leadership in Postwar Japan." In *Political Leadership in Contemporary Japan*, edited by Terry Edward MacDougall, 1–31. Ann Arbor: University of Michigan, 1982.

———. *Singapore: Smart City, Smart State*. Washington, DC: Brookings Institution Press, 2016.

———. *Strategic Capitalism: Private Business and Public Purpose in Japanese Industrial Finance*. Princeton, NJ: Princeton University Press, 1993.

———. "The Japanese Model of Industrial Policy." Presentation at the Beijing Forum 2007, Beijing, China, 2007.

———. *The New Continentalism: Energy and Twenty-First Century Eurasian Geopolitics*. New Haven, CT: Yale University Press, 2012.

———. "The Turbulent Path to Social Science: Japanese Political Analysis in the 1990s." In *The Postwar Development of Japanese Studies in the United States*, edited by Helen Hardacre, 336–353. Boston: Brill, 1998.

Calder, Kent E., and Roy Hofheinz, Jr. *The Eastasia Edge.* New York: Basic Books, 1982.

Callon, Scott. *Divided Sun: MITI and the Breakdown of Japanese High-Tech Industrial Policy, 1975–1993.* Stanford, CA: Stanford University Press, 1995.

Cargill, Thomas F., and Takayuki Sakamoto. *Japan Since 1980.* Cambridge, UK: Cambridge University Press, 2008.

Carlile, Lonny E., and Mark C. Tilton, eds. *Is Japan Really Changing Its Ways? Regulatory Reform and the Japanese Economy.* Washington, DC: Brookings Institution Press, 1998.

Chaudhry, Kiren Aziz. "The Myths of the Market and the Common History of Late Developers." *Politics and Society* 21, no. 3 (September 1993): 245–274.

Cohen, Jerome B. *Japan's Economy in War and Reconstruction.* Minneapolis: University of Minnesota Press, 1949.

Colignon, Richard A., and Chikako Usui. *Amakudari: The Hidden Fabric of Japan's Economy.* Ithaca, NY: Cornell University Press, 2003.

Curtis, Gerald L. *The Japanese Way of Politics.* New York: Columbia University Press, 1988.

Dahrendorf, Ralf. *Class and Class Conflict in Industrial Society.* Stanford, CA: Stanford University Press, 1959.

———. *Society and Democracy in Germany.* Garden City, NY: Doubleday, 1967.

Dore, Ronald. *British Factory, Japanese Factory: The Origins of National Diversity in Industrial Relations.* Berkeley: University of California Press, 1973.

———. *Flexible Rigidities: Industrial Policy and Structural Adjustment in the Japanese Economy 1970–80.* London: Athlone Press, 1986.

———. *Stock Market Capitalism, Welfare Capitalism: Japan and Germany versus the Anglo-Saxons.* Oxford, UK: Oxford University Press, 2000.

Dreher, Axel, Noel Gaston, and Pim Martens. *Measuring Globalisation: Gauging its Consequences.* New York: Springer, 2008.

Emmott, Bill. *The Sun Also Sets: Why Japan Will Not Be Number One.* New York: Simon & Schuster, 1990.

Estévez-Abe, Margarita. *Welfare and Capitalism in Postwar Japan.* Cambridge, UK: Cambridge University Press, 2008.

Ferguson, Niall, Charles S. Maier, Erez Manela, and Daniel J. Sargent, eds. *The Shock of the Global: The 1970s in Perspective.* Cambridge, MA: Harvard University Press, 2011.

Fligstein, Neil. *The Architecture of Markets: An Economic Sociology of Twenty-First-Century Capitalist Societies.* Princeton, NJ: Princeton University Press, 2001.

Fligstein, Neil, and Doug McAdam. *A Theory of Fields.* Oxford, UK: Oxford University Press, 2012.

Freeman, Laurie Anne. *Closing the Shop: Information Cartels and Japan's Mass Media.* Princeton, NJ: Princeton University Press, 2000.

Frieden, Jeffry A. *Global Capitalism: Its Fall and Rise in the Twentieth Century.* New York: W. W. Norton, 2006.

Fruin, W. Mark. *The Japanese Enterprise System: Competitive Strategies and Cooperative Structures.* Oxford, UK: The Clarendon Press, 1992.

Fukada, Shinichi, and Satoshi Koibuchi. "The Impacts of 'Shock Therapy' under a Banking Crisis: Experiences from Three Large Bank Failures in Japan." *Japanese Economic Review* 57, no. 2 (June 2006): 232–256. doi:10.1111/j.1468-5876.2006.00375.x.

Gao, Bai. *Economic Ideology and Japanese Industrial Policy: Developmentalism from 1931 to 1965.* Cambridge, UK: Cambridge University Press, 1997.

————. *Japan's Economic Dilemma: The Institutional Origins of Prosperity and Stagnation*. Cambridge, UK: Cambridge University Press, 2001.

Garon, Sheldon. *Molding Japanese Minds: The State in Everyday Life*. Princeton, NJ: Princeton University Press, 1997.

Genther, Phyllis A. *A History of Japan's Government-Business Relationship: The Passenger Car Industry*. Ann Arbor: University of Michigan Center for Japanese Studies, 1990.

Gerlach, Michael. *Alliance Capitalism: The Social Organization of Japanese Business*. Berkeley: University of California Press, 1997.

Gerschenkron, Alexander. *Economic Backwardness in Historical Perspective*. Cambridge, MA: Harvard University Press, 1962.

Gilpin, Robert. *The Political Economy of International Relations*. Princeton, NJ: Princeton University Press, 1987.

Ginkō Kyōkai 20-nen Shi Hensanshitsu, ed. *Ginkō Kyōkai 20-nen Shi [A Twenty-Year History of the Japanese Bankers' Association]*. Tokyo: Zenkoku Ginkō Kyōkai Rengōkai, 1965.

Granovetter, Mark. "Economic Action and Social Structure: The Problem of Embeddedness." *American Journal of Sociology* 91, no. 3 (November 1985): 481–510. www.jstor.org/stable/2780199.

Grewal, David Singh. *Network Power: The Social Dynamics of Globalization*. New Haven, CT: Yale University Press, 2008.

Grimes, William W. "Japan and Globalization: From Opportunity to Constraint." *Asian Perspective* 23, no. 4, Special Issue on Globalization in East Asia (1999): 167–198. www.jstor.org/stable/42704238.

Grossman, Gene M., and Elhanan Helpman. *Special Interest Politics*. Cambridge, MA: MIT Press, 2001.

Haggard, Stephen, Wonhyuk Lim, and Euysung Kim, eds. *Economic Crisis and Corporate Restructuring in Korea: Reforming the Chaebol*. Cambridge, UK: Cambridge University Press, 2003.

Haley, John Owen. *Authority without Power: Law and the Japanese Paradox*. New York: Oxford University Press, 1991.

Hall, Ivan P. *Cartels of the Mind: Japan's Intellectual Closed Shop*. New York: W. W. Norton, 1998.

Hall, Peter A., and David Soskice, eds. *Varieties of Capitalism: The Institutional Foundations of Comparative Advantage*. Oxford, UK: Oxford University Press, 2001.

Hatch, Walter, and Kozo Yamamura. *Asia in Japan's Embrace: Building a Regional Production Alliance*. Cambridge, UK: Cambridge University Press, 1996.

Hayasaka, Shigezō. *Hayasaka Shigezō no Tanaka Kakuei Kaisōroku [Memoirs of Tanaka Kakuei by Shigezō Hayasaka]*. Tokyo: Shogakukan, 1987.

Hoeckel, Kathrin, and Robert Schwartz. *OECD Reviews of Vocational Education and Training: A Learning for Jobs Review of Germany 2010*. Paris: OECD Publishing, 2010. doi:10.1787/9789264113800-en.

Hoshi, Takeo, and Anil K. Kashyap. *Corporate Financing and Corporate Governance in Japan: The Road to the Future*. Cambridge: MIT Press, 2001.

Huntington, Samuel. *Political Order in Changing Societies*. New Haven, CT: Yale University Press, 1968.

Inamoto, Yōnosuke, Shunichirō Koyanagi, and Toshikazu Sutō. *Nihon no Tochihō: Rekishi to Genjō [Japan's Land Law: History and Current Situation]*. 2nd ed. Tokyo: Seibundoh, 2009.

Inoguchi, Takashi, and Tomoaki Iwai. *Zoku Giin no Kenkyū: Jimintō Seiken wo Gyūjiru Shuyakutachi [A Study on "Tribal Dietmen": The Leading Players Who Manipulate the LDP Government]*. Tokyo: Nikkei Inc., 1987.

Ishi, Hiromitsu. *The Japanese Tax System*. 2nd ed. Oxford, UK: The Clarendon Press, 1993.

Johnson, Chalmers. *MITI and the Japanese Miracle: The Growth of Industrial Policy, 1925–1975*. Stanford, CA: Stanford University Press, 1982.

Kabeya, Nobuyuki, and Yoshio Itaba. "Tochi Zeisei to Chihō Zaisei Shūnyū: Nōchi ni taisuru Yūgūzeisei wo Megutte [Land Taxation and Local Public Finance Income: Farmland Tax Breaks]." *Kaikei Kensa Kenkyū* 40 (September 2009): 79–96.

Katz, Richard. *Japanese Phoenix: The Long Road to Economic Revival*. Armonk, NY: M. E. Sharpe, 2003.

———. *Japan, the System That Soured: The Rise and Fall of the Japanese Economic Miracle*. Armonk, New York: M. E. Sharpe, 1998.

Katzenstein, Peter J., ed. *Between Power and Plenty: Foreign Economic Policies of Advanced Industrial States*. Madison: University of Wisconsin Press, 1978.

———. *Corporatism and Change: Austria, Switzerland, and the Politics of Industry*. Ithaca, NY: Cornell University Press, 1984.

———. *Policy and Politics in West Germany: The Growth of a Semisovereign State*. Philadelphia: Temple University Press, 1987.

———. *Small States in World Markets: Industrial Policy in Europe*. Ithaca, NY: Cornell University Press, 1985.

Khanna, Tarun, Jaeyong Song, and Kyungmook Lee. "The Globe: The Paradox of Samsung's Rise." *Harvard Business Review*, July–August 2011. https://hbr.org/2011/07/the-globe-the-paradox-of-samsungs-rise.

King, Gary, Robert O. Keohane, and Sidney Verba. *Designing Social Inquiry: Scientific Inference in Qualitative Research*. Princeton, NJ: Princeton University Press, 1994.

Krauss, Ellis S. *Broadcasting Politics in Japan: NHK and Television News*. Ithaca, NY: Cornell University Press, 2000.

Krauss, Ellis S., and Robert J. Pekkanen. *The Rise and Fall of Japan's LDP: Political Party Organizations as Historical Institutions*. Ithaca, NY: Cornell University Press, 2011.

Kume, Ikuo. *Disparaged Success: Labor Politics in Postwar Japan*. Ithaca, NY: Cornell University Press, 1998.

Lamoreaux, Naomi R., Daniel M. G. Raff, and Peter Temin. "Beyond Markets and Hierarchies: Toward a New Synthesis of American Business History." *American Historical Review* 108, no. 2 (April 2003), 404–433.

Lesbirel, S. Hayden. *NIMBY Politics in Japan: Energy Siting and the Management of Environmental Conflict*. Ithaca, NY: Cornell University Press, 1998.

Levenstein, Margaret C., and Valerie Y. Suslow. "What Determines Cartel Success?" *Journal of Economic Literature* 64 (March 2006): 43–95.

Lijphart, Arend. *Patterns of Democracy: Government Forms and Performance in Thirty-Six Countries*. New Haven, CT: Yale University Press, 1999.

Lincoln, Edward J. *Arthritic Japan: The Slow Pace of Economic Reform*. Washington, DC: Brookings Institution Press, 2001.

Lockwood, W. E. *The State and Economic Enterprise in Japan: Essays in Political Economy*. Princeton, NJ: Princeton University Press, 1965.

Loriaux, Michael, Meredith Woo-Cumings, Kent E. Calder, Sylvia Maxfield, and Sofia A. Pérez. *Capital Ungoverned: Liberalizing Finance in Interventionist States.* Ithaca, NY: Cornell University Press, 1997.

Lynn, Leonard H., and Timothy J. McKeown. *Organizing Business: Trade Associations in America and Japan.* Washington, DC: American Enterprise Institute for Public Policy Research, 1988.

Mabuchi, Masaru. *Ōkurashō Tōsei no Seiji-Keizaigaku [The Political Economics of Ministry of Finance Controls].* Tokyo: Chuokoron, 1994.

Maclachlan, Patricia L. *Consumer Politics in Postwar Japan: The Institutional Boundaries of Citizen Activism.* New York: Columbia University Press, 2002.

Magaziner, Ira C., and Thomas M. Hout. *Japanese Industrial Policy: A Descriptive Account of Postwar Developments with Case Studies of Selected Industries.* London: Policy Studies Institute, 1980.

Matsumoto, Koji. *The Rise of the Japanese Corporate System: The Inside View of a MITI Official.* Translated by Thomas I. Elliott. London: Kegan Paul International, 1991.

McMillan, John. "Dango: Japan's Price-Fixing Conspiracies." *Economics & Politics* 3, no. 3 (November 1991): 201–218.

McNamara, Dennis L. *Textiles and Industrial Transition in Japan.* Ithaca, NY: Cornell University Press, 1995.

Metzler, Mark. *Capital as Will and Imagination: Schumpeter's Guide to the Postwar Japanese Miracle.* Ithaca, NY: Cornell University Press, 2013.

Mill, John Stuart. *A System of Logic, Ratiocinative and Inductive: Being a Connected View of the Principles of Evidence, and Methods of Scientific Investigation.* London: J. W. Parker, 1843.

Ministry of Agriculture, Forestry and Fisheries. "Nōkyōhō Kaisei ni tsuite [About Agricultural Cooperative Law Reform]." January 2016. www.maff.go.jp/j/keiei/sosiki/kyosoka/k_kenkyu/pdf/1_nokyohou_kaisei.pdf.

———. "Nōringyogyō no 6-ji Sangyōka [The 6th Industrialization of Agricultural, Forestry, and Fisheries Industries]." www.maff.go.jp/j/shokusan/sanki/6jika.html.

Ministry of Economy, Trade and Industry Agency for Natural Resources and Energy. *Enerugī Hakusho 2015 [Energy White Paper 2015].* Tokyo: Keizai Sangyō Chōsa Kai, 2016.

Ministry of Finance. "Annualized rate of changes from the previous quarter (at current prices: seasonally adjusted series)." *Quarterly Estimates of GDP Jan.–Mar. 2016 (The 2nd preliminary).* 2016, Tokyo, Japan.

Ministry of Finance Budget Bureau Research Section. *Zaisei Tōkei Showa 61-nendo [Financial Statistics 1986].* Tokyo: Đkura-shō Insatsu-kyoku, 1986.

———. *Zaisei Tōkei Heisei 2-nendo [Financial Statistics 1990].* Tokyo: Đkura-shō Insatsu-kyoku, 1990.

Ministry of Finance Policy Research Institute. "Investment in plant and equipment and inventories." *Financial Statements Statistics of Corporations by Industry, Quarterly.*

Ministry of Internal Affairs and Communications Statistics Bureau. *Heisei 20-nendo Koteishisan no Kakaku-nado no Gaiyō Chōsho [Outline Report of Fixed Asset Prices 2008].* www.soumu.go.jp/main_sosiki/jichi_zeisei/czaisei/czaisei_seido/ichirano8_8.html.

———. *Historical Statistics of Japan.* www.stat.go.jp/english.

———. *Japan Statistical Yearbook, 2011–2016.* Tokyo: Statistics Bureau. www.soumu.go.jp/english/data/handbook/c0117.hm#c04.

Ministry of Strategy and Finance. *The Budget System of Korea,* March 2014. http://english.mosf.go.kr/upload/pdf/TheBudgetSystemofKorea.pdf.

Miwa, Yoshiro, and J. Mark Ramseyer. *The Fable of the Keiretsu: Urban Legends of the Japanese Economy.* Chicago: University of Chicago Press, 2006.

Miyazaki, Yoshikazu. "Rapid Economic Growth in Post-War Japan: With Special Reference to 'Excessive Competition' and the Formation of 'Keiretsu.'" *Developing Economies* 5, no. 2 (June 1967): 329–350.

Morinobu, Shigeki. "The Rise and Fall of the Land Myth in Japan—some implication to the Chinese Land Taxation." *PRI Discussion Paper Series No. 06A-08.* Tokyo: Ministry of Finance, Policy Research Institute, 2006.

Mulgan, Aurelia George. *Japan's Failed Revolution: Koizumi and the Politics of Economic Reform.* Canberra, AU: Asia Pacific Press, 2002.

———. *Japan's Interventionist State: The Role of the MAFF.* London: Routledge, 2005.

Nakamura, Takafusa. *Nihon no Keizai Tōsei: Senji, Sengo no Keiken to Kyōkun [Japan's Economic Controls: Prewar and Postwar Experiences and Lessons].* Tokyo: Nikkei, Inc., 1974.

Nakane, Chie. *Japanese Society.* Berkeley: University of California Press, 1970.

Nihon Kōgyō Ginkō Nenshi Hensan Iinkai, ed., *Nihon Kōgyō Ginkō 75-nen Shi [A Seventy-Five-Year History of the Industrial Bank of Japan].* Tokyo: Industrial Bank of Japan, 1982.

———. *Nihon Kōgyō Ginkō 50-nen Shi (A Fifty-Year History of the Industrial Bank of Japan).* Tokyo: Nihon Kōgyō Ginkō Rinji Shiryoshitsu, 1957.

Noguchi, Yukio. *1940-nen Taisei: Saraba Senji Keizai [The 1940 System: Farewell to Wartime Economy].* Tokyo: Toyo Keizai Inc., 1995.

North, Douglass C. *Institutions, Institutional Change, and Economic Performance.* Cambridge, UK: Cambridge University Press, 1990.

———. *Structure and Change in Economic History.* New York: W. W. Norton, 1981.

Ohkawa, Kazushi, and Henry Rosovsky. *Japanese Economic Growth: Trend Acceleration in the Twentieth Century.* Stanford, CA: Stanford University Press, 1973.

Okimoto, Daniel. *Between MITI and the Market: Japanese Industrial Policy for High Technology.* Stanford, CA: Stanford University Press, 1989.

Olson, Mancur. "A Theory of the Incentives Facing Political Organizations: Neo-Corporatism and the Hegemonic State." *International Political Science Review* 7, no. 2 (April 1986): 165–189. doi: 10.1177/019251218600700205.

———. *The Logic of Collective Action: Public Goods and the Theory of Groups.* Cambridge, MA: Harvard University Press, 1965.

———. *The Rise and Decline of Nations: Economic Growth, Stagflation, and Social Rigidities.* New Haven, CT: Yale University Press, 1982.

Organisation for Economic Co-operation and Development (OECD). *Agricultural Policies in OECD Countries 2003: Monitoring and Evaluation.* Paris: OECD Publishing, 2003. doi: 10.1787/agr_oecd-2003-en.

———. *Agricultural Policy Monitoring and Evaluation 2014: OECD Countries.* Paris: OECD Publishing, 2014. doi: 10.1787/agr_pol-2014-en.

———. *Agricultural Support Estimates,* ed. 2015. doi: 10.1787/data-00737-en.

———. *Evaluation of Agricultural Policy Reforms in Japan.* Paris: OECD Publishing, 2009. doi: 10.1787/9789264061545-en.

———. *Evaluation of Agricultural Policy Reforms in Korea,* 2008, 70. www.oecd.org/tad/agricultural-policies/40383978.pdf.

———. *OECD Communications Outlook 2013.* Paris: OECD Publishing, 2013. doi: 10.1787/comms_outlook-2013-en.

———. *OECD Economic Surveys: Japan 2015.* Paris: OECD Publishing, 2015.

————. *PISA 2012 Results: What Students Know and Can Do*, vol. 1, revised edition. Paris: OECD Publishing, 2014. doi: 10.1787/9789264208780-en.

————. "Regulatory Reform in Telecommunications." In *OECD Reviews of Regulatory Reform: Regulatory Reform in Germany*, 2004, 167–190. www.oecd.org/regreform/32408088 .pdf/.

————. "Singapore: Rapid Improvement Followed by Strong Performance." In *Lessons from PISA for the United States*. Paris: OECD Publishing, 2011. doi: 10.1787/9789264096660-en.

Ostrom, Elinor. *Governing the Commons: The Evolution of Institutions for Collective Action*. Cambridge, UK: Cambridge University Press, 1990.

Patrick, Hugh T., and Yung Chul Park, eds. *The Financial Development of Japan, Korea, and Taiwan: Growth, Repression, and Liberalization*. New York: Oxford University Press, 1994.

Pekkanen, Robert. *Japan's Dual Civil Society: Members Without Advocates*. Stanford, CA: Stanford University Press, 2006.

Pempel, T. J. *Regime Shift: Comparative Dynamics of the Japanese Political Economy*. Ithaca, NY: Cornell University Press, 1998.

Piketty, Thomas. *Capital in the Twenty-First Century*. Translated by Arthur Goldhammer. Cambridge, MA: Harvard University Press, 2014.

Ramseyer, J. Mark, and Frances McCall Rosenbluth. *Japan's Political Marketplace*. Cambridge, MA: Harvard University Press, 1993.

————. *The Politics of Oligarchy: Institutional Choice in Imperial Japan*. Cambridge, UK: Cambridge University Press, 1995.

Ravenhill, John, ed. *Global Political Economy*. 2nd ed. Oxford, UK: Oxford University Press, 2008.

Reischauer, Edwin O. *Japan: The Story of a Nation*. 4th ed. Tokyo: Tuttle Publishing, 2004.

Reischauer, Edwin O., and Marius B. Jansen. *The Japanese Today: Change and Continuity*. Cambridge, MA: Harvard University Press, 1995.

Richter, Frank-Jürgen. *Strategic Networks: The Art of Japanese Interfirm Cooperation*. Binghamton, NY: Haworth Press, 2000.

Rosenbluth, Frances McCall. *Financial Politics in Contemporary Japan*. Ithaca, NY: Cornell University Press, 1989.

Rosenbluth, Frances McCall, and Michael F. Thies. *Japan Transformed: Political Change and Economic Restructuring*. Princeton, NJ: Princeton University Press, 2010.

Schaede, Ulrike. *Choose and Focus: Japanese Business Strategies for the 21st Century*. Ithaca, NY: Cornell University Press, 2008.

————. *Cooperative Capitalism: Self-Regulation, Trade Associations, and the Antimonopoly Law in Japan*. Oxford, UK: Oxford University Press, 2000.

————. "The 'Old Boy' Network and Government-Business Relationships in Japan." *Journal of Japanese Studies* 21, no. 2 (Summer 1995): 293–317. www.jstor.org/stable/133010.

————. "The Strategic Logic of Japanese *Keiretsu*, Main Banks and the Cross-Shareholdings, Revisited." Working Paper No. 247, Working Paper Series, Center on Japanese Economy and Business, Columbia Business School, October 2006.

Schaede, Ulrike, and William Grimes, eds. *Japan's Managed Globalization: Adapting to the Twenty-first Century*. Armonk, NY: M. E. Sharpe, 2003.

Scheiner, Ethan. *Democracy Without Competition in Japan: Opposition Failure in a One-Party Dominant State*. Cambridge, UK: Cambridge University Press, 2006.

Schmitter, Philippe C., and Gerhard Lehmbruch, eds. *Trends Toward Corporatist Intermediation*. Beverly Hills, CA: Sage Publications, 1979.

Schoppa, Leonard J. *Bargaining with Japan: What American Pressure Can and Cannot Do*. New York: Columbia University Press, 1997.

Schwartz, Frank J. *Advice and Consent: The Politics of Consultation in Japan*. Cambridge, UK: Cambridge University Press, 1998.

Schwartz, Frank J., and Susan J. Pharr, eds. *The State of Civil Society in Japan*. Cambridge, UK: Cambridge University Press, 2003.

Shindō, Muneyuki. *Gyōsei Shidō: Kanchō to Gyōkai no Aida [Administrative Guidance: Between Government Agencies and the Business World]*. Tokyo: Iwanami Shoten, 1992.

Stigler, George J. "The Extent and Bases of Monopoly." *American Economic Review* 32, no. 2, part 2 (June 1942): 1–22. www.jstor.org/stable/1805346.

———. "The Theory of Economic Regulation." *Bell Journal of Economics and Management Science* 2, no. 1 (Spring 1971): 3–21. www.jstor.org/stable/3003160.

Sutton, John. *Technology and Market Structure: Theory and History*. Cambridge, MA: MIT Press, 1998.

Suzuki, Yasushi. *Japan's Financial Slump: Collapse of the Monitoring System under Institutional and Transition Failures*. Basingstoke, UK: Palgrave Macmillan, 2011.

Suzuki, Yoshio, ed. *The Japanese Financial System*. Oxford, UK: Oxford University Press, 1987.

Tachibana, Takashi. *Nōkyō [The Agricultural Cooperative]*. Tokyo: Asahi Shimbun Publications, Inc., 1980.

Takahashi, Nozomu, and Muneki Yokomi. *Earain/Eapōto Bijinesu Nyūmon [An Introduction to Airline and Airport Business]*. Tokyo: Horitsubunka Sha, 2011.

Tanaka, Kakuei. *Building A New Japan: A Plan for Remodeling the Japanese Archipelago*. Tokyo: Simul Press, 1973.

Tett, Gillian. *Saving the Sun: A Wall Street Gamble to Rescue Japan from Its Trillion-Dollar Meltdown*. New York: Harper Business, 2003.

Tiberghien, Yves. *Entrepreneurial States: Reforming Corporate Governance in France, Japan, and Korea*. Ithaca, NY: Cornell University Press, 2007.

Tirole, Jean. *The Theory of Industrial Organization*. Cambridge, MA: MIT Press, 1988.

Tsebelis, George. *Nested Games: Rational Choice in Comparative Politic*. Berkeley: University of California Press, 1990.

———. *Veto Players: How Political Institutions Work*. Princeton, NJ: Princeton University Press, 2002.

Tsuru, Shigeto. *Japan's Capitalism: Creative Defeat and Beyond*. Cambridge, UK: Cambridge University Press, 1993.

Uriu, Robert M. *Troubled Industries: Confronting Economic Change in Japan*. Ithaca, NY: Cornell University Press, 1996.

Vogel, David. "Consumer Protection and Protectionism in Japan." *Journal of Japanese Studies* 18, no. 1 (Winter 1992): 119–154. www.jstor.org/stable/132709.

Vogel, Steven K. "Can Japan Disengage? Winners and Losers in Japan's Political Economy, and the Ties that Bind Them." *Social Science Japan Journal* 2, no. 1 (April 1999): 3–21. www.jstor.org/stable/30209743.

———. *Freer Markets, More Rules: Regulatory Reform in Advanced Industrial Countries*. Ithaca, NY: Cornell University Press, 1996.

———. *Japan Remodeled: How Government and Industry Are Reforming Japanese Capitalism*. Ithaca, NY: Cornell University Press, 2006.

———. "Japan's Information Technology Challenge." In *The Third Globalization: Can Wealthy Nations Stay Rich in the Twenty-First Century?*, edited by Dan Breznitz and

John Zysman. Oxford, UK: Oxford University Press, 2013. doi:10.1093/acprof :oso/9780199917822.003.0016.

———. "The Crisis of German and Japanese Capitalism: Stalled on the Road to the Liberal Market Model?" *Comparative Political Studies* 34, no. 10 (December 2001): 1103–1133. doi: 10.1177/0010414001034010001.

———. "When Interests are Not Preferences: The Cautionary Tale of Japanese Consumers." *Comparative Politics* 31, no. 2 (January 1999): 187–207. www.jstor.org/stable/422144.

Williamson, Oliver E. *The Economic Institutions of Capitalism: Firms, Markets, Relational Contracting.* New York: The Free Press, 1985.

———. *Markets and Hierarchies: Analysis and Antitrust Implications: A Study in the Economics of Internal Organization.* New York: Free Press, 1975.

———. *The Mechanisms of Governance.* New York: Oxford University Press, 1996.

Woo-Cumings, Meredith, ed. *The Developmental State.* Ithaca, NY: Cornell University Press, 1999.

Woodall, Brian. *Japan Under Construction: Corruption, Politics, and Public Works.* Berkeley: University of California Press, 1996.

Yamamura, Kōzō, ed. *Policy and Trade Issues of the Japanese Economy: American and Japanese Perspectives.* Seattle: University of Washington Press, 1982.

———. "The Japanese Political Economy after the 'Bubble': Plus Ca Change?" *Journal of Japanese Studies* 23, no. 2 (Summer 1997): 291–331. www.jstor.org/stable/133159.

Yanaga, Chitoshi. *Big Business in Japanese Politics.* New Haven, CT: Yale University Press, 1968.

Yano Tsuneta Kinenkai, ed. *Nihon Kokusei Zue 2011–2012: Nihon ga wagaru Detabukku [Japan in Graphics 2011–2012].* Tokyo: Yano Tsuneta Kinenkai, 2011.

Yoshikawa, Hiroshi. *Japan's Lost Decade.* Translated by Charles H. Stewart. Tokyo: International House of Japan, 2001.

Zeigler, Harmon. *Pluralism, Corporatism, and Confucianism: Political Association and Conflict Regulation in the United States, Europe, and Taiwan.* Philadelphia: Temple University Press, 1988.

Index

Pages in *italics* refer to figures and tables.